MW00812294

Cambridge Studies in US Foreign Relations

Edited by

Paul Thomas Chamberlin, *Columbia University*
Lien-Hang T. Nguyen, *Columbia University*

This series showcases cutting-edge scholarship in US foreign relations that employs dynamic new methodological approaches and archives from the colonial era to the present. The series will be guided by the ethos of transnationalism, focusing on the history of American foreign relations in a global context rather than privileging the US as the dominant actor on the world stage.

Also in the Series

Renata Keller, *Mexico's Cold War: Cuba, the United States, and the Legacy of the Mexican Revolution*

Elisabeth Leake, *The Defiant Border: The Afghan-Pakistan Borderlands in the Era of Decolonization, 1936–65*

Michael Neagle, *America's Forgotten Colony: Cuba's Isle of Pines*

Tuong Vu, *Vietnam's Communist Revolution: The Power and Limits of Ideology*

Vietnam's Lost Revolution

Ngô Đình Diệm's Failure to Build An Independent Nation, 1955–1963

GEOFFREY C. STEWART

University of Western Ontario

CAMBRIDGE
UNIVERSITY PRESS

CAMBRIDGE
UNIVERSITY PRESS

University Printing House, Cambridge CB2 8BS, United Kingdom
One Liberty Plaza, 20th Floor, New York, NY 10006, USA
477 Williamstown Road, Port Melbourne, VIC 3207, Australia
4843/24, 2nd Floor, Ansari Road, Daryaganj, Delhi – 110002, India
79 Anson Road, #06-04/06, Singapore 079906

Cambridge University Press is part of the University of Cambridge.

It furthers the University's mission by disseminating knowledge in the pursuit of
education, learning, and research at the highest international levels of excellence.

www.cambridge.org
Information on this title: www.cambridge.org/9781107097889
DOI: 10.1017/9781316160992

© Geoffrey C. Stewart 2017

First published 2017

Printed in the United States of America by Sheridan Books, Inc.

A catalogue record for this publication is available from the British Library.

ISBN 978-1-107-09788-9 Hardback

For Michelle

Contents

Illustrations

Maps

Acknowledgments

As I have come to realize over the process of writing this book, such an enterprise is far more than the work of one individual. Over the long process of developing this manuscript, I have racked up many debts. I would like to take this opportunity to thank all the people who have helped along the way. First and foremost, I would like to thank my doctoral supervisor, Andrew Johnston, who has been a true mentor and friend and whose invaluable suggestions have helped steer what started out as a pretty cool dissertation topic (at least to me) into the book it has now become. At my own institution, the University of Western Ontario, I have been extremely fortunate to work in a tremendously supportive intellectual environment where I have benefited from the friendship and advice of Frank Schumacher, Karen Priestman, Francine McKenzie, Jonathan Vance, Eli Nathans, Shelley McKellar, Liz Mantz, Mike Dove, Michelle Hamilton, Brock Millman, Rob MacDougall, Tyler Turek, Daniel Manulak and Keith Fleming. I must also include a shout out to Mary Beth Start for her digital expertise.

Beyond my campus I have been introduced to a fantastic cohort of scholars who have read and commented on various drafts and excerpts of this manuscript or offered their support, timely help and suggestions: Pierre Asselin, Matt Masur, Nu-Anh Tran, Jessica Chapman, David Biggs, Lien-Hang Nguyen, Hue-Tam Ho Tai, Keith Taylor, Fred Logevall and Daniel Immerwhar. Special thanks must go to Van Nguyen-Marshall and Ed Miller. Van has seen this project evolve from the beginning and has provided excellent feedback along the way. Ed has been tremendously generous with his time, commenting on earlier drafts, offering great guidance and demonstrating a willingness to answer any question on Vietnam, no matter how mundane. As well, I am very appreciative of the input of Rufus Phillips, who may not agree with my conclusions, but was willing to listen.

In terms of the research, I am indebted to the staffs at the National Archives and Records Administration at College Park, National Archives Number 2 and the General Sciences Library in Hồ Chí Minh City, the Eisenhower and Kennedy Presidential Libraries, the Hoover Institution at Stanford University, Libraries and Archives Canada and the Michigan State University Archives. I would also like to extend my gratitude to my sponsor institution in Hồ Chí Minh City, the University of Social Sciences and Humanities. Of special note are my Vietnamese language instructors, Cô Chi, Cô Quyên and Cô Hà, who listened with good humor and a tremendous degree of patience as I tried to learn to read, write and speak their language over two summers at the Southeast Asian Summer Studies Institute at the University of Wisconsin.

I am extremely grateful to Lien-Hang Nguyen and Paul Chamberlain for including this work in their US Foreign Relations series. This has been a labor of love that has been most patiently shepherded through the production process by my editor Debbie Gershenowitz and her team at Cambridge, including Kristina Deusch and Ian McIver. Additionally, I must thank the two anonymous reviewers whose suggestions have made this work a much better product.

Finally, there's been the support of my friends and family. David "Freddy" Duncan helped out with the design of the cover. The group at Amherst Shore provided much needed and, at times, puerile (Harold) relief from the revision process. When the revisions were complete, my neighbor Joël Campbell was there with a jack-hammer to help me decompress. My brother-in-law Sean Brown and his wife Heather McKay, my sister-in-law Lesley Brown and her partner Chad McAlpine, my sister Robin Stewart and her husband Chris Trella, my step-sister Sarah Watson and step-brother Phil Watson have all been (mostly) welcome diversions. Growing up I could always count on the support of my mother Gail Stewart and I know it was there in some form throughout the process of writing the book. My father and my step-mother Don and Mary Stewart were always there for me. My mother- and father-in-law Linda and Hugh Brown have continued to show an unquestioning (or misguided) faith in my abilities and offered all manner of support to help sustain this project.

Finally, there's my immediate family who've made this whole ride worthwhile. My daughter Abigail and my two boys Elliot and Ross have kept me grounded and served as constant reminders of what's really important in life. Most importantly, I have to thank my beautiful wife Michelle whose love and enthusiasm have kept me going. Words are not enough to express my love for her. This book is dedicated to her.

THE DEMOCRATIC REPUBLIC OF VIETNAM

Quang Tri
Quang Tri
Hue
Thua Thien
Da Nang

LAOS

Quang Nam

Quang Ngai

Kontum

Binh Dinh
Qui Nhon

Pleiku

Phu Yen

Darlac

CAMBODIA

Khanh Hoa
Nha Trang

Quang Duc
Tuyen Duc
Da Lat
Ninh Thuan

Phuoc Long

Lam Dong

Binh Long

Binh Thuan

Tay Ninh
Binh Duong
Long Khanh

Bien Hoa

Binh Tuy

Long An
Gia Dinh
Saigon
Cholon
Kien Tuong
Kien Phong
Phuoc Tuy

Chau Doc
Dinh Tuong
Go Cong
Vung Tau

An Giang
Sa Dec
Kien Hoa

Kien Giang
Can Tho
Vinh Long

Phong Dinh
Vinh Binh

Ba Xuyen

Bac Lieu

An Xuyen

**Province Map of
THE REPUBLIC
OF VIETNAM,
*ca.*1959–60**

0   50   100   150   200   250 km

0   25   50   75   100   125   150 miles

MAP 1 Province map of the Republic of Vietnam, ca. 1959–1960

Introduction

On November 17, 1956, one thousand government cadres were transferred to the Special Commissariat for Civic Action (*Đặc Ủy Phủ Công Dân Vụ* or CDV) with great fanfare in Sài Gòn.[1] Presiding over the event was the Secretary of State for the Office of the Presidency, Nguyễn Hữu Châu. In his remarks commemorating the occasion, he placed these cadres at the vanguard of the government's plan to "bring together the whole population in a revolutionary spirit" by charging them with carrying out "the mission of the Constitution of the Republic." He proclaimed that they would return "democracy in every aspect, throughout the region" and ensure that "every Vietnamese person" would become "a modern citizen."[2]

This statement neatly encapsulates the various objectives that lay at the heart of South Vietnamese President Ngô Đình Diệm's ambitions for nation-building during the nine tumultuous years of his leadership. Throughout, he aspired to create a viable nation in the southern half of Vietnam that would be capable of standing independently among the other nations of the so-called "free world."[3] It would be founded on the

[1] Lễ Chuyển Giao Cán Bộ của các Bộ sang Đặc Ủy Phủ Công Dân Vụ [Transfer Ceremony for Cadres of the Ministries sent to the Special Commissariat for Civic Action], November 17, 1956, Folder 16068, Phủ Tổng Thống Đệ Nhất Cộng Hòa [Office of the President of the First Republic] (hereafter PTTĐICH), Trung Tâm Lưu Trữ Quốc Gia II [National Archives 2] (hereafter TTLTQG2).

[2] Điện Văn của Ông Bộ Trưởng Nguyễn Hữu Châu, Đại Diện Dai Tổng Thống [Address of Secretary Nguyen Huu Chau, Speech for the President], November 17, 1956, Folder 16068, PTTĐICH, TTLTQG2.

[3] Presidency of the Republic of Vietnam, *Toward Better Mutual Understanding*, Vol. 1, *Speeches Delivered by President Ngo Dinh Diem during his State Visits to Thailand,*

backs of a new civic-minded populace that was aware of its obligations
to one another, the community and the nation at large.[4] It would be
democratic insofar as it assured to "all citizens the right of free development and of maximum initiative, responsibility and spiritual life."[5] And
it would be realized by a national and social revolution propagated at
the grassroots. Beginning in 1957, the Special Commissariat for Civic
Action would be charged with fomenting this revolution across the South
Vietnamese countryside.

The Special Commissariat for Civic Action was a rural development initiative intended to enlist the support of the peasant population
of southern Vietnam in both the physical and ideological construction
of Ngô Đình Diệm's South Vietnamese nation. It had its origins in a
December 1954 National Security Action Plan drafted with the assistance of the Central Intelligence Agency to fill the administrative vacuum
that emerged in parts of the countryside following the withdrawal of
the Việt Minh at the end of the First Indochina War. Officially launched
in the spring of 1955, the CDV employed teams of young cadres to go
down to the village level, live amongst the peasantry and mobilize them
to voluntarily work together to modernize their local institutions and
infrastructure to improve their overall welfare. The Civic Action cadres
would be a vital link between Sài Gòn and the countryside through which
Diệm could disseminate propaganda and build local support for his government. Initially, this effort was intended to win enough adherents to
enable Diệm to defeat Hồ Chí Minh's communist regime in Hà Nội in
national elections slated for 1956 to determine the political future of a
newly independent Vietnam. The national elections were never held and
the mission of the Special Commissariat was significantly altered.

This book traces the development of Ngô Đình Diệm's revolution
through the lens of the Special Commissariat for Civic Action. The revolution itself was rooted in the humanist philosophy of Personalism which
emerged from the French-Catholic left during the interwar period. It was
adapted by Diệm's brother, Ngô Đình Nhu, to contend with what he perceived to be the inadequacy of the existing social, cultural and political

---

Australia, Korea, 2nd ed. (Saigon: Presidency of the Republic of Vietnam, Press Office,
1958), 20, 30 and 35.
[4] John C. Donnell, "Politics in South Vietnam: Doctrines of Authority in Conflict,"
Ph.D. diss. (University of California, Berkley, CA, 1964), 118–121; and Philip E. Catton,
Diem's Final Failure: Prelude to America's War in Vietnam (Lawrence, KS: University
Press of Kansas, 2002), 49–50.
[5] Quoted in Clive J. Christie, Ideology and Revolution in Southeast Asia, 1900–
1975: Political Ideas of the Anti-Colonial Era (Richmond, UK: Curzon, 2001), 150.

means of organizing a new national community in the wake of the French colonial experience. But Diệm's nationalism was more than just a means of uniting a community based on the concept of the nation, it was, as Nicholas Tarling contends, a way of organizing the people to interact in the global community.[6]

At the midpoint of the twentieth century, the global community was fast becoming a world of nation-states as many of the African and Asian states which collectively made up the Third World – in contrast to the First and Second Worlds of nations that fell into the American and Soviet-led camps respectively – were emerging from a century or more of colonialism.[7] The leaders of these developing states were each looking for a means to transfer to their respective nations "the political loyalty which they previously gave to some other structure."[8] In the postcolonial world, however, this structure was supposed to guarantee some form of popular sovereignty that would protect these new polities from the ebb and flow of the competing interests of the more developed powers. The trick for the Ngôs, as it was for many other Third World nationalists, was to get the Vietnamese people to embrace the nationalist structure they were proffering. In this sense Civic Action, and the broader Personalist Revolution, to which it was attached, may be seen as an example of what Benedict Anderson refers to as "bound seriality": a means to create a distinct set of individuals who were self-aware, loyal and productive citizens of the Vietnamese nation that Diệm envisioned.[9] In other words, this would be a community of Vietnamese people who lived within the territorial boundaries of the Republic of Vietnam and recognized this, dutifully adhered to the laws laid down by the government in Sài Gòn, and worked toward building a strong and viable nation. The difficulty he faced, of course, was that in attempting to build *his* nation, he was competing with a rival state entrenched in the northern half of Vietnam that was offering an alternative vision of a modern Vietnamese nation that had its own set of adherents in the South. Not to mention the countless other members of the South Vietnamese populace with their own distinct notions of what a modern Vietnamese nation should provide.

---

[6] Nicholas Tarling, *Nationalism in Southeast Asia: "If the People are with Us"* (London: RoutledgeCurzon, 2004), 5–10.
[7] Vijay Prashad, *The Darker Nations: A People's History of the Third World* (New York: The New Press, 2007), xv–xvi.
[8] F.H. Hinsley quoted in Tarling, *Nationalism in Southeast Asia*, 6.
[9] Benedict Anderson, *The Spectre of Comparisons: Nationalism, Southeast Asia and the World* (London: Verso, 1998), 36–45.

This book sits at the cusp of a historiographic shift in the scholarship of the Vietnam War. Most early accounts rely primarily on American sources and situate the conflict firmly within a Cold War framework. Much of their focus has been devoted to explaining why American and South Vietnamese efforts failed to staunch the communist-led insurgency. As vast as this body of literature is, it has tended to revolve around the needs of American scholarship, trying, in effect, to explain that nation's fateful immersion in a long and bloody quagmire. These studies inevitably – and understandably – privilege the American perspective of the conflict which considers Southeast Asia as a vital Cold War battleground and South Vietnam as an American-created bulwark against communist expansion.[10] One consequence of this is that the national hopes and aspirations of South Vietnamese actors have been largely ignored.

Ngô Đình Diệm's regime is a particular case in point. In much of the literature he is depicted as either a hopelessly inept and autocratic leader, notoriously unwilling to accept US advice or a staunch nationalist driven by a knee-jerk anticommunism who was ultimately sold out by his American patrons.[11] With the opening of archives in Hà Nội and Hồ Chí

[10] See for example Robert Shaplen, *The Lost Revolution: The U.S. in Vietnam, 1946–1966*, rev. ed. (New York: Harper Colophon Books, 1966); George C. Herring, *America's Longest War: The United States and Vietnam, 1950–1975* (New York: Wiley, 1979); Marilyn B. Young, *The Vietnam Wars, 1945–1990* (New York: HarperCollins, 1991); James S. Olson and Randy Roberts, *Where the Domino Fell: America and Vietnam, 1945 to 1990* (New York: St. Martin's Press, 1991); and James R. Arnold, *The First Domino: Eisenhower, The Military and America's Intervention in Vietnam* (New York: W. Morrow, 1991); Robert Schulzinger, *A Time for War: The United States and Vietnam, 1941–1975* (New York: Oxford University Press, 1997); and David Kaiser, *American Tragedy: Kennedy Johnson, and the Origins of the Vietnam War* (Cambridge, MA: The Belknap Press of Harvard University Press, 2000).

[11] For the former view see, for example, Frances Fitzgerald, *Fire in the Lake: The Vietnamese and the Americans in Vietnam* (Boston: Little, Brown and Company, 1972); William J. Rust and the Editors of U.S. News Books, *Kennedy in Vietnam* (New York: Charles Scribner's Sons, 1985); George McTurnan Kahin, *Intervention: How America Became Involved in Vietnam* (New York: Knopf, 1986); Neil Sheehan, *A Bright Shining Lie: John Paul Vann and America in Vietnam* (New York: Random House, 1988); David L. Anderson, *Trapped by Success: The Eisenhower Administration and Vietnam, 1953–1961* (New York: Columbia University Press, 1991); David Halberstam, *The Best and the Brightest*, twentieth anniversary ed. (New York: Ballantine Books, 1992); Stanley Karnow, *Vietnam: A History*, 2nd rev. ed. (New York: Penguin, 1997); Gary R. Hess, *Vietnam and the United States: Origins and Legacy of War*, rev. ed. (New York: Twayne Publishers, 1998); Seth Jacobs, *Cold War Mandarin: Ngo Dinh Diem and the Origins of America's War in Vietnam* (Lanham, MD: Rowman & Littlefield Publishers, Inc., 2006); and James M. Carter, *Inventing Vietnam: The United States and State Building, 1954–1968* (New York: Cambridge University Press, 2008). For the latter perspective see, for example, Denis Warner, *The Last Confucian: Vietnam, Southeast Asia and the West* (New York: Macmillan, 1963); Anthony Bouscaren, *The Last of the Mandarins: Diem*

Minh City and an increased emphasis on interdisciplinarity and internationalizing the study of American foreign relations scholars are beginning to move away from the Cold War paradigm in trying to understand the Vietnam Conflict. They are drawing from area studies, postcolonial theory and global history in their analysis. This has had the effect of revealing the agency of Vietnamese actors and reframing the war as part of a long drawn-out struggle for national independence and unity. Such new and exciting works provide richer and more nuanced analyses of the war in which internal struggles over national identity, self-determination and even modernity itself are central.[12]

This study follows the lead of scholars like Matthew Connelly, Odd Arne Westad and Heonik Kwon by starting to take the "Cold War lens" off of our view of the Vietnam Conflict.[13] By decentering the Cold War in our field of view, Matthew Connelly has demonstrated

---

of Vietnam (Pittsburgh: Duquesne University Press, 1965); Ellen J. Hammer, *A Death in November: America in Vietnam 1963* (New York: Oxford University Press, 1987); Francis X. Winters, *The Year of the Hare: America in Vietnam, January 25, 1963–February 15, 1964* (Athens, GA: University of Georgia Press, 1997); and Mark Moyar, *Triumph Forsaken: The Vietnam War, 1954–1965* (Cambridge: Cambridge University Press, 2006).

[12] Robert Brigham, *Guerrilla Diplomacy: The NLF's Foreign Relations and the Viet Nam War* (Ithaca, NY: Cornell University Press, 1999) and *ARVN: Life and Death in the South Vietnamese Army* (Lawrence, KS: University Press of Kansas, 2006); Mark Bradley, *Imagining Vietnam and America: The Making of Postcolonial Vietnam, 1919–1950* (Chapel Hill, NC: University of North Carolina Press, 2000), and *Vietnam at War* (Oxford: Oxford University Press, 2009); Catton, *Diem's Final Failure*; Pierre Asselin, *A Bitter Peace: Washington, Hanoi, and the Making of the Paris Agreement* (Chapel Hill, NC: University of North Carolina Press, 2002), and *Hanoi's Road to the Vietnam War, 1954–1965* (Berkeley, CA: University of California Press, 2013); David W.P. Elliott, *The Vietnamese War: Revolution and Social Change in the Mekong Delta, 1930–1975* (Armonk, NY: M.E. Sharpe, 2003); David Hunt, *Vietnam's Southern Revolution: From Peasant Insurrection to Total War* (Amherst, MA: University of Massachusetts Press, 2008); Matthew Masur, "Exhibiting Signs of Resistance: South Vietnam's Struggle for Legitimacy," *Diplomatic History* 33(2) (April 2009): 293–313; Geoffrey C. Stewart, "Hearts, Minds and Công Dân Vụ: The Special Commissariat for Civic Action and Nation-Building in Ngô Đình Diệm's Vietnam, 1955–1957," *Journal of Vietnamese Studies* 6(3) (Fall 2011): 44–100; Lien-Hang T. Nguyen, *Hanoi's War: An International History of the War for Peace in Vietnam* (Chapel Hill, NC: University of North Carolina Press, 2012); Jessica Chapman, *Cauldron of Resistance: Ngo Dinh Diem, the United States, and 1950s Southern Vietnam* (Ithaca, NY: Cornell University Press, 2013); Edward Miller, *Misalliance: Ngo Dinh Diem, the United States, and the Fate of South Vietnam* (Cambridge, MA: Harvard University Press, 2013); and Nhu-An Tran, "Contested Identities: Nationalism in the Republic of Vietnam (1954–1963)," Ph.D. diss. (University of California, Berkley, CA, 2013).

[13] Matthew Connelly, "Taking Off the Cold War Lens: Visions of North-South Conflict during the Algerian War for Independence," *The American Historical Review* 105(3) (June 2000): 739–769.

that a "diplomatic revolution" was at work in the international system, where non-state actors in the developing world used world opinion and international institutions like the United Nations to challenge the Cold War visions for world order held by the Great Powers.[14] In this light, Odd Arne Westad argues that the political and revolutionary struggles for decolonization in the developing world were equally as important for shaping the Cold War order as the actions of either of the dominant superpowers. The Cold War interventions of both the United States and Soviet Union, he argues, "shaped both the international and domestic framework within which political, social, and cultural changes in Third World countries took place."[15] Heonik Kwon contends that there was no singular Cold War. Rather, it was experienced in different ways throughout the globe which cannot be "forced into a single coherent conceptual whole."[16] To understand the Cold War on the periphery, we must consider the "postcolonial visions" of the newly emerging states.[17]

I situate the Vietnam War at the intersection of the Cold War international order with the phenomenon of decolonization. When examining the broad international forces at work in Southeast Asia at the midpoint of the twentieth century, it provides equal weight to the phenomenon of decolonization and the Cold War in shaping Ngô Đình Diệm's efforts to establish a viable independent state south of the seventeenth parallel. It considers the interaction of these forces as mutually constitutive in Vietnam. To paraphrase Kwơn, I view the ideological divide between Ngô Đình Diệm's Personalist Revolution and the Marxist-Leninism vision that lay deep at the roots of the National Liberation Front's platform as different paths to "national liberation and self-determination" that, in the maelstrom of the Cold War, were "transformed into the ideology of civil strife and war, in which achieving national unity became equivalent to annihilating one or the other side from the body politic."[18]

This study relies extensively on South Vietnamese sources from Archives Number II in Hồ Chí Minh City as well as archives in the United States and Canada to examine Ngô Đình Diệm's effort to foment his

---

[14] Matthew Connelly, *A Diplomatic Revolution: Algeria's Fight for Independence and the Origins of the Post-Cold War Era* (Oxford: Oxford University Press, 2002), 278–279.
[15] Odd Arne Westad, *The Global Cold War: Third World Interventions and the Making of Our Times* (Cambridge: Cambridge University Press, 2007), 3.
[16] Heonik Kwon, *The Other Cold War* (New York: Columbia University Press, 2010), 6–7.
[17] *Ibid.*, 89.
[18] *Ibid.*, 116.

Personalist Revolution at the grassroots. It uses these materials to reveal the agency of South Vietnamese actors in three important ways. First, it demonstrates the regime in Sài Gòn and its policies were more than simply the machinations of the Ngô family. Other individuals, like Kiều Công Cung, the head of the Special Commissariat for Civic Action, were integral in trying to interpret the wishes of the regime and formulating policy accordingly. Second, it places the nation-building effort, to which the Personalist Revolution was attached, in a transnational framework by exploring its connection to the global community development movement. This movement, which had its origins in New Deal urban renewal projects and a rural development scheme in the state of Uttar Pradesh in India came to the Republic of Vietnam by way of a variety of sources including American advisers working with the International Cooperation Administration and Michigan State University, Europeans working for the United Nations, and the literature of community development experts emerging from the Indian experience. It was based on the notion – what I refer to as the community development idea – that local human and material resources could be used for reconstruction projects aimed at satisfying the "felt needs" of a particular community.[19] Third, it contrasts American developmental prescriptions designed to fashion a state capable of meeting both the communist challenge from the North and the needs of the perceived revolution of rising expectations in the South with Diệm's efforts to create what he considered to be a modern and viable nation capable of exercising its international sovereignty to the best of its ability in the global arena. Though Diệm was as intent on nation-building as his US allies, he was determined to do it on his own terms.

This book develops the story of the Special Commissariat for Civic Action over six chapters. The opening chapter looks at the circumstances surrounding the establishment of the Special Commissariat for Civic Action, exploring how it was initially conceived as a temporary expedient for the Sài Gòn government to extend its reach down to the village level following the Franco-Việt Minh War. The chapter places particular emphasis on the national election scheduled to be held in the summer of 1956 to determine whether the Hà Nội government of Hồ Chí Minh or Diệm's government in Sài Gòn would preside over a unified Vietnam. It demonstrates that the South Vietnamese government hoped the cadres of the Special Commissariat could win support for Diệm in the electoral

---

[19] Daniel Immerwahr, *Thinking Small: The United States and the Lure of Community Development* (Cambridge, MA: Harvard University Press, 2015), 71–75.

contest by helping to mitigate the effects of South Vietnam's social, political and economic dislocation on the morale of the peasantry following
the French colonial experience and the subsequent war of decolonization.

The second chapter examines the origins of Ngô Đình Diệm's revolution in the context of his efforts to consolidate his hold on power during
his first year in office. In addition to clandestine communist agents loyal
to the Hà Nội government, Diệm was faced with a host of enemies ranging from dissident generals to politico-religious sects and an organized
crime syndicate to holdovers from the French colonial apparatus all vying
for influence. Branding them enemies under a formula which identified
communists, feudalists and colonialists as opponents of the government,
Diệm began to define his vision of a postcolonial Vietnamese nation in
opposition to what he saw as the retrograde qualities of these adversaries.
At the same time, Diệm elected to make the Special Commissariat for
Civic Action a permanent arm of the government. Once Diệm had elected
not to hold the 1956 election on unification, Civic Action's mandate was
significantly broadened to promoting the ideals behind his national vision.
Under the twin concepts of "Raising the People's Intellectual Standards"
and "Welfare Improvement" the Civic Action cadres mobilized the rural
population to both identify the enemies of the regime and actively participate in the modernization of their village institutions and infrastructure.
The regime's intent was to foster a sense of solidarity between the people
and the Sài Gòn government by instilling them with the virtues of good
citizenship while bringing material improvement to their standard of living. Unfortunately, the Special Commissariat suffered from a perennial
lack of funding and the efforts of its Commissioner, Kiều Công Cung, to
solicit assistance from the United States Mission in Sài Gòn ran afoul of
the prejudices and bureaucratic rigidity of the American organization.

The third chapter examines the Ngôs' Personalist Revolution and how
the palace wanted to use it as a guide for nation-building. Personalism's
emphasis on personal sacrifice for the common good jibed with the voluntarism and spirit of self-help that underpinned the Welfare Improvement
work. It also meshed with the principle of community development which
had been filtering into South Vietnam through a variety of sources. This
made community development a perfect fit for the palace's ambitious
nation-building agenda. The Republic of Vietnam's community development plan, however, was decidedly at odds with Washington's developmental designs, particularly the Ngôs' decision to entrust it to the Special
Commissariat for Civic Action. This sparked deliberations on whether or
not to support it that were informed by the Eisenhower administration's

perception of colonialism and the global south as well as the fiscal conservatism of its New Look foreign policy. In the end, these policymakers concluded that Sài Gòn's community development plan was beyond the scope of what was an acceptable enterprise to support financially.

Chapter 4 explores Kiều Công Cung's efforts to make South Vietnam's community development plan his own. Though the Special Commissariat for Civic Action was to be the organ to administer the plan, community development was to be kept independent from Civic Action with creation of separate community development teams. For two years Cung worked to bring the community development effort into the fold of the Special Commissariat in order to keep it in line with what he perceived to be the revolutionary aims of the Diệm regime. In the process, he transformed the mission of the Special Commissariat from "Welfare Improvement" to "Bettering the People's Conditions of Existence" – which, in his mind, was synonymous with community development – and drafting his own community development plan, complete with a National Community Development Training Centre. By the start of 1959, Cung anticipated all of the Civic Action cadres being converted to community development cadres over the course of the following year.

Chapter 5 looks at the origins of the southern insurgency and the challenges this posed for the Special Commissariat for Civic Action just as it reached its apotheosis as a community development organ for Kiều Công Cung. It accepts the argument that the insurgency was a southern phenomenon born of the alienation elements of the southern population felt towards the more nefarious aspects of the Sài Gòn regime such as the most insidious component of the "three enemies" formula, the (*Tố Cộng*) communist denunciation campaign, a brutally effective means to weed out suspected communists from the villages. Chronically underfunded and short of manpower, the CDV struggled to stay ahead of the insurgency as southern communists were able to exploit the disaffection of the peasantry to organize a sustained campaign of violence against the Sài Gòn government.

The final chapter looks at the formation of the National Liberation Front (NLF) at the end of 1961 and the implications this had for Diệm's revolution. As this was occurring it became apparent that the CDV was incapable of meeting this new challenge. The cadres' activity became more reactionary, shifting away from community development to population control and, in some cases, armed propaganda campaigns. No longer capable of using the Civic Action cadres to foment the Personalist Revolution at the local level, the palace adopted the Strategic Hamlet

Program as a means to continue this work in an ostensibly more secure environment. Though it showed some signs of progress in countering the insurgency from 1962 to 1963, the Strategic Hamlet Program was ultimately incapable of inculcating the peasantry with the revolutionary ardor the palace hoped it could. When the Diệm government was overthrown in November 1963, the whole program collapsed under its own weight. The book concludes with a brief discussion of the shortcomings of the Personalist Revolution and an explanation of why it failed to resonate with the South Vietnamese people.

ONE

A Temporary Expedient

The Origins of Civic Action in Vietnam

When Ngô Đình Diệm assumed power as prime minister of the State of Vietnam on July 7, 1954 he inherited a politically and geographically divided state. Since December 1946 the Việt Minh – an amalgam of Vietnamese nationalist groups led clandestinely by the Vietnamese communists – had been fighting a brutal war of decolonization against French and colonial forces attempting to hold on to their Southeast Asian colony. Unable to overcome the Việt Minh's nationalist appeal by force of arms, the French, in concert with the former Vietnamese emperor, established the State of Vietnam with Bảo Đại as the chief of state on March 8, 1949. This new government would receive limited independence as an Associated State within the French Union – a successor organization to the French empire whose associative nature was intended to be more collaborative in governance than the old imperial structure. Under this new regime, the Vietnamese would be permitted more freedom to manage their domestic affairs, but foreign and defense policy would remain firmly under French control. Both Bảo Đại and the French hoped his standing as what they conceived to be a more legitimate Vietnamese leader would undercut the Việt Minh's claim to represent the national aspirations of the Vietnamese people in light of their communist ties which, in a Cold War context, could make them appear beholden to the machinations of a foreign power – the USSR.[1] Unfortunately this was not the case and the war

---

[1] For a discussion of the creation of the State of Vietnam see Kathryn C. Statler, *Replacing France: The Origins of American Intervention in Vietnam* (Lexington, KY: The University Press of Kentucky, 2007), 16–17; Fredrik Logevall, *Embers of War: The Fall of an Empire and the Making of America's Vietnam* (New York: Random House, 2012), 210–212; Jessica Chapman, *Cauldron of Resistance: Ngo Dinh Diem, the United States, and 1950s*

raged on until representatives of France and the Democratic Republic of Vietnam (DRV) – the independent Vietnamese political entity established by the leadership of the Việt Minh at the end of World War II – met in Geneva in the spring of 1954 to negotiate an end to the hostilities.

The Geneva Accords, signed on July 21, 1954, two weeks after Diệm's appointment as prime minister, brought the fighting to a close and divided Vietnam into two regroupment zones for Việt Minh and French forces on either side of the seventeenth parallel.[2] This territorial division was intended to be a temporary measure that would be resolved within two years by national elections to determine the political future of a unified Vietnam. Under the provisions of the Accords, the Vietnamese people would have a choice between the leadership of the Democratic Republic of Vietnam or the government Ngô Đình Diệm led, the French-sponsored State of Vietnam.

To win these elections, Diệm would have to convince the population of Vietnam that he was the leader of a government that could both provide for the people and serve as a national unifying force capable of bringing a fragmented society together. This was no easy task given that the deck was heavily stacked against Diệm in Vietnam. In the north, he could count on virtually no popular support as any individuals likely to choose his government in the 1956 referendum were "voting with their feet" and using the regroupment provision of the Geneva Accords to move south. Over a period of 300 days following the implementation of the Accords, nearly one million refugees including approximately 800,000 of Diệm's Catholic co-religionists from north of the seventeenth parallel moved south fearing the prospect of life under a communist regime.[3] This left the south, where Diệm's government should have been able to wield its influence, as the main source of potential support. But due to a combination of circumstance, French design and the legacies of war

Southern Vietnam (Ithaca, NY: Cornell Universsity Press, 2013), 44–47; and Edward Miller, *Misalliance: Ngo Dinh Diem, the United States and the Fate of South Vietnam* (Cambridge, MA: Harvard University Press, 2013), 34–35.

[2] According to Fredrik Logevall, the Accords were signed in the morning of July 21, but dated July 20 to allow Pierre Mendès France, the French premier who had staked his premiership on reaching an agreement by July 20, to "save face." Logevall, *Embers of War*, 605.

[3] George McTurnan Kahin, *Intervention: How America Became Involved in Vietnam* (New York: Alfred A. Knopf, 1986), 76–77; David L. Anderson, *Trapped by Success: The Eisenhower Administration and Vietnam, 1953–1961* (New York: Columbia University Press, 1991), 77–78; and Seth Jacobs, *America's Miracle Man in Vietnam: Ngo Dinh Diem, Religion, Race, and U.S. Intervention in Southeast Asia* (Durham, NC: Duke University Press, 2004), 129–138.

his government actually exerted very little control below the seventeenth parallel. The vast and sparsely populated Mekong Delta had only just come under ethnic Vietnamese control prior to the arrival of the French, making it a polyglot territory of distinct and isolated communities with little allegiance to any central state. Elsewhere, huge swaths of land were controlled by millenarial religious sects that emerged in opposition to the French or isolated ethnic minorities that had occupied their land for generations. In both cases, they had been able to enjoy some semblance of autonomy as part of the colonial regime's divide-and-rule tactics.[4] Finally, the Việt Minh, which had demonstrated its nationalist mettle by forcing the French to abandon the northern half of Vietnam, enjoyed considerable sympathy among the remainder of the southern population. This was particularly disconcerting as Diệm could make no such claim while the government he headed and the bureaucracy he inherited were both products of the French colonial system. Many administrators were part of the French colonial apparatus and Diệm had very little confidence in their abilities, viewing them as *fonctionnaires* with little interest in pursuing the nationalist cause he would be advancing. Overcoming these obstacles to his authority would require a government initiative to convince the southern population that there was an alternative Vietnamese authority in Sài Gòn worth rallying around. Diệm's Civic Action program was intended to fill that role.

NGÔ ĐÌNH DIỆM AND THE LEGACY
OF THE FIRST INDOCHINA WAR

The South Vietnamese nation that Ngô Đình Diệm would attempt to fashion over the course of his tenure had its origins in the Geneva Accords. They represented the international complexities occasioned by the intersection of the forces of decolonization with the global Cold War. The Accords were the result of an international conference convened in the Swiss city to try to bring the bloodletting between the French and Việt Minh forces on the Indochinese peninsula to a halt. By the summer of 1953 it was evident that neither side could deliver the knock-out blow to the other to achieve a decisive victory while significant war-weariness was setting in on both sides. Complicating the matter was the fact that the Việt Minh and the French had courted international support

---

[4] The challenges these posed to Ngô Đình Diệm's authority will be examined in the next chapter.

for their respective causes from the two camps of the Cold War. The Việt Minh's government of the Democratic Republic of Vietnam had been recognized as the legitimate government of the entire territory of Vietnam by the Soviet Union and the People's Republic of China, while the French-backed State of Vietnam had received the same recognition from the United States and Great Britain. With recognition came military and economic aid and a commitment of international credibility, increasing the potential stakes of this war of decolonization considerably. Rather than see the conflict in Southeast Asia spin out of control and risk triggering a superpower confrontation in an area considered peripheral to the Cold War, leaders from the Great Powers – Britain, France, the United States and the Soviet Union – agreed at an international summit in Berlin in early 1954 to add the matter to a conference scheduled to be held in Geneva to try to resolve outstanding matters arising from the armistice that had recently ended the Korean War.[5]

The Indochinese portion of the conference opened in May 1954 and was chaired by Great Britain and the Soviet Union. The Democratic Republic of Vietnam was represented by Pham Văn Đồng, while France was represented by Georges Bidault and Pierre Mendès France.[6] The outcome of the deliberations reflected the realities on the ground. A day before the conference started the French received a staggering blow to their fortunes in Indochina when their airbase at Điện Biên Phủ fell to Việt Minh forces after more than three months of intense, bloody fighting.[7] A significant psychological defeat for the French Union, it was not decisive for their military effort. The French still maintained a significant military presence in northern Vietnam while the Việt Minh presence in the south was quite weak. Moreover, the DRV's best forces were exhausted from the battle of Điện Biên Phủ and needed time to recover.[8] Months of grueling combat would still be needed to achieve victory on the Việt Minh's terms. There was considerable doubt within the government of

---

[5] For a good account of the events leading up to the Geneva Conference see James Waite, *The End of the First Indochina War: A Global History* (London: Routledge, 2012), 15–34. See also Statler, *Replacing France*, 51–84.

[6] Georges Bidault, the French foreign minister in Joseph Laniel's government, was replaced by Pierre Mendès France when Laniel's government fell in the middle of the negotiations. Mendès France, the new premier, elected to handle the foreign ministry portfolio himself and dramatically promised to reach an agreement at the conference in thirty days or resign. Statler, *Replacing France*, 102.

[7] For an excellent account of the battle of Điện Biên Phủ see Logevall, *Embers of War*, especially 381–546.

[8] *Ibid.*, 537.

the DRV that the Vietnamese people could sustain this. The French, for their part, were well aware that a majority of the people in the metropole were resigned to abandoning their Southeast Asian colonies and simply wanted an end to what was now considered *la geurre sale*, or dirty war.[9]

After six weeks of hard bargaining, facilitated to a great degree by Zhou En-Lai of the People's Republic of China, who was in attendance due to his nation's position as the largest power in the region,[10] both sides agreed to halt the fighting and temporarily divide Vietnam into two regroupment zones for forces representing either side at the seventeenth parallel. Soldiers fighting for the Việt Minh would regroup to the north of the demarcation line, while the armed forces of the French Union would move to the south. Within two years, a referendum would be held to determine under which government Vietnam would be reunified, the Democratic Republic of Vietnam located in Hà Nội or the State of Vietnam in Sài Gòn. Civilians were also allowed 300 days following the signing of the Accords to move across the seventeenth parallel in order to live under the government of their choice.[11]

For the new premier of the State of Vietnam, the outcome of the Geneva Conference was extremely disappointing. Ngô Đình Diệm was a fierce nationalist and vehemently opposed to communism. As far as he was concerned, his was the legitimate government of the entire territory of Vietnam and it had been betrayed by the French. He refused to recognize either the Accords or the existence of the DRV. This stance represented the independent position he was attempting to carve out for Vietnam between the perpetuation of the colonial apparatus and adoption of the communist system maintained by the leadership of the Việt Minh. This position, in turn, was a reflection of Diệm himself.

Ngô Đình Diệm (see Figure 1) had been born to a prominent Catholic family in 1901. His father, Ngô Đình Khả, had been a member of the Imperial

---

[9] Miller, *Misalliance*, 88–89.

[10] The fighting in Indochina was occurring on the doorstep of the People's Republic of China, giving Beijing a vested interest in the outcome. Additionally, China's inclusion in the Geneva Conference reflected Soviet Foreign Minister Vyachaslav Molotov's desire to promote the legitimacy of the Beijing government as representing a great power allied with Moscow as well as French premier Georges Bidault's preference to negotiate with the USSR and PRC rather than the Việt Minh as he felt they might be more amenable to meeting French demands in the global interest of world peace versus the local concerns of the Vietnamese; Waite, *End of the First Indochina War*, 29.

[11] Agreement on the Cessation of Hostilities in Vietnam, July 20, 1954, *Foreign Relations of the United States*, Vol. 16, *The Geneva Conference 1952–1954* (Washington, DC: United States Government Printing Office, 1981), *1505–1520*.

Court at Huế and instilled both Confucian and Catholic values in his children. Diệm had originally intended to dedicate his life to the church, but found monastic life to be too rigid and pursued a career in the civil service. A driven, energetic and studious individual, Diệm rose quickly through the colonial administration, becoming a provincial governor by the age of twenty-eight. In May of 1933, Vietnam's young emperor, Bảo Đại, made Diệm the Minister of the Interior. His service as a member of the Imperial Cabinet was short-lived, however. After a period of only three months, Diệm resigned in protest when his request to the French for more political autonomy for the Vietnamese government went unfulfilled. This courageous act of defiance demonstrated a stubborn, self-righteous integrity that bordered on obstinacy and enhanced his reputation as an incorruptible nationalist.[12]

During World War II, Diệm engaged in various anti-French intrigues which nearly got him arrested by the *Sûreté*. He was saved by his efforts to exploit the sympathies of some of Vietnam's more "idealist" Japanese occupiers who bristled at the fact that Tokyo, despite its stated aim of an "Asia for Asians," permitted the Vichy French colonial government to maintain control over Vietnam. The Japanese Consul in Huế helped him escape to Sài Gòn where he remained politically active.[13] In early 1946, Diệm was brought before Hồ Chí Minh, the founder of the Việt Minh, who asked him to join them. Diệm refused, apparently citing as reason the death of his older brother at the hands of the Việt Minh the year before and a suspicion that he would not be a full partner in any future government.[14] In the short run, Diệm's opposition to both the Việt Minh and the French did him few favors. Once World War II ended and the war with the French commenced, Diệm's refusal to support either side garnered him the reputation as an *attentiste*, or fence-sitter.[15]

Over the next few years, Diệm shrewdly used this opportunity to try to establish an independent position between the two poles of communism

---

[12] Catton, *Diem's Final Failure*, 6; Miller, *Misalliance*, 26; Statler, *Replacing France*, 118; See also Dennis Warner, *The Last Confucian: Vietnam, Southeast Asia and the West* (New York: Macmillan, 1963), 69–71.

[13] Miller, *Misalliance*, 29–31.

[14] Ellen J. Hammer, *The Struggle for Indochina: 1940–1955: Viet Nam and the French Experience* (Stanford, CA: Stanford University Press, 1966), 101 and 149–150. Ngô Đình Khôi had preceded Diệm into the civil service. He was equally as opposed to communism as Diệm and had been executed by being buried alive, along with his son, by the Việt Minh for his views. For a more spirited account of Khôi's death and Diệm's confrontation with Hồ Chí Minh see Warner, *The Last Confucian*, 66–68.

[15] Miller, *Misalliance*, 32.

FIGURE 1 Ngô Đình Diệm reading the proclamation of the Republic of Vietnam, 1955. Bettmann, Getty Images

and colonialism. He approached other like-minded leaders and groups to join him, including members of the Việt Minh who were not enamored with some of its communist inclinations. When the Elysée Accords were announced in June 1949, Diệm publicly denounced them, releasing his own statement that indicated he possessed an alternative vision for Vietnam to that of the French or the Vietnamese communists that was tantamount to a "social revolution." Though this was only a protean vision, it would evolve, as we shall see, and form the basis of his platform for national development.[16] Just as importantly, it reflected Diệm's remarkable confidence in himself and his abilities, suggesting that he saw himself as holding the key to the creation of a viable, independent Vietnamese state. Unfortunately, at the time it only earned Diệm the enmity of both the Việt Minh and the French. He found himself on a Việt

[16] *Ibid.*, 36.

Minh hit-list and, without the protection of the colonial government, he was forced to leave Vietnam in 1950.

Even though Diệm's exile removed him from direct engagement with the political scene in Vietnam, his time away proved to be extremely important for his political fortunes. During this period, Diệm spent time in Japan, Europe and the United States. In the two-and-a-half years he spent in the United States, he made several entreaties to various officials in the State Department. Unfortunately, officials there showed little interest in what Diệm had to say. Diệm did, however, earn points with other prominent officials in the United States including Francis Cardinal Spellman, Democratic Senate Majority Leader Mike Mansfield, former Office of Strategic Services chief William Donovan and Justice William O. Douglas. While these individuals could relate to Diệm's adherence to a Western religion and laud his opposition to communism – especially at a time when they were mired in their own devastating efforts to root out alleged domestic subversives – they were particularly impressed by Diệm's pleas for a "Third Force" in Indochina between communism and colonialism. Many American officials worried that French efforts to cling to their colonial possessions were only aiding the communists, who could use this to their advantage by claiming they were the true champions of national liberation. Diệm was a refreshing alternative whose credentials appeared to match their desires for a postcolonial leader.[17]

In the meantime, members of Diệm's family worked behind the scenes to further his political prospects in Vietnam. A key player was his immediate junior in the family, his brother Ngô Đình Nhu.[18] Nhu was the family intellect, having attended France's École de Chartes. In the early 1950s, Nhu promoted Diệm's cause among the Vietnamese noncommunist intelligentsia through the journal *Xã Hội (Society)*. At the same time, he proved to be quite adept at political organization, forming a Trade Union movement and the nucleus of a political party based on Diệm's nascent ideas for nationhood. This latter organization, initially created

[17] Joseph Buttinger, *Vietnam: A Dragon Embattled*, Vol. II, *Vietnam at War* (New York: Frederick A. Praeger, 1967), 846–847; Catton, *Diem's Final Failure*, 6; Miller, *Misalliance*, 31–41; Statler, *Replacing France*, 118.

[18] Other members in his immediate family who were important in Diệm's rise to power were his eldest surviving brother, Ngô Đình Thục, the Bishop of Vĩnh Long province; his younger brother Ngô Đình Cẩn, who ruled Central Vietnam as his personal fief from the family home in Huế; and his youngest brother, Ngô Đình Luyện, who spoke several languages and lived in Europe, which facilitated access to certain dignitaries and made him a vital conduit to the Emperor Bảo Đại who preferred the decadence of the French Riviera to ruling in Vietnam; Miller, *Misalliance*, 42.

to lobby on Diệm's behalf, became the *Đảng Cần Lao Nhân Vị* (The Vietnamese Personalist Labor Party), more commonly known as the *Cần Lao* – a semi-secret party whose members were organized into cells that, once Diệm assumed power, infiltrated the state bureaucracy to better control it.

By 1953, Nhu was able to seize on rising impatience among noncommunist nationalists toward Bảo Đại's gradualist approach to acquiring outright independence from the French. He manipulated the situation to force the emperor to consider appointing an individual with Diệm's anti-French and anticommunist stature to command a prominent role in his cabinet to quell the rising discontent. Neither Diệm nor Bảo Đại held each other in very high regard. Diệm saw Bảo Đại as a weak leader, readily willing to supplicate himself to the French and the trappings of his exalted position at the expense of the Vietnamese people. For Bảo Đại, Diệm was too high-minded and stubborn. Nevertheless, both could use the other to achieve what he wanted. Diệm could finally attain a position of power through which he could begin the process of realizing his nationalist vision for an independent noncommunist Vietnam. Bảo Đại could use Diệm for both his nationalist credentials and his American connections, which the emperor deemed increasingly important as France's imperial forces in Indochina continued to wane at the hands of the Việt Minh. On June 16, 1954, the two entered into a marriage of convenience when Diệm formally agreed to Bảo Đại's request that he form a cabinet.[19] Even with the emperor's endorsement, however, Diệm found himself at a decided disadvantage in the impending contest to lead an independent Vietnam.

By compelling the French forces to sue for peace and, by extension, recognize Vietnamese independence above the seventeenth parallel, Hồ Chí Minh, the leader of the Democratic Republic of Vietnam, had legitimized his nationalist credentials in the eyes of many of the Vietnamese people and seized the upper hand. Diệm viewed Hồ Chí Minh as a communist dupe who was interfering in Vietnam's progression from colonial state to sovereign nation. If Hồ was allowed to succeed, Diệm feared, Vietnam would disappear as an independent political entity and become nothing more than "a southern province of Communist China."[20] However, for

[19] Catton, *Diem's Final Failure*, 7 and 15–16; Miller, *Misalliance*, 49–53.

[20] See Catton, *Diem's Final Failure*, 27–28 for the quotation. See also the Speech of the Head of Vietnam's Delegation to the Bandung Conference, April 29, 1955, Item number 2321503034, Texas Tech Virtual Vietnam Archive, www.virtualarchive.vietnam.ttu.edu (hereafter referred to as TTVVA) (accessed March 25, 2009).

Diệm to have any chance of countering Hồ Chí Minh's appeal he would need to contend with the myriad challenges to his authority that were a product of Vietnam's colonial experience and produce some semblance of a national vision of his own to rival that of Hồ's socialist republic. But before he could even do that, he needed to find a way extend his political reach beyond the capital city of Sài Gòn and the other locations where his regime enjoyed a modicum of political control.

Expanding his government's writ into the countryside was crucial for Diệm to have any chance of advancing his national vision of an independent, noncommunist Vietnam, much less winning the elections scheduled for July 1956. This would be difficult as seven-and-a-half years of war with the French had left significant portions of the countryside devoid of any government presence. Moreover, the countryside contained a population that was in ferment. Individual members of the peasantry were wrestling with their own questions about the state, society and what an independent Vietnam might look like.[21] The new premier would have to find a means to fill the gap between the government and the people and try to respond to their needs as quickly as possible.

KIỀU CÔNG CUNG AND THE ORIGINS OF CIVIC ACTION

With only two years to establish a firm presence throughout the countryside before the national elections, the Sài Gòn government needed to work quickly. Of particular concern were the so-called "liberated areas." These were two areas in central and southern Vietnam that had been administered by the Việt Minh during the war with the French that were now to be placed under the control of the southern government as stipulated by the Geneva Accords.[22] The Sài Gòn government needed to fill the administrative vacuum left by the departing Việt Minh and counter what Diệm saw as Việt Minh efforts to "embarrass" his new regime through tax moratoriums, land redistribution and construction projects, such as new schools, to improve the lot of the peasantry.[23]

---

[21] David Hunt, *Vietnam's Southern Revolution: From Peasant Insurrection to Total War* (Amherst, MA: University of Massachusetts Press, 2008), 10–28.

[22] The two areas consisted of the central Vietnamese provinces of Quảng Nam, Quảng Ngãi, Phú Yên and Bình Định and some districts of the southern provinces of Quảng Trị and Bình Thuận.

[23] Re-establishing civil administration in liberated areas of Central Vietnam, ND, Subject Files 1954–1958 (hereafter referred to as SF 54–58), Box 1, Record Group 469 (hereafter

The government was in a poor position to fill this void. The central government had failed to reach beyond the towns under the French colonial system, resulting in the neglect of the villages where the mass of the people lived.[24] Eighty percent of government employees were concentrated in the Sài Gòn-Chợ Lớn area alone.[25] Many of what the Diệm regime referred to as "modern public services," such as those of the Ministries of Public Works and Information, failed to reach beyond the provincial capitals.[26] This scenario perpetuated itself because many members of the administrative organizations Diệm had inherited had been trained in accordance with the old colonial methods and regulations and maintained the same hierarchical structure that concentrated services and staff in the provincial centers. Those that had entered the bureaucracy after the French returned in 1945, Diệm believed, had learned to defer to French judgment and rarely attained any position that required meaningful decision-making. This *"fonctionnaire* spirit" made them little more than appendages of the colonial state.[27] Consequently, Diệm did not hold them in high regard, questioning their moral acumen.[28] With such poor and dysfunctional leadership, the government believed, the rural population remained in a politically, socially and culturally backward and benighted state.[29] Their loyalties had "been extended to whatever party, religious sect or local warlord ... seemed to care for their welfare," while the lack of public services in the villages had prevented the local population from being kept abreast of "the social and economic changes which have taken place in larger towns and cities."[30]

referred to as RG 469), National Archives and Records Administration (hereafter referred to as NARA).

[24] Critical Note and Proposals of the Secretary of State at the Presidency, ND, SF 54–58, Box 1, RG 469, NARA; and Report on the Organization of the Special Commissariat for Civic Action, June 1957, Folder 82, Box 660, Michigan State University Vietnam Advisory Group (hereafter MSUVAG), Michigan State University Archives (hereafter MSUA).

[25] Civic Action, ND, SF 54–58, Box 1, RG 469, NARA; and Report on the Organization of the Special Commissariat for Civic Action, June 1957, Folder 82, Box 660, MSUVAG, MSUA.

[26] Critical Note and Proposals of the Secretary of State at the Presidency, ND, SF 54–58, Box 1, RG 469, NARA.

[27] For a discussion of the *fonctionnaire* spirit, see Robert Scigliano, *South Vietnam: Nation Under Stress: An Important Look at the Trouble Spot of Asia* (Boston: Houghton Mifflin Company, 1964), 38.

[28] Miller, *Misalliance*, 89 and 134. See also William Colby with James McCargar, *Lost Victory: A Firsthand Account of America's Sixteen-Year Involvement in Vietnam* (Chicago: Contemporary Books, 1989), 86; and Catton, *Diem's Final Failure*, 127.

[29] Critical Note and Proposals of the Secretary of State at the Presidency, ND, SF 54–58, Box 1, RG 469, NARA.

[30] Civic Action, ND, SF 54–58, Box 1, RG 469, NARA.

To make matters worse, the Diệm regime was acutely aware that the departing Việt Minh were leaving undercover "stay-behind" agents in their wake to agitate on behalf of the communist government in Hà Nội in preparation for the upcoming elections. It saw itself at a decided disadvantage in this competition. Communist agents could easily exploit the rural poverty caused by seven-and-a-half years of war and roughly eighty years of French colonial rule to highlight the inability of the Sài Gòn government to help its citizens. The central government feared these communist agitators would also be able to capitalize on the limited presence of the government administrators at the local level to more easily infiltrate anti-regime elements into the ranks of the village community.[31]

As David Hunt has shown, much of the South Vietnamese peasantry was grappling with the question of how best to "safeguard their lives and futures" at the mid-point of the twentieth century.[32] They were dependent on "fragile" household economies for survival that were often based on subsistence farming, low wage jobs or trade in marketplaces that could be far away. In some cases, they were the products of single-parent families that had endured the disruption of the French war and lost relatives in the fighting.[33] In the wake of the Geneva Accords, Hunt continues, many in the province of Định Tường (Mỹ Tho),[34] frustrated with what they felt to be the confines of this rural existence, took it upon themselves to "control their own destiny" and set out for the more urban centers in the hopes of a "better life." For some, the district capitals offered a way out. Others found an insurmountable gulf existed between the rural ways they were accustomed to and the urban demands they were met with. Rather than material gain and social justice, these peasants encountered alienation and hardship. As Hunt argues, these positive and negative encounters with the urban centers broadened the consciousness of a generation of the Định Tường peasantry, providing them with a greater awareness of the urban–rural divide and the multiple possibilities it offered for alternative ways of living that escaped those who had only been exposed to life in the towns and cities.[35]

---

[31] Critical Note and Proposals of the Secretary of State at the Presidency, ND, SF 54–58, Box 1, RG 469, NARA; and Civic Action, ND, SF 54–58, Box 1, RG 469, NARA.

[32] Hunt, *Vietnam's Southern Revolution*, 9.

[33] *Ibid.*, 13–14.

[34] During the period of French rule this province was known as Mỹ Tho, following the end of the Franco-Việt Minh war it was called Định Tường.

[35] Hunt, *Vietnam's Southern Revolution*, 9–21. The first quote can be found on page 9 and the second one can be found on page 15.

At the same time, Hunt demonstrates that a generational shift was at work as a new youth culture began to emerge among the peasantry. Encouraged by the development of a consumer culture and the opportunities it offered for "self-transformation," youth challenged what they saw as antiquated patterns of filial piety, choosing their own partners rather than entering into arranged marriages or finding an alternative source of livelihood from the family farm.[36] All of this restiveness produced a potentially fertile environment for opponents of the regime to sow the seeds of revolt.[37]

To address this situation, Ngô Đình Diệm issued a directive on national security action for the Vietnamese Army on December 31, 1954 that placed all of the unsecured provinces in South Vietnam under military authority. This program, also known as "pacification" by the Americans, was drafted with the assistance of Rufus Phillips, a second lieutenant in the US Army detailed to the Central Intelligence Agency. It would be run through the South Vietnamese Ministry of Defense and was initially intended to use *Groupes Administratifs Mobiles* (GAM) to try to establish a governmental administrative presence in the districts and villages of the liberated zones. The GAM portion of this directive, however, was never implemented as Diệm realized shortly thereafter that during the Franco-Vietnamese War the French had attempted to use GAMs in their effort to defeat the Việt Minh in the north and central provinces to no avail.[38]

Ironically, Diệm's concern was not motivated by the fact that the GAMs were attempting to extend the reach of a foreign occupier down to the village level. As he saw it, the Việt Minh, under the control of the communists, were simply puppets of Moscow or Beijing and therefore attempting to do much the same. His opposition to the plan stemmed

---

[36] *Ibid.*, 26–27.

[37] *Ibid.*, 8.

[38] Instruction Presidentiale, December 31, 1954, Folder 14651, Phủ Thủ Tướng Chính Phủ [Office of the Prime Minister of the Government] (hereafter PTTCP), Trung Tâm Lưu Trữ Quốc Gia II [National Archives Number 2] (hereafter TTLTQG2); and Note: Sur la Creation et L'Organisation d'un Commissariat General a L'Action Civique (charge de gagner la population a la cause nationale) [Note on the Creation of the Special Commissariat for Civic Action (charged with winning the population to the national cause)], ND, Folder 1463, Phủ Tổng Thống Đệ Nhất Cộng Hòa [Office of the President of the First Republic] (hereafter PTTĐICH), TTLTQG2. For Phillips' assistance in the drafting of the National Security Action Memorandum see Rufus Phillips, "Before We Lost in South Vietnam," in *Prelude to Tragedy: Vietnam, 1960–1965*, eds. Harvey Neese and John O'Donnell (Annapolis, MD: Naval Institute Press, 2001), 14; and Rufus Phillips, *Why Vietnam Matters: An Eyewitness Account of Lessons Not Learned* (Annapolis, MD: Naval Institute Press, 2008), 32–33.

from the perceived strategic and administrative shortcomings of the GAMs. For one thing, their presence in the villages had been so fleeting compared to that of the Việt Minh, who were already entrenched there, that the Việt Minh could easily reassert themselves once the GAMs had left. For another, the strictly administrative nature and organizational structure of the GAMs was inadequate for the task as Diệm conceived it. He felt it had been too top-heavy and therefore incapable of forging any meaningful and lasting connection with the villagers on a personal level. The GAMs had not allowed the French to extend the base of their administrative organization to the grassroots level, making the effort largely ineffective as far as Ngô Đình Diệm was concerned.[39]

Americans on the ground in Vietnam supported Diệm's proposed pacification plan. One of the most prominent was Rufus Phillips' boss, Colonel Edward Lansdale, an Air Force officer detailed to the Central Intelligence Agency. A close confidant of Diệm's and self-proclaimed expert on psychological and unconventional warfare, Lansdale had been sent by Washington to help the South Vietnamese premier thwart the perceived communist threat. Many of the ideas presented in the pacification plan had been drawn from Lansdale's experiences in the Philippines where he had helped the Secretary of Defense, Ramon Magsaysay, defeat the communist-led Huk insurgency in the early 1950s. Lansdale hoped he could work the same magic in South Vietnam and strongly endorsed the "National Action" Plan as an "integral part" of the larger effort to "establish government" and its "benefits" below the seventeenth parallel.[40]

The United States Operations Mission (USOM) – the International Cooperation Administration's (ICA) representative organ in Sài Gòn – showed similar support. They pushed strongly for American aid for the

[39] Civic Activities of the Military, Southeast Asia, March 13, 1959, Item number 12050107012, TTVVA (accessed January 29, 2007); Critical Note and Proposals of the Secretary of State at the Presidency, ND, SF 54–58, Box 1, RG 469, NARA; Report on the Project No. 2 on the creation and organization of the Commissionership of Civic Action, ND, SF 54–58, Box 1, RG 469, NARA; Civic Action, ND, SF 54–58, Box 1, RG 469, NARA; Memorandum for Collins from John E. Dwan, March 8, 1955, Lansdale, Edward G. (Colonel) 2, Box 28, Collins Papers (hereafter CP), Dwight D. Eisenhower Library (hereafter DDEL); and Wesley R. Fishel, *Vietnam: Anatomy of a Conflict* (Itasca, IL: F.E. Peacock Publishers, 1968), 597.
[40] Memorandum to Collins from Edward G. Lansdale, January 3, 1955, Lansdale, Edward G. (Colonel) 2, Box 28, CP, DDEL. See also Jonathan Nashel, *Edward Lansdale's Cold War* (Amherst, MA: University of Massachusetts Press, 2005), 49–76. For the significance of Lansdale's role in the Philippines on the National Security Action Plan see Thomas L. Ahern, Jr., *CIA and Rural Pacification in South Vietnam* (Langley, VA: Center for the Study of Intelligence, declassified 2007), 5–7 and Phillips, *Why Vietnam Matters*, 32–33.

program. A draft document entitled "Re-establishing Civil Administration in Liberated Areas of Central Vietnam" articulated the hope that this effort would "have long-range significance as a step in broadening the democratic base of the national government." Pacification, the document argued, could improve the line of communication between Sài Gòn and the countryside that the highly centralized French colonial apparatus had weakened. This improved communication, in turn, could have a "significant effect on the local sense of participation in, and responsiveness to, the national government and upon the Regional and National Government's knowledge of and responsiveness to local needs and desires." Such coordination and improved governance, it concluded, were "necessary prerequisites for the effective implementation of Foreign Operations Administration projects in all fields that involve local participation."[41]

In the interim, a former member of the Việt Minh, Kiều Công Cung, was approached by Hồ Thông Minh, the South Vietnamese Minister of Defense, to study the problems in the countryside and come up with a new pacification plan to replace the defunct GAM proposal. The Diệm government had been directed to Cung by Edward Lansdale. According to Lansdale, Cung approached the CIA operative at his Sài Gòn quarters in January 1955. During this encounter, Cung told Lansdale that he had heard the American "was trying to help Vietnam and that he [Cung] had some ideas of what needed doing." As Lansdale recalls, Cung began outlining a plan he had conceived to train members of South Vietnam's civil service to go out into the villages, dress like the peasantry and engage in manual labor to "serve the people" and help establish "self-government." This plan was intended to help lay a foundation of rural support for South Vietnamese premier Ngô Đình Diệm in preparation for the national elections scheduled to be held in the summer of 1956. Lansdale records that he was intrigued about the plan and its potential and brought it to the attention of Diệm.[42]

Cung's personal history encapsulates the complexities of life in postcolonial Vietnam. At the outbreak of World War II Cung had been a lieutenant in the French Army. Following the French surrender he resigned his commission. In June 1945 he became the director of police and security for Sài Gòn-Chợ Lớn under the pro-Japanese government of Trần

---

[41] Re-establishing civil administration in liberated areas of Central Vietnam, ND, SF 54–58, Box 1, RG 469, NARA. The Foreign Operations Administration was the forerunner to the International Cooperation Administration.

[42] Edward Geary Lansdale, *In the Midst of Wars: An American's Mission to Southeast Asia* (New York: Harper & Row, 1972), 206–210.

Trọng Kim. After the war he joined the Việt Minh as a nationalist. When the French returned in 1946 Cung became the leader of a resistance unit that opposed them. By 1951 he had attained the rank of Brigadier General within the resistance forces, but refused to join the communist party. This refusal bred suspicion and he was ultimately placed on a list of noncommunists to be purged. Catching wind of this, Cung deserted from his command located near the border with China and managed to escape with his family. Over the following year he and his family slowly made their way southward evading both the French and the Việt Minh, using forged papers that identified him as a peasant farmer. Between 1952 and 1954 he and his family remained underground in a Mekong Delta village where his wife had relatives. With the end of the Franco-Việt Minh War, Cung emerged from hiding and, impressed with Diệm's nationalism, offered to assist the new government in reasserting its control over the countryside.[43]

Cung's ideas, experience with the Việt Minh and his loyalty as a nationalist certainly made him an appealing candidate to orchestrate the Diệm government's effort to reach out to the countryside. But despite all this experience he proved to need some guidance in formulating a feasible plan. The initial approach he devised for the government was so broad and affected so many different ministries that Diệm asked Trần Trung Dung, Secretary of State to the Presidency and later Minister of Defense, to take over and use Cung as his assistant. Together they incorporated ideas from Lansdale's experiences in the Philippines and American economic and information officers in Sài Gòn into a more modest program that would accelerate central government assistance to regional and provincial officials and help counter communist influence over the villages. This plan, viewed as a temporary expedient, essentially attempted to place the resources of the South Vietnamese state behind an effort to duplicate the tactics of the communist agents at the village level and beat them at their own game.[44] It called for the creation of a flexible, mobile

---

[43] Civic Action, ND, SF 54–58, Box 1, RG 469, NARA (most likely written after November 7, 1955 and no later than January 31, 1956); Phillips, "Before We Lost in South Vietnam," 20–21; Phillips, *Why Vietnam Matters*, 76; Lansdale, *In the Midst of Wars*, 207–210; Memorandum from D.C. Lavergne to Leland Barrows, November 28, 1955 SF 54–58, Box 1, RG 469, NARA; and Fishel, *Anatomy of a Conflict*, 597.

[44] Civic Action, ND, SF 54–58, Box 1, RG 469, NARA; Ahern, *CIA and Rural Pacification in South Vietnam*, 8–9; and Phillips, *Why Vietnam Matters*, 74–75. For comparisons with Việt Minh techniques see Civic Action: Role, Activities, Results, ND, SF 54–58, Box 1, RG 469, NARA; and Memorandum from D.C. Lavergne to Leland Barrows, December 3, 1955, SF 54–58, Box 1, RG 469, NARA.

civilian organization drawn from the existing pool of civil servants that would go out into the countryside and fill the vacuum that was present between the central government ministries and the village population.[45]

The activities of this mobile organization, as envisioned by its creators, would be coordinated by commissars serving alongside their governmental counterparts at the regional, district, and provincial levels, but under the authority and control of a Commissioner General. This parallel structure, it was hoped, would facilitate relations between the local authorities and the central government by promoting greater cooperation and mediating conflicts that might arise between the members of the mobile organization and the regional, provincial or district governments.[46] The mobile groups would establish a grassroots connection with the people by living and working alongside villagers to recruit local cadres and guide them in carrying out useful local projects to improve their overall welfare, something the GAMs had failed to do.[47] As we shall see, the concept of harnessing local human resources to a self-help effort was quite consistent with ideas underpinning a broad rural development movement that was circulating throughout the Third World known as community development.[48]

[45] Huấn Lệnh Tổng Quất Tạm Thời Về Công Dân Vụ [Temporary Comprehensive Directions for Civic Action], March 7, 1955, Folder 1463, PTTĐICH; Untitled Document justifying Civic Action, ND, Folder 38, PTTCP, TTLTQG2; Report on the Organization of the Special Commissariat for Civic Action, June 1957, Folder 82, Box 660, MSUVAG, MSUA; Civic Activities of the Military, Southeast Asia, March 13, 1959, Item number 12050107012, TTVVA (accessed January 29, 2007); and Civic Action, ND, SF 54–58, Box 1, RG 469, NARA.

[46] Report on the Project No. 2 on the creation and organization of the Commissionership of Civic Action, ND, SF 54–58, Box 1, RG 469, NARA.

[47] Untitled Document justifying Civic Action, ND, Folder 38, PTTCP, TTLTQG2; Report on the Organization of the Special Commissariat for Civic Action, June 1957, Folder 82, Box 660, MSUVAG, MSUA; Civic Activities of the Military, Southeast Asia, March 13, 1959, Item number 12050107012, TTVVA (accessed January 29, 2007); Report on the Project No. 2 on the creation and organization of the Commissionership of Civic Action, ND; and Civic Action, January 31, 1956; SF 54–58, Box 1, RG 469, NARA.

[48] Community development, which shall be discussed in greater detail in the following chapters, was an American-inspired initiative that had its origins in New Deal urban renewal programs. It was adapted to rural conditions in post-independence India where it was held up as a model for other postcolonial states to emulate in their efforts to establish themselves as viable, independent nations. According to the Indian example, a trained community development worker would catalogue the perceived needs of the community, which could include anything from improving village health and sanitation to animal husbandry, and then enlist the voluntary help of its inhabitants in addressing these needs. Lane E. Holdcroft, "The Rise and Fall of Community Development: 1950–1965" (M.Sc. thesis, Michigan State University, East Lansing, MI, 1976), 1–3 and 9–16; Nicole Sackey, "Passage to Modernity: American Social Scientists, India, and the Pursuit

The Civic Action program, unfortunately, met with resistance from all sides. At a series of inter-ministerial conferences held throughout January and February, many province chiefs objected to it on the grounds that it would usurp their power, despite arguments to the contrary. As far as they were concerned, they believed the central government should simply provide them with money and allow them to carry out the program as they saw fit.[49]

Interested American observers, such as President Eisenhower's Special Representative to Vietnam, General J. Lawton Collins and his assistant Lieutenant Colonel John E. Dwan, were equally concerned. Though they were encouraged Civic Action's effort to extend the Sài Gòn government's presence down to the village level, they were slightly disturbed by the fact that the American Mission received no advanced word of the new National Action Plan developed by Cung and Dung prior to its hotly contested presentation to the province chiefs.[50] Moreover, they bristled at the extent of the program's organizational structure, which they perceived to be far too ambitious for the national budget of the State of Vietnam to sustain, while needlessly creating a parallel system of government.[51] Concerned that this duplication of effort could lead to "creation of another ministerial empire," Dwan suggested that the plan be revised so Civic Action would be implemented through the existing government agencies.[52]

of Development, 1945–61'" (Ph.D. diss., Princeton University, Princeton, NJ, 2004),181–183; Francis X. Sutton, "Nation-Building in the Heyday of the Classic Development Ideology: Ford Foundation Experiences in the 1950s and 1960s," in *Nation-Building: Beyond Afghanistan and Iraq*, ed. Francis Fukuyama (Baltimore, MD: The Johns Hopkins University Press, 2006), 53–55; Nick Cullather, *The Hungry World: America's Cold War Battle Against Poverty in Asia* (Cambridge, MA: Harvard University Press, 2010), 76–83; and Daniel Immerwahr, *Thinking Small: The United States and the Lure of Community Development* (Cambridge, MA: Harvard University Press, 2015), 71–75.

49 Report on the Organization of the Special Commissariat for Civic Action, June 1957, Folder 82, Box 660, MSUVAG, MSUA; Civic Activities of the Military, Southeast Asia, March 13, 1959, Item number 12050107012, TTVVA (accessed January 29, 2007); and Civic Action, ND, SF 54–58, Box 1, RG 469, NARA; and Ahern, *CIA and Rural Pacification in South Vietnam*, 9.

50 Memorandum of a Conversation with Ho Thong Minh, March 11, 1955, Memos for Record, Box 29, CP, DDEL.

51 Civic Action, ND, SF 54–58, Box 1, RG 469, NARA; Memorandum for Collins from John E. Dwan, March 8, 1955, Lansdale, Edward G. (Colonel) 2, Box 28, CP, DDEL; Memorandum of a Conversation with Ho Thong Minh, March 11, 1955, Memos for Record, Box 29, CP, DDEL; and Ahern, *CIA and Rural Pacification in South Vietnam*, 9.

52 Memorandum for Collins from John E. Dwan, March 8, 1955, Lansdale, Edward G. (Colonel) 2, Box 28, CP, DDEL.

Undaunted by this lack of overwhelming support for the National Plan, Diệm went ahead and on March 7, 1955 established within the Office of the Prime Minister a provisional Special Commissariat for Civic Action (*Đặc Ủy Phủ Công Dân Vụ* or CDV) with Kiều Công Cung as its Commissioner General.[53] The Special Commissariat consisted of two parts. One was the Central Services, which were responsible for liaising with the relevant ministries and services, drawing up plans and training the cadres for field work. It was originally housed in a temporary headquarters provided by the Ministry of Defense along with furniture, materiel, vehicles, equipment and military recruits on loan as administrative staff. The other part of the CDV was made up of the mobile provincial groups assigned to carry out the work of civic action and win the peasantry over.[54]

The Commissioner General set out immediately to recruit and train candidates for field duty to assist in the ongoing pacification operation following Việt Minh regroupment in the Cà Mau peninsula.[55] Cung hoped to find his first volunteers in the civil service, most likely assuming that current government employees would exhibit the spirited patriotism such a role warranted. When no volunteers appeared forthcoming he turned to a small group of young, university-trained men who had recently left the north as part of the post-Geneva resettlement.[56] These initial recruits were rapidly trained in the dissemination of propaganda; communal organization; and proper conduct, which meant dressing in

---

[53] Huấn Lệnh Tổng Quát Tạm Thời Về Công Dân Vụ [Temporary Comprehensive Directions for Civic Action], March 7, 1955, Folder 1463, PTTĐICH; Ordre de Service [Directions for the Service], March 7, 1955, Folder 4065, PTTCP, TTLTQG2; and Civic Action, ND, SF 54–58, Box 1, RG 469, NARA. It is interesting to note, and perhaps this is indicative of the level of active American interest in the internal Vietnamese affairs, that the American document on Civic Action referred to here, along with many subsequent American documents and works to reference Civic Action erroneously state that the Special Commissariat for Civic Action was established on May 7, 1955.

[54] Draft Copy of a Decree, ND, SF 54–58, Box 1, RG 469, NARA.

[55] Báo Cáo Hoạt Động Công Dân Vụ từ ngày thành lập đến nay (7.3.1955 đến 30.4.1955) [Report on the Operations of Civic Action from its establishment until the present (March 7, 1955 to April 30, 1955)], May 3, 1955, Folder 29155, PTTCP, TTLTQG2; Civic Activities of the Military, Southeast Asia, March 13, 1959, Item number 12050107012, TTVVA (accessed January 29, 2007); and Civic Action, ND, SF 54–58, Box 1, RG 469, NARA.

[56] Civic Activities of the Military, Southeast Asia, March 13, 1959, Item number 12050107012, TTVVA (accessed January 29, 2007). See also Lansdale, *In the Midst of Wars*, 210–213.

the "calico noir" of the farmers and laborers and helping the people in their daily activities.[57]

Despite the rapid training of this first group of Civic Action cadres, the Cà Mau operation never materialized. The Prime Minister's Office did not deem the political situation in the region "favorable," most likely because of the threat the entrenched presence of "stay behind" elements posed to the security of the newly minted CDV cadres. The first group of cadres was instead deployed on April 15, 1955 to the province of Gia Định, which surrounded Sài Gòn, followed subsequently by groups dispatched to Bình Định and Biên Hòa provinces on completion of their training.[58]

These initial deployments became part of a three-month pilot project intended to gain practical experience in coordinating the activities of the various ministries for subsequent CDV teams.[59] Their work consisted mainly of demonstrating the government's interest in the well-being of its citizens. Such tasks included providing gifts from the government for the people, establishing information rooms in the villages in order to propagandize on the behalf of the government, investigating the political allegiances of the various rural communities, and distributing desperately needed medicine and medical equipment from the Ministry of Health.[60]

Over the next six weeks, the CDV continued to expand and by the beginning of June, 117 cadres had been trained. Of these new cadres, 100 were divided evenly into ten mobile groups, while the remaining seventeen were given staff and supervisory roles in the Central Services. As the number of CDV cadres began to grow, it became readily apparent that

---

[57] Báo Cáo Hoạt Động Công Dân Vụ từ ngày thành lập đến nay (7.3.1955 đến 30.4.1955) [Report on the Operations of Civic Action from its establishment until the present (March 7, 1955 to April 30, 1955)], May 3, 1955, Folder 29155, PTTCP, TTLTQG2; Civic Activities of the Military, Southeast Asia, March 13, 1959, Item number 12050107012, TTVVA (accessed January 29, 2007); and Lansdale, *In the Midst of Wars*, 210–213.

[58] Báo Cáo Hoạt Động Công Dân Vụ từ ngày thành lập đến nay (7.3.1955 đến 30.4.1955) [Report on the Operations of Civic Action from its establishment until the present (March 7, 1955 to April 30, 1955)], May 3, 1955, Folder 29155, PTTCP, TTLTQG2.

[59] Báo Cáo Hoạt Động tháng 5, 1955 [May 1955 Operation Report], June 9, 1955; Báo Cáo Hoạt Động tháng 6 [June 1955 Operation Report], July 12, 1955; and Báo Cáo Hoạt Động tháng 7 1955 [July 1955 Operation Report], August 8, 1955, Folder 29155, PTTCP, TTLTQG2.

[60] Báo Cáo Hoạt Động Công Dân Vụ từ ngày thành lập đến nay (7.3.1955 đến 30.4.1955) [Report on the Operations of Civic Action from its establishment until the present (March 7, 1955 to April 30, 1955)], May 3, 1955; and Báo Cáo Hoạt Động tháng 5, 1955 [May 1955 Operation Report], June 9, 1955, Folder 29155, PTTCP, TTLTQG2. For an American account of the early stages of the Civic Action program see Phillips, "Before We Lost in South Vietnam," 21–22.

it would need a larger infrastructure to manage its constituent elements more efficiently. In the Central Services, Civic Action staff attempted to coordinate their work with representatives from the Ministries of Information and Propaganda, Education, Youth and Social Action, and Health. These ministries sent some of their own specialized cadres to join the CDV cadres in the villages.[61]

While a Vietnamese organization in design and execution, the Special Commissariat for Civic Action did receive some initial support from American sources. Lansdale provided valuable input to Cung regarding how the program should be conceived and obtained some additional "seed money" for training cadres from the Central Intelligence Agency.[62] At the same time, the Central Services liaised with the American-directed Training Relations and Instruction Mission (TRIM), USOM, the United States Information Service (USIS), and CARE (the Cooperative for Assistance and Relief Everywhere) in order to keep them informed of their work and obtain whatever financial and material support they could.[63] Rufus Phillips was assigned by Lansdale to facilitate this process. According to Phillips, USIS was very cooperative, loaning movie projectors to the Civic Action teams and helping them train projectionists. USOM, however, was far less amenable. USOM officials bristled at what they saw as the program's potential for a wasteful duplication of effort. They were far more interested in working directly with existing Vietnamese ministries in Sài Gòn.[64]

Where Phillips did have a more positive impact was in training the Civic Action cadres. A protégé of Lansdale, Phillips was well-versed in what he and Lansdale called "military civic action" – ensuring that members of the military adhered to an ethical code of conduct with regard to their relations with the civilian population using the armed forces to carry out activities that would contribute to the people's overall well-being, such as distributing blankets and mosquito nets or using army

---

[61] Báo Cáo Hoạt Động tháng 5, 1955 [May 1955 Operation Report], June 9, 1955, Folder 29155, PTTCP, TTLTQG2.

[62] Phillips, "Before We Lost in South Vietnam," 21.

[63] Báo Cáo Hoạt Động tháng 5, 1955 [May 1955 Operation Report], June 9, 1955, Folder 29155, PTTCP, TTLTQG2.

[64] Phillips, *Why Vietnam Matters*, 76–77; Civic Action, ND, SF 54–58, Box 1, RG 469, NARA; Memorandum for Collins from John E. Dwan, March 8, 1955, Lansdale, Edward G. (Colonel) 2, Box 28, CP, DDEL; and Memorandum of a Conversation with Ho Thong Minh, March 11, 1955, Memos for Record, Box 29, CP, DDEL. According to Thomas Ahern, Lansdale would later persuade "USIS to commit three-fourths of its operating budget to support the civic action program's public information efforts." Ahern, *CIA and Rural Pacification in South Vietnam*, 14.

engineers to repair bridges and roads. Phillips had accompanied the
South Vietnamese Army to help in this capacity during the reoccupation
of the Việt Minh regroupment zones.[65] With these experiences in hand,
Phillips personally assisted Cung in establishing a training and operations
program for the cadres.[66] More specific training involved instruction by
specialists from the Ministries of Information and Propaganda, National
Education, Youth and Social Action, and law enforcement from the
Ministry of Interior to educate the cadres about the tasks of their respective sphere. The ideological aspect of this training was designed to mimic
that of the communist cadres. Each member of the team was "instructed
in the major political lines of the government" – such as Diệm's views
on communism, colonialism and an independent Vietnam – and how to
"cope with the subversive maneuvers of the adversary."[67]

Given the limited budget for the program and the perceived demand
for cadres to act in the field (initial estimates put the need at 6,340 people) they could only afford to be trained for two-week terms. To help
ease the burden the Ministry of Defense provided the CDV with an additional and much larger building at Tân Sơn Nhứt airport to serve as both
a headquarters and a new cadre training school. With this new school
they anticipated being able to train anywhere from 300 to 400 students
every two weeks, but contended that to be really effective they should
be increasing the number of training classes to be able to start one each
week.[68]

The evolution of the Central Services allowed the Commissariat to
more clearly define the cadres' roles and responsibilities in the field. At

---

[65] Phillips, *Why Vietnam Matters*, 26–27, and 40–50; Thomas L. Ahern, Jr., *CIA and the House of Ngo* (Langley, VA: Center for the Study of Intelligence, declassified 2009), 61–65; and Ahern, *CIA and Rural Pacification in South Vietnam*, 5–6.

[66] Phillips, "Before We Lost in South Vietnam," 21.

[67] The quotation is from Civic Action: Role, Activities, Results, ND, SF 54–58, Box 1, RG 469, NARA. See also Critical Note and Proposals, ND; and Civic Action, ND, SF 54–58, Box 1, RG 469, NARA. Unfortunately we do not have any evidence of what message the cadres were to convey to the peasantry. We can surmise from the language of many Civic Action reports that they involved denouncing the communist line as traitorous while lauding the Diệm regime as humane and attentive to the people's welfare. See for exam- ple Báo Cáo Hoạt Động tháng 6 [June 1955 Operation Report], July 12, 1955; and Báo Cáo Hoạt Động tháng 7, 1955 [July 1955 Operation Report], August 8, 1955, Folder 29155, PTTCP, TTLTQG2; Báo Cáo Hàng Tháng: Tháng 11 năm 1955 của Đặc Ủy Phủ Công Dân Vụ [Monthly Report: November 1955 of the Special Commissariat for Civic Action], December 12, 1955; and Báo Cáo Hoạt Động Công Dân Vụ trong năm 1955 [1955 Operation Report], January 21, 1956, Folder 15982, PTTĐICH, TTLTQG2.

[68] Báo Cáo Hoạt Động tháng 5, 1955 [May 1955 Operation Report], June 9, 1955, Folder 29155, PTTCP, TTLTQG2.

the village level, they were operationally responsible to the province chief and instructed to get close to the community in order to gain their trust: living, eating, sleeping and working alongside the peasantry in the fields when necessary during the harvest season. Initially their efforts remained focused on demonstrating the government's benevolence. This continued to take the form of dispensing gifts, medical supplies and political tracts. Over time, the responsibilities were broadened to holding popular education classes, explaining the mission of the government ministries and how they could help the village population, and re-establishing administrative councils in areas that had been abandoned by the Việt Minh.

As part of their role, the Civic Action cadres were expected to ensure each village had a primary school, village hall for the village council to meet, a medical dispensary and information rooms where news and information about the government and its programs and policies would be available for members of the community to access easily. Where such facilities were unavailable, one of the cadres' first orders of business was to construct them with local materials and whatever volunteers were forthcoming.[69] Additionally, the cadres were also expected to bring a measure of security and order to the villages by convincing the community to accept some responsibility for its own self-defense and, more ominously, investigating the political allegiance of individual village members and their families and reporting on the activities of suspected communist agents or other dissident elements.[70] All of this was aimed to make the people realize that the leadership in Sài Gòn was attentive to their needs, with the hope that, when compared to the clandestine efforts of the communists, they would see that the new government in Sài Gòn was genuinely concerned about their interests.[71]

---

[69] Civic Action, ND, SF 54–58, Box 1, RG 469, NARA; Báo Cáo Hoạt Động tháng 5, 1955 [May 1955 Operation Report], June 9, 1955; and Báo Cáo Hoạt Động tháng 6 [June 1955 Operation Report], July 12, 1955, Folder 29155, PTTCP, TTLTQG2; and Memorandum for the Record, July 15, 1958, Item number 2321726007, TTVVA (accessed January 29, 2007).

[70] Civic Action, ND, SF 54–58, Box 1, RG 469, NARA; Báo Cáo Hoạt Động tháng 5, 1955 [May 1955 Operation Report], June 9, 1955; and Báo Cáo Hoạt Động tháng 8, 1955 [August 1955 Operation Report], September 14, 1955, Folder 29155, PTTCP, TTLTQG2.

[71] See for example Báo Cáo Hoạt Động tháng 5, 1955 [May 1955 Operation Report], June 9, 1955; and Báo Cáo Hoạt Động tháng 6, 1955 [June 1955 Operation Report], July 12, 1955 Folder 29155, PTTCP, TTLTQG2.

EARLY ASSESSMENTS

The first reports on the work of Civic Action were quite optimistic about the potential of the program. They offered an upbeat picture of measured success, contending that while the cadres were received with initial suspicion by the villagers, after realizing the nature of the mission they quickly warmed to the cadres' presence.[72] In each village the cadres passed through they made the people realize that the government was concerned with their welfare and sincerely looking for ways to help them.[73] According to one report, the people began to realize that they were being "exploited" by "the cunning propaganda of the Việt Minh" that claimed the Sài Gòn government was ineffective.[74] In some cases, the cadres' actions instilled new confidence in the national government, encouraging the members of the village councils in their jobs and injecting new life into the local authorities.[75]

Despite these buoyant reports there were some fundamental weaknesses that needed to be addressed for the program to demonstrate any lasting success. First, the cadres were still very inexperienced. As the program was new, they had very little practical experience to draw upon in their training; consequently, much of what they learned was theoretical. Second, a lack of the financial and material means to recruit, train and employ cadres on the scale they envisioned severely limited the scope of the program.[76] Third, most of the cadres recruited were from the north of

[72] Báo Cáo tổng quất về hoạt động của Công Dân Vụ từ ngày thánh lên đến ngày nay [Comprehensive report about the operations of Civic Action from its establishment until the present], June 20, 1955; Báo Cáo Hoạt Động tháng 5, 1955 [May 1955 Operation Report], June 9, 1955; Báo Cáo Hoạt Động tháng 7, 1955 [July 1955 Operation Report], August 8, 1955; and Báo Cáo Hoạt Động tháng 8, 1955 [August 1955 Operation Report], September 14, 1955, Folder 29155, PTTCP, TTLTQG2.

[73] Kính gửi Bộ Phủ Tổng Thống [Memorandum from the Special Commissariat for Civic Action to the Office of the President], June 4, 1955, Folder 29155, PTTCP, TTLTQG2.

[74] The quotations are taken from Báo Cáo Hoạt Động tháng 7, 1955 [July 1955 Operation Report], August 8, 1955, Folder 29155. The government's perspective on the substance of communist propaganda appears in Thuyết Trình về dự án sắc lệnh thiết lập Phủ Đặc Ủy Công Dân Vụ [Report on the decree establishing the Special Commissariat for Civic Action], September 24, 1955, Folder 1463, PTTCP, TTLTQG2.

[75] Memorandum from John Gates, TRIM to Edward G. Lansdale, August 7, 1956, SF 54–58, Box 1, RG 469, NARA; and Báo Cáo Hoạt Động tháng 5 [May 1955 Operation Report], 1955, June 9, 1955, Folder 29155, PTTCP, TTLTQG2.

[76] Báo Cáo tổng quất về hoạt động của Công Dân Vụ từ ngày thánh lên đến ngày nay [Comprehensive report about the operations of Civic Action from its establishment until the present], June 20, 1955; Báo Cáo Hoạt Động tháng 7, 1955 [July 1955 Operation Report], August 8, 1955; and Báo Cáo Hoạt Động tháng 8, 1955 [August 1955 Operation Report], September 14, 1955, Folder 29155, PTTCP, TTLTQG2.

Vietnam and possessed dialects, accents and mores that were unfamiliar
to the population in the south, making the communication and trans-
mission of ideas difficult.[77] Finally, power struggles and disagreements
between some regional authorities and their Civic Action counterparts
over the course of action remained a hindrance to cooperation in areas
where cadres were active.[78] In many cases, the local officials still resented
having to share some of their authority with outsiders sent down from
Sài Gòn and viewed the Civic Action cadres with suspicion.[79] According
to one report, provincial authorities refused to recognize Civic Action
personnel as government representatives due to their "plebian dress." It
was not until Cung himself dressed in the same manner and toured the
provinces as "a high functionary close to" Diệm that the program began
to gain some acceptance.[80]

These clashes were most likely the result of the greater autonomy
Vietnamese officials had received in running the country just prior to
the departure of the French. Throughout the colonial period a glass ceil-
ing had existed for the Vietnamese members of the colonial apparatus.
These officials were denied posts as administrators in Sài Gòn and permitted only to rise as high as district chief within the provincial governing system. As Roy Jumper observes, that began to change during the
French-Indochina War, when Vietnamese officials were finally "promoted

---

[77] Civic Activities of the Military, Southeast Asia, March 13, 1959, Item number 12050107012, TTVVA (accessed January 29, 2007); David W.P. Elliott, *The Vietnamese War: Revolution and Social Change in the Mekong Delta, 1930–1975*, Vol. 1 (Armonk, NY: M.E. Sharpe, 2003), 188; and Phillips, *Why Vietnam Matters*, 79. Though no specific examples of these difficulties were cited in the reports for this initial period of Civic Action, representative examples may be found in Tỉnh Tường Bến Tre Kính gởi Ông Bộ Trưởng tại Phủ Tổng Thống [Memorandum from the Ben Tre Province Chief to the Secretary of State for the Office of the President], August 18, 1956; and Tỉnh Tường Tânan Kính gởi Ông Bộ Trưởng tại Phủ Tổng Thống [Memorandum from the Tanan Province Chief to the Secretary of State for the Office of the President], September 4, 1956, Folder 16065, PTTĐICH, TTLTQG2.
[78] Báo Cáo tổng quát về hoạt động của Công Dân Vụ từ ngày thánh lên đến ngày nay [Comprehensive report about the operations of Civic Action from its establishment until the present], June 20, 1955; Báo Cáo Hoạt Động tháng 7, 1955 [July 1955 Operation Report], August 8, 1955; and Báo Cáo Hoạt Động tháng 8, 1955 [August 1955 Operation Report], September 14, 1955, Folder 29155, PTTCP, TTLTQG2.
[79] Báo Cáo Hoạt Động tháng 6, 1955 [June 1955 Operation Report], July 12, 1955; and Báo Cáo Hoạt Động tháng 7, 1955 [July 1955 Operation Report], August 8, 1955, Folder 29155, PTTCP, TTLTQG2.
[80] See Civic Activities of the Military, Southeast Asia, March 13, 1959, Item number 12050107012, TTVVA (accessed January 29, 2007). See also Civic Action, ND, SF 54–58, Box 1, RG 469, NARA for a corroborating account of this report.

to the top rungs of the administrative ladder."[81] Vietnamese officials who replaced the retreating French were able to enjoy much of the same autonomy and power that the *Administrateurs* had before them.[82]

Unfortunately, they were also the products of a system that stifled initiative, exhibiting the *fonctionnaire* spirit Diệm so derided. Rather than be perceived as a system for governance, administration was primarily viewed as a means for "ensuring accountability of bureaucratic transactions and the control of both government officials and the subject population."[83] As Diệm saw it, the bureaucracy was filled with "automatons" who were "slaves of routine." Civic Action offered him a means to inject it with a new vitality. Naturally, such moves encountered resistance as they threatened the status quo.[84] Ironically, Diệm contributed directly to this problem. In order to quell the "storm of protest" that had initially greeted the program when it was introduced in early 1955, Diệm had compromised and placed the Civic Action teams under provincial jurisdiction. This meant that many of the "working-level supervisors" who were holdovers from the system Diệm inherited from the French retained authority over the Civic Action cadres despite the fact that the "ineffectiveness" of these functionaries was something the CDV teams were intended to "circumvent."[85] In such a tense environment, Diệm's efforts to enlist the help of the various ministries and regional authorities in facilitating the work of Civic Action only served to further threaten these individuals who were already on the defensive; and they sought to protect their turf.[86]

Many of these underlying problems were discussed in a May 20, 1955 report of a recent trip to a village in Biên Hòa province by Randall Frakes, a Field Representative with USOM stationed in the Mekong Delta city of Cần Thơ. Although he saw great potential in the program as a means to reach many villages in a minimum period of time, Frakes contended that there had been little cooperation provided by the various government ministries and noted the "problem of duplication of effort." According

[81] Roy Jumper, "Mandarin Bureaucracy and Politics in South Viet Nam," *Pacific Affairs* 30(1) (March 1957): 47.
[82] Edward Garvey Miller, "Grand Designs: Vision, Power and Nation Building in America's Alliance with Ngo Dinh Diem, 1954–1960," Ph.D. diss. (Harvard University, Cambridge, MA, 2004), 244–245.
[83] Scigliano, *Nation Under Stress*, 38.
[84] Jumper, "Mandarin Bureaucracy and Politics," 53; and John C. Donnell, "National Renovation Campaigns in Vietnam," *Pacific Affairs* 32(1) (March 1959): 74–75.
[85] Ahern, *CIA and Rural Pacification in South Vietnam*, 9.
[86] Scigliano, *Nation Under Stress*, 39.

to his report, the Civic Action cadres had established a dispensary and begun training a first-aid worker, but the village already had a fully trained first-aid worker along with a complete first aid kit. He also did not feel qualified personnel could be trained within the fifteen days the cadres were in the village to be able to continue the teaching and health work. More generally, he felt it would be very difficult for the CDV to be able to obtain enough qualified volunteers to fill the anticipated number of Civic Action teams, which he stated to be 100. Finally, he doubted that there would be enough funds or equipment available to pay their salaries and carry out the proposed activities once the cadres moved on.[87]

Frakes' final observation proved to be the most enduring problem of the Civic Action program: maintaining continuity in the areas where the cadres had been active. As the USOM Field Representative observed, cadres were only assigned to villages for two- to four-week periods. One of the most pressing concerns was the training of appropriate individuals at the village level to serve as regional cadres who would continue the work of the Civic Action mobile group once it had moved on.[88] These individuals were selected for their enthusiasm and devotion to the national cause and were rewarded with minor seats on the village councils and exemption from local taxes. They were trained through oral instruction, the use of printed texts, and by working closely with the Civic Action cadres prior to their departure. Civic Action cadres would return periodically to check on the progress being made in their absence. Despite this backing, the perks and the training, these regional cadres were ostensibly volunteers and, in order to be willing to serve the Sài Gòn regime, they needed to be instilled with a sense of "self-sacrifice" that would ultimately require an iron faith in the benevolence of the government and its ability to lead.[89]

This proved to be a formidable task. In some areas where the cadres had managed to get close to the peasants and earn their trust, they found their efforts to maintain this bond were hampered by a chronic shortage of resources and a lack of trained personnel.[90] In a number of other places that had formerly been under Việt Minh control, the cadres found

[87] Memorandum from Randall V. Frakes to M.H.B. Adler, Chief, Field Service USOM, May 20, 1955, SF 54–58, Box 2, RG 469, NARA.
[88] Báo Cáo Hoạt Động tháng 6, 1955 [June 1955 Operation Report], July 12, 1955, Folder 29155, PTTCP, TTLTQG2.
[89] Báo Cáo Hoạt Động tháng 5, 1955 [May 1955 Operation Report], June 9, 1955; Báo Cáo Hoạt Động tháng 7, 1955 [July 1955 Operation Report], August 8, 1955, Folder 29155, PTTCP, TTLTQG2; and Civic Action, ND, SF 54–58, Box 1, RG 469, NARA.
[90] Báo Cáo Hoạt Động tháng 6 [June 1955 Operation Report], 1955, July 12, 1955; Báo Cáo Hoạt Động tháng 7, 1955 [July 1955 Operation Report], August 8, 1955; and Báo

very little support. The local administration was either nonexistent, or still in exile. The communist members of the Việt Minh who remained behind still managed to wield enough influence to effectively prevent the Civic Action cadres from establishing any meaningful government presence amongst the population.[91] Compounding this was the fact that despite the efforts of the Civic Action cadres Diệm, for the most part, remained an unproven commodity to much of the peasantry. Members of the rural population looking for some semblance of stability in their lives and hoping for a better future were hesitant to throw their support behind the South Vietnamese premier, as he had yet to demonstrate that he was capable of providing for their needs. The communists, on the other hand, had already proven their nationalist mettle as members of the Việt Minh and could point to having defeated the French as evidence of what they were capable of.[92] For Civic Action to succeed and show the people of South Vietnam that they had more to gain by supporting the Sài Gòn government than Hồ Chí Minh in Hà Nội before the 1956 elections it was imperative that it overcome the shortcomings that emerged in these early assessments.

Cáo Hoạt Động tháng 8, 1955 [August 1955 Operation Report], September 14, 1955, Folder 29155, PTTCP, TTLTQG2.

[91] Báo Cáo Hoạt Động tháng 6, 1955 [June 1955 Operation Report], July 12, 1955; and Báo Cáo Hoạt Động tháng 7, 1955 [July 1955 Operation Report], August 8, 1955, Folder 29155, PTTCP, TTLTQG2.

[92] Douglas Pike, *Viet Cong: The Organization and Techniques of the National Liberation Front of South Vietnam* (Cambridge, MA: MIT Press, 1967), 58–59, 75–76 and 83.

TWO

Nationalism and Welfare Improvement in the Republic of Vietnam

On July 10, 1955 the "experimental" period for the Civic Action program came to a close. In September its work was temporarily halted as it was reorganized to try to deal with some of its shortcomings.[1] While it is difficult to determine the exact chain of events that led to the reorganization, as well as what experience was gleaned from the three months when Civic Action was a pilot project, it is clear that on September 26 the first of what was to be a series of monthly inter-ministerial meetings were held between the CDV, the Ministries of Information, the Interior, Education, Youth and Social Action, Land Registration and Agrarian Reform to better coordinate their activities at the village level.[2]

Prior to this restructuring, Civic Action had been little more than a propaganda wing of the central government in practice. It had provided the rural masses with some reassurance that the Sài Gòn government was more interested in their welfare than the communists, but in material terms it had done little to raise the living standards of the people in the countryside or resolve outstanding individual questions about what the future may have in store for them. That began to change throughout the autumn of 1955 as the scope of the CDV's responsibilities was considerably enlarged. In November, the Special Commissariat for Civic Action

[1] Báo Cáo Hoạt Động tháng 7, 1955 [July 1955 Operation Report], August 8, 1955; and Báo Cáo Tổng Quát tháng 9 năm 1955 [September 1955 Comprehensive Operation Report], October 19, 1955, Folder 29155, Phủ Thủ Tướng Chính Phủ [Office of the Prime Minister of the Government] (hereafter PTTCP), Trung Tâm Lưu Trữ Quốc Gia II [National Archives Number 2] (hereafter TTLTQG2).
[2] Báo Cáo Tổng Quát tháng 9 năm 1955 [September 1955 Comprehensive Operation Report], October 19, 1955, Folder 29155, PTTCP, TTLTQG2.

was given a new mandate and more permanence to enable it to accord more with Ngô Đình Diệm's desire to consolidate his hold on power and pave the way for the revolution he and Nhu had been envisioning since the Elysée Accords.

As we have already seen, Ngô Đình Diệm had some ideas about what a postcolonial Vietnamese nation should look like. It needed to be socially just, economically viable and politically unified under one government free from either communist or colonial control. In his mind, he was the only person with the moral fortitude and vision of purpose to lead the Vietnamese people toward it. Unfortunately, this vision received a sharp blow from the Geneva Accords which temporarily divided Vietnam at the seventeenth parallel into two regroupment zones administered in the north by Hồ Chí Minh's communist government and the French-backed State of Vietnam in the south. The question of reunification would be resolved by national plebiscite to be held no later than July 1956 to determine under which government the nation would be unified. The Special Commissariat for Civic Action had been established to help win the southern population over to Diệm's government in time for the elections.

Ngô Đình Diệm, however, did not recognize the legitimacy of the Geneva Accords. They did not fit with his national vision and, more importantly, his government had not been a signatory to them. In the summer of 1955 he went so far as to repudiate their provision for a national plebiscite, announcing, in a July 16 radio broadcast, that his government would not participate in the national elections to reunify Vietnam the following year unless the Hà Nội government abandoned its "totalitarian methods of terror" to guarantee that they would be truly free and fair above the seventeenth parallel.[3] As a virulent nationalist Diệm no doubt legitimately believed he was under no obligation to honor the provision as his government had not signed the Accords. However, he also recognized that under the circumstances of the summer of 1955 his government would be wholly incapable of mustering enough national support to defeat Hồ Chí Minh's Democratic Republic of Vietnam in the coming election.[4] Not only did he have the clandestine communist agents who remained in the south to deal with but he had other more immediate threats to his authority to contend with, including the French, ambitious members of his own government and other elements of the

[3] Kathryn C. Statler, *Replacing France: The Origins of American Intervention in Vietnam* (Lexington, KY: The University Press of Kentucky, 2007), 170.
[4] Nhu-An Tran, "Contested Identities: Nationalism in the Republic of Vietnam (1954–1963)," Ph.D. diss. (University of California, Berkeley, CA, 2013), 39.

fractious political makeup of South Vietnam. Each of these groups harbored their own vision of what a noncommunist Vietnam should look like to rival Diệm's. For Diệm to be able to have even a hope of realizing his vision he would need to eliminate these opponents and consolidate his grip on power. Over the course of 1955, Diệm moved to eliminate these opponents and consolidate his grip on power. With his new mandate in November, Kiều Công Cung seized the initiative and made the Special Commissariat for Civic Action complicit in the process.

At the same time, the budget for Civic Action was set to expire. Throughout the fall of 1955 policymakers in the United States Operations Mission in Sài Gòn grappled with the decision of whether they should fund this initiative. US officials on the ground in Vietnam questioned the efficacy of the program as they perceived it. While Diệm envisioned the Civic Action program to be a means to extend his government's authority into the countryside and improve the material wellbeing of the Vietnamese people, key members of the American mission in Sài Gòn believed it incapable of achieving these far ranging goals in its current form. They considered Diệm's aims through the lens of community development – a grassroots approach to overcoming the impoverishment of the Third World through self-help initiatives that would increase local productivity and improve the overall welfare of the village population. They were skeptical that the Special Commissariat for Civic Action was the appropriate organ to carry out community development based on what they had actually seen. Despite Kiều Công Cung's interest in applying some aspects of the community development approach to the Civic Action program, these Americans viewed the Special Commissariat as little more than a propaganda device that needlessly duplicated the efforts of other ministries within the South Vietnamese government. Receiving US funding for the program would depend on whether or not the Americans could be brought around to accept that the CDV could, in reality, accord with their own preconceived notions of community development – a highly dubious prospect given the inflexibility of the United States Operations Mission in Sài Gòn.

THE ROOTS OF A REVOLUTION

As mentioned in the opening of the previous chapter, when Ngô Đình Diệm was invested as prime minister of the State of Vietnam in July 1954 he became the leader of a society that was wracked with division.[5] The

---

[5] The following discussion on the political divisions of South Vietnam in the first year of Ngô Đình Diệm's leadership draws heavily from Jessica Chapman, *Cauldron of*

French, who were in the process of relinquishing their Indochinese possessions as a result of treaties signed at Geneva, were still in a position to wield considerable influence over Vietnamese politics in the southern zone of regroupment.[6] The Chief of State, the former emperor Bảo Đại, maintained close connections with the French, continuing to reside in Cannes; the French representative to the State of Vietnam retained the title of High Commissioner; and the French Expeditionary Corps (FEC) remained in South Vietnam to train the Vietnamese National Army and keep order as part of Paris' obligations to the Geneva Accords.[7] The French were also adamantly opposed to Diệm and his vehement nationalism, with its stubborn resistance to any infringement on Vietnamese sovereignty. They schemed repeatedly to have him shunted aside, if not removed from power altogether.[8] More serious, however, was the threat posed by the Army Chief of Staff General Nguyễn Văn Hinh. Disgruntled by the nepotism of the cabinet and the narrowness of Diệm's political base, Hinh arrogantly boasted that he could seize control of the government at any time.[9]

Hinh found a sympathetic ear in members of two millennial politico-religious sects, the Cao Đài and Hòa Hảo, which controlled nearly one-third of the territory of southern Vietnam. This area, which one scholar has referred to as Vietnam's "Wild South," was considered frontier territory which had only been populated by the Vietnamese just prior to the arrival of the French. This was reflected in the disparate and widespread settlement pattern of "loosely connected communities" that stood

Resistance: Ngo Dinh Diem, the United States, and 1950s Southern Vietnam (Ithaca, NY: Cornell University Press, 2013).

[6] On June 4, 1954, just prior to Diệm's acceptance of the post of premier, two treaties were signed between representatives of the governments of France and the State of Vietnam. These treaties recognized the State of Vietnam as a "fully independent and sovereign state invested with all the competence recognized by international law." They abrogated the controls the French placed over Vietnam's defense and foreign policy, stating that the two governments would mutually agree to new conventions on these matters on an equal basis. Statler, *Replacing France*, 99.

[7] *Ibid.*, 117–216 *inter alia.*

[8] Kathryn Statler, "The Diem Experiment: Franco-American Conflict over South Vietnam, July 1954–May 1955," *The Journal of American-East Asian Relations* 6(2–3) (Summer–Fall, 1997): 151–154; and David L. Anderson, *Trapped by Success: The Eisenhower Administration and Vietnam, 1953–1961* (New York: Columbia University Press, 1991), 80.

[9] Statler, *Replacing France*, 128–129; and Edward Miller, *Misalliance: Ngo Dinh Diem, the United States, and the Fate of South Vietnam* (Cambridge, MA: Harvard University Press, 2013), 90 and 104.

in stark contrast to the dense village communities of northern and central Vietnam. These demographics, coupled with the diverse geography of the area, which included coastal plains, mountainous jungle highlands and the "mazelike waterways" of the Mekong Delta, had made this region notoriously difficult to govern by any central authority. When combined with the "social, spiritual, and economic" dislocation to the rhythm of everyday life caused by the French imperial project it made for a fertile environment from which rival centers of power could grow.[10]

The Cao Đài and Hòa Hảo had taken advantage of these circumstances in the 1920s and late 1930s, respectively, to carve niches for themselves and, in the process, come to dominate the religious, social and political affairs of great swathes of the southern countryside and command the allegiance of much of the population. Though they both claimed to be anticommunist and anticolonial, they had been able to exploit the French and the Việt Minh during World War II and the subsequent war of decolonization to play both sides off of one another to acquire their own armies and defend their own interests. Each possessed its own vision of what a postcolonial Vietnam should look like. Some members of the Cao Đài wanted to make their syncretic religion[11] the national religion of Vietnam, while the Hòa Hảo "sought to reform Buddhist practices that were inherently critical of French colonial and economic policies."[12]

Finally, there was the Bình Xuyên crime syndicate which controlled all the vice industries in the Sài Gòn-Chợ Lớn area including its prostitution rings and the Grande Monde Casino which was one of the largest in Asia. Its leader, Lê Văn Viễn (Bảy Viễn), had been made a brigadier general in the auxiliary forces of the Vietnamese National Army and had purchased the Sài Gòn-Chợ Lớn police concession from Bảo Đại in 1953 giving him effective control of the State of Vietnam's capital city.[13] All of these groups were potent forces in post-Geneva southern Vietnam's national politics. All of them posed an added and more immediate challenge to Diệm's authority during his first year in office. And all of them would

---

[10] Chapman, *Cauldron of Resistance*, 13–14. See also Li Tana, *Nguyễn Cochinchina: Southern Vietnam in the Seventeenth and Eighteenth Centuries* (Ithaca, NY: Southeast Asia Program Publications, Southeast Asia Program, Cornell University, 1998), 110.

[11] The Cao Đài religion drew from an eclectic array of religious beliefs including Confucianism, Christianity, Buddhism, Islam and Taoism and its adherents worshipped a pantheon of saints that ranged from Joan of Arc to William Shakespeare to Sun Yat Sen. Chapman, *Cauldron of Resistance*, 15.

[12] *Ibid.*, 15–23; the quote is from pages 22–23. See also and Tran, "Contested Identities," 53–58.

[13] Chapman, *Cauldron of Resistance*, 74–75.

need to be reckoned with for Diệm to have any chance of realizing his national vision for a viable Vietnamese nation. It was in the process of contending with this volatile political matrix that the contours of Ngô Đình Diệm's revolution began to emerge.

Diệm's troubles with these groups began almost immediately after taking office. In August and September Hinh joined with members of the Cao Đài and Hòa Hảo in a plot to approach Bảo Đại to get him to remove Diệm from office. They received support from French High Commissioner General Paul Ély and the minister in charge of relations with the Associated States, Guy La Chambre. Their concerns were three-fold. First, they questioned Diệm's abilities to contend with the commu-nist threat. Having spent much of the First Indochina War in exile, they did not think Diệm could serve as a unifying force around which the Vietnamese people would rally in opposition to the communists. Second, they perceived Diệm as a legitimate threat to their interests. They were well aware of Diệm's incorruptibility and desire to promote his vision of a united Vietnam at the expense of theirs. Finally, they opposed the nar-row base of his government. As mentioned above, Diệm had an undying faith in his abilities and firmly believed his to be the best way forward for Vietnam. But it would need a firm and reliable hand at the top. With little confidence in his own bureaucracy and an awareness that political enemies lurked everywhere, he packed his initial cabinet with individuals he felt he could trust, which meant people close to either him or members of his family. With the exception of a few token appointments, virtually all members of the religious sects, Bình Xuyên or the pre-existing govern-ment establishment were excluded from holding any political power.[14]

The ensuing crisis lasted for nearly eight months in which Diệm tried to divide and conquer his enemies, co-opting some with political appoint-ments and rewards and isolating others like Nguyễn Văn Hinh who was forced to leave the country in the late autumn of 1954. The denouement came in the spring of 1955 with a government assault on the remain-ing opposition elements of the sects and the Bình Xuyên that turned Sài Gòn into a battleground that at times threatened to pitch South Vietnam into civil war.[15] This was followed by the 7,000-man-strong Nguyễn Huệ Campaign launched in late May to root out the remaining political and religious opposition that had fled Sài Gòn to find sanctuary in the jungles

---

[14] *Ibid.*, 72–85.
[15] For accounts of the "Hinh" and so-called "Sect" crises see *ibid.*, 86–115; Miller, *Misalliance*, 95–123 and Anderson, *Trapped by Success*, 77–119.

of the surrounding provinces. While the military action, which lasted until April 1956, dealt with the leadership and military wings of Diệm's opposition, he still had to contend with the multitudes who supported them.[16] It was in trying to pacify these elements that some of the ideas regarding national identity, citizenship and democracy that would underpin his national revolution were revealed.

On April 19, 1955, in the midst of the assault on the Bình Xuyên and the sects in Sài Gòn, Ngô Đình Diệm complained to General J. Lawton Collins, Eisenhower's Special Representative to Vietnam, about French collusion with Bảy Viễn's gangsters which he likened to a retrograde feudal entity out of step with the modern nation he hoped to fashion. Their joint opposition to his leadership would only weaken the state, he argued, paving the way for a communist victory. Vietnam had to oppose communists, feudalists and colonialists.[17] Countering this triad of enemies to Diệm's postcolonial state would form the basis of an official Vietnamese nationalism that the South Vietnamese leader hoped to create.[18]

Antifeudalism and anticolonialism were the first tropes to emerge in Diệm's "three enemies" formula. They were a direct response to the challenges posed by the noncommunist opposition to Diệm's rule. Feudalists consisted of the Cao Đài, Hòa Hảo, Bình Xuyên, Nguyễn Văn Hinh, Bảo Đại and other southern elites sympathetic to the French colonial apparatus. Ngô Đình Diệm accused them of moral depravity and possessing selfish interests they were willing to put before those of the state. Colonialists referred to the French and the French troops stationed in Vietnam to provide security as per the Geneva Accords. As Diệm's experiences in the preceding eight months had demonstrated, these two groups were all too willing to collaborate with one another to bring down Diệm's regime which, in his mind, was synonymous with the best interest of any future Vietnamese nation.

Anticommunism quickly emerged as the heart of the national revolution. It certainly reflected Ngô Đình Diệm's ideological proclivities and was an important component of the pacification campaign of which the Special Commissariat for Civic Action was a part. It was made manifest

---

[16] Chapman, *Cauldron of Resistance*, 114–128 and Tran, "Contested Identities," 70 and 73–74.

[17] Telegram From the Embassy in Vietnam to the Secretary of State, April 19, 1955, *Foreign Relations of the United States, 1955–1957*, Vol. 1, *Vietnam* (hereafter *FRUS*) (Washington, DC: US Government Printing Office, 1985), 269.

[18] This interpretation of nationalism is based on the work of Nhu-An Tran; Tran, "Contested Identities."

in the denounce the communist (*Tố Cộng*) campaign launched on July 20, 1955 – the date by which Diệm's government was to have opened discussions with Hồ Chí Minh's government about the plebiscite on national reunification.[19] In its initial stages, the campaign used anticommunism as a vehicle to rally nationalist support behind the regime. It was soon broadened to the rest of the population as part of Diệm's efforts to root out the clandestine network of stay-behind communists. In theory, the denunciation campaign provided a forum where the village community could gather to expose the crimes of alleged communists and report subversive activities to the government. In practice, it was easily subject to abuse by overzealous government officials and exploited by local authorities. According to one first-hand account from an American observer a local community of between 800 and 1,000 people gathered near the coastal village of Nha Trang for a people's tribunal to try two men "accused of Vietminh agitation both before and after the Geneva Accords." Following the national anthem, tributes to the state colors and the prime minister, and a "point by point criticism" of Hồ Chí Minh's post-Geneva policies regarding national reunification, the accused were brought before the crowd to explain their actions. Before they could speak a signal was given and members of the crowd rushed forward to beat the defenseless victims. Once order was restored the accused were sentenced to prison and warned any repeat offence would be met by the death penalty.[20]

At the same time, Diệm's campaign against his noncommunist opponents also revealed some of his thoughts about citizenship and democracy which were both rooted in recent reconceptions of Confucian thought regarding virtue and self-improvement.[21] For Diệm, the ideal citizen had certain obligations before the state. He or she had to act ethically and responsibly, putting the interests of society ahead of his or her own. In a democracy, he believed that the citizens were to be popularly engaged with the state, but only insofar as they participated in efforts to improve

[19] This date was deliberately chosen as a symbol of Diệm's repudiation of the Geneva Accords in general and the provision for the national elections in particular. Chapman, *Cauldron of Resistance*, 119; Tran, "Contested Identities," 70; Miller, *Misalliance*, 132.

[20] Memorandum from USIS Hue (Picknell) to USIS Saigon, August 19, 1955, Subject Files 1954–1958 (hereafter referred to as SF 54–58), Box 3, Record Group 469 (hereafter referred to as RG 469), National Archives and Records Administration (hereafter referred to as NARA).

[21] Edward Miller demonstrates that Ngô Đình Diệm was heavily inspired by the anticolonial activist Phan Bội Châu's ideas about the relevance of Confucian thought in the modern era. According to Miller, Phan Bội Châu situated the Confucian conception of achieving "self-improvement" within the broader context of the community; Miller, *Misalliance*, 138.

themselves and society at large. As Edward Miller puts it, democracy for Diệm was based more on an "assertion of moral *duties*" than a "protection of political *rights*."[22] The state, of course, had certain responsibilities for realizing the aspirations of the body politic, such as ensuring "all citizens the right of free development and of maximum initiative, responsibility and spiritual life."[23] But the polity was duty-bound to pursue only those "aspirations" deemed "legitimate" by the government.[24] Thus, the people's aspirations were somewhat circumscribed by a paternalistic government. The actions of the religious sects, the Bình Xuyên, General Hinh and the elite and *fonctionnaires* of the State of Vietnam clearly put them beyond the pale of what Diệm conceived to be responsible citizenship and democratic practices. The regime's response, in articulating the "three enemies" formula established, in a negative sense, the parameters of the revolution Ngô Đình Diệm conceived himself fomenting. It would be nationalist, noncommunist and executed by a progressive, engaged and virtuous citizenry.

These ideas received a full hearing in what some scholars contend to be the pivotal moment in Diệm's revolution: the October 1955 referendum that deposed Bảo Đại.[25] For Diệm, one of the main obstacles standing in the way of his nation-building project was the State of Vietnam's continued attachment to France. Bảo Đại remained the chief of state of an associate state of the French Union. Diệm needed to irrevocably sever the tie in order to accord himself the national legitimacy he believed he needed to realize his national vision.[26] Now that Diệm had consolidated his hold on power over the sects and the Bình Xuyên he was in a position to deal with Bảo Đại and the French. Diệm announced in the summer that he would hold a referendum for the people to decide whether they wished to retain the former emperor as their chief of state or be replaced by him. Diệm exploited his privileged position in Vietnam to manipulate the referendum heavily in his favor. He only gave Bảo Đại three weeks to campaign, which placed the former emperor who was firmly ensconced

---

[22] *Ibid.*, 139. Emphasis in the original.

[23] These are Diệm's words, quoted in Clive J. Christie, *Ideology and Revolution in Southeast Asia, 1900–1975: Political Ideas of the Anti-Colonial Era* (Richmond, UK: Curzon, 2001), 150.

[24] What is Civic Action, ND, Folder 58, Box 660, Michigan State University Vietnam Advisory Group (herafter MSUVAG), Michigan State University Archives (hereafter MSUA). Though there is no date on this document the material discussed indicates that is from 1955.

[25] Miller, *Misalliance*, 125 and Chapman, *Cauldron of Resistance*, 151.

[26] Miller, *Misalliance*, 125.

on the French Riviera at a tremendous disadvantage. He used his security forces to round up pro-Bảo Đại elements and any potential extremists who could pose a threat to his victory. And he rigged the balloting so that everyone who voted by a supposedly secret ballot would have to reveal their choice by discarding the part of their ballot indicating the candidate they were not supporting on the floor in front of the watchful eyes of the regime's stooges. Unsurprisingly, Diệm received more than 98 percent of the vote.

What is more revealing with respect to Diệm's revolution was the nature of the campaign. Diệm employed the three enemy formula in his attacks on his opponent. He accused Bảo Đại of conspiring with the sects, the Bình Xuyên, the communists and the colonialists to subvert Vietnam's independence. He derided the former emperor's debaucherous and degenerative behavior, exhibited through his womanizing, drinking and gambling on the Riviera all the while serving as the State of Vietnam's chief of state. He suggested that Bảo Đại simply perpetuated an anachronistic and antiquated monarchical structure hopelessly out of touch with the needs of a modern democratic state. And, invoking Confucian notions of leadership which held that only those who ruled fairly and justly were deemed fit to rule the people, he contended that through his actions, Bảo Đại had lost the "mandate of heaven" making him unworthy to lead. Diệm, in contrast, was everything Bảo Đại was not. He was offering progressive, forward-looking leadership dedicated to upholding virtue and ensuring the well-being of the Vietnamese people according to democratic principles – at least as far as he conceived them. His victory set the stage for the promulgation of a new political entity, the Republic of Vietnam, three days later with Diệm as its president.[27]

"RAISING THE PEOPLE'S INTELLECTUAL STANDARDS" AND "WELFARE IMPROVEMENT"

Against this political backdrop, the Special Commissariat for Civic Action underwent its first significant reorganization. On November 18, 1955, President Diệm responded to a number of appeals from the Special Commissariat for Civic Action to be given more permanence by signing Presidential Decree Number 22, which made the CDV an official

---

[27] Chapman, *Cauldron of Resistance*, 146–167.

government organ belonging to the Office of the President.[28] Not only did this Decree remove the Commissariat's temporary status, but it established a bureaucratic framework that would be used to lay the foundation for the regime's national revolution at the local level.[29]

From its inception the previous March, the stated aim of the Special Commissariat had been to "raise the intellectual level and standard of living of the population."[30] This formed the basis of the regime's strategy of winning the people over to the "national cause" of the Diệm government.[31] The Civic Action cadres' mission had been to go out and demonstrate that the regime was genuinely concerned with the people's well-being and could provide a better future than the communists in time for the Geneva-mandated national plebiscite slated for July 1956. Now that Diệm had announced the referendum was not going to occur and had begun to place his stamp of authority on the southern zone, Kiều Công Cung began to reorganize the Special Commissariat for Civic Action to align it more closely to the other more revolutionary aims of the regime outlined above.

Added to the Special Commissariat's responsibilities of getting close to the people was a greater emphasis on filling the technical and administrative gaps at the local level. This included coming up with proposals for "improving the standard of living, of safeguarding security and of rebuilding communities"; actually assisting the ministries and technical services in carrying out their work – not simply coordinating the activities of these bodies; and participating in "community administrative affairs," which could involve sitting on the village council when requested by local officials.[32] To keep up with this expanded mission and

[28] Sắc Lệnh [Decree], November 18, 1955, Folder 797, Phủ Tổng Thống Đệ Nhất Cộng Hòa [Office of the President of the First Republic] (hereafter PTTĐICH), TTLTQG2. For the appeals for Civic Action to be made a permanent government organ see Báo Cáo Hoạt Động tháng 7, 1955 [July 1955 Operation Report], August 8, 1955, Folder 29155, PTTCP, TTLTQG2; Thuyết Trình về dự án sắc lệnh thiết lập Phủ Đặc Ủy Công Dân Vụ [Report on the decree establishing the Special Commissariat for Civic Action], September 24, 1955, Folder 1463, PTTĐICH, TTLTQG2; and Báo Cáo Tổng Quát tháng 10 năm 1955 [October 1955 Comprehensive Operation Report], November 9, 1955, Folder 29155, PTTCP, TTLTQG2.

[29] Report on the Organization of the Special Commissariat for Civic Action, June 1957, Folder 82, Box 660, MSUVAG, MSUA.

[30] Draft copy of a Decree, ND, SF 54–58, Box 1, RG 469, NARA.

[31] Draft copy of General Directive on the Structure and Operation of the Commissariat for Civic Action, ND, Folder 83, Box 660, MSUVAG, MSUA.

[32] Sắc Lệnh [Decree], November 18, 1955, Folder 797, PTTĐICH, TTLTQG2. See also Report on the Officialization of Civic Action, ND, Folder 57, Box 660, MSUVAG, MSUA.

rectify some of the organizational shortcomings that had emerged since Civic Action's inception, the organ's operational structure was considerably overhauled (see Figure 2). In the southern provinces, the Central Services continued to serve as the administrative hub of Civic Action and maintain direct control over operations. To better coordinate action beyond the southern provinces, the Commissariat designated two agents to serve this control function in the southern highlands and central Vietnam. At the province level, CDV officials were to be installed as control cadres, or "expediters," to liaise with the province chief, decide where the Civic Action teams were to be sent, supervise and inspect their work, and determine where the material aid available for the province should be distributed for maximum effect. These control cadres were under the authority of the province chief, but reported either directly to the Commissioner General or his representative if they were assigned to central Vietnam or the southern highlands. In theory, these "expediters" could mitigate the deleterious impact of the friction that existed between the Civic Action cadres and the province chiefs and functionaries who continued to view the Special Commissariat as a threat to their own positions of power. As for the mobile cadre units, they would now work at the district level, with the size of the team depending on the needs of the region.[33] The cadre group chief would liaise with the district chief to coordinate the work of the mobile unit and report directly to the controller at the province level.[34]

These changes were intended to better meet the needs of the government in the countryside given the realities on the ground. As we have seen, at this early stage the bureaucratic and administrative apparatuses of the various services and ministries at the local level was virtually nonexistent, particularly where the communists and other groups that rivaled the regime still maintained a significant presence. Decree 22 highlighted the Special Commissariat's role as a "complementary and reinforcement organism" for the existing government apparatus in the countryside.[35] How this would occur was laid out in the "General Directive on the

---

[33] Government administration in Vietnam is divided hierarchically into the hamlet/village, district, provincial and national levels.

[34] Sắc Lệnh [Decree], November 18, 1955, Folder 797, PTTĐICH, TTLTQG2; and Quy Chế Cán bộ Công Dân Vụ [Regulations for Civic Action Cadres], December 20, 1955, Folder 1036, PTTĐICH, TTLTQG2.

[35] Sắc Lệnh [Decree], November 18, 1955, Folder 797, PTTĐICH, TTLTQG2. The quote can be found in Draft copy of General Directive on the Structure and Operation of the Commissariat for Civic Action, ND, Folder 83, Box 660, MSUVAG, MSUA.

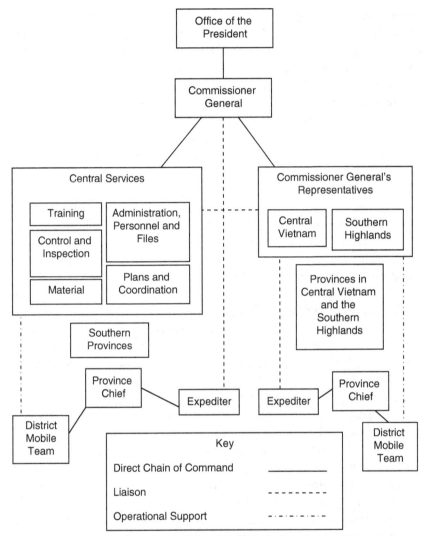

FIGURE 2 Operational structure of the Special Commissariat for Civic Action

Structure and Operation of the Commissariat for Civic Action" that was circulated after Decree 22 was issued.[36] This document emphasized the collaborative nature of the project between the Special Commissariat and the various organs on the ground.[37] In the event there was no government

[36] Draft copy of General Directive on the Structure and Operation of the Commissariat for Civic Action, ND, Folder 83, Box 660, MSUVAG, MSUA.
[37] The Background of Civic Action, ND, Folder 57, Box 660, MSUVAG, MSUA.

presence, the cadres would establish the local offices for the various
branches of government that were to be providing for the community
such as Health and Social Action, Popular Education, Propaganda and
Information, Security and Order and Land Reform. Where these organs
were in a nascent form, the Special Commissariat would assist them in
coming up with plans of action designed to improve "the material and
moral conditions of the population." Once the plans had been drafted
and were ready for execution the Special Commissariat would then work
with the ministries and technical services to implement them. The mobile
cadres would also be available to fill the gaps and provide the necessary
manpower wherever and whenever it was needed.[38]

The General Directives also reinforced the dynamic nature of the
Special Commissariat. In keeping with the mission of pacification, it stipulated that the activities of the CDV would "vary" according to the level
of security in the regions in which it was operating. In "zones of pacification" where there was still significant opposition to the regime, the
mobile Civic Action groups would operate under the command of the
military and have the added responsibility of "contributing to the resettlement and consolidation of the administration in the districts and villages which have recently been liberated." In "transition zones" which had
been recently pacified, the mobile groups would be under the "direct control" of either the province chief or the military commander acting as the
interim province chief. They would carry out their regular duties. Finally,
in the "civilian zones," the mobile teams would be placed at the disposal
of the provincial authorities to perform tasks designed to improve the
overall welfare of the people. These mobile groups would operate according to the needs of the area. In some cases, they would be combined into
regional mobile groups that would move between provinces to help set up
provincial groups with the assistance of the local population. Provincial
mobile groups would serve a similar role, but would act within a particular province, organizing groups in each district. The district mobile
groups would be "the backbone of the organization." Their cadres would
function at the village level. Training of new cadres would continue to
be "in concert with the Ministries" as well as the appropriate "administrative and military agencies" – civil service and army. In time, each

[38] Draft copy of General Directive on the Structure and Operation of the Commissariat for
Civic Action, ND, Folder 83, Box 660, MSUVAG, MSUA. See also Sắc Lệnh [Decree],
November 18, 1955, Folder 797, PTTĐICH, TTLTQG2; and Quy Chế Cán bộ Công Dân
Vụ [Regulations for Civic Action Cadres], December 20, 1955, Folder 1036, PTTĐICH,
TTLTQG2.

province would establish its own training center, which would employ "the heads of the provincial services or specialized functionaries" – local representatives of the ministries or technical services – to carry out the instruction.[39]

As mentioned in the previous chapter, the ideas that underpinned the work of the Civic Action cadres were consistent with the idea of community development – a voluntary self-help initiative that harnessed the power of local human resources for rural reconstruction – that was sweeping the Third World at the midpoint of the twentieth century.[40] The community development idea was appealing to members of the developing world because the coordination of these reconstruction projects allowed the central government to extend its reach out into the countryside. By offering to support various development schemes from land reform and development to reconstruction of local infrastructure, such as roads, bridges and waterways, newly formed national governments that premised their existence on representing the will of the people could boost their legitimacy.[41] This was particularly important in fractured societies like South Vietnam where various groups were vying with each other for power. From the manner in which the mobile teams were already operating, it no doubt informed Cung's thinking about the Special Commissariat for Civic Action.[42] Upon assignment to a village the Civic Action team would meet with the local leaders and survey the situation to see what tasks were most urgent – such as dispensing medical kits, constructing a school or establishing an information hall. The cadres would then work alongside the population to satisfy these needs while

---

[39] Draft copy of General Directive on the Structure and Operation of the Commissariat for Civic Action, ND, Folder 83, Box 660, MSUVAG, MSUA.

[40] This definition comes from Nick Cullather, *The Hungry World: America's Cold War Battle Against Poverty in Asia* (Cambridge, MA: Harvard University Press, 2010), 76–78. See also Lane E. Holdcroft, "The Rise and Fall of Community Development: 1950–1965" (M.Sc. thesis, Michigan State University, East Lansing, MI, 1976), 1–3; Nicole Sackey, "Passage to Modernity: American Social Scientists, India, and the Pursuit of Development, 1945–61" (Ph.D. diss., Princeton University, Princeton, NJ, 2004), 181–183; Francis X. Sutton, "Nation-Building in the Heyday of the Classic Development Ideology: Ford Foundation Experiences in the 1950s and 1960s," in *Nation-Building: Beyond Afghanistan and Iraq*, ed. Francis Fukuyama (Baltimore, MD: The Johns Hopkins University Press, 2006), 53–55; and Daniel Immerwahr, *Thinking Small: The United States and the Lure of Community Development* (Cambridge, MA: Harvard University Press, 2015), 71–75.

[41] Sutton, "Nation-Building in the Heyday of the Classic Development Ideology," 53–54.

[42] According to Rufus Phillips, Kiều Công Cung had taken an interest in community development, reading up on it and seeking "American experts to advise him." Rufus Phillips, *Why Vietnam Matters: An Eyewitness Account of Lessons Not Learned* (Annapolis, MD: Naval Institute Press, 2008), 75.

recruiting and instructing volunteers who would later serve as regional cadres once the mobile cadres' work was finished.

The community development idea had another element that was conducive to the situation in Vietnam: its ability to tie the rural population to the concept of the nation. In India, where the "high profile" community development program served as a model for much of the postcolonial world in the 1950s, Prime Minister Jawaharlal Nehru hoped its emphasis on voluntary self-help would overcome the acute divisions of language, religion and caste that plagued his country and integrate his people into one nation.[43] This was manifest in the mutually reinforcing objectives of "Raising the People's Intellectual Standards" (*Nâng Cao Dân Trí*) and "Welfare Improvement" (*Cải Thiện Dân Sinh*), which Cung made the core of the Special Commissariat's mission following Decree 22.[44]

The first objective, Raising the People's Intellectual Standards, marked an effort to extend some of the Diệm regime's ideas about civic virtue out into the countryside. Jessica Chapman has shown Ngô Đình Diệm believed that the colonial experience, World War II and war against the French had left the Vietnamese population in a state of "moral decay." This had sapped them of the civic fortitude he believed was necessary to counter the three enemies of feudalism, colonialism and communism that lurked in their midst and engage in the rigorous task of national reconstruction that lay ahead. Compounding the matter were concerns arising from Diệm's rather paternalistic view of the peasantry that held them as a somewhat backward and benighted group who were not wholly cognizant of their perceived plight. These were significant problems for the South Vietnamese leader given his particular view of both citizenship and democracy where the South Vietnamese population possessed certain political and social obligations toward the state. As we have seen, in Diệm's mind, the ideal South Vietnamese citizen should be a morally upstanding individual, immune to the lure of vice and corruption. He or she had to be virulently anticommunist and willing to sacrifice certain material and ideological interests deemed antithetical by the state for the

[43] Sutton, "Nation-Building in the Heyday of the Classic Development Ideology," 53–54. See Cullather, *The Hungry World*, 77 for reference to the Indian Community Development program as "high profile."

[44] Cải thiện dân sinh often appears directly translated in documents as People's Life Improvement or People's Living Improvement, however the term Welfare Improvement is more appropriate as the aims of the various initiatives undertaken through this concept were aimed at improving the overall welfare of the people. Báo Cáo Hàng Tháng Tháng 11 1955 [November Monthly Report], December 12, 1955, Folder 15982, PTTĐICH, TTLTQG2.

greater good of society.[45] This was crucial for Diệm's nation-building program because it would ultimately rely on the one resource he had in great abundance: the people. The cadres, therefore, had to instruct the rural population about their political and social obligations to one another and the state. This primarily involved political indoctrination to alert them to the potential dangers they could encounter. They needed to be vigilant in their conduct lest they inadvertently succumb to the machinations of the three enemies. Communist denunciation was the principle where the cadres organized demonstrations festooned with anticommunist banners and centered on testimonials of former communists who had seen the errors in their ways and rallied to the side of the government.[46] The cadres were also responsible for using popular education and propaganda to eradicate what the government considered "superstitious" practices and promote its anti-vice campaign which targeted the four social evils of drinking, gambling, prostitution and opium – all of which were associated with the Bình Xuyên.[47]

Welfare Improvement referred to the more tangible aspects of nation-building that were implicit in the work of the Civic Action cadres.[48] It

[45] Chapman, *Cauldron of Resistance*, 117–124. See also Miller, *Misalliance*, 136–140.

[46] Báo Cáo Tổng Quát tháng 9 năm 1955 [September 1955 Comprehensive Operation Report], October 19, 1955; Báo Cáo Tổng Quát tháng 10 năm 1955 [October 1955 Comprehensive Operation Report], November 9, 1955, Folder 29155, PTTCP, TTLTQG2; Báo Cáo Hàng Tháng: Tháng 11 năm 1955 của Đặc Ủy Phủ Công Dân Vụ [Monthly Report: November 1955 of the Special Commissariat for Civic Action], December 22, 1955, Folder 15982, PTTĐICH, TTLTQG2; Background of Civic Action, ND, Folder 57, Box 660, MSUVAG, MSUA, though there is no date, the material suggests the document was drafted in early 1957; and Thành Tích Bốn Năm Hoạt Động Công Dân Vụ [Four Years of Achievements of Civic Action], 1958, Item number 0721002003, Texas Tech Virtual Vietnam Archive, www.virtualarchive.vietnam.ttu.edu (hereafter referred to as TTVVA) (accessed November 13, 2015)

[47] For a discussion of the four social evils see Tran, "Contested Identities," 88; Miller, *Misalliance*, 132. For examples of the Civic Action cadres' role in this campaign see Công Dân Vụ Mục Đích và Nhiệm Vu [Objective and Mission of Civic Action], ND, Folder 1463, PTTĐICH, TTLTQG2.

[48] The tasks related to the two objectives of Raising the People's Intellectual Standards and Welfare Improvement were often broken down in the Civic Action team reports into the categories of information and propaganda, social and health work, popular education, security and people's living improvement. Order regarding Civic Action Reporting with Template, November 25, 1955, Folder 77, Box 660, MSUVAG, MSUA. Distinguishing between activities that explicitly educated the people about the government and their obligations to it or improved their welfare was often difficult and some overlap naturally occurred; General Observation on Civic Action, ND, Folder 76, Box 660, MSUVAG, MSUA. See also Report on Campaign for Life Improvement in Ca-mâu, October 10, 1955, Folder 78, Box 660, MSUVAG, MSUA.

consisted mainly of village reconstruction tasks and medical and social work. Village reconstruction, as we have seen, involved the cadres enlisting volunteers from the local population and coordinating their efforts to dig wells, canals and ditches, and repair roads in an effort to fill the population with a sense of civic pride in working for their own betterment. In the fields of health and social improvement, the cadres would guide the people in constructing medical dispensaries, public lavatories, maternity hospitals and schools; organize meetings regarding public health and conduct inoculation campaigns; help local families with the harvest; and provide the impoverished with financial and material support if it was available. The cadres would also establish popular education classes to eradicate illiteracy and introduce the people to the state apparatus and its role in the villages as well as open information offices where the villagers could read the news and learn about their government in Sài Gòn.[49]

On the surface, all of this was designed to teach the people the importance of self-sacrifice and self-help as a collective effort at the local level would be crucial for rebuilding South Vietnam following the war with the French. But it also gave the regime an avenue to lay the foundation for a revolutionary agenda that would be based, in part, on the community development idea. Following the November reorganization the twin aims of Raising the People's Intellectual Standards and Welfare Improvement would come to serve as the cornerstone for the Sài Gòn government's broader nation-building agenda. The former was intended to bring the peasant world into congruence with that which the state operated in by identifying enemies of the regime and establishing appropriate codes of conduct. The latter aimed to improve the standard of living for the community and give them a vested interest in maintaining it. Combined they would establish an appropriately civic-minded and motivated population that could be mobilized to participate in a revolution that was both national and social in its scope and ultimately geared toward transforming South Vietnam into Diệm's vision of an economically and politically viable nation.

---

[49] Civic Action, ND; Memorandum from John Gates, TRIM to Edward G. Lansdale, August 7, 1956, SF 54–58, Box 1, RG 469, NARA; The Background of Civic Action, ND, Folder 57, Box 660, MSUVAG, MSUA. See also Báo Cáo Hoạt Động tháng 5, 1955 [May 1955 Operation Report], June 9, 1955; Báo Cáo Tổng Quát tháng 10 năm 1955 [October 1955 Comprehensive Operation Report], November 9, 1955, Folder 29155, PTTCP; and Báo Cáo Hàng Tháng: Tháng 11 năm 1955 của Đặc Ủy Phủ Công Dân Vụ [Monthly Report: November 1955 of the Special Commissariat for Civic Action], December 22, 1955, Folder 15982, PTTĐICH, TTLTQG2.

How, exactly, all of this would occur still remained to be determined. But what was obvious was that the right kind of people be employed as cadres. They had to demonstrate a desire to serve the people, an ability to bear tremendous hardship and overcome adversity, and a willingness to serve as a model of moral turpitude, forsaking decadence and vice "to represent the spirit of the new era."[50] They were to be young and healthy individuals between twenty-two and forty years old. They were obligated to obey the Government of the Republic of Vietnam, respect the authority of the Commissioner General, execute every policy and instruction assigned to them with an "exemplary fighting spirit" and commit to at least one year of service with an understanding that that could be extended if the situation demanded it. To weed out undesirable elements potential candidates had to pass an entrance exam.[51] Once selected, these new cadres were then subject to a training regimen that, in a certain respect, mimicked the tactics the communists used to create their disciplined cells of cadres. Not only were they expected to learn about the techniques of the various ministries and technical services they were supposed to work with, but they had to endure self-criticism sessions and political indoctrination to be sure they possessed an "ardent and patriotic spirit" and full understanding of the policies and "just cause" of the new republican government.[52]

Despite these efforts to overhaul the Special Commissariat and give the cadres more national purpose the effectiveness of the Civic Action program was still limited by problems beyond its control. First, Civic Action had relied heavily on the South Vietnamese army for logistical support in these early stages. This had been possible due to the territorial

---

[50] Civic Action: Role, Activities, Results, ND, SF 54–58, Box 1, RG 469, NARA.

[51] Unfortunately we do not presently know what the entrance exam entailed, but it could not have been overly rigorous as all cadres had to have the equivalent of at least a primary education.

[52] The two quotes regarding the "spirit" of the cadres can be found in Quyết Định [Resolution], August 14, 1958, Folder 1463, PTTĐICH, TTLTQG2. Though from August 1958, these stipulations regarding the selection of cadres remained virtually unchanged since the selection process was first systematized in 1955. The quote regarding the "just cause" can be found in Civic Action: Role, Activities, Results, ND, SF 54–58, Box 1, RG 469, NARA. For other details of the selection and training of the cadres see Draft copy of General Directive on the Structure and Operation of the Commissariat for Civic Action, ND, Folder 83, Box 660, MSUVAG, MSUA; and Civic Action, ND, SF 54–58, Box 1, RG 469, NARA. In addition to holding self-criticism sessions in training, self-criticism was an integral part of the reporting of the Civic Action teams as each monthly report concluded with a section on strengths and weaknesses. See for example Báo Cáo Hoạt Động tháng 5, 1955 [May 1955 Operation Report], June 9, 1955, Folder 29155, PTTCP.

role the army had played in the reoccupation of the Việt Minh controlled territories. This support evaporated as the army was reorganized as part of the American advisory effort's plan to prepare it to fight a conventional war against a Korean-style invasion across the seventeenth parallel, rather than a nonconventional one where its primary responsibility would be internal security against an insurgency.[53] Second, under-funding remained a chronic problem. At the Central Services office, the staff was seconded from existing government organs rather than hired directly from the population to prevent expanding the governmental payroll.[54] On the very day that Diệm issued the decree reorganizing the CDV, he submitted a letter to Kiều Công Cung warning him to proceed slowly in fulfilling his new orders. Cung was to concern himself primarily with establishing a local infrastructure and organizing mobile groups. The remaining structure, such as designating control cadres at the provincial level, or even representatives of the Commissioner General in the southern highlands or central Vietnam, could wait until their presence was considered absolutely necessary. Districts that did receive the mobile action groups often failed to see a controller arrive at the province level to better coordinate their work with the province chief, or oversee the work that was being carried out.[55]

More troubling, the lack of funding inhibited Civic Action's ability to train able recruits. Though there were operational Civic Action groups working across twenty-one provinces in southern Vietnam by December 1955 (see Map 2), new mobile cadres could not be produced fast enough to meet the demand for their services coming from the countryside.[56] Time was too great a factor to be overcome as the mobile groups that were available could only afford to stay in one spot for a maximum of four weeks before moving on. This made it extremely difficult to gain local support in areas where the anti-regime forces were armed. The peasantry knew that once the Civic Action group withdrew, there would no longer be anyone to prevent reprisals against those who chose to help the Sài Gòn

---

[53] Phillips, *Why Vietnam Matters*, 82 and 85.

[54] Tổng Thống Việt Nam Cộng Hòa Kính gởi Kiều Công Cung [President of the Republic of Vietnam to Kieu Cong Cung], November 18, 1955, Folder 4122, PTTCP, TTLTQG2.

[55] Report on the Organization of the Special Commissariat for Civic Action, June 1957, Folder 82, Box 660, MSUVAG, MSUA.

[56] Report on the Organization of the Special Commissariat for Civic Action, June 1957, Folder 82, Box 660, MSUVAG, MSUA. For the number of Civic Action groups working in the provinces see Tổng Kết Thành Thích 6–56 đến 6–57 [Summary of Achievements 6–56 to 6–57], June 21, 1957, Folder 16294, PTTDICH, TTLTQG2.

THE DEMOCRATIC REPUBLIC OF VIETNAM

Areas where Civic Action
mobile groups were active
as of October 1955

Quang Tri
Quang Tri
Hue
Thua Thien
Da Nang

Quang Nam

LAOS

Quang Ngai

Kontum

Binh Dinh
Qui Nhon

Pleiku

Phu Yen

Darlac

CAMBODIA

Khanh Hoa
Nha Trang

Quang Duc
Tuyen Duc
Da Lat
Ninh Thuan

Phuoc Long
Lam Dong

Binh Long
Binh Thuan

Tay Ninh
Binh Duong
Long Khanh
Binh Tuy

Long An
Saigon
Cholon
Gia Dinh
Bien Hoa
Phuoc Tuy

Kien Tuong
Kien Phong
Dinh Tuong
Go Cong
Vung Tau

Chau Doc
An Giang
Sa Dec
Kien Hoa

Can Tho
Vinh Long

Kien Giang
Phong Dinh
Vinh Binh

Ba Xuyen

Bac Lieu

An Xuyen

**Territory with
Civic Action
mobile groups as
of October 1955**

0   50   100   150   200   250 km
0   25   50   75   100   125   150 miles

MAP 2 Territory with Civic Action mobile groups as of October 1955 overlaid on
a province map of the Republic of Vietnam ca. 1959–1960

government.[57] Consequently, it was almost always impossible to recruit and train able successors to continue their work when they left.[58]

Finally, there was the question of actually translating the theoretical aspects of Raising the People's Intellectual Standards and Welfare Improvement into practice. Theoretically, these mutually reinforcing concepts were perfectly laudatory aims, but whether they could actually lay the material and spiritual foundation for national development at the community level remained to be seen. This would prove to be a major point of contention when it came to the question of both the type and level of support the Special Commissariat for Civic Action could expect to receive from the Diệm regime's principle foreign backer.

USOM, COMMUNITY DEVELOPMENT AND
THE CDV

While Civic Action was undergoing its reorganization throughout the fall of 1955, members of the American Mission in Vietnam debated whether the US government should support it if – but more likely – when asked by the Commissioner General to do so.[59] Aside from the small amount of seed money provided by the CIA and assistance from USIS, it had not received any significant US funding. But its operating budget would be exhausted by the end of 1955 and the South Vietnamese government lacked the resources to pay for it.[60] It had been decided that USOM would be responsible for providing economic aid to the program.[61] They had very specific guidelines and procedures for the procurement and distribution of American aid. Rufus Phillips had been assigned by Lansdale to help Kiều Công Cung come up with a budget and try to get USOM to approve it.[62] Given USOM's initial reluctance to support Civic Action, it was going to be a tough sell.

[57] Phúc Trình Đặc Biệt, Đoàn Trưởng 202 Công Dân Vụ Lưu Động Kính gởi Ông Đặc Ủy Trưởng Công Dân Vụ [Special Report, Civic Action Group 202 Chief to the Commissioner General for Civic Action], March 10, 1956, Folder 16064, PTTĐICH, TTLTQG2.

[58] Tóm tắt Thuyết Trình Chỉ Thị Đặc Ủy Trưởng Công Dân Vụ [Summary Report of the Instructions for the Special Commissariat for Civic Action], ND, Folder 16293, PTTĐICH, TTLTQG2.

[59] Memorandum from United States Embassy, Saigon to the Department of State, December 19, 1955, SF 54–58, Box 1, RG 469, NARA.

[60] Draft Response to ICATO-701, November 29, 1955, SF 54–58, Box 1, RG 469, NARA.

[61] Phillips, *Why Vietnam Matters*, 85.

[62] *Ibid.*, 77.

Within USOM the funding debate hinged on three issues: Kiều Công Cung, the potential for a wasteful duplication of effort with existing ministries and the question of community development. D.C. Lavergne, USOM's Assistant Director for Rural Resettlement and Rehabilitation and the point man for deliberations in Sài Gòn, did not hold the Commissioner General of Civic Action in particularly high esteem, questioning both his loyalty and his competence. In a November 28, 1955 memo to Leland Barrows, the Chief of USOM, Lavergne pointed out that Cung had served as the Chief of Police for Sài Gòn-Chợ Lớn in the pro-Japanese (but anti-French) government of Trần Trọng Kim during World War II, been a member of the Việt Minh, and, more troublingly in the eyes of the American, attended a military conference in the highland city of Đà Lạt with the noted Việt Minh – now DRV – General Võ Nguyên Giáp during the First Indochina War. Cung's professional and ideological loyalties no doubt reflected the fluid nature of the anti-French war, and the broad appeal of the Việt Minh's ardent nationalism. Lavergne, like many US officials in Vietnam, had trouble making these distinctions and concluded that "while intelligent and seemingly sincere, [he] seems to have changed his affiliations often, if not his basic thinking." He was "not convinced" that Cung should be the individual to head the program.[63]

Lavergne was also growing frustrated with Cung's obfuscation. Cung repeatedly informed Lavergne that he would be requesting US aid when Civic Action's operating budget was exhausted at the end of 1955.[64] But he took a great deal more time coming up with a proposed budget than Lavergne anticipated and when he did, the American found it dubious. Citing Cung's lack of concern over budget constraints and neglect for

[63] Memorandum from D.C. Lavergne to Leland Barrows, November 28, 1955, SF 54–58, Box 1, RG 469, NARA. Though it is not explicitly stated in any memoranda, Lavergne's opposition to Kiều Công Cung may also have stemmed from his association with Edward Lansdale and his team. Lansdale and his team did not hold USOM in particularly high regard. They disagreed with its "centralized" and "top down" approach to rural development and felt that the mission was not only "incapable of understanding the bottom up idea of village development" they espoused, but perceived it as a threat to their own programs; Phillips, *Why Vietnam Matters*, 76–77. Additionally, according to Lansdale, some members of USOM were "afraid" that Civic Action was another of his schemes "to flood the country with secret agents, of which it wanted no part." Edward Geary Lansdale, *In the Midst of Wars: An American's Mission to Southeast Asia* (New York: Fordham University Press, 1991), 211.

[64] Memorandum from D.C. Lavergne to Leland Barrows, December 3, 1955; Correspondence from Leland Barrows to Louis Miniclier, December 12, 1955; and Memorandum from United States Embassy, Saigon to the Department of State, December 19, 1955, SF 54–58, Box 1, RG 469, NARA.

correct appropriations protocol with regard to requesting foreign aid, Lavergne complained to M.H.B. Adler, USOM's Chief of Field Services, that he did not see it as a budget at all, simply "a formula by which he [Cung] arrives at the amount of money he wants," which "does not appear entirely realistic since materials he proposed to buy could be provided by already established Ministries."[65]

This reflects the second issue USOM had with the CDV: the perennial concern over the Special Commissariat's tendency to cut across administrative boundaries. As the Sài Gòn office of the International Cooperation Administration, USOM was particularly concerned that American foreign aid funding was being spent as efficiently as possible. Based on the reports he was getting from USOM personnel in the field, Lavergne had his doubts. Rather than a means for the central government to reach out and fill the administrative vacuum at the village level, Lavergne concluded that "Civic Action is basically a propaganda effort."[66] From what he had seen, the CDV had been doing two things: disseminating propaganda and distributing medical supplies. Each of these tasks were the responsibilities of the Ministries of Information and Health – two administrative organs currently receiving US funding. If Civic Action remained limited to these functions, it was not worthy of US support as an independent administrative entity.[67] At most, Lavergne recommended, it should be a program of an existing government institution, such as the Ministry of Information whose activities most closely resembled the CDV's.[68] Even then the Civic Action program should function on a temporary basis to provide technical services at the village level until the established arm of the government is capable of providing those services on its own.[69] If the Special Commissariat for Civic Action were to receive funding, USOM would need to be certain that it avoided any needless duplication of effort. This would mean that, as he told Kiều Công Cung, "certain revisions [would] need to be made for the program to make its objectives conform more closely to a realistic appraisal of what it is possible to achieve."[70]

[65] Memorandum from D.C. Lavergne to M.H.B. Adler, Chief, Field Service USOM, February 1, 1956, SF 54–58, Box 1, RG 469, NARA.
[66] Draft Memorandum from D.C. Lavergne to Gardner Palmer, November 17, 1955, 1955, SF 54–58, Box 1, RG 469, NARA.
[67] An Evaluation of Civic Action, November 28, 1955, SF 54–58, Box 1, RG 469, NARA.
[68] Draft Memorandum from D.C. Lavergne to Gardner Palmer, November 17, 1955, 1955, SF 54–58, Box 1, RG 469, NARA.
[69] An Evaluation of Civic Action, November 28, 1955, SF 54–58, Box 1, RG 469, NARA.
[70] Memorandum from United States Embassy, Saigon to the Department of State, December 19, 1955, SF 54–58, Box 1, RG 469, NARA.

This was the most significant issue USOM had with the Civic Action program: the "reported dissimilarity between the theoretical proposals of the plan and its practical application in the villages."[71] No one in the American mission disputed the fundamental principle of bringing the government directly to the people that lay at the heart of the Civic Action program. USIS, which supplied the Civic Action teams with the bulk of the propaganda matter to distribute to the people and occasionally "used the Civic Action structure to reach the village level," envisioned making the organization "a major arm of [a] USIS rice roots campaign in uncertain areas."[72] Alfred Cardineaux of the USOM Resettlement Division called the CDV's "guiding idea" of extending the central government down to the village level "praiseworthy."[73] Wolf Ladejinsky, the American Mission's Land Reform expert who would soon become a close confidant of Ngô Đình Diệm,[74] lauded the cadres' zeal, manners and conduct, and stated that "the mere presence of such eager-beaver groups in the villages, speaking in the name of the Government where few others do, is on the plus side."[75] Even D.C. Lavergne could not "deny the need to reach and involve the people in a program designed to attain the objective of Civic Action."[76] What Cardineaux, Ladejinsky and Lavergne all envisioned, however, was that Civic Action should be something more along the lines of a community development program where the people, through "self-help and outside assistance" develop the infrastructure of their local community to improve their overall standard of living, not an "ideological propaganda" agency that relied "too much upon 'giving away' things as a basic stock in trade."[77]

As Daniel Immerwhar has demonstrated, the appeal of the idea of community development in the postwar world was such that it could be

[71] An Evaluation of Civic Action, November 28, 1955, SF 54–58, Box 1, RG 469, NARA.
[72] Memorandum from George M. Hellyer to Kenneth Landon, December 2, 1955, OCB 091 Indo-China (File #5) 3 (September 1955–January 1957), Box 39, OCB Central Files Series, NSC Staff Papers, Dwight D. Eisenhower Library.
[73] Memorandum from Alfred Cardineaux to Leland Barrows, September 28, 1955, SF 54–58, Box 1, RG 469, NARA.
[74] Ladejinsky would leave USOM in January 1956 to become Diệm's personal land reform advisor, a position he would hold until 1961. Louis J. Walinsky, ed., *Agrarian Reform as Unfinished Business: The Selected Papers of Wolf Ladejinsky* (New York: Oxford University Press, 1977), 6–7. See also Miller, *Misalliance*, 158–159.
[75] Memorandum from Wolf Ladejinsky to Leland Barrows, October 6, 1955, SF 54–58, Box 1, RG 469, NARA.
[76] An Evaluation of Civic Action, November 28, 1955, SF 54–58, Box 1, RG 469, NARA.
[77] Memorandum from Wolf Ladejinsky to Leland Barrows, October 6, 1955, SF 54–58, Box 1, RG 469, NARA.

referred to as a movement throughout the developed and underdeveloped world.[78] The roots of community development can be found in New Deal social welfare and slum clearance projects.[79] In the 1930s Albert Mayer, a civil engineer, was involved in massive urban renewal projects which would replace the run-down dwellings of impoverished areas with planned public housing that would improve the well-being of the people who lived there. More than just a public works project, Mayer aimed to redress what he perceived to be the ills of modern urban living, which he believed contributed to a more commodified, impersonal and, ultimately, decayed civil society. He envisioned replacing the slums with "urban villages" that would restore, in the words of Nick Cullather, "the intimate, participatory community that had been lost in the depersonalized modern city."[80] For Mayer and other urban planners, the idea of the "village" was both a key to urban renewal and an antidote to the alienation of the individual that he believed came with life in the modern city.[81]

During World War II, Mayer was dispatched to India with the Tenth Air Force, where he designed airfields for the southern end of the notorious "Burma Hump." During his time there, his ideas resonated strongly with important Indian nationalists like Mohandas Gandhi and Jawaharlal Nehru who were both interested in using the village as a basic building block for establishing a new and independent India. For Gandhi, who eschewed the grand top-down modernization projects that were associated with the imperial project, rural reconstruction had to start at the village level where it would "focus on local conditions, grassroots issues and renewable sources of energy" and require "decentralized planning, community input and development decisions."[82] Nehru, who is often associated with centralized, technocratic and sweeping "high-impact infrastructural projects" quite at odds with local community development schemes, had a far more nuanced understanding of modernization than has been attributed to him in previous accounts. According to Daniel Immerwahr, Nehru's thinking about development is symbolic of the fact "that the urge to modernize and the quest for community"

---

[78] Immerwahr, *Thinking Small*, 9. See also Holdcroft, "The Rise and Fall of Community Development," 3–4

[79] Much of the following discussion on community development is drawn from Cullather's *The Hungry World*, 76–94 and Immerwahr's *Thinking Small*, 66–85.

[80] Cullather, *The Hungry World*, 80.

[81] *Ibid.*, 80–81

[82] Michael Adas, *Dominance by Design: Technological Imperatives and America's Civilizing Mission* (Cambridge, MA: The Belknap Press of Harvard, 2006), 272–273.

can coexist "alongside or even within each other."[83] Nehru was struck with the possibility of applying Mayer's ideas to India and introduced the American planner to Gandhi. What was particularly appealing to Nehru was Mayer's holistic approach to improving human welfare, which translated into building up all aspects of "community life" from village infrastructure to hygiene to agriculture.[84]

In 1946, Mayer began a community development pilot project in the villages of the Etawah district of Uttar Pradesh province. Reflecting its Gandhian influence, the pilot project took a bottom-up approach to rural reconstruction that started out small in scale, emphasized local "folk-solutions" to problems rather than outside expert advice, and relied on the material resources of the community wherever possible. The bulk of the development work was done by the local population whose services were enlisted by a Rural Life Analyst – an individual with "sociological or anthropological training" to observe local customs and employ them in the various reconstruction projects. The Rural Life Analyst was assisted by the "village-level workers" who had no real "technical aptitude" but specialized in determining the "felt needs" of the community through meetings and deliberations.

The Etawah project was remarkably successful, transforming the district's ramshackle villages into vibrant communities by the early 1950s to such a degree that it "became the international symbol for community development."[85] Not only did it dramatically improve village life through the construction of school houses, community centers, roads, wells and increased agricultural output, but it revitalized the sociological basis of the community, tying the people together in a common cause. It was this aspect of the project that was so appealing to Nehru. Community development ultimately aimed at bringing about "a collective psychological awakening" throughout the village "after which progress would accelerate through the peasants' own initiative."[86] For post-independence India, promoting community development would allow the Delhi government to connect with the people and draw them into an undertaking that had the potential to both materially and spiritually construct a new national community.

Nehru wasted little time. On October 2, 1952 – Gandhi's birthday – the prime minister launched a national Community Development Plan to

[83] Immerwahr, *Thinking Small*, 71.
[84] *Ibid.*, 72–73.
[85] *Ibid.*, 75.
[86] Cullather, *The Hungry World*, 78.

construct upward of 15,000 new model villages. Funding for the ambitious program came from $50 million of Point Four aid and a substantial grant from the Ford Foundation. From here the idea quickly took off. Indonesia, the Philippines, Iran and Pakistan all embraced it. In 1956, the UN adopted the term as its official designation for rural development initiatives. By the following decade it had spread even further. The UN estimated that by 1960 more than sixty developing states in Africa, Latin America and Asia had established community development programs.

Community development's appeal across the postcolonial world was its potential to harness the supposedly idle labor of the peasantry to the task of nation-building. For many of these states the colonial experience, World War II, or both, had left them quite impoverished. Though the imperial edifice was crumbling in this age of decolonization, there was the constant risk that the state of their political and economic development left them vulnerable to the predations of a new imperial or neoimperial power. By relying on local human and material resources, community development appeared to offer these newly emerging nations an affordable way to build themselves into viable states from the ground up that was based on local realities. At the very least, it represented a means for the state to connect with the grassroots and demonstrate its interest in the people's well-being.

The American foreign aid apparatus was an integral part of the community development movement. In 1954, the ICA established a community development division, headed by Louis Miniclier.[87] By October 1956 it was supporting twenty-three different community development programs.[88] Advocates of community development saw it "as a democratic social movement embracing the idea of the balanced, integrated development of the whole of community life."[89] According to community development guidelines transmitted to US missions that were supporting such programs they were to conceptualize it as "a process of social action in which the people of a community organize themselves for planning and action." They would meet, identify communal and individual problems, plan on how to address them and "execute these plans with a maximum reliance upon community resources." As Albert Mayer and Nehru had anticipated, the process of social action was to be conceived of as more than simply a self-help program, but the basis for a fundamental

[87] Holdcroft, "The Rise and Fall of Community Development," 20.
[88] Airgam, Community Development Guidelines, October 15, 1956, SF 54–58, Box 2, RG 469, NARA; and Holdcroft, "The Rise and Fall of Community Development," 3.
[89] Holdcroft, "The Rise and Fall of Community Development," 4.

shift in the ways communities organized themselves as social entities that took responsibility for ensuring the overall welfare of their members. The ICA believed that "when local people have a chance to decide how they can better their own local conditions ... desirable improvements are more easily introduced and have a more lasting effect."[90]

One aim of these measures was to contend with the so-called revolution in rising expectations in the developing world. As Nick Cullather shows, policymakers in the Truman administration perceived the village to be the locus of a postcolonial threat to American interests. It "represented a dangerous combination of poverty, population and isolation" that created the type of community isolation that was the first step in "the formation of self-contained autarkies" that had spawned World War II. In the postwar world, the consequences could be even more dire, particularly as so many newly emerging states were exhibiting such strong nationalist tendencies in an age of increased geopolitical uncertainty. Drawing from the example of the Chinese Revolution, some officials, such as Isidor Lubin, Truman's foreign aid adviser, believed the isolated village, cut off from government contact, could be the spawning ground for a host of ideologies – some more menacing than international communism – that threatened the American ideal of a liberal-internationalist world order. Making the situation more problematic was the fact that social scientists and members of the intelligence community warned that the villages were most vulnerable to radical ideas when their "historic seclusion" was broken and "modern ideas and technology" challenged "traditional cultural bonds." Community development was seen as a cost-effective way to contend with this danger.[91] This is clearly seen in the ICA guidelines, which conclude that community development is "an efficient way of multiplying U.S. technical assistance, a constructive way of developing an enduring base for a sound national economy, a successful way of giving the people a greater stake in their own development, and a sound way of meeting the increasing demand for a better life."[92]

This belief in the possibilities of community development informed the evaluation of Civic Action that was occurring in the fall of 1955. Because the establishment of Civic Action had been primarily a Vietnamese initiative, USOM had very little first-hand knowledge of the program on which

[90] Airgam, Community Development Guidelines, October 15, 1956, SF 54–58, Box 2, RG 469, NARA.

[91] Cullather, *The Hungry World*, 78–79.

[92] Airgam, Community Development Guidelines, October 15, 1956, SF 54–58, Box 2, RG 469, NARA.

to base its assessment.[93] The two main sources of information available to it were a memorandum by Edward Lansdale and a field report from Wolf Ladejinsky.[94] Lansdale, who, as we have seen was involved with Civic Action from the outset – and a firm believer of what it could achieve – wrote a detailed and glowing survey of the history of the program to date. Each Civic Action team, he explained, contained "specialists in the fields of medicine, information, education, social welfare and civil administration." Their mission was to "help provide a fuller life" for the peasantry to demonstrate that a free government in Vietnam could offer them "a brighter future" – something the Việt Minh had promised, but "failed to produce." When describing the team's method of work, he did so explicitly in terms of community development. On entering the village, the team would survey the situation and establish "a schedule of action priorities" to meet the people's "most pressing needs." "Public works improvements" would be accomplished "through community self-help." Medical dispensaries and community information halls, if not existent, would be built with "volunteer labor and materials provided by the village." Easier tasks would be "tackled first" so they could be completed quickly "to demonstrate what self-help can accomplish and encourage the villagers to take on bigger tasks." The intent being, such work would develop "within the community a sense of civic pride which is engendered by having the villagers work for their own betterment." Continuity would be maintained, Lansdale went on, by screening volunteers "for their enthusiasm and devotion to the national cause." They would be "trained" and "expected to keep alive the spirit of civic action after a team leaves and to continue with programs of community development." This was a "dynamic program" to strengthen the bonds between the technical and administrative apparatuses in Sài Gòn and the villages which, he concluded, "could be useful both to the government of Vietnam and to the nations engaged in assisting her become a free, independent and secure state."[95]

Alfred Cardineaux, who had been asked to comment on Lansdale's report, was far more circumspect. He stated that Civic Action, as laid out

---

[93] Memorandum from M.H.B. Adler, Chief, USOM, Field Service to D.C. Lavergne, August 17, 1956, SF 54–58, Box 1, RG 469, NARA.

[94] Memorandum From American Embassy Saigon to Department of State, December 19, 1955, SF 54–58, Box 1, RG 469, NARA.

[95] Civic Action, ND, SF 54–58, Box 1, RG 469, NARA. Though the document is undated, it is revealed as being written on September 6, 1955 in Memorandum from Leland Barrows to Louis Miniclier, December 12, 1955, SF 54–58, Box 1, RG 469, NARA.

by the Lansdale report, oversimplified the problems faced in the countryside and tended "to encompass too wide a field." There "appears," he
wrote, "a dangerous trend of promoting new needs in the villages which,
from the villagers' point of view, do not exist and which would not come
into existence without outside interference." From what he could glean,
teams arrived and started to establish new buildings regardless of the
village's need for them or the village's ability to create qualified staff to
operate them. More significantly, he doubted the ability of the CDV to
fulfill the larger nation-building expectations that Lansdale placed upon
it. From a practical perspective, he questioned whether the CDV team
would be able "to create the incentives and initiatives which are the roots
from which the program must grow" in just two to four weeks. From a
nation-building perspective, he argued, any successful program would
need to "confine itself to such activities which can easily be supported
by the village and which fit into the existing village pattern"; if not, "the
program, instead of helping the community and ultimately the nation will
create new burdens for both of them." In its current form, Civic Action
was on its way to becoming a bureaucratic behemoth that would "eventually only enlarge the national family of functionaries."[96]

Cardineaux's observations were subsequently corroborated by
Ladejinsky's findings from the field. Addressing whether or not the Civic
Action teams could successfully achieve the stated aim of demonstrating
that the Sài Gòn government could provide a better life than the Việt
Minh, Ladejinsky claimed that it could not. What the Civic Action teams
would like to achieve, he argued, "is popularly referred to as a 'community
development program.'" The CDV teams, while "well-meaning," "well-
mannered" and "obviously zealous for the cause they espouse" were "not
fitted by background or experience" to meet these aims. "Contrary to the
prevalent view of the organizers of the program," they were not "made
up of specialists in any real meaning of the term." Compounding the
problem was that the government in Sài Gòn was, in its present state,
bureaucratically and administratively ill-equipped to support the cadres
in their endeavors. Supplies were in short demand. The "rigmarole" in
facilitating the delivery of those goods that were available was prohibi-
tive. They lacked the necessary funding to compensate people for assisting them. According to one example, a CDV team member reported that
his group was unable to mobilize the population to build a community

---

[96] Memorandum from Alfred Cardineaux to Leland Barrows, September 28, 1955, SF 54–
58, Box 1, RG 469, NARA.

center, which, he stated, "would have stood as both a symbol of local self-help and the government's interest in the well-being of the population," because the Commissariat could not compensate them for any work and the people were too poor to make any contributions themselves. The people involved in "promoting" the effort, he continued, "must be in a position to show the farmers, how, for example, to build a better road, dig a better well, introduce improved farm methods, animal husbandry, and so forth." But even this might not be enough, he warned. The "work of the team must go beyond an attempt to develop within the community a sense of civic pride that leads to voluntary community action." Ladejinsky believed "the single most important test of a team's good performance is whether it can insure continuity of its activities upon leaving the village." Even if the teams were "masterly indoctrinators," the two to four weeks they spent in each village was simply not enough time "to inculcate the spirit which moves one to a higher purpose even at the price of sacrifice or inconvenience." In sum, Ladejinsky noted, the cadres were placed "in an equivocal position by issuing promissory notes all over the place which cannot be made good in the next year or so, no matter how often the promises are made."[97]

Despite all the pessimism in his report, Ladejinsky concluded that "as an instrument to try and actively bring the Government and the people closer together it is valuable and to that extent it deserves support" from USOM. However, "with aims so grandiose as to lose touch with realities [Civic Action] should be subject to careful re-examination from the standpoint of the national Government's and our own priorities" and that support "should be considered accordingly." USOM would need to have "a fairly clear idea of what 'Civic Action' can and should or cannot and shouldn't do." It should not be a "cure-all" for the ills of Vietnam, nor should it be the organ "that binds the people to the Government" as conceived of by the organizers. It acts like a "shock brigade" where "patient, step by step and day by day methodical work is called for." One or two members of the team should be kept in the village on a more permanent basis. The Civic Action teams should not be responsible for distributing gifts or equipment to the peasantry such as medical kits or water pumps. That should be the province of the responsible ministries. Having the cadres do so would set an unhealthy precedent that they were simply providers rather than facilitators of self-help. Finally, he suggested,

---

[97] Memorandum from Wolf Ladejinsky to Leland Barrows, October 6, 1955, SF 54–58, Box 1, RG 469, NARA.

most likely with an eye to communist denunciation, the cadres should be more attentive to emphasizing "what the Government stands for rather than what the Government is against."[98]

Drawing from these reports, D.C. Lavergne's assessment bleakly concluded that Civic Action would "probably move from bad to worse unless we stop it absolutely, which is probably not advisable or even possible; or we press for re-appraisal and possible revision." If Civic Action limited itself to the "application of the community development process following a pattern suitable to the situation in Vietnam," then it would be worthy of USOM's support. Lavergne recommended that if USOM decided to support the Civic Action program it would need to define exactly what Civic Action should and should not do. Approved activities could include: serving as the "eyes and ears" of the national government; clearly explaining the Vietnamese government's efforts to improve the lot of the peasantry; pointing out "understandable problems" facing the government and soliciting the local population's aid in suggesting means to solve them; discussing "realizable" plans for the solution of rural problems and being honest in stating that "immediate rewards may be meager"; promoting interest in education and youth organization; encouraging self-betterment on a voluntary and positive basis in areas touching daily life, health, sanitation, local government and information; stressing what the government is for rather than against; and devoting an intense effort to selecting and training capable local individuals to carry on the work once the team leaves the community. In terms of what Civic Action should *not* do, Lavergne repeated each of Ladejinsky's recommendations: Civic Action should not be a "give away program," should not make promises it cannot keep, and should not be a mere "shock brigade" but a long-term plan. Above all, it should not be considered a "cure-all" or the sole program for directly reaching the people – drawing a sharp distinction between what USOM believed Civic Action was capable of achieving and what Lansdale argued it was achieving.[99]

Based on the various assessments he had received, Leland Barrows concluded in a December 1955 letter to Louis Miniclier, the Chief of the ICA's Community Development Division, that Civic Action was simply "an outgrowth of psychological warfare." As far as the USOM chief could tell, Civic Action only offered a "trained and disciplined body of agents"

---

[98] *Ibid.*
[99] Memorandum from D.C. Lavergne to Leland Barrows, November 28, 1955, SF 54–58, Box 1, RG 469, NARA.

that would move from village to village in an effort to "win the villages' support of the Diem government" against the Việt Minh and "other dissident elements in the country by distributing 'relief goods' " and carrying out "propaganda efforts to counteract the effect of infiltration by Viet Minh agents." This was "not primarily intended to stimulate local initiative and village self-development, rather to establish some measure of central government influence and control over village attitudes and activities." This left Barrows highly reluctant to fund the CDV.[100]

What is particularly interesting about the discussion over the theory and practice of Civic Action is Kiểu Công Cung's position. While Lansdale was discussing the program in terms of actually doing community development work, Cung was not. Throughout the whole deliberation over funding, Cung adhered to the position that Civic Action was simply a means of extending the reach of the government down to the countryside to counter the communist presence.[101] This no doubt contributed to the problems he had with the Americans at the top of USOM in Sài Gòn. Though Cung was clearly versed in some of the ideas of community development he saw them as one means to the larger end of winning the people over to the Diệm government, particularly with an eye to the impending July 1956 national election on the unification of Vietnam.[102] Even though Ngô Đình Diệm had effectively rejected holding them in July 1955, arguing that they could not possibly be conducted fairly in Việt Minh controlled areas, Cung believed that the South Vietnamese government still might be compelled by foreign powers to hold them at a future date. Given this potential danger, Cung wanted to be certain that the government had a recognizable presence in the countryside.[103] This explains why, as late as May 1956, Cung stated the CDV's "purposes are not to be considered in terms of a technical assistance program but purely as a psychological warfare program."[104]

---

[100] Correspondence from Leland Barrows to Louis Miniclier, December 12, 1955, SF 54–58, Box 1, RG 469, NARA.

[101] See Civic Action: Role, Activities, Results, ND, SF 54–58, Box 1, RG 469, NARA.

[102] Phillips, *Why Vietnam Matters*, 74–77 and 85–86.

[103] See Memorandum from D.C. Lavergne to Leland Barrows, December 3, 1955, SF 54–58, Box 1, RG 469, NARA for a discussion of the need to prepare for elections. See Telegram from the Secretary of State to the Embassy in Vietnam, August 3, 1955, *FRUS, 1955–57*, Vol. 1, 505, FN 5 for further discussion on Diệm's decision not to hold the national elections.

[104] Memorandum from M.H.B. Adler, Chief, Field Service USOM to D.C. Lavergne, May 3, 1956, SF 54–58, Box 1, RG 469, NARA.

Moreover, Kiều Công Cung appears to have believed that at its core Civic Action only had the resources to put the cadres in the villages to convince the people that the Sài Gòn government could better provide for them than the communists, and not embark on a wholesale community development program as advocated by the Americans. As far as he was concerned, in their current state, the government ministries and technical services lacked the appropriate personnel – he shared Diệm's disdain for the *fonctionnaires* in the government[105] – the resources and the ability to reach down to the countryside to provide the support such a community development program would require – the very reason why he had proposed the Civic Action in the first place.[106] But this then raises the question of the discrepancy between his conception of Civic Action as akin to psychological warfare and Edward Lansdale's, which spoke of it specifically in terms of community development. The answer appears to be that Lansdale oversold the community development aspect of it in his September memorandum because he saw in the program a means to promote his vision of grassroots development. This highlights the fundamental differences in conceiving development that existed within the American foreign aid apparatus during the 1950s.

As Edward Miller has demonstrated, American foreign policymakers were in no way unified on how best to achieve the social transformation of South Vietnam.[107] Some individuals, such as Lansdale, Phillips and Ladejinsky, whom Miller identifies as "low modernists," favored a bottom-up approach to development that relied on "small-scale, locally based initiatives aimed at particular groups and communities." Such low modernist schemes as community development would target the grassroots, instilling the local population with "new rational and democratic habits of mind." Societal change would come as these new attitudes spread outward from the village.[108] Other individuals, such as Leland Barrows, who may be dubbed "high-modernists", adhered to massive, often state-driven developmental schemes that relied on centralized planning and the application of scientific knowledge and technical expertise. The sheer scale and top-down approach of the projects envisioned by

---

[105] See for example, Memorandum Nguyễn Quan to Walter Mode, March 11, 1957, Folder 76, Box 660, MSUVAG, MSUA.

[106] Report on the Officialization of Civic Action, ND, Folder 57; Memorandum for the Record, November 29, 1956, Folder 84, Box 660, MSUVAG, MSUA; and Civic Action: Role, Activities, Results, ND, SF 54–58, Box 1, RG 469, NARA.

[107] Miller, *Misalliance*, 54–84.

[108] *Ibid.*, 58–59.

high-modernists often caused "them to denigrate local and traditional practices and beliefs."[109] In the discussion over whether or not to fund Civic Action, Phillips contends that Barrows felt "the major focus of economic development should be on industrialization," as this, presumably, would propel South Vietnam toward self-sufficiency and alleviate the chronic impoverishment that made the people so susceptible to radical ideas. This inclination toward broad-scale industrialization, rather than an emphasis on more modest local means of production to cure South Vietnam's perceived ills, went directly against the grain of what Civic Action was attempting to achieve. But for Barrows, Phillips argues, it meant that "community development, while worthwhile, was a secondary consideration."[110]

In the end this wrangling over funding appears to have left Cung more wary about dealing with USOM, and the upper echelon of the American mission more skeptical about the efficacy of the program in its current form. Cung wanted the American mission to provide funding in cash which he could use as he deemed fit. But this was inconsistent with standard USOM operating procedures, which labeled Civic Action a "political necessity" and "not a typical USOM development or reconstruction project."[111] A compromise of sorts was reached in the spring of 1956. The Sài Gòn government agreed to provide the funding to meet the internal operating costs of the Civic Action program. USOM, after much pressure from Ambassador Frederick Reinhardt, would offer a one-time grant of $500,000 in the form of "materials and equipment" rather than cash. The CDV would continue to operate, but USOM was absolved of future "responsibility for [its] execution."[112] But, as we will see, this was not the end of USOM's, much less the American, relationship with Civic Action. The "lure of community development" was so strong that the Special Commissariat could not escape its pull. This would once again raise questions of American support – this time all the way at the top in Washington – and more importantly, have tremendous consequences for Diệm's revolution as he sought his own formula for nation-building.

---

[109] Miller, *Misalliance*, 57. For a more thorough discussion of high modernism see James Scott, *Seeing Like a State: How Certain Schemes to Improve the Human Condition Have Failed* (New Haven, CT: Yale University Press, 1998), 87–102.

[110] Phillips, *Why Vietnam Matters*, 86.

[111] Memorandum from M.H.B. Adler to D.C. Lavergne, August 17, 1956, SF 54–58, Box 1, RG 469, NARA.

[112] Telegram United States Operations Mission Saigon to the Department of State, April 27, 1956, SF 54–58, Box 3, RG 469, NARA. See Phillips, *Why Vietnam Matters*, 86 for Reinhardt's involvement in getting USOM to compromise.

THE CDV, NGÔ ĐÌNH DIỆM AND NATION-BUILDING
IN SOUTH VIETNAM

As the deliberations over what kind of financial aid USOM should offer
Civic Action were coming to a head at the end of April 1956, the Special
Commissariat attempted to address the pervasive problems of maintaining some sort of meaningful presence in the countryside and instilling in
the peasantry a sense of belonging to something greater than the village
community.[113] At the same time, the Special Commissariat was hoping
to broaden the reach of the cadres to other parts of the country. Based
on some of the Civic Action field reports drafted in late 1955 and early
1956, the cadres' activities in the villages had been meeting with considerable success in the regions where they had been active. By this time,
there were more than 1,000 cadres acting in the Sài Gòn – Chợ Lớn area
and seventeen provinces in South Vietnam.[114] They had been connecting
with the local population with various Welfare Improvement activities
such as helping with the harvest, repairing roads, improving local sanitation and, in the case of a village in Gò Cộng, delivering thirty sewing
machines to the people to bolster local industry and help to improve their
economic situation. As well, they accelerated the communist denunciation campaign by holding more meetings and going deeper into territory
where the communists – termed "Việt Cộng" in the reports – had considerable influence, such as Tây Ninh, Biên Hòa, Long Xuyên and Bac
Liêu.[115] March 4, 1956 saw the election of the Republic of Vietnam's first

[113] Report on the Organization of the Special Commissariat for Civic Action, June 1957,
Folder 82, Box 660, MSUVAG, MSUA.
[114] These provinces were: Gia Định, Biên Hoà, Bình Dương, Tây Ninh, Bến Tre, Bà Rịa, Mỹ
Tho, Vĩnh Long, Vĩnh Bình, Ba Xuyen, Bắc Liêu, Kiên Giang, Phong Dinh, An Giang, Châu
Đốc and Sa Đéc; Báo Cáo Tổng Kết Thành Tích Vận Động Tổng Tuyển Cử Quốc Hội 4-3-
1956 của Đặc Ủy Phủ Công Dân Vụ [Summary Report of Achievements of the March 4,
1956 National Assembly Election Campaign of the Special Commissariat for Civic Action],
March 3, 1956, Folder 16064, PTTĐICH, TTLTQG2. The number of cadres in the Special
Commissariat comes from Báo Cáo Hoạt Động Đặc Ủy Trưởng Công Dân Vụ trong năm
1955 [Operation Report of the Special Commissariat for Civic Action for 1955], January
21, 1956 Folder 15982, PTTĐICH, TTLTQG2. This latter report also indicates that by
the end 1955 the number of provinces the cadres had been active in reached twenty-one.
Unfortunately, there is no explanation for why the number of provinces had been reduced
to seventeen by April. It could be a product of the amalgamation of several provinces into
one, which happened somewhat frequently as the regime tried to consolidate its administrative grip over the countryside. See for example Báo Cáo Hoạt Động Đặc Ủy Trưởng
Công Dân Vụ trong Tháng 3, 1956 [Operation Report of the Special Commissariat for
Civic Action for March 1956], April 1956, Folder 16063, PTTĐICH, TTLTQG2.
[115] Báo Cáo Hoạt Động Đặc Ủy Trưởng Công Dân Vụ trong Tháng 2, 1956, [Operation
Report of the Special Commissariat for Civic Action for February 1956], March 1956,

National Assembly and in the weeks leading up to it the Civic Action cadres carried out a widespread campaign to educate the people about the meaning and goals of both the election and the new governing body. Of particular emphasis in their explanations was imparting on the people the fact that it was the civic duty of every citizen to exercise the franchise.[116] All of these activities were intended to reinforce the idea that the Sài Gòn government was there to help the people and, according to the reports, increase their confidence in the Diệm regime.

Despite this success, the reach of the cadres was still quite limited. The provinces where Civic Action was active were restricted to the southern end of the country. Neglected were the provinces in the center and the Central Highlands. Communists and other opponents of the regime still exerted significant control in parts of the south, particularly in the Mekong Delta and areas along the border with Cambodia to the northeast of Sài Gòn. Additionally, it was apparent that these opponents of the regime still exerted a negative influence on the population in certain areas where the cadres were active as their four-week presence in the village remained too transitory to instill the people with a lasting faith in the government. In April the mobile cadres were recalled to Sài Gòn and reassigned into province groups that would operate at the district level. Each province group consisted of a small supervisory staff with a modest reserve of cadres located at district headquarters. The remaining mobile cadres were then divided into units of two agents each. Each unit would be assigned to a particular village for eight weeks before moving on. Continuity would theoretically be maintained by the reserve group of cadres at the district headquarters who would follow up on the various villages that had already been visited. This would continue until every village in a district had been reached by one of the mobile units.

During their first week in the village, the two cadres of each mobile unit would try to get close to the people. They would establish what the people's "living situation" was like and what the perceived needs of the community were, such as improved sanitation or better roads and canals. Over the ensuing weeks, they would mobilize the people to participate

---

Folder 16063, PTTĐICH, TTLTQG2. See also Báo Cáo Hàng Tháng 11, 1955 [Monthly Report, November 1955], December 12, 1955, Folder 15982, PTTĐICH, TTLTQG2.

[116] Phúc Trình Kính Gởi Ông Đặc Ủy Trưởng Công Dân Vụ [Report to the Special Commissioner of Civic Action], February 28, 1956; and Bản Sao Báo Cáo Đặc Biệt của Kiểm Tra Viên Nguyễn Ngọc Hồ về Công Tác Vận Động Tổng Tuyển Cử tại Tỉnh Bạc Liêu [Copy of a Special Report of Verifier Nguyễn Ngọc Hồ about theElection Work in Bạc Liêu Province], March 2, 1956, Folder 16064, PTTĐICH, TTLTQG2.

in self-help projects to address these needs. One means of doing this was through the "family mutual help system," in which certain families would be organized into groups of five with each family given responsibility for a particular role in improving the entire group's welfare such as popular education, hygiene or economic matters. The head family of the group would have the added duty of keeping tabs on the comings and goings of the group and ensuring each member remained loyal to the government.[117] They would also spend a considerable amount of time informing the people of the government's policies and programs and indoctrinating them in the appropriate political line of the regime which involved regular communist denunciation sessions. Finally, they would recruit local agents from the population who demonstrated the necessary zeal and character to continue overseeing this work once the cadres moved on to another village. The central purpose of the cadres' work was to make the people realize that the government was there to help them if they were willing to seize the initiative and help themselves.[118]

The fact that the members of the CDV believed the state had to tell the rural elements to help themselves is particularly telling. On the one hand, one could argue that the government took a rather dim view of the peasantry and saw them as incapable of individually ensuring their own welfare.[119] On the other, one could also argue that it reflects Diệm's conception of a modern Vietnam as a perpetual work in progress.

As a postcolonial leader Diệm had some fairly substantial notions of what he believed a modern South Vietnamese state should look like. At the core of this design was Diệm's notion that the entire population needed to be involved in the nation-building process. Not only would this provide his countrymen with a common bond, but it would also give them a vested interest in ensuring the nation's continued viability. In other words, the physical construction of a Vietnamese nation came to be part of the Vietnamese national identity that Diệm was trying to create. Kiều Công Cung, most likely due to his past experiences, appears to have been very much in tune with Diệm's desires. As noted previously,

---

[117] See for example, Report on the Ceremony Held in the Village of Hòa Khánh province of Chợ Lớn, on December 29, 1955, Folder 76, Box 660, MSUVAG, MSUA. See also Catton, *Diem's Final Failure*, 14.

[118] Tóm tắt Thuyết Trình Chỉ Thị Đặc Ủy Trưởng Công Dân Vụ [Summary Report of the Instructions for the Special Commissariat for Civic Action], ND, Folder 16293, PTTĐICH, TTLTQG2; Report on the Organization of the Special Commissariat for Civic Action, June 1957, Folder 82, Box 660, MSUVAG, MSUA.

[119] Thomas L. Ahern, Jr., *CIA and Rural Pacification in South Vietnam* (Langley, VA: Center for the Study of Intelligence, declassified 2007), 27.

Kiều Công Cung was a staunch nationalist. He resigned his commission from the French Army following its surrender to the Japanese and then joined the Việt Minh in its struggle for independence when the French tried to return. He subsequently abandoned this organization over his unwillingness to join the communist party, which he most likely perceived to be directed by Moscow or Beijing. After an arduous journey southward he became very enamored by Diệm and the national cause he espoused, devoting himself to propagating it across the Vietnamese countryside. This latest reorganization of the Special Commissariat was therefore intended to ensure that the Civic Action cadres would be the vanguard for this national vision.

By reducing the number of cadres acting in the villages to two, the Special Commissariat would be able to spread itself more widely, increasing the influence of the government in the countryside. Having so few cadres at the village level would place a premium on getting members of the village population to come out and participate in the daily tasks of Welfare Improvement in a manner consistent with these larger national designs. Local participation in these village self-help projects, Cung felt, would unite the people at the grassroots. This would reinforce the propagandistic work of Raising the People's Intellectual Standards through popular education to create a new more civic-minded citizenry that would form the basis of Diệm's infrastructure for democracy.[120]

Such ideas were rooted in Diệm's view of Vietnam's past. Dennis Duncanson, a member of the British Advisory Mission to Vietnam, contends that Diệm always believed the "intensity of communal relationships" that stemmed from the compact rural farming settlements that were prevalent in his native Central Vietnam "gave rise to ... the foundation of the Vietnamese way of life."[121] According to Diệm, this had contributed to a tradition of local autonomy that led to a "decentralized system" of corporate villages. Such a social system, Diệm argued, had "met the economic conditions of its time." It "worked smoothly" due to a "moral cohesion" and "strong spiritual unity which was a counterweight to centrifugal tendencies." Diệm hoped to re-establish this decentralized corporate village structure which, as we shall see, he

---

[120] Brief Summary on the Civic Action Background, November 1956; and Background of Civic Action, ND, Folder 57 Box 660, MSUVAG, MSUA. Though there is no date on the second document, the material suggests it was drafted in early 1957.

[121] Dennis J. Duncanson, *Government and Revolution in Vietnam* (New York: Oxford University Press, 1968), 313.

believed held the key to achieving enough self-sufficiency to decrease South Vietnam's dependence on a foreign power for its continued viability.[122] The use of fewer cadres spread more broadly marked a concerted effort by Cung to get the Civic Action cadres to "tap these deep roots" at the village level and lay the "local foundations" for a new state as widely as possible.[123] The challenge, however, was that the modern South Vietnamese nation that Diệm was envisioning was based on his idealized reading of the past. Whether this would resonate with other particularist notions of Vietnamese modernity held by the members of the rural population the Civic Action cadres were intended to win over remained to be seen.

The idea of distributing the cadres more broadly across the Vietnamese countryside on which the restructuring rested made a good deal of sense given the limited number of cadres available for the Special Commissariat for Civic Action. The initial reports coming in indicated that these reforms were having some positive effect. In its characteristically upbeat tone, the Special Commissariat for Civic Action contended that coordination between the local administrative organs and the cadres was improving, as the regional authorities were better understanding the mission of Civic Action. The cadres in the provinces of Bến Tre (Kiến Hòa), Vĩnh Long and Bà Rịa were reporting significant help from the administrative councils in carrying out their work of Welfare Improvement. Such progress was reflected in a reportedly more positive attitude of the peasantry toward the "Black Shirt Cadres" – a reference to the calico noir they wore – as in one case where the local population contended that "in nine years of war we have just now been able to find the Government and the help of the Government toward the people." With such confidence, the cadres reported, the people were seemingly more willing to participate in the work of rural development and, in certain cases, start turning their backs on the communists.[124]

---

[122] Presidency of the Republic of Vietnam, *Toward Better Mutual Understanding*, Vol. 1, *Speeches Delivered by President Ngo Dinh Diem during his State Visits to Thailand, Australia, Korea*, 2nd ed.(Saigon: Presidency of the Republic of Vietnam, Press Office, 1958), 19–21. See also Marguerite Higgins, *Our Vietnam Nightmare: The Story of U.S. Involvement in the Vietnamese Tragedy, with Thoughts on a Future Policy* (New York: Harper & Row, 1965), 166 and 173.

[123] The first quote is from Higgins, *Our Vietnam Nightmare*, 166; the second quote is from Catton, *Diem's Final Failure*, 49.

[124] Báo Cáo Hoạt Động của Đặc Ủy Phủ Công Dân Vụ trong tháng 4 năm 1956 [Operation Report of the Special Commissariat for Civic Action in April 1956], May 9, 1956, Folder 16063, PTTĐICH, TTLTQG2.

The following month, the Commissariat reported even more progress with regard to the competition with the communists and other anti-regime groups, as demonstrated by heightened action against the cadres in the field. In some extreme instances this resulted in the overt targeting of mobile cadres with violent actions such as kidnapping and murder. But in the majority of cases it simply involved subversive elements penetrating the local organizations – such as the mutual aid family groups – and using them to spread disinformation to cause alarm and discredit the Sài Gòn government.[125] One such technique employed by southern party cadres was known as "whispering propaganda" whereby they discretely spread messages discrediting the regime, or feigned drunkenness to obnoxiously denounce the regime publicly.[126]

While the Special Commissariat was being reorganized it began to extend its operations into the Central Highlands. In April the first cadres were dispatched to Kon Tum.[127] By December they were also operating in Đà Lat, Darlac, Đồng Nai Thương and Pleiku.[128] Officially, the government's aim in reaching out to the highland provinces was to eradicate the French influence over the local ethnic groups – termed *Montagnards* by the French – and bring them into the government fold. During the colonial period the highlands had been organized as the *Pays Montagnards du Sud* (PMS), a semiautonomous zone which had afforded the ethnic highland minorities considerable freedom.[129] In practice, this meant a policy of cultural assimilation, or "Vietnamization," where the Civic Action cadres were responsible for teaching highlanders the Vietnamese language, educating them about the republican system of government in Sài Gòn – who was Diệm, how the National Assembly operated – and their obligations to it, and eliminating any "harmful superstitions and customs

---

[125] Báo Cáo Hoạt Động của Đặc Ủy Phủ Công Dân Vụ trong tháng 5 năm 1956 [Operation Report of the Special Commissariat for Civic Action in May 1956], June 4, 1956, Folder 16063, PTTĐICH, TTLTQG2. While the mutual family groups were created to mobilize the peasantry to participate in rural development projects, they were in reality used as much to inform on the activities of family members who had fallen under the suspicion of the regime, Catton, *Diem's Final Failure*, 14.

[126] David W.P. Elliott, *The Vietnamese War: Revolution and Social Change in the Mekong Delta 1930–1975*, Vol. 1 (Armonk, NY: M.E. Sharpe, 2003), 178.

[127] Tỉnh Trưởng Tỉnh Kon Tum Kính gởi Ông Bộ Trưởng tại Phủ Tổng Thống [Memorandum from the Kon Tum Province Chief to the Secretary of State in the Office of the President], August 8, 1956, Folder 16065, PTTĐICH, TTLTQG2

[128] Báo Cáo Hoạt Động của Đặc Ủy Phủ Công Dân Vụ trong tháng 12 năm 1956 [Operation Report of the Special Commissariat for Civic Action in December 1956], January 14, 1957, Folder 16063, PTTĐICH, TTLTQG2.

[129] Catton, *Diem's Final Failure*, 57.

which caused living standards to remain low."[130] Initially, the operating procedure was the same as it was in the southern provinces, only they employed "Montagnard Cadres" wherever they could. Unsurprisingly, they encountered resistance as their efforts to bring them under the control of Sài Gòn challenged their traditional autonomy. The ethnic minorities required "more persuasion and education to embrace the program." The cadres' stay was reduced to one month in each village and more flexibility was afforded the province group chief to plan and organize his operations. This meant abandoning the practice of establishing mutual family groups, as the highland populations had "a similar tribal organization," and placing greater emphasis on "language instruction, health and sanitation demonstrations and political indoctrination."[131]

While all of the restructuring that had begun in April had been intended to extend the reach of Civic Action into the countryside, the Special Commissariat was still handicapped by the number of available cadres. At the midpoint of 1956, there were only 1,622 cadres operating in the countryside. They had been divided into 104 groups acting across twenty-six provinces.[132] Though they could report greater receptivity to the presence of the cadres in the field and gains in the competition with the communists, it was unclear as to whether this would have a lasting effect. Would the peasantry continue to support the Sài Gòn government once the cadres' work was completed and they had moved on? Unfortunately, the answer to this question would have to wait as all of the cadres were recalled from the field in June and reorganized into joint-province groups that would participate in the Trương Tấn Bửu and Thoại Ngọc Hầu pacification campaigns which were launched on July 19.[133]

This was not the first time the Civic Action mobile groups had been drafted into military campaigns. As we have seen, the Special Commissariat was created in March 1955 to help with the pacification of the countryside and its subsequent general directive had specific provisions for its contribution to this type of military activity, particularly in the "zones of

---

[130] Memorandum from John Gates, TRIM to Edward G. Lansdale, August 7, 1956, SF 54–58, Box 1, RG 469, NARA. For the quote on superstition see Background on the Civic Action Program, ND, Folder 57, Box 660, MSUVAG, MSUA.

[131] Background on the Civic Action Program, ND, Folder 57, Box 660, MSUVAG, MSUA.

[132] Tổng Kết Thành Thích 6–56 đến 6–57 [Summary of Achievements 6–56 to 6–57], June 21, 1957, Folder 16294, PTTDICH, TTLTQG2.

[133] Báo Cáo Hoạt Động của Đặc Ủy Phủ Công Dân Vụ trong tháng 7 năm 1956 [Operation Report of the Special Commissariat for Civic Action in July 1956], August 3, 1956, Folder 16063, PTTĐICH, TTLTQG2; and Special Commissariat for Civic Action History Part II of the Draft Report, ND, Folder 83, Box 660, MSUVAG, MSUA.

pacification." More specifically, twenty Civic Action mobile groups had recently worked with the military in the Nguyễn Huệ campaign to flush out the remaining elements of the Bình Xuyên and the Cao Đài and Hòa Hảo sects in the Plain of Reeds.[134] What was different in the case of these two campaigns is the sheer scope of Civic Action's involvement. Virtually every cadre was involved in these campaigns which lasted until February 1957.[135] Existing province groups were reorganized into joint-province groups which consisted of a joint group staff and four combined province groups made up of four teams of ten cadres each.[136] The Trương Tấn Bửu campaign was carried out in the eastern provinces of southern Vietnam and initially involved 300 cadres. They were all placed at the disposal of the operation's commander in chief, Major General Mai Hữu Xuân, and carried out activities designed by the campaign's directing committee. The Thoại Ngọc Hầu campaign, commanded by Major General Đương Văn Minh, initially consisted of three joint-province groups made up of twelve province groups totaling 600 cadres. Its base of operations originated in the western provinces of Cà Mau, Sóc Trăng and Phong Thạnh. They undertook projects worked out by the directing committee, but received their direction from the Special Commissariat for Civic Action in Sài Gòn. The remaining cadres made up the general staffs of the joint, province and mobile team groups.[137]

In general, the projects created by the campaign directing committees accorded with the tenets of Raising the People's Intellectual Standards and Welfare Improvement. They consisted of communist denunciation sessions to highlight the crimes of the enemy; the creation and

---

[134] Báo Cáo Hoạt Động của Đặc Ủy Phủ Công Dân Vụ trong tháng 3 năm 1956 [Operation Report of the Special Commissariat for Civic Action in March 1956], April 1956, Folder 16063, PTTĐICH, TTLTQG2; and Press Release "Achievements Accomplished by the Government Ngo Dinh Diem after 2 Years of Power," July 26, 1956, Folder 55, Box 660, MSUVAG, MSUA.

[135] The Background of Civic Action, ND, Folder 57, Box 660, MSUVAG, MSUA.

[136] Special Commissariat for Civic Action History Part II of the Draft Report, ND, Folder 83, Box 660, MSUVAG, MSUA.

[137] Báo Cáo Hoạt Động của Đặc Ủy Phủ Công Dân Vụ trong tháng 7 năm 1956 [Operation Report of the Special Commissariat for Civic Action in July 1956], August 3, 1956, Folder 16063; Ông Bộ Trưởng tại Phủ Tổng Thống Kính gởi Thiếu Tướng Mai Hữu Xuân, Tư Lịnh Chiến Dịch Trương Tấn Bửu, Thiếu Tướng Dương Văn Minh, Tư Lịnh Chiến Dịch Thoại Ngọc Hầu [Memorandum from the Secretary of State for the Office of the President to Major General Mai Huu Xuan, Commander of the Tan Buu Campaign and Major General Duong Van Minh, Commander of the Thoai Ngoc Hau Campaign], October 30, 1956, Folder 16068, PTTĐICH, TTLTQG2; Special Commissariat for Civic Action History Part II of the Draft Report, ND, Folder 83; and The Background of Civic Action, ND, Folder 57, Box 660, MSUVAG, MSUA.

"strengthening" of mutual family groups; popular education activities, such as indoctrination classes to inform the recently liberated people about the structure and function of the Sài Gòn government and how it had been established to work for their interests; and local construction projects to help raise the standard of living, such as bridge and road repairs. The main difference with previous work was that they were carried out in conjunction with a military effort to bring order and security to these particular areas of the countryside.[138]

Two specific examples of the Special Commissariat's ability to demonstrate to the people that they stood to gain more by placing their allegiance behind the Sài Gòn government than its myriad enemies stand out from the campaigns. In late November, two Civic Action province groups were rushed to Trà Vinh and Tam Cần provinces to help the people rebuild in the wake of a devastating typhoon and the subsequent flooding. In just under ten days, from November 21 to November 30, they rebuilt 316 houses; repaired 254 houses, three schools, two military posts and fifty foot bridges; cleared debris and felled trees from roadways; and reopened irrigation canals. They were able to reap considerable propaganda value from this action work by exposing an alleged communist plot to take credit for the relief work. Just as importantly, they took advantage of the situation to demonstrate the merits of mutual help as the cadres' efforts to "use their own hands" was a source of inspiration to get other people to help one another to rebuild or repair their own houses. It paid off as the Special Commissariat could report to the Office of the President that this emergency assistance gave the affected people "great confidence in the Republican system" as they pledged "to unite closely around President Ngo for security and therefore freedom and democracy."[139]

---

[138] See, for example, Báo Cáo Hoạt Động của Đặc Ủy Phủ Công Dân Vụ trong tháng 7 năm 1956 [Operation Report of the Special Commissariat for Civic Action in July 1956], August 3, 1956; Báo Cáo Hoạt Động của Đặc Ủy Phủ Công Dân Vụ trong tháng 8 năm 1956 [Operation Report of the Special Commissariat for Civic Action in August 1956], September 20, 1956, Báo Cáo Hoạt Động của Đặc Ủy Phủ Công Dân Vụ trong tháng 12 năm 1956 [Operation Report of the Special Commissariat for Civic Action in December 1956], January 14, 1957, Folder 16063; Tỉnh Trưởng Mỹ Tho Kính gởi Bộ Trưởng tại Phủ Tổng Thống [Memorandum from the My Tho Province Chief to the Secretary of State for the Office of the President], August 13, 1956; Tỉnh Trưởng Vĩnh Long Kính gởi Bộ Trưởng tại Phủ Tổng Thống [Memorandum from the Vinh Long Province Chief to the Secretary of State for the Office of the President], August 22, 1956, Folder 16065, PTTĐICH, TTLTQG2.
[139] Đặc Ủy Phủ Công Dân Vụ Kính gởi Bộ Trưởng tại Phủ Tổng Thống [Memorandum from the Special for Civic Action to the Secretary of State for the Office of the President] December 12, 1956, Folder 16064, PTTĐICH, TTLTQG2. See also Báo Cáo Hoạt Động của Đặc Ủy Phủ Công Dân Vụ trong tháng 11 năm 1956 [Operation Report of the

In December cadres from the Thoại Ngọc Hầu campaign halted a supposed communist effort to sabotage rice crops in the Mekong Delta. In the village of Mỹ Lâm in the province of Mỹ Tho (Định Tường) they mobilized the people of the village of to re-embank a dam that had been sabotaged by the "Việt Cộng," saving over 2,000 hectares of rice paddies from being flooded by sea water. Destroying the crops would have made the farmers dependent on the communists for rice, which would have been subject to an exploitive tax. These and other efforts made the cadres targets of the enemy. The following month, Civic Action cadre Lương Đức Thoan was ambushed and assassinated alongside a member of the Civil Guard in Rạch Giá province. Such sacrifice reportedly earned the cadres considerable praise from the peasantry. This was matched by the alleged surrender of forty-eight clandestine communist agents to regional authorities.[140]

On the whole the Civic Action cadres comported themselves quite well throughout the campaigns. According to the September 1956 monthly report of the Special Commissariat the Civic Action cadres drew highly favorable comparisons with their counterparts in the military due to the fact that they would "also accept each physical hardship and were willing to sacrifice themselves in the provinces like an official soldier."[141] Observers with the Michigan State University Advisory Group, which were conducting an evaluation of the Civic Action program at the time as part of their effort to help the Sài Gòn government streamline its operations corroborated this, citing reports that the cadres "had been of great help and outstanding elements in the operations."[142]

To get his own assessment of the Civic Action program, the president issued a request to all of the province chiefs for an evaluation of the strengths and weaknesses of the CDV cadres early in the campaigns.[143]

Special Commissariat for Civic Action in November 1956], December 11, 1956, Folder 16063, PTTĐICH, TTLTQG2.

[140] Báo Cáo Hoạt Động của Đặc Ủy Phủ Công Dân Vụ trong tháng 1 năm 1957 [Operation Report of the Special Commissariat for Civic Action in January 1957], February 12, 1957, Folder 16295, PTTĐICH, TTLTQG2. See also Báo Cáo Hoạt Động của Đặc Ủy Phủ Công Dân Vụ trong tháng 12 năm 1956 [Operation Report of the Special Commissariat for Civic Action in December 1956], January 14, 1957, Folder 16063, PTTĐICH, TTLTQG2.

[141] Báo Cáo Hoạt Động của Đặc Ủy Phủ Công Dân Vụ trong tháng 9 năm 1956 [Operation Report of the Special Commissariat for Civic Action in September 1956], October 9, 1956, Folder 16063, PTTĐICH, TTLTQG2.

[142] Brief Summary on the Civic Action Background, November 1956, Folder 57, Box 660, MSUVAG, MSUA.

[143] Bộ Trưởng tại Phủ Tổng Thống Kính gởi Quý Ông Tỉnh Trưởng [Memorandum from the Secretary of State for the Office of the President to the Province Chiefs], August 10, 1956, Folder 16065, PTTĐICH, TTLTQG2.

In virtually every province where a CDV province group was active, the province chief was supportive of the program and claimed it had a beneficial impact on the population. Nevertheless, several of these reports did identify shortcomings that suggested some of the significant weaknesses evident in 1955 remained. For example, regional differences between the cadres and the peasantry proved, at times, to be a hindrance to cooperation. Many of the cadres were Catholics who had moved to the South as part of the exodus of refugees following the Geneva Accords.[144] They had come from a part of Vietnam that had been inhabited by indigenous Vietnamese for centuries. Those who lived further to the south, particularly in the Mekong Delta, had come from families that had settled there in the eighteenth or nineteenth century – many arriving less than a hundred years before the French. As we have seen, this had been considered Vietnam's frontier and the population there was dispersed and more independent, while their northern brethren came from more densely populated and integrated farming communities.[145]

The difficulties this created most often manifest themselves in the failure of the cadres and the peasants to understand one another's dialect and mores.[146] In both the provinces of Tân An and Bến Tre, the respective province chiefs complained that the peasantry had difficulty understanding the CDV cadres because of the way they spoke, while the cadres were unable to identify with the individuals they were sent to help. In Tân An the ensuing misunderstandings openly hindered the province group's ability to propagate the ideology of the government as the cadres could not effectively communicate with the local population.[147] In Bến Tre the problem was much worse. Not only were the cadres and the villagers having difficulty understanding one another, but some of the cadres bullied the peasantry, sometimes physically abusing, grabbing, punching and otherwise intimidating the people. In other places, they forced their

---

[144] According to a memorandum by D.C. Lavergne, up to 75 percent of the Civic Action cadres had come from the north, Memorandum from D.C. Lavergne to Leland Barrows, November 28, 1955, SF 54–58, Box 1, RG 469, NARA.

[145] Li Tana, "An Alternative Vietnam? The Nguyen Kingdom in the Seventeenth and Eighteenth Centuries," *Journal of Southeast Asian Studies* 29(1) (March 1998): 111–121; Bernard Fall, *The Two Vietnams: A Political and Military Analysis*, 2nd. rev. ed. (New York: Frederick A. Praeger, 1968), 4 and 12–14; and Duncanson, *Government and Revolution in Vietnam*, 38–39.

[146] See for example, Phillips, *Why Vietnam Matters*, 79.

[147] Tỉnh Trưởng Tânan Kính gởi Ông Bộ Trưởng tại Phủ Tổng Thống [Memorandum from the Tanan Province Chief to the Secretary of State for the Office of the President], September 4, 1956, Folder 16065, PTTĐICH, TTLTQG2.

way into positions of regional authority by invoking the name of the president.[148]

It is unclear from the reports why these individuals acted this way, but the evidence from the other provinces suggests that these were isolated incidents carried out by unscrupulous and power-hungry ne'er-do-wells and not indicative of the overall behavior of the cadres, which was, for the most part, quite exemplary. When these problems occurred, they could be rectified by more open dialogue or, if necessary, disciplinary measures. Unfortunately, other reports pointed to more significant issues that struck at the very nature of Civic Action.

In Gò Công, its province chief highlighted continuity as a significant problem. He praised the cadres for their spirit and advice, contending that they had improved life in the countryside, convinced communist cadres to turn themselves in, and strengthened the regional government overall. But he also hinted at an unhealthy dependency on the cadres, concluding that their presence had become crucial for the development of his province. Once the cadres had left, the regional administrative organs lost efficient co-workers, indicating that all the good work performed to date threatened to be undone.[149]

More concerning was the situation in Bà Rịa. In his report, the province chief commended the affable manner of the cadres and lauded their close coordination with the regional administration. But he also pointed to a troubling reality that struck at the very heart of the nation-building agenda Diệm was attempting when he complained that many of the farmers, laborers and fishermen resented the fact that the Welfare Improvement projects were actually "increasing their deprivation," as they had to voluntarily offer their manpower, when they could otherwise be using it to earn a living.[150] It was on this spirit of voluntarism and self-sacrifice toward the greater good of rebuilding the country that Diệm's hopes for fashioning a new national ideal rested. The peasants' reluctance to buy into this system in Bà Rịa indicated that despite the good work of the Civic Action cadres the segments of the peasantry possessed

[148] Tỉnh Tưởng Bến Tre Kính gởi Ông Bộ Trưởng tại Phủ Tổng Thống [Memorandum from the Ben Tre Province Chief to the Secretary of State for the Office of the President], August 18, 1956, Folder 16065, PTTĐICH, TTLTQG2.

[149] Tỉnh Tưởng Gòcông Kính gởi Ông Đồng Lý Bộ Trưởng tại Phủ Tổng Thống [Memorandum from the Gocong province Chief to the Secretary of State for the Office of the President], September 3, 1956, Folder 16065, PTTĐICH, TTLTQG2.

[150] Tỉnh Tưởng Bária Kính gởi Ngài Bộ Trưởng tại Phủ Tổng Thống [Memorandum from the Baria Province Chief to the Secretary of State for the Office of the President], August 29, 1956, Folder 16065, PTTĐICH, TTLTQG2.

a lingering resistance to abandoning their own self-interest to embrace a new communal order imposed from above.

While these particular instances were by no means reflective of the program as a whole, they did indicate that some problems remained. Cadres were certainly extending the reach of the government into the countryside, reaching out into the Central Highlands and penetrating the strongholds of the opponents of the regime. In both cases, these black-shirted agents of the regime were systematically demonstrating that the government was legitimately concerned with their welfare. But as the situation in Bà Rịa demonstrates, significant work remained in making the people understand their role in the new society that Diệm envisioned while satisfying their individual aspirations for what a modern state could provide: stability, personal autonomy and the promise of a better future. This, as we shall see, required a revolutionary effort on behalf of the government which ended up bringing Kiều Công Cung to terms with the international community development movement.

THREE

Revolution, Community Development and the Construction of Diệm's Vietnam

On July 7, 1957, the third anniversary of his ascension to power, Ngô Đình Diệm addressed the National Assembly of the Republic of Vietnam (RVN). He spoke in terms of a revolution having occurred. This revolution, he stated, had begun when his country's national sovereignty had "been wrest from the hands of colonial and feudal forces, making possible the establishment of a republican regime." Much progress had been made with respect to the creation of "a new political and economic structure" highlighted by the establishment of "democratic institutions and a democratic constitution." But despite these achievements, the "relentless efforts from one and all" were still required in order to complete "the work of national reconstruction, of improvement of the people's living standard, and the achievement of an independent economy."[1]

The ideas that underpinned South Vietnam's stated developmental aspirations, particularly self-sufficiency and improved social welfare, were common throughout postcolonial Southeast Asia. The leaders of two of the Republic of Vietnam's neighbors, also contending with the economic, political and social dislocation that accompanied independence from a colonial power, had articulated such goals for nation-building. In Cambodia, Prince Norodom Sihanouk expressed a desire to concentrate his nation-building efforts on the existing human capital available in his country. According to one favorable account of his rule, the prince attempted to instill in the Cambodian people "a sense of responsibility for

---

[1] Ngô Đình Diệm, Authorized Translation of the President of the Republic's Message on Double Seven Day, July 10, 1957, Item number 2321507007, Texas Tech Virtual Vietnam Archive, www.virtualarchive.vietnam.ttu.edu (hereafter referred to as TTVVA) (accessed February 2, 2007).

and participation in the process of social and political modernization."
One concrete example of this were the biannual National Congresses he
instituted in 1955 where the people were given the opportunity to discuss issues of concern with the government.[2] Another was the *Sangkum*,
or People's Socialist Community, a government-sponsored movement
that cut across party lines and took as its themes "loyalty to the Nation,
Buddhism and Monarchy."[3]

In Burma, Premier U Nu presented a clear forerunner to the development model of the RVN when he coined the term *"Pyidawtha"* in the early
1950s. Roughly translated, *"Pyidawtha"* could be defined as "building a
'happy and prosperous nation.'" In more concrete terms it attempted to
rouse the people and mobilize them for rehabilitation and development
of their nation through self-help by establishing *Pyidawtha* committees in
each town to propose practical, economically sound projects of immediate
benefit to the village communities. This was part of a much larger national
development plan that aimed at "the full development of Burma's human
and material resources and improvement of the people's livelihood through
fair distribution and effective government-sponsored welfare services" in
order to create what they perceived to be a true "welfare state."[4]

Since the November 1955 reorganization, the Special Commissariat
for Civic Action (CDV) had been laying the groundwork for such a societal transformation to occur across South Vietnam based on the concepts of Raising the People's Intellectual Standards (*Nâng Cao Dân Trí*)
and Welfare Improvement (*Cải Thiện Dân Sinh*). The task of Raising
the Intellectual Standards of the people was intended to create a politically engaged populace of progressive, patriotic and anticommunist citizens upon which Diệm's national revolution could be mounted. Welfare
Improvement work would establish the institutions and infrastructure
for such an endeavor. What was missing, however, was national purpose.

The Civic Action cadres' work was still only being performed on a
case-by-case basis determined by the specific needs of the region and the
number of personnel available.[5] Such an ad hoc approach, according to

[2] Roger M. Smith, "Prince Norodom Sihanouk of Cambodia," *Asian Survey* 7(6) (June
1967): 356–357.
[3] William Shawcross, *Sideshow: Kissinger, Nixon and the Destruction of Cambodia*
(New York: Touchstone, 1981), 49. See also Roger Kershaw, *Monarchy in South-East
Asia: The Faces of Tradition in Transition* (London: Routledge, 2001), 55–56.
[4] Maung Maung, "Pyidawtha Comes to Burma," *Far Eastern Survey* 22(9) (August
1953): 117–119.
[5] Đặc Ủy Phủ Công Dân Vụ Kính gởi Quý Ông Tỉnh Trưởng [Memorandum from the
Special Commissariat for Civic Action to the Province Chiefs], May 25, 1957; Hoạt Động

the regime, was inadequate to "build the nation in every aspect." What was needed, was a broad and cohesive effort to "awaken the people to the government's politics," and plans, and "make them clearly understand what is the just cause and what is the false cause." If the cadres could "encourage and guide the people" in the way Kiều Công Cung, the Commissioner of the Special Commissariat, believed, they could "build support for the authorities in the undertakings of national salvation and founding the state."[6] In other words: encouraging popular participation in these nation-building projects to instill in the people a sense of nationhood.

To meet this aim, Civic Action began what Cung would later refer to as a more "revolutionary" program of development to theoretically alter the burgeoning South Vietnamese state politically, socially and economically. This was manifest in the government's community development (*phát triển cộng đồng*) plan, launched in March 1957. It was part of a broader five-year plan for social and economic development that attempted to provide substance to the philosophical ruminations Diệm's younger brother Ngô Đình Nhu had long harbored regarding how best to realize the vision of a postcolonial Vietnam that Diệm possessed.

The Sài Gòn government's turn to community development was met by internal and external resistance. Bureaucratic rivalry and Kiều Công Cung's proclivities about the direction of the Special Commissariat for Civic Action kept him from embracing it wholeheartedly. Cung and the Special Commissariat initially maintained a peripheral role in its execution despite the government's desire to see Civic Action assume responsibility for the plan. Diệm's international patron, the US government, was also wary. The question of Civic Action's involvement prompted another round of debate over the level of support Washington should afford the plan, this time extending all the way up to the executive branch of the

---

Công Dân Vụ tại Các Tỉnh [Action of Civic Action in the Provinces], May 25, 1957, Folder 16302; Báo Cáo Tổng Kết Năm 1957 [1957 Comprehensive Report], January 10, 1958, Folder 16294; and Nhiệm vụ chủ trương đường lối hoạt động thành tích và chương trình công tác của Phủ Đặc Ủy Công Dân Vụ [Achievements from the line of action and program of Action for the Special Commissariat for Civic Action], October 3, 1959, Folder 16919, Phủ Tổng Thống Đệ Nhất Cộng Hòa [Office of the President of the First Republic] (hereafter PTTĐICH), Trung Tâm Lưu Trữ Quốc Gia II [National Archives 2] (hereafter TTLTQG2). See also Evaluation of Viet-Nam Program, August 15 1957, Mutual Security and Assistance 1959 (14) (hereafter MSA 59), Box 40, Confidential File Series (hereafter CFS), White House Central Files (hereafter CF), Dwight D. Eisenhower Library (hereafter DDEL) for a favorable American appraisal of the achievements of Civic Action.

[6] Hoạt Động Công Dân Vụ tại Các Tỉnh [Action of Civic Action in the Provinces], May 25, 1957, Folder 16302, PTTĐICH, TTLTQG2.

Eisenhower administration. These internal tensions and external deliberations reflected differing interpretations of the community development idea, particularly its aims for and application to South Vietnam. This demonstrates that while the community development movement was global in scope, the principles that lay at its root were not above contestation. For Cung it was a matter of control over the direction of Diệm's postcolonial vision. For Sài Gòn and Washington it was a question of where this postcolonial vision fit within a Cold War world.

CIVIC ACTION AND THE PERSONALIST REVOLUTION

While the Trương Tấn Bửu and Thoại Ngọc Hầu pacification campaigns were underway the Special Commissariat for Civic Action continued to evolve both institutionally and in practice into a permanent vehicle for nation-building. This was a result of both changing circumstances in the countryside as the pacification campaigns brought more and more of the people into the government's fold and Kiểu Công Cung's efforts to bring the program in line with Ngô Đình Diệm's national vision. On September 5, 1956, President Diệm issued Decree No. 116 which conferred on the Special Commissariat for Civic Action the added responsibility of managing and training all cadres from the existing branches of government such as Information, Youth, Labor, Agrarian Reform and Popular Education.[7] These cadres would be transferred over to the Special Commissariat for training – which would be carried out by instructors seconded from the relevant branches of the government – and then kept available for the use of any ministry or technical service in the field. The decree was established to meet two concerns: the persistent problem of clashes between the ministries and technical services and their counterparts in Civic Action; and the inefficiency of uncoordinated actions by government officials overlapping in the countryside.[8] According to John Gates, Edward Lansdale's assistant, it was intended to "centralize government action in the villages under one head."[9] Other American observers were somewhat

---

[7] Sắc Lệnh [Decree], September 5, 1956, Folder 1359, PTTĐICH, TTLTQG2.

[8] Thông Tư gỏi Quý Ông Bộ Trưởng [Circular sent to the Ministers], September 7, 1956, Folder 1359, PTTĐICH, TTLTQG2.

[9] Memorandum from John Gates, TRIM to Edward G. Lansdale, August 7, 1956, Subject Files 1954–1958 (hereafter referred to as SF 54–58), Box 1, Record Group 469 (hereafter referred to as RG 469), National Archives and Records Administration, (hereafter referred to as NARA)

more circumspect. M.H.B. Adler contended that the decree may have been proposed "to button down the large number of 'cadres' employed by several of the ministries and assigned to village areas more for political reasons than reasons of technical assistance or the development of public services."[10]

This may well have been the case given the low opinion the Diệm regime had for the bureaucracy it had inherited from the French.[11] While recognizing that these functionaries were highly educated and trained individuals, the regime felt that they showed "little initiative, no internal flame, no self-sacrificing spirit." They were "contaminated by all the usual colonial defects: corruption, promotion and decoration seeking, fear of responsibility, absence of self-confidence" as they were "accustomed to relying upon the French supervisor." The cadres, in contrast, were seen in a much higher light than these regressive *fonctionnaires*. Though of a "lower educational background" and "less fluent in administrative matters," they were "well-indoctrinated," "progressive, courageous," showed a "great deal of initiative" and "younger" and therefore free of the taint of colonialism. Entrusting the Special Commissariat with the responsibility of training, administering and managing all field operatives of the various government branches would ensure that they were suitably forward-looking individuals filled with the requisite "can–bô" or cadre "spirit."[12]

In its new role, the CDV was responsible for drawing up plans for joint operations with the various ministries and services in the field; ensuring the necessary personnel from those branches were present for use in a mobile Civic Action group if their particular area of expertise were needed; coordinating the training of the cadres within their specific government organs; overseeing their work; and paying, promoting and disciplining them as necessary. The specialized cadres of each ministry or technical service would continue to work in their respective field, but could be called upon for assignment to a Civic Action mobile team at any moment, though officials in the Central Services would continue to consult closely with their home branch in the execution of the joint

---

[10] Memorandum from M.H.B. Adler, Chief, Field Service USOM to D.C. Lavergne, August 17, 1956, SF 54–58, Box 1, RG 469, NARA.

[11] Dennis J. Duncanson, *Government and Revolution in Vietnam* (New York: Oxford University Press, 1968), 228–229.

[12] Memorandum Nguyễn Quan to Walter Mode, March 11, 1957, Folder 76, Box 660, Michigan State University Vietnam Advisory Group (hereafter MSUVAG), Michigan State University Archives (hereafter MSUA).

operations. Approval of these operations would come from the president, ensuring the palace a modicum of control over the cadres' activities.[13]

As expected, this proposal met stiff resistance throughout the civil service. The various ministries and services involved opposed ceding administrative control of their staff to another government organ. The individual cadres slated to be seconded to the CDV resented the inconvenience of being transferred and having to accept a lower salary and more arduous working conditions. Many resigned in protest.[14] As for the Special Commissariat, it was forced to temporarily suspend recruiting new cadres while it recalled a number of existing cadres from the field to Sài Gòn for retraining.[15] Despite the outcry, the government's news agency reported that a number of black-dressed cadres pledged their allegiance to the President of the Republic in a transfer ceremony in Sài Gòn on November 17, 1956.[16] Here, Nguyễn Hữu Châu, Secretary of State for the Office of the President, challenged the cadres, contending that it was their job to make sure that every Vietnamese person "becomes a progressive citizen" who clearly understands their obligation to "carry out the mission of the Constitution of the Republic" recently promulgated on October 26.[17]

In real terms, the transfer of cadres to the Special Commissariat failed to have the impact the palace desired. The Vietnamese News Agency reported that over a thousand cadres were transferred to the Special Commissariat on November 17. Other reports, however, indicate that the number was half that suggesting that the government was attempting to gloss over the divisions that existed within the bureaucracy over the

[13] Sắc Lệnh [Decree], September 5, 1956; Thông Tư gởi Qúy Ông Bộ Trưởng [Circular sent to the Ministers], September 7, 1956, Folder 1359, PTTĐICH, TTLTQG2; and Report on the Organization of the Special Commissariat for Civic Action, June 1957, Folder 82, Box 660, MSUVAG, MSUA.

[14] Report on the Organization of the Special Commissariat for Civic Action, June 1957, Folder 82, Box 660, MSUVAG, MSUA.

[15] Sắc Lệnh [Decree], September 5, 1956; and Thông Tư gởi Qúy Ông Bộ Trưởng [Circular sent to the Ministers], September 7, 1956, Folder 1359; and Đặc Ủy Phủ Công Dân Vụ Kính gởi Bộ Trưởng tại Phủ Tổng Thống [Memorandum from the Special Commissariat for Civic Action to the Secretary of State in the Office of the President], October 15, 1956, Folder 16068, PTTĐICH, TTLTQG2.

[16] Lễ Chuyển Giao Cán Bộ của các Bộ sang Đặc Ủy Phủ Công Dân Vụ [Transfer Ceremony for Cadres of the Ministries sent to the Special Commissariat for Civic Action], November 17, 1956, Folder 16068, PTTĐICH, TTLTQG2.

[17] Điện Văn của Ông Bộ Trưởng Nguyễn Hữu Châu, Đại Diện Dai Tổng Thống [Address of Secretary Nguyen Huu Chau, Speech for the President], November 17, 1956, Folder 16068, PTTĐICH, TTLTQG2.

controversial maneuver.[18] Indeed, the Michigan State University Group, in its report on the Special Commissariat for Civic Action, stated that as of June 1957, when the report was issued, the decree remained in place, "but efforts to implement it have lapsed."[19] Symbolically, however, the decree should be considered significant as it coincided with other changes at work in the methodology of the Special Commissariat in 1956.

Throughout the year Kiều Công Cung had been making a concerted effort to push the Civic Action program in the direction of community development.[20] As we have seen the original mode of action for Civic Action was informed by the community development movement. Now that the Civic Action cadres had established a greater presence in the countryside, Cung apparently felt even more emphasis should be placed on self-help projects to give the peasantry more of a vested interest in the success of the nation they were building. This could be seen in the April 1956 reorganization which assigned only two cadres to a village in a district. While intended to help spread the Civic Action cadres more widely across the districts of South Vietnam, it had the concomitant effect of making the villages more self-reliant. No longer could local councils rely solely on the mobile Civic Action groups to come and do the work for them. Now they were required to show more initiative and "build a consciousness in the people to launch a popular movement to automatically improve their existence."[21] From this point forward the Special Commissariat gradually move in the direction of a community development-type program.[22]

---

[18] One official report from October 1956 suggested that only 521 cadres would be transferred; Đặc Ủy Phủ Công Dân Vụ Kính gởi Bộ Trưởng tại Phủ Tổng Thống [Memorandum from the Special Commissariat for Civic Action to the Secretary of State in the Office of the President], October 15, 1956, Folder 16068, PTTĐICH, TTLTQG2. A memorandum written by Nguyễn Quan for the Michigan State University Advisory Group in March 1957 puts the number at 518 cadres transferred "on paper." In reality, he continues the number is closer to one hundred as many of those cadres resigned rather than receive a cut in wages; Memorandum Nguyễn Quan to Walter Mode, March 11, 1957, Folder 76, Box 660, MSUVAG, MSUA.

[19] Report on the Organization of the Special Commissariat for Civic Action, June 1957, Folder 82, Box 660, MSUVAG, MSUA.

[20] Civic Action and Community Development, ND, Folder 75, Box 660, MSUVAG, MSUA, though there is no date on this document, the material in the document indicates it is from 1957. See also The Civic Action Program, ND, Folder 85, Box 660; The Background of Civic Action, ND, Folder 57, Box 660, MSUVAG, MSUA, like the preceding document, the material in these two documents indicates it is from 1957; Memorandum from John Gates, TRIM to Edward G. Lansdale, August 7, 1956, SF 54–58, Box 1, RG 469, NARA.

[21] Báo Cáo Tổng Kết Năm 1957 [Summary Report for 1957], January 10, 1958, Folder 16294, PTTĐICH, TTLTQG2.

[22] Civic Action and Community Development, ND; and Memorandum from Normand Poulin to Russell Frakes, March 20, 1958, Folder 75, Box 660, MSUVAG, MSUA.

One way of understanding the movement of Civic Action toward community development is to see it as part of a broader effort by Kiều Công Cung to keep the program in lockstep with the development of Ngô Đình Diệm's nation-building plan. Already the methodology employed by the Civic Action cadres through the twin concepts of Raising the People's Intellectual Standards and Welfare Improvement reflected the influence of the global community development movement on Kiều Công Cung's thinking. Their emphasis on creating a morally just and civic-minded population capable of working self-reliantly for their own betterment accorded very much with the principles at the heart of Ngô Đình Diệm's revolution. This notion of self-sacrifice for the greater good, in turn, reflects the ideological underpinning of the Diệm regime which was based on the philosophy of Personalism (*Nhân Vị*).[23]

Personalism is associated with the French Catholic thinker Emmanuel Mounier. Mounier, who was writing in the midst of the Great Depression, was disenchanted with the state apparatuses to emerge from the prevailing ideologies of liberal-capitalism and communism. In both cases, he believed, their rush for social order had effectively dehumanized the individual. Liberal-capitalism's emphasis on individual pursuit at the expense of others produced selfish "anarchy." Communism produced an oppressive regime that reduced the individual to a "material and vegetative existence" through both its collectivization and atheism.[24] Mounier's philosophy presented a middle ground between the two ideologies that placed more emphasis on protecting the interests of the person.

Personalists conceived of the person as an inherently social creature who was bound together with other human beings by a sense of community. The community formed the basic unit of societal order and its constituent members had certain obligations to one another to work together for the common good. The person was conceived of as distinct from the individual in that the person had both a spiritual and material component, where the former refers to the immortal soul and the latter the corporeal body. Personalist philosophy emphasized the development of the spiritual

[23] Đại Cương về Việt Nam [General Overview of Vietnam], ND, Folder 371, PTTĐICH, TTLTQG2, though there is no date on the document there is evidence that it was written some time around June 1959.

[24] Emmanuel Mounier, *Personalism*, translated by Philip Mairet (London: Routledge and Kegan Paul Ltd., 1952), 18–19, 32 and see page xxvi for the first quote and page 52 for the second quote. See also Edward Miller, *Misalliance: Ngo Dinh Diem, the United States, and the Fate of South Vietnam* (Cambridge, MA: Harvard University Press, 2013), 43–44; and Philip E. Catton, *Diem's Final Failure: Prelude to America's War in Vietnam* (Lawrence, KS: University Press of Kansas, 2002), 41.

over the material in order to achieve one's full potential. The impersonal nature of the liberal-capitalist or communist state impeded this type of spiritual development by placing greater emphasis on the material nature of the individual, either through the pursuit of selfish goals for personal profit or as an automaton in a collective. Only the spiritual nature of the Personalist community could provide a bulwark against these dehumanizing forces and "emancipate the person from every oppressive exploitation." Working for the common good provided both a social safety net as well as an avenue for spiritual fulfillment, while the communal bonds that tied the people together ensured everyone had a stake in preserving and furthering the interests of the community.[25]

This philosophy, which Diệm's brother Ngô Đình Nhu (see Figure 3) discovered while studying in France in the 1930s, resonated strongly with the Ngôs on a number of levels. Its spiritualism offered both a theistic element that they, as Catholics, could easily relate to, and a necessary moral compass to guide the people. Its humanism conformed to what they saw as Vietnamese society's latent Confucian tendencies regarding the importance of self-cultivation and working for the common good. And its emphasis on community, social responsibility and providing for the well-being of one another offered a model of self-reliance that gelled with their perception of the village as the lifeblood of the Vietnamese nation.[26] Most importantly, from a nation-building perspective it offered a means to balance political and social development in order to "create a society where" everyone could enjoy "the necessary conditions to fulfill its material, cultural and spiritual needs."[27] In this way, Diệm argued, Vietnam could "quickly achieving the industrial revolution without the evil consequences" of either capitalism or communism. Like many members of the developing world they rejected the dominant ideologies of the Western powers. In Diệm's mind "the free capitalist and forced communist solutions" had "achieved great industrial progress,

---

[25] Mounier, *Personalism*, 3–53; and John C. Donnell, "Politics in South Vietnam: Doctrines of Authority in Conflict," Ph.D. diss. (University of California, Berkley, CA, 1964), 86–87, 108 and 578–583. The quote is from Kiến Nghị của KhóaSinh Trung Tâm Huấn Luyện Nhân Vị (Khóa XI) [Petition of the Personalist Training Centre Ninth Class], June 12, 1958 Folder 20895, PTTĐICH, TTLTQG2.

[26] Bức Thư [Letter], November 2, 1959, Folder 20895 PTTĐICH, TTLTQG2; Donnell, "Politics in South Vietnam," 34–41, 86–87, 108; Catton, *Diem's Final Failure*, 41–43; and Miller, *Misalliance*, 43–46.

[27] Our Concept of Development: An Address by The Honorable Vu Van Thai, Director-General of the Budget and Foreign Aid, October 23, 1959, Item number 1780612031, TTVVA (accessed February 2, 2007). See also Đại Cương về Việt Nam [General Overview of Vietnam], June 1959, Folder 371, PTTĐICH, TTLTQG2.

FIGURE 3 Ngô Đình Nhu, adviser and brother of President Ngô Đình Diệm, 1963. Photo by Larry Burrows, The LIFE Picture Collection, Getty Images

but both, especially the communist solution ... inflicted great damage on man."[28] Liberal-capitalism was too unpredictable a model for an underdeveloped state like Vietnam and had the potential of making the country dependent on foreign or private capital. Communism was even less appealing as Diệm believed adherence to this ideology would make South Vietnam subservient to Moscow or Beijing.[29] Personalism was an ideal third way.

Personalist thought had been evident in Diệm's thinking since he assumed power. It could be seen in Civic Action's stated aim of bringing "direct spiritual and material assistance" to the people.[30] It was evident in

[28] Quoted in Donnell, "Politics in South Vietnam," 113.
[29] Catton, *Diem's Final Failure*, 38–39; Speech of the Head of Vietnam's Delegation to the Bandung Conference, April 29, 1955, Item number 2321503034, TTVVA (accessed March 25, 2009); and John C. Donnell, "Personalism in Vietnam," in *Problems of Freedom: South Vietnam Since Independence*, ed. Wesley R. Fishel (New York: Free Press of Glencoe, 1961), 39–40.
[30] Sắc Lệnh [Decree], November 18, 1955, Folder 797, PTTĐICH, TTLTQG2.

the emphasis on moral turpitude, which was part of Raising the People's Intellectual Standards. And it was reflected in the spirit of communal voluntarism that lay at the heart of Welfare Improvement. Nevertheless, it was not until the government adopted its Constitution at the end of 1956 that explicitly Personalist language began to permeate the official pronouncements of the regime.[31] As seen in the Double Seven Day address at the outset of the chapter, Diệm believed that with the new constitution the nationalist stage of the revolution was complete as the Republic of Vietnam theoretically had all the institutional trappings of a sovereign nation. What was still required was the social transformation of the state to ensure it possessed all the functional elements of an independent nation: national unity, a relative level of economic self-sufficiency, political legitimacy and the ability to determine its own destiny on the world stage. It was at this point that what had been termed a "national" revolution became the Personalist Revolution (*Cách Mạng Nhân Vị*).

Given the state of Vietnam's social and economic development, the Ngôs were aware that such an enterprise posed a tremendous challenge to their country's existing resources. This was further complicated by the internal pressures the process of decolonization in a Cold War world placed upon Diệm's room to maneuver. As a staunch nationalist leading a postcolonial state in an age when the Western empires were crumbling, Diệm was wary of becoming overly dependent on an outside power to fund Vietnam's development. Relying too heavily on the West for assistance ran the risk of sacrificing his country's newly won independence as he was certain that any aid he received would arrive with strings attached.[32] More significantly, he feared that it would lend credence to charges from Hà Nội that his government was simply a colonial puppet. The best way for the Ngôs to realize their national ambitions appeared to be to convince the population of South Vietnam to play an active role in this process.[33]

Promulgating the Personalist Revolution was one way to do this. It could serve as a counterweight to the challenge posed to the South Vietnamese government by the Marxist-Leninist revolution being promulgated by Hà Nội and communists agents below the seventeenth

---

[31] Miller, *Misalliance*, 148.

[32] Catton, *Diem's Final Failure*, 25–26, 31 and 94; Miller, *Misalliance*, 234–235.

[33] Catton, *Diem's Final Failure*, 31–33, and 44; Our Concept of Development: An Address by The Honorable Vu Van Thai, Director-General of the Budget and Foreign Aid, October 23, 1959, Item number 1780612031, TTVVA (accessed February 2, 2007); and Donnell, "Politics in South Vietnam," 578–583.

parallel – meeting the ideological needs of a Free World state in the Cold War. Just as importantly, it would satisfy Nhu's postcolonial demand for an authentic Vietnamese "cultural formula" to imbue the population with the appropriate sense of national spirit to willingly participate in the nation-building process. While Nhu never offered a precise definition of what he meant by the term cultural formula, it was clearly a response to what he saw as one of the greatest threats to South Vietnam's existence: the lack of an "authentic culture." Without this, he believed, Vietnam would be rendered as irrelevant in the international arena as it had been during its colonial period.[34] The Personalist emphasis on communal self-sacrifice for the greater good gave the revolution a positive element of national purpose that had been absent from the "three enemies" formula articulated earlier. It added popular participation in the construction and maintenance of the nation as an essential component of what the Ngôs conceived to be a distinctly Vietnamese national identity in the South. Not only would this further their developmental aims by encouraging the people to participate in their modernization project, but it would also afford the Ngôs the opportunity to address what they saw as one of the fundamental weaknesses that they believed had plagued Vietnam in the first place: the lack of a national consciousness.

The Ngôs were of a generation that believed that Vietnam had lost its independence because the leaders of the Nguyễn Dynasty had failed to foster a unified response to the French imperial conquest. While Vietnam's political independence had essentially been regained by the time Diệm ascended to a position of power, Vietnamese nationalists like the Ngôs – along with some members of a restive peasantry, as we have seen – still believed there remained an absence of the kinds of social structures that would connect the individual with the rest of society and establish what they conceived to be a *modern* Vietnamese national polity.[35] Affixing the Personalist philosophy to the revolutionary idea gave the Ngôs an ideology around which they could organize the people. Though Personalism's conservatism and spiritualism may be considered decidedly antimodern from a liberal Western perspective, from a postcolonial view it made a certain kind of sense.[36] In the West,

---

[34] Donnell, "Politics in South Vietnam," 104–105; and Catton, *Diem's Final Failure*, 36–41. John Donnell discusses Nhu's conception of a cultural formula, quoting Nhu's use of the term. However, he does not provide a Vietnamese translation of the term.

[35] Catton, *Diem's Final Failure*, 35–38.

[36] Postcolonialism is used in the sense of what Robert Young refers to as "postcoloniality," viewing the world from the perspective of the subaltern. Robert Young J.C.

modernity meant, *inter alia*, secularization, urbanization and democratization. Modern society was cosmopolitan and welcoming of change, "a manifestation of postwar liberalism" based on "a particular rendition of the dichotomy of 'the traditional' and 'the modern.' "[37] For the Ngôs it meant stability, national self-determination and the ability to act independently in the international arena.[38] They were painfully aware that they were attempting to compete with two other "modern" ideologies – communism and liberalism – in their efforts to develop their postcolonial state, and wished to avoid placing their country in a dependent or even subservient position to the nations which were their main proponents – the Soviet Union and China on the one hand and the United States on the other.

Kiều Công Cung was attuned to all of this. The mutually reinforcing concepts of Raising the People's Intellectual Standards (*Nâng Cao Dân Trí*) and Welfare Improvement (*Cải Thiện Dân Sinh*) effectively lay the groundwork for the Personalist Revolution as they worked together to create the spiritual and material conditions for nationalist development at the community level. Spiritually, they would create a citizenry of morally just peasants, willing to sacrifice their individual pursuits for the betterment of the community. Materially, they would establish the local infrastructure that would form the basis for an economically diverse and modern nation-state. Combined, the spiritual and material rewards would continuously encourage the people to develop their community, society and nation, as well as themselves as individuals in what would become a self-perpetuating cycle. This, Cung believed, would ultimately

Young, *Postcolonialism: An Historical Introduction* (Oxford: Blackwell Publishers, Inc., 2007), 57.

[37] Nils Gilman, *Mandarins of the Future: Modernization Theory in Cold War America* (Baltimore, MD: Johns Hopkins University Press, 2003), 4–5. See also Frank Ninkovich, *Modernity and Power: A History of the Domino Theory in the Twentieth Century* (Chicago: The University of Chicago Press, 1994), xi–xii; Michael E. Latham, *Modernization as Ideology: American Social Scientists and "Nation Building" in the Kennedy Era* (Chapel Hill, NC: The University of North Carolina Press, 2000), 30–46.

[38] See for example Kiến Nghị [Petition], June 12, 1958, Folder 20895, PTTĐICH, TTLTQG2. This is a petition from students of the Personalist Training Centre in Vĩnh Long – which was established in 1957 – requesting the government establish a satellite campus in Sài Gòn. In the petition they stated it was the purpose of the Sài Gòn government to "strengthen Personalism over every domain," to promote humanity, to make independence and democracy its "motto" and make social justice the norm. They also pledged to make each government organ a "Personalist strong hold with the aim of National Salvation and Nation Building."

overcome South Vietnam's underdevelopment and disunity with minimum reliance on outside assistance.[39]

THE COMMUNITY DEVELOPMENT PLAN:
PHÁT TRIỂN CỘNG ĐỒNG

While Kiều Công Cung was busy transforming the Special Commissariat for Civic Action into a community development-type initiative throughout 1956, other members of the Sài Gòn government were actively exploring the possibility of establishing a separate and far-reaching community development program for the fledgling state. As early as February 1955, the Ministry of the Interior had come up with the draft of "a broad plan for the economic, moral, and administrative development of communities" which it had distributed to the other ministries for comment.[40] Nothing came of this plan, but it represented one of many efforts by various officials in the South Vietnamese government to come up with a coherent community development plan throughout 1955 and 1956. According to D.C. Lavergne, these "uncoordinated first attempts" reflected more of a belief that US aid would be more forthcoming for a community development effort than an "understanding of the significance of such a program for [the] overall national economic and social development."[41] Given Kiều Công Cung's experience with USOM, this is hardly surprising. In the spring of 1956, however, Nguyễn Hữu Châu, the Secretary of State to the Presidency, began considering proposals for a broad-based, interministerial community development program.[42] According to Kiều Công Cung, Diệm was not initially interested in community development and left the matter entirely in Châu's hands.[43] Though, Diệm did reportedly ask his sister-in-law Trần Lệ Xuân – who would go onto greater notoriety as Madame Nhu – to coordinate the planning. She declined, stating that she had enough other responsibilities, including serving as the hostess for the president and sitting in the National Assembly. While genuinely busy,

[39] Hoạt Động Công Dân Vụ tại Các Tỉnh [Action of Civic Action in the Provinces], May 25, 1957, Folder 16302, PTTĐICH, TTLTQG2. See also Báo Cáo Tổng Kết Năm 1957 [Summary Report for 1957], January 10, 1958, Folder 16294, PTTĐICH, TTLTQG2.

[40] Memorandum Joseph Starr to Leland Barrows, February 15, 1955, SF 54–58, Box 1, RG 469, NARA.

[41] Airgram from USOM/Saigon to ICA/W, April 15, 1957, SF 54–58, Box 2, RG 469, NARA.

[42] Letter from D.C. Lavergne to Nguyen Huu Chau, April 24, 1956, SF 54–58, Box 1, RG 469, NARA.

[43] Memorandum from Normand Poulin to Russell Frakes, March 20, 1958, Folder 75, Box 660, MSUVAG, MSUA.

she may also have not wanted to share the responsibility for the program with Châu.[44]

USOM, according to D.C. Lavergne, was quite interested in the proposal, though it wanted to be certain that it met its criteria of what community development was. One concern he had were reports that Civic Action would coordinate this effort. While he acknowledged that both he and the US mission would like to see Civic Action move toward a community development-type approach to rural reconstruction, he still did not think it fit "the generally accepted definition of this process." To try to steer the Secretary's thinking more along the lines of what he felt was appropriate, Lavergne offered "three distinct approaches to the application" of community development to Vietnam. The first, was a voluntary village works program which would subsidize provincial government efforts to obtain the resources – "material and skills" – necessary to undertake village self-help projects. The second was a "traditional community development program" where "village level multi-purpose workers" would be trained in coordination with a UNESCO education program already underway in Vietnam. The third would employ individuals from the voluntary services working in Vietnam "to demonstrate village improvement through local initiative."[45] Each of these approaches emphasized the spirit of self-help at the local level, but the second one stressed training local leaders in the "principles and techniques" of community development to ensure its longevity once the external support was withdrawn. Notably absent was any mention of the Special Commissariat for Civic Action's involvement.[46]

At the same time D.C. Lavergne was offering his advice to Châu, the Michigan State University Advisory Group (MSUG) was also at work on its own community development program proposal for South Vietnam. The MSUG was a technical assistance program sponsored by the International Cooperation Administration to send experts from the faculty of Michigan State University to advise the South Vietnamese government on effective state formation. From 1955 to 1962, the MSUG engaged in numerous reform projects in areas from public administration

---

[44] Memorandum from D.C. Lavergne to Leland Barrows, May 22, 1956, SF 54–58, Box 2, RG 469, NARA.

[45] Letter from D.C. Lavergne to Nguyen Huu Chau, April 24, 1956, SF 54–58, Box 1, RG 469, NARA.

[46] Memorandum from Robert Slusser to Charles Mann, May 4, 1956, SF 54–58, Box 1, RG 469, NARA.

to refugee resettlement to policing.[47] In late 1955, Walter Mode, the Field Administration team leader for the MSUG, began studying community development techniques for their applicability to Vietnam. He drew a variety of resources that included material from USOM and the United Nations as well as US community development experts working in India.[48]

Over the following year, Mode worked on a study on the application of community development for Vietnam.[49] One of the sources that he appears to have used was a report drafted by L.J. Farrell entitled "Evaluation of a Community Development Program in Vietnam."[50] Farrell had been in charge of community development projects for the US Mission in Vietnam prior to Mode's study, but had departed, bringing USOM's community development effort to a halt.[51] Farrell concluded that community development would be useful for Vietnam, but the population would need to be "educated to accept the principle of self-help." This effort would need to start at the top, where government officials needed to "appreciate" the value of self-help in "economic and village facilities improvement." Citing various examples, Farrell demonstrated that volunteers willing to offer their services free of charge for communal aid projects were not forthcoming. To achieve this, he recommended the "gradual introduction" of the principle of self-help through an "educational approach." This would occur throughout the remainder of the 1956 fiscal year, preparing them to undertake a "National Development Program" which would begin in fiscal 1957. The national program

[47] John Ernst, *Forging a Fateful Alliance: Michigan State University and the Vietnam War* (East Lansing, MI: Michigan State University Press, 1998).

[48] These include USOM studies like "Principles of Community Development," "A Report on Community Development to USOM Vietnam," and the UN's "Fifteenth Report of the Administrative Committee on Coordination to the Economic and Social Council" USOM; see Correspondence from Walter Mode to Ernest Neal, December 20, 1955; Memorandum D.C. Lavergne to Walter Mode, December 27, 1955; and Correspondence from D.C. Lavergne to Walter Mode, December 28, 1955, Folder 75, Box 660, MSUVAG, MSUA.

[49] Memorandum from Walter Mode to Alfred Hausrath, December 19, 1956, Folder 75, Box 660, MSUVAG, MSUA.

[50] Evaluation of a Community Development Program in Vietnam, January 12, 1956, Folder 64, Box 660, MSUVAG, MSUA. Other reports written for the study include "Some Thoughts on Community Development Possibilities for Free Vietnam", ND; and "Community Development as Seen by a Vietnamese", ND, Folder 74, Box 660, MSUVAG, MSUA which both endorse a community development program to overcome Vietnam's underdevelopment.

[51] Memorandum from Normand Poulin to J.A. Hackett, November 21, 1956, SF 54–58, Box 1, RG 469, NARA.

would be overseen by an organization consisting of "service members" of the US mission and their counterparts in the Vietnamese government and would be housed in the appropriate – but unspecified – Vietnamese minister's office. It would undertake projects on an area basis, where each area would employ the local human and material resources under the guidance of the appropriate operational service or services to develop it according to its needs. Upon the completion of the development of one area, a new area would be developed according to its particular needs.[52]

By the end of 1956, Mode had reached his own conclusion that a community development program would benefit Vietnam. But before finalizing any recommendations, he wanted to wait for the completion of another study the Michigan State Group was working on: a report on the Special Commissariat for Civic Action. Mode was aware that USOM had been trying to steer Civic Action along the lines of community development and his own reading of the materials appears to have brought him to the conclusion that the Special Commissariat might be an appropriate body to coordinate the program.[53] This was supported by the ongoing work of the MSUG on Civic Action which noted that the work of the Special Commissariat, at the present time, was "activated by the concept of guided self-help." Due to the "similarity in operating techniques" between the two concepts – and the fact that the MSUG was aware that Civic Action under Kiểu Công Cung was embracing the philosophical spirit of community development – the MSUG felt that "serious study should be devoted" to the use of the Special Commissariat "as the basic element in the national administration of Community Development."[54]

In the meantime, Nguyễn Hữu Châu proceeded with his own efforts to coordinate a community development program. He delegated responsibility to the Director General of Planning within the Office of the

[52] Evaluation of a Community Development Program in Vietnam, January 12, 1956, Folder 64, Box 660, MSUVAG, MSUA.

[53] Memorandum from Walter Mode to Alfred Hausrath, December 19, 1956, Folder 75, Box 660, MSUVAG, MSUA. For Mode's awareness of USOM's position on Civic Action and community development see a note on a distribution list presumably accompanying the USOM studies Principles of Community Development and A Report on Community Development to USOM Vietnam which states "U.S.O.M. thinks Civic Action should be a community development project." Distribution List, December 6, 1955, Folder 75, Box 660, MSUVAG, MSUA.

[54] Discussion Paper, ND, Folder 75, Box 660, MSUVAG, MSUA. By the time the study on Civic Action was released in June 1957, the MSUG had changed its position somewhat to arguing that "in practice community development and civic action *could* operate separately without duplication of effort and division of responsibility." Report on the Organization of the Special Commissariat for Civic Action, June 1957, Folder 82, Box 660, MSUVAG, MSUA, emphasis in the original.

Presidency, Huỳnh Văn Diệm, to come up with a community development plan. They established, within the Directorate General of Planning, a Central Committee for Community Development with Châu as Chair, Kiều Công Cung as Vice Chairman and Huỳnh Văn Diệm as the Secretary-General to coordinate "the interests of the various government ministries and technical departments." The committee itself consisted of representatives from the Ministries of Agriculture, National Education, Public Health, Social Action, National Economy and Agrarian Reform and the Special Commissariat for Civic Action.[55]

Though he had been given an important position on the committee, Cung was apparently "not impressed" with the direction the South Vietnamese government was headed regarding community development. According to a 1958 USOM memorandum which discussed, among other things, the South Vietnamese community development program, Cung felt the Special Commissariat for Civic Action was already engaged in community development work. What the central committee was proposing amounted to the establishment of a new organization to undertake community development, a move Cung saw as "unnecessary and illogical." He favored "the normal evolution of civic action teams into community development teams." Huỳnh Văn Diệm, however, was "adamant" in his opposition to Cung's position and "insisted on a complete separation between the two organizations." Because of the disagreement, Cung removed himself from much of the planning, leaving Huỳnh Văn Diệm and the Planning Bureau, as the "dominant" influences over the process.[56]

The Directorate of Planning saw the utility of community development for a five-year plan for the social and economic development of South Vietnam that was being studied by the Sài Gòn government.[57] It aimed to exploit the human capital available to them to bring about a relatively self-sufficient and moderately industrialized society in the south that would overcome the damage caused to its economy by Vietnam's turbulent past. Roughly eighty years of colonial rule and fifteen years of violent decolonization had left South Vietnam in a horribly backward state industrially. As the French colony of Indochina had been viewed as a market for manufactured goods from the "mother" country, little significant effort had been made to develop Vietnam's

[55] Airgram from USOM/Saigon to ICA/W, April 15, 1957, SF 54–58, Box 2, RG 469, NARA; and Memorandum from Normand Poulin to Russell Frakes, March 20, 1958, Folder 75, Box 660, MSUVAG, MSUA.
[56] Memorandum from Normand Poulin to Russell Frakes, March 20, 1958, Folder 75, Box 660, MSUVAG, MSUA.
[57] Airgram from USOM/Saigon to ICA/W, April 15, 1957, SF 54–58, Box 2, RG 469, NARA.

industry.[58] Where the French had made such efforts they did so in the areas of the country where sources of fuel and raw materials were in greater abundance, which were predominantly located in the north. Whatever industry existed in the south was dependent on the north for such items as coal, concrete and fertilizer. When war came, first with Japan and then with the French, the shipping routes for goods flowing to the south were disrupted. Roads, railroads and inland waterways were severely damaged or destroyed during the fighting and needed to be rebuilt. Following the Geneva Accords these routes were cut-off entirely as nothing could cross the seventeenth parallel.[59]

The agricultural sector had also suffered under the French and held little immediate promise for future development. Prior to World War II rice and rubber had been the predominant exports. Many of the rubber plantations had been owned by French companies like Michelin and would have seen all their profits return to the metropole during the colonial period. Following Geneva, many of the managers, skilled personnel and capital that were essential for their operation were repatriated to France. Rice production was also subject to a similar monopolization.[60] In Cochin China, 2 percent of the landowning population possessed 45 percent of the land, while 72 percent of the population could only lay claim to 15 percent of the land.[61] The rise of the Việt Minh dramatically changed all of this as the peasant–landlord relationship was fundamentally altered by the Việt Minh's socialist land redistribution policies. In some areas, landlords, fearing for their lives, retreated to the safety of the cities, leaving their land in the hands of the tenants who farmed it. In other areas, where fighting put both owner and cultivator at risk, the land was abandoned altogether, leaving 400,000 acres of fertile land to be reclaimed by the jungles. The net result was a significant decline in rice exports and the revenue they would generate for the national economy.[62]

---

[58] Robert Scigliano, *South Vietnam: Nation Under Stress: An Important Look at the Trouble Spot of Asia* (Boston: Houghton Mifflin Company, 1964), 107.

[59] Milton C. Taylor, "South Viet-Nam: Lavish Aid, Limited Progress," *Pacific Affairs* 34(3) (August 1961): 243.

[60] David L. Anderson, *Trapped by Success: The Eisenhower Administration and Vietnam, 1953–1961* (New York: Columbia University Press, 1991), 140; and Taylor, "Lavish Aid, Limited Progress," 243.

[61] Anderson, *Trapped by Success*, 140.

[62] Scigliano, *Nation Under Stress*, 104; and Taylor, "Lavish Aid, Limited Progress," 243.

The five-year plan should be seen as a concrete manifestation of the Ngôs' Personalist Revolution in both its intent and execution. It attempted to stake a middle ground between socialism and liberal-capitalism and capitalize on Vietnam's agricultural sector – which was considered its major economic strength as it supported 80 percent of the population – in order to "develop the productive capacity of the country." It involved "adopting a process of growth of agricultural development complemented by a progressive industrialization" to "build the solid and economic infrastructure" on which they could base their "future industrial development." The Vietnamese believed their developmental plan's emphasis on agricultural production "with a complementary industrialization" would allow them to "accelerate" their "capital formation without passing through a phase of concentration of capital in the hands of a few." To achieve this they intended to promote the diversification of the agricultural sector by reducing its dependence on rice and rubber exports, while redistributing the ownership of large landholdings to the tenants who farmed them.[63]

This thinking was wholly consistent with Diệm's broader aims of establishing a citizenry of economically independent, middle-class farmers who owned their own land – what David Elliott refers to as the "middle peasantization" of the countryside.[64] It also meshed with the Personalist emphasis on self-reliance and self-sacrifice for the collective good. The five-year plan sought to rally the rural population to take an active role in agricultural development in the hope that this would lead to an increase in rural income and purchasing power across the board, not to mention make them beholden to the state which redistributed land on their behalf. This "stage of social capitalism" would then theoretically be translated into a greater demand for manufactured goods produced by indigenous light industries, which would be satisfied by an increased source of labor that had been freed up by technological improvements in agricultural

---

[63] Our Concept of Development: An Address by The Honorable Vu Van Thai, Director-General of the Budget and Foreign Aid, October 23, 1959, Item number 1780612031, TTVVA (accessed February 2, 2007). The 80 percent figure is from Scigliano, *Nation Under Stress*, 107. See also Ngô Đình Diệm, Authorized Translation of the President of the Republic's Message on Double Seven Day, July 10, 1957, Item number 2321507007, TTVVA (accessed February 2, 2007); Ellen J. Hammer, "Progress Report on Southern Viet Nam," *Pacific Affairs* 30(3) (September 1957): 234; Roy Jumper, "Problems of Public Administration in South Viet Nam," *Far Eastern Survey* 26(12) (December 1957): 189; and Douglas C. Dacy, *Foreign Aid, War, and Economic Development* (New York: Cambridge University Press, 1986), 3–4.
[64] David Elliott, *The Vietnamese War: Revolution and Social Change in the Mekong Delta, 1930–1975*, Vol. 1(Armonk, NY: M.E. Sharpe, 2003), 166 and 180.

production.[65] In time, this would lead to an economy that would not be dependent on foreign aid for its continued viability. This was consistent with ideas circulating among other newly emerging and noncommunist states of the postcolonial world. As Odd Arne Westad contends, many what he calls "nativist" (as distinct from Marxist) anticolonial leaders "saw rebuilding the economic, social and military strength of their countries as the key objective" in determining their people's future direction once their independence had been won.[66] In Vietnam, the Ngôs anticipated their nation-building project below the seventeenth parallel being so successful that it would inspire their compatriots in the north to defect in numbers so great that it would eventually bring about the collapse of the northern regime.[67] Community development, with its emphasis on communal self-help, would be a means to harness the human capital of South Vietnam at the village level for this broad undertaking.[68]

In the fall of 1956, the Directorate of Planning began to put a plan together that would make community development an integral part of South Vietnam's five-year development plan.[69] It drafted an eighty-seven-page manual that laid out the concepts and principles behind community development and various methods and approaches to implementation.[70]

[65] Our Concept of Development: An Address by The Honorable Vu Van Thai, Director-General of the Budget and Foreign Aid, October 23, 1959, Item number 1780612031, TTVVA (accessed February 2, 2007).

[66] Odd Arne Westad, *The Global Cold War: Third World Interventions and the Making of Our Times* (Cambridge: Cambridge University Press, 2007), 81. Vijay Prashad makes a similar argument indicating that the "radical democracy" offered by the newly emerging nations of the "Third World" promised that "every person would be constituted by the state as a citizen" and that "every citizen in turn would act through the state to construct a national society, economy and culture." Vijay Prashad, *The Darker Nations: A People's History of the Third World* (New York: The New Press, 2007), 122.

[67] Ngô Đình Diệm, Authorized Translation of the President of the Republic's Message on Double Seven Day, July 10, 1957, Item number 2321507007, TTVVA (accessed February 2, 2007); Đại Cương về Việt Nam [General Idea of Vietnam], June 1959, Folder 317, PTTĐICH, TTLTQG2; From the Central Intelligence Agency Station in Saigon to the Agency, November 20, 1962, General 11/11/62 – 11/25/62, Countries: Vietnam, Box 197, National Security Files, John F. Kennedy Library; and Catton, *Diem's Final Failure*, 46–47.

[68] Circular No.106-TTP, October 10, 1956, Folder 75, Box 660, MSUVAG, MSUA.

[69] Airgram from USOM/Saigon to ICA/W, April 15, 1957, SF 54–58, Box 2, RG 469, NARA; and Memorandum from Normand Poulin to Russell Frakes, March 20, 1958, Folder 75, Box 660, MSUVAG, MSUA.

[70] Nha Tổng Giám Đốc Kê Hoạch [Directorate of Planning], *Phát Triển Công Đong* [Community Development] (Saigon: RVN Office of the Presidency, ND). Though the manual itself bears no date of publication other documents indicate it was published some time in 1956; see Circular No.8-TTP, January 15, 1957, Folder 75, Box 660, MSUVAG, MSUA.

This was accompanied by a circular to the province chiefs laying out their obligations toward the burgeoning community development plan. The circular is as revealing for its emphasis on the importance of community development to the government's thinking as it is for its use of Personalist language. It opened by referring to the proposed community development program as "one of the basic plans for the renaissance of the country." For it to succeed, it continued, it would need "a stable and wide foundation." This could only come by "infusing in the people a constructive spirit, a desire for progress and good knowledge of the citizen's position in the general reconstruction work" so the people could be mobilized to "work together toward self-improvement." It then requested the province chiefs select appropriate areas which could be used as experimental sites for community development pilot projects and cadre training. The criteria for each province was that they could have no more than three experimental sites and they needed to comprise at least one fishing village, agricultural village or handicraft village, and at least one large, prosperous village or a "small and needy village."[71]

The government followed this up in January 1957 with two more circulars further clarifying the government's expectations. The first requested the provinces come up with a plan of action for implementing community development on a three-month experimental basis that took into account local realities and proposed a means to encourage the people to carry it out.[72] The second specified the five fields in which the chiefs should focus their efforts: health, public works, education, agriculture and veterinary medicine.[73] This was all part of establishing the proper mental framework in the peasantry for the program, as part of the aim of these experimental initiatives was to demonstrate to the people of South Vietnam that community development could work and improve their lives.

While the province chiefs were surveying areas for experimental community development work in the provinces, Nguyễn Hữu Châu got Huỳnh Văn Diệm to enlist the aid of R. Uit Den Bogard, a Dutchman, who was the United Nations Community Development expert in Sài Gòn, and Marcel De Clerc from UNESCO to help the Directorate of Planning. The UN experts began working with the Directorate of Planning in January and established an advisory group consisting of

[71] Circular No.106-TTP, October 10, 1956, Folder 75, Box 660, MSUVAG, MSUA.
[72] Circular No.8-TTP, January 15, 1956, Folder 75, Box 660, MSUVAG, MSUA.
[73] Circular, January 29, 1957 Folder 75, Box 660, MSUVAG, MSUA. There was no number on this copy of the circular.

representatives from USOM, MSUG, UNESCO and the United Nations Technical Assistance Administration.[74] A crucial element of their work would be to ensure the provincial staffs which were responsible for conducting the community development plan were properly trained and organized. So much of community development's success depended on instilling the right mindset in the people. They had to have faith that the communal work would lead to an overall improvement in their living conditions – something which could not happen overnight. Moving too quickly or setting unrealistic goals could easily lead to discouragement and eventual disillusionment among the population, leaving the government vulnerable to charges that it was failing to meet the needs of the revolution of rising expectations that was believed to be occurring across the Vietnamese countryside. This was a real danger as the planners found that the preliminary work of surveying sites at the province level for community development projects was leading to confusion as some overzealous province officials attempted to "move ahead and achieve quick results," demonstrating that they were "not sufficiently cognizant of the principles and concepts of community development and its methods and techniques of implementation."[75]

Part of the problem was that the Vietnamese and their Western counterparts had very different perspectives on what these "principles and concepts" were. Within the Office of the President there were people like Nguyễn Hữu Châu who wanted the Special Commissariat for Civic Action to oversee the implementation of the community development program in South Vietnam; even though Kiều Công Cung opposed the direction the Directorate of Planning was taking. The desire to use the Special Commissariat, which already had a considerable reach across South Vietnam, suggests that the South Vietnamese government was looking for community development to have a more immediate and far-reaching impact. Given that community development's emphasis on community, voluntarism and self-sacrifice resonated so strongly with the central tenets of the Ngôs' Personalist Revolution it is hardly surprising the government would want to see it implemented as far and wide as it could in as short a period as possible. This was essential for the Ngôs' nation-building agenda.

[74] Airgram from USOM/Saigon to ICA/W, April 15, 1957, SF 54–58, Box 2, RG 469, NARA; and Memorandum from Normand Poulin to Russell Frakes, March 20, 1958, Folder 75, Box 660, MSUVAG, MSUA.
[75] Airgram from USOM/Saigon to ICA/W, April 15, 1957, SF 54–58, Box 2, RG 469, NARA. See also Memorandum to Nguyen Huu Chau from Marcel De Clerc and R. Uit Den Bogard, March 30, 1957, SF 54–58, Box 2, RG 469, NARA.

As we have seen, Ngô Đình Diệm's Personalist Revolution was intended to mobilize the South Vietnamese populace to participate in what he considered to be the physical and spiritual construction of a self-sufficient nation. Self-sufficiency was the key as this is what would make South Vietnam a viable national entity in the international realm. Community development offered a concrete framework for achieving this aim. But the impetus for self-sufficiency also added an element of urgency to the community development ideal in Sài Gòn that was absent from other programs throughout the developing world.[76] For Diệm, instilling the community development spirit in the people meant making them see it as their duty to contribute their manpower and material to the construction of the Vietnamese nation he envisioned. His government was not above employing near-coercive measures to enlist popular participation in development projects that he believed it was their obligation to fulfill. This flew in the face of Western conceptions of community development which saw it as a long-term process that ultimately made the community responsible for determining its own needs and the appropriate means to meet them based as much as possible on the resources available locally.

Over the winter of 1957, Den Bogard and De Clerc attempted to steer the Directorate of Planning "toward a more orthodox type [of community development] program than was envisioned" by some in the Vietnamese government.[77] A principle concern was the relationship between community development and the Special Commissariat for Civic Action. They felt that there was a fundamental difference in the "work and methods" of community development and the Civic Action cadres, with the latter being "of short duration" and aiming "at immediate results." Using the Civic Action cadres to try to carry out both their own Civic Action work and community development would inevitably lead to confusion and possibly "create *a rupture in the process of Community Development.*" Instead, they recommended that some Civic Action cadres be temporarily seconded to community development where they could be kept on a permanent basis once they had received the appropriate training and education.[78]

By the spring, they had come up with a plan which reflected both the desires of the South Vietnamese government and the requirements of

[76] Miller, *Misalliance*, 164–165.
[77] Airgram from USOM/Saigon to ICA/W, April 15, 1957, SF 54–58, Box 2, RG 469, NARA.
[78] Memorandum to Nguyen Huu Chau from Marcel De Clerc and R. Uit Den Bogard, March 30, 1957, SF 54–58, Box 2, RG 469, NARA, emphasis in the original.

the community development experts.[79] It was presented to the members of USOM in early April to get their feedback. According to documents related to the presentation community development was pitched as the "component" of the government's "national economic and social development plans" that would provide "for the active participation of the people" and "the mobilization of latent community resources." It was intended to "promote" "harmonious" coordination between the various technical services and ministries of the government as well as their "cooperation" with "the people towards progressive achievement of the economic and social development objectives," which meant according with the palace's Personalist philosophy. The plan had to "fully recognize the democratic rights of the people" as well as "respect" their "human dignity and foster the feeling of self respect." Among its aims were educating "the people in civic consciousness," instilling in them "the desire and sense of capability to take an active part in the economic and social development process" and guiding them "in identifying their common needs and problems" and taking the necessary actions to "meeting these needs and solving these problems through community action on a self help basis."[80] From the South Vietnamese government's perspective, the Special Commissariat had to be the operational organ responsible for administering the program.[81]

Operationally, the community development program would be directed by the central committee chaired by Huỳnh Văn Diệm and housed in the Office of the Secretary of State to the Presidency, Nguyễn Hữu Châu (see Figure 4). This body would coordinate the activities of the government ministries and technical services as well as the work of private associations, such as the 4-T clubs – the Vietnamese equivalent of the 4-H club – and farmers' and women's associations. These technical services and private associations

---

[79] According to Ngô Đình Diệm's Double Seven Day address of 1957 the community development movement was launched on March 1, 1957, though little appears to have been done beyond the continued surveying of the provinces for appropriate experimental sites as the community development plan was still in the works. President Ngo Dinh Diem's Speech on Third Anniversary of Accession to Office, July 7, 1957, Item Number 2321507007, TTVVA (accessed January 29, 2007).

[80] Discussion Paper, ND, SF 54–58, Box 2, RG 469, NARA. Though there is no date on the actual discussion paper it was delivered to the US Mission on April 4, 1957 in advance of the April 5 meeting; Memorandum from D.C. Lavergne, April 4, 1957, SF 54–58, Box 2, RG 469, NARA.

[81] Though the UN advisers and individuals in USOM like D.C. Lavergne and Leland Barrows tried to discourage the South Vietnamese government from giving the Special Commissariat for Civic Action the responsibility for administering the program their advice was not heeded.

would work closely with the village or, in the cities, local urban (quarter) committees for community development. In the countryside the community development teams would be under the direct supervision of the province chief, while in cities they would be divided into quarters with the work of each community development team overseen by an executive board in the quarter. Training would occur in either a National Community Development Training Center, which would be established in Tân An or more local provincial and regional "Training Institutes." The Special Commissariat for Civic Action would be responsible for executing the "program instructions" issued by either the province chief or the quarter committee, "administering and training" the cadres and managing all training centers except the national one at Tân An and the training center for the staff of the central committee. The pilot projects, currently being investigated in each province, were slated to begin in July. They were intended to be experimental in order to determine the strengths and weaknesses of the plan as well as expose the people to the potential benefits of the program in a controlled environment. Implementation of the actual community development plan was not anticipated to start until 1958 once the results of the experimental stage had been assessed.[82]

USOM's response was supportive. Vietnamese officials would return to their various ministries and technical departments to determine how best to organize their activities with the community development workers on the ground. The appropriate USOM officials would "be invited to participate in these meetings" to offer their input on how US funding could best be applied if the mission was approved.[83] From D.C. Lavergne's perspective having some American officials involved in the program would be a welcome turn of events. Following a May 22 meeting with Nguyễn Bích Liên, the Secretary-General of the central committee, about more involved ICA participation than simply offering advice, Lavergne cabled Washington to recommend their approval as it offered them an opportunity to steer the program in a direction more consistent with American designs for South Vietnam. Echoing his earlier concerns about wastage that emerged when negotiating over funding Civic Action with Kiều Công Cung he argued that this would allow the US government "to get across to the [South Vietnamese] government an understanding that Community Development programs are intended to do more than

[82] Organization Chart for the Community Development Program and Notes, ND, Folder 75, Box 660, MSUVAG, MSUA; Discussion Paper, ND; and Airgram from USOM/Saigon to ICA/W, April 15, 1957, SF 54–58, Box 2, RG 469, NARA.
[83] Airgram from USOM/Saigon to ICA/W, April 15, 1957, SF 54–58, Box 2, RG 469, NARA.

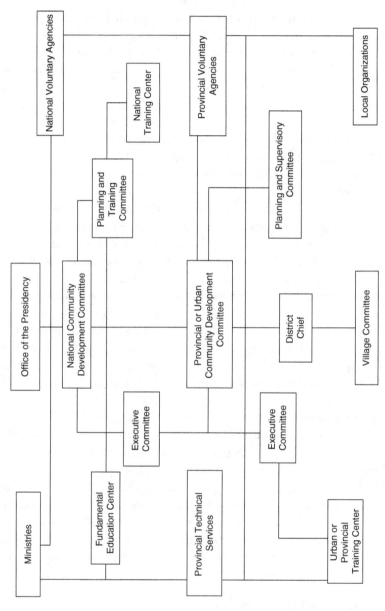

FIGURE 4 Organizational structure of the National Community Development Plan

simply re-channel previously agreed upon technical assistance aid." More importantly, he continued, with the proper guidance community development "in Vietnam might very well capitalize upon the existing villagers' historic appreciation of self-help in matters that are of village interest," making the program run more efficiently.[84] How and when the American mission would get involved with the community development program would have to wait for the eventual implementation of the program which, as we shall see, was dependent on the South Vietnamese personalities involved. But before getting to that, we must consider the view from Washington.

COMPETING CONCEPTIONS OF DEVELOPMENT: PHÁT TRIỂN CỘNG ĐỒNG AND THE EISENHOWER ADMINISTRATION

As the Sài Gòn government's most important ally and principal source of economic and material aid, the Eisenhower administration had a vested interest in ensuring that South Vietnam was not absorbed by North Vietnam. Following Diệm's successful defeat of the sects, such a policy meant supporting him as the best nationalist around whom the Eisenhower administration hoped to see a noncommunist state built.[85] Individuals like Eisenhower's Secretary of State, John Foster Dulles, believed Diệm's anticommunist credentials were impeccable and, when combined with his Catholicism, made him appear to be a known commodity.[86] But meaningful American support for Diệm would prove to require more than just a shared religion and opposition to communism on behalf of the two governments. It would require comprehension of Diệm's larger aims for nation-building, something which was in short supply.

According to some scholars, this myopia reflected a tendency among American policymakers in the Eisenhower administration to view the peoples of the Far East through an Orientalist prism. Authors like Mark Bradley and Seth Jacobs have argued that Americans tended to classify and define the Vietnamese as a benighted, childlike and exotic people.

---

[84] Memorandum from D.C. Lavergne to Leland Barrows, May 22, 1957, SF 54–58, Box 2, NARA.

[85] Anderson, *Trapped by Success*, 91–119.

[86] Seth Jacobs, *America's Miracle Man in Vietnam: Ngo Dinh Diem, Religion, Race, and U.S. Intervention in Southeast Asia: 1950–1957* (Durham, NC: Duke University Press, 2004), 25–59 and 172–216.

Eisenhower and Dulles, both born in the late nineteenth century, were not immune to erroneously seeing the Vietnamese as both unprepared for the rigors of self-government in a Cold War world and willing to supplicate themselves to American advice and tutelage. Since these Americans saw themselves as benevolent actors attempting to uplift a benighted people by invitation, they were completely oblivious to the neoimperial realities of their actions.[87] As policymakers of all levels in Washington and Sài Gòn began to deliberate how best to support Diệm's efforts to increase his government's influence throughout the countryside these exceptionalist notions about America's relations with Vietnam certainly influenced the tone and direction of these discussions to some degree. But Orientalism was not the only factor at work. Examining the top-level debates over the direction of US aid to the South Vietnamese government as it pertained to Civic Action and community development in particular and the overall nation-building effort in general reveals that a far more nuanced understanding of the situation was also at work in the corridors of power in Washington. The Eisenhower administration's view of the state of affairs in South Vietnam in 1957 was filtered through a number of different lenses in addition to its construction of "the other." These included the administration's understanding of the postcolonial moment and the potential dangers it posed to the developed world; the developmental tradition in the United States; and the potential consequences of the expense of foreign aid to the conduct of US foreign policy.

The discussions on the degree of US support for community development in South Vietnam can be considered on two levels. The first focused specifically on the relationship between the community development program and the Special Commissariat for Civic Action. Sometime in late 1956 or early 1957, the Eisenhower administration established an "Ad Hoc Working Group on Community Development and Civic Action" comprised of representatives from the ICA, United States Information

[87] Mark Philip Bradley, *Imagining Vietnam and America: The Making of Postcolonial Vietnam, 1919–1950* (Chapel Hill, NC: The University of North Carolina Press, 2000), 45–106, 162, 170 and 186–187; and Jacobs, *America's Miracle Man in Vietnam*, 14–18. See also Christina Klein, *Cold War Orientalism: Asia in the Middlebrow Imagination, 1945–1961* (Berkeley, CA: University of California Press, 2003) which details how postwar American popular culture reinforced this image of "the Orient" for the American mainstream. Other works which explore the impact of "American Orientalism" on American foreign policy, though toward the Middle East, are Douglas Little, *American Orientalism: The United States and the Middle East since 1945* (Chapel Hill, NC: The University of North Carolina Press, 2002) and Melani McAlister, *Epic Encounters: Culture Media, and U.S. Interests in the Middle East, 1945–2000* (Berkeley, CA: University of California Press, 2001).

Agency, CIA and State Department, in order "to clarify the relationship between civic action and community development" based on the evolving situation in Southeast Asia. Like their counterparts in the US mission in Sài Gòn, the members of the ad hoc committee concluded that Civic Action was "primarily related to security and propaganda to achieve political objectives in a brief period of time" while "Community Development" was "a long-range program primarily concerned with improving the living conditions of villagers" and "providing them with a method of helping themselves." As a result, "they reached a general consensus that there is not and should not be any planned relationship between the two types of programs." The committee recommended that Civic Action be phased-out once it had served its short-term purpose and ICA should be the only US agency involved in community development.[88]

The second level of the debate was far more involved and reveals all of the complexities regarding in the Eisenhower administration's approach to offering assistance to the Third World. Many of Eisenhower's advisers believed that the underdeveloped nations were of significant importance to the future of the Free World as well as the maintenance of international peace. They provided many of the raw materials that were necessary for industrial and defense production. The political instability of these states threatened to devolve into minor local wars that could easily turn into larger conflicts fueled by the symbolic and material competition of the Soviet Union, China and the United States. But there was more to this concern than the dictates of the Cold War.

As Matthew Connelly has demonstrated, the Eisenhower administration's response to the shifting political fortunes of the Third World was also informed by an appreciation of the potential for North–South conflict that the unpredictable forces unleashed by decolonization could spark as postcolonial leaders sought to satisfy the revolution of rising expectations sweeping the global south.[89] Looking at the language of individuals like President Eisenhower and his Secretary of State John Foster Dulles reveals that they – just as much as their predecessors in the

---

[88] Memorandum of a Meeting of the Ad Hoc Working Group on Community Development and Civic Action, April 2, 1957, OCB 091 Indo-China (File #6) 4 (February-April 1957), Box 40, OCB Central Files Series, NSC Staff Papers, DDEL.

[89] Matthew Connelly, "Taking Off the Cold War Lens: Visions of North-South Conflict during the Algerian War for Independence," *The American Historical Review* 105(3) (June 2000): 739–769. See also Matthew Connelly, *A Diplomatic Revolution: Algeria's Fight for Independence and the Origins of the Post-Cold War Era* (Oxford: Oxford University Press, 2002), especially 34–35, 37, 85, 119–120 and 164–165.

Truman administration – were acutely aware of the postcolonial implications of decolonization.

Most of the newly emerging states were considered to be quite poor and, members of an International Development Advisory Board to the President believed, under great internal pressure to achieve economic progress having been exposed to Western political and economic ideas that "taught them that man can, within very wide limits, remake his life to achieve greater material benefit for himself and greater power for his nation." National leadership groups would be "virtually compelled to speed millions of their countrymen into the twentieth century." As these nations possessed very limited capital to invest in such modernization projects there was the fear that they might approach either Moscow or Beijing, the alleged champions of anticolonial resistance, for direct aid or worse. They might adopt more extreme measures, which could lead to the replacement of more moderate governments by totalitarian regimes "of communist or indigenous origin," that would be more inclined "to resort to external adventurism" and further destabilize the international system.[90] Such fears had already prompted the Eisenhower administration to intervene covertly in Iran and Guatemala, where left-leaning nationalist revolutionaries had emerged to assert indigenous control over their countries' national resources which had heretofore been exploited by foreign corporations.[91]

---

[90] A New Emphasis on Economic Development Abroad, March 1957, OF8-Q-2 ICA, IDAB (3), Box 145, Official Files Series (hereafter OFS), CF, DDEL. See also Memorandum from Kevin McGann to Clarence Randall, August 14, 1956, Fairless Committee (7) (hereafter FC), Box 5, Series IV: Randall Series, Subject Subseries (hereafter IV:RS), U.S. Council on Foreign Economic Policy (hereafter FEP), Office of the Chairman, Records (hereafter OCFEPR), DDEL; Latham, *Modernization as Ideology*, 27; Irene L. Gendzier, *Managing Political Change: Social Scientists and the Third World* (Boulder, CO: Westview Press, 1985), 27–28; Gilman, *Mandarins of the Future*, 175; and Westad, *The Global Cold War*, 80.

[91] In both cases the Central Intelligence Agency coordinated coups to remove the "offending" leaders. In Iran Mohammad Mossadegh had risen to power and challenged the monopoly held over Iranian oil by the British controlled Anglo-Iranian Oil Company. When Mossadegh moved to seize the British company's resources and earn more than the 20 percent in earnings the British had been providing them, the CIA acted. In 1953 they organized massive street demonstrations that threw Tehran into chaos and provided the opportunity to have Mossadegh arrested and subsequently removed from power. Barry Rubin, *Paved with Good Intentions: The American Experience and Iran* (New York: Oxford University Press, 1980), 54–90. In June 1954 the CIA led an army of Guatemalan exiles to oust the nationalist President Jacobo Arbenz Guzman who had attempted to nationalize the United Fruit Company (UFCO). UFCO owned 42 percent of Guatemala's arable land, but used less than 10 percent. Arbenz targeted the company in an effort to redistribute the land it owned to the nation's poor. Richard H. Immerman,

It seemed apparent to the US government that these developing nations needed to achieve "a satisfactory pace of economic growth" to quell any destabilizing revolutionary fervor. Only through sustained and accelerated economic development could they achieve the internal stability required to redirect the people's energies toward internal progress rather than external aggression. With accelerated growth, they believed, would come more jobs and more economic and social opportunities for the leadership groups in these countries. This economic stimulus, in turn, would serve as "a major source for national pride" and "a major incentive for stability and peace."[92] It would make these nations far less susceptible to the communist threat as it was extremely difficult for "Communist psychological and subversive programs to make substantial headway in nations which are economically strong, or among people who enjoy material and spiritual advantages that are to be found through full freedom of opportunity."[93] American policymakers felt that these nations would "find much of value to their own situation in the methods developed out of the American experience," particularly as the United States had dedicated itself to "finding techniques of economic and social advance which do not compel the sacrifice of freedom of choice or freedom of opportunity."[94]

With regard to Vietnam, the Americans believed the Vietnamese were doubly cursed as they also had to contend with the damage done during their recent colonial experience. As far as the Americans were concerned the French, during their imperial occupation, had done nothing to help. Despite the notion of a *mission civilisatrice*, members of the Eisenhower administration argued that the French presence had failed to modernize the traditional social pattern of the village, which had retained an "almost unchanged pattern of living from generation to generation." Now that the country had been "catapulted since independence into the

The CIA in Guatemala: The Foreign Policy of Intervention (Austin, TX: University of Texas Press, 1982), 68–186.

[92] A New Emphasis on Economic Development Abroad, March 1957, OF8-Q-2 ICA, IDAB (3), Box 145, OFS, CF, DDEL; See also Latham, *Modernization as Ideology*, 27; Gendzier, *Managing Political Change*, 27–28; and Gilman, *Mandarins of the Future*, 175.

[93] Fairless Committee Report, March 1, 1957, Fairless Committee Photo Album, 1956–1957 (hereafter FCPA 56–57), Box 76, Collins Papers (hereafter CP), DDEL.

[94] Draft Letter for the President's signature, ND, FC (7), Box 5, IV:RS, FEP, OCFEPR, DDEL. It is unclear who this letter is to, though it is in response to a suggestion by someone of having a full and frank discussion of possible measures by which the United States can promote economic progress in Southeast Asia. This draft copy was sent to Clarence Randall and appears to have been written by Elliot Richardson. See also A New Emphasis on Economic Development Abroad, March 1957, Box 145, OFS, CF, DDEL.

complex task of managing a nation state, the Vietnamese are suffering the consequences of the prewar educational system which denied them training in managerial, technical, and vocational skills." All was not lost however, as they credited the Vietnamese with a great "capacity to learn" and "an energy seldom encountered in tropical climes" – concluding this neo-Lamarckian comparison to other post colonial Southeast Asian nations by arguing that "whatever their other handicaps, indolence or lethargy cannot be said to retard Viet-Nam's forward motion."[95]

Development would not be easy since the French had not helped the Vietnamese foster the attitudes necessary for progress like "a group of values ... associated with the Christian ethic, or rooted in the concepts of 'natural law' that assert the dignity of the individual, the existence of responsibilities as well as the rights on the part of the citizen and the state, and the vast concept of public welfare." The French had also failed to provide their colonial charges with "a heritage of institutional arrangements" to "advance these values and concepts" such as "the organization of impartial public administration at national and local levels, a scheme of productive economic organization operating in the public welfare either through private or public ownership, and a body of highly trained public and private officers who administer the community's affairs" – all elements that were seen in the United States as *normal* features of a modern society.[96]

Such a worldview reflected a number of cultural and intellectual assumptions that underpinned US development policy toward the developing world.[97] Since the opening decades of the twentieth-century

[95] Evaluation of Viet-Nam Program, August 15 1957, MSA 59, Box 40, CFS, CF, DDEL.
[96] *Ibid.* Frank Ninkovich contends that "modernity" in the United States "was characterized by a legal-rational outlook dominated by science, the professionalization and bureaucratization of institutions, and, not least, the emergence of a global division of labor as a result of the workings of the market economy," while Nils Gilman argues that it "suggested a God-fearing but secular society in which race and gender were of little import; a privately run full-employment economy of well-paid workers, all of whom owned a house and a car and lived in a nuclear family; and a formal democratic system in which consensus existed about societal goals." Ninkovich, *Modernity and Power*, xi–xii. See also Gilman, *Mandarins of the Future*, 15.
[97] There is a vast international scholarship on the history of development. See, for example, Nick Cullather, "Development? It's History," *Diplomatic History* 24(4) (2000): 641–653 and Marc Frey and Sönke Kunkel, "Writing the History of Development: A Review of the Recent Literature," *Contemporary European History* 20(2) (2011): 215–232. Some of the works focusing on American-style development which the following discussion draws upon are: Latham, *Modernization as Ideology*; Michael Latham, "Modernization, International History, and the Cold War World," in *Staging Growth: Modernization Development, and the Global Cold War*, ed. David C. Engerman, Nils Gilman, Mark H. Haefele and Michael E. Latham (Amherst, MA: University of Massachusetts Press,

American private citizens from missionaries to philanthropists had been involved in reconstruction efforts intended to raise the standard of living in the impoverished areas of the world, often out of a humanitarian impulse. Many of these early developmental projects drew on lessons from the post-Civil War efforts to reconstruct the war-torn south and advance its economy beyond its dependence on the old slave system as well as some of the reform experiments of the Progressive Era to promote the social and economic advancement of the indigenous populations. One of the most involved initiatives was the work of the Rockefeller Foundation in China where American experts engaged in a variety of rural reconstruction efforts to overcome the nation's perennial impoverishment. These were often massive modernization projects, like damming rivers for better water management, to try to improve the overall well-being of the rural population. Not only did they involve transforming the landscape, but they were also intended to alter the psychology of the rural population. By demonstrating the ability of modern technology to tame nature, American engineers hoped to instill in the Chinese a new, more rational and "scientific" way of thinking about the world that would allow them to effectively embrace modernity.[98]

The Great Depression offered a host of new sites for American experimentation with relief and reconstruction efforts domestically as seen in the New Deal. Franklin Roosevelt's scheme to try to mitigate the fate of the global economic collapse was particularly significant as it demonstrated that that some of society's problems were too vast to be solved by private initiative alone and government intervention would be necessary as seen with the various programs he implemented. Of the alphabet soup of New Deal measures introduced development scholars have identified the TVA (Tennessee Valley Authority) as paramount – the epitome of

2003), 1–23; Gilman, *Mandarins of the Future*; Francis X. Sutton, "Nation-Building in the Heyday of the Classic Development Ideology: Ford Foundation Experience in the 1950s and 1960s," in *Nation-Building: Beyond Afghanistan and Iraq*, ed. Francis Fukuyama (Baltimore: The Johns Hopkins University Press, 2006), 42–63; Michael Adas, *Dominance by Design: Technological Imperatives and America's Civilizing Mission* (Cambridge, MA: The Belknap Press of Harvard University Press, 2006); and David Ekbladh, *The Great American Mission: Modernization and the Construction of an American World Order* (Princeton, NJ: Princeton University Press, 2010).

[98] For a detailed study see David Ekbladh, "To Reconstruct the Medieval: Rural Reconstruction in Interwar China and the Rise of an American-Style Modernization, 1921–1961," *Journal of American-East Asian Relations* 9(3–4) (Fall-Winter 2000): 169–196.

high modernist development schemes.[99] The Tennessee Valley Authority attempted to tackle the twin problems of the Great Depression and the rural underdevelopment of the United States by employing tens of thousands of out-of-work Americans in a massive engineering project to bring about the modernization of the Tennessee Valley. This was a massive top-down endeavor that relied on the centralized planning and technical expertise of social scientists and engineers to build a slate of dams and hydroelectric plants that would bring electricity to rural homes for the first time, potentially transforming the lives and livelihoods of millions of Americans.

Following World War II, this development impulse received a new and heightened impetus by the perceived crisis of decolonization and its intersection with the Cold War as policymakers in Washington and elsewhere began to see the newly emerging states as threats to world peace or geopolitical pawns to be kept from siding with their ideological adversaries in Moscow or Beijing. Both the Marshall Plan and Harry Truman's Point Four Program demonstrated the shift to government involvement by both providing economic assistance for reconstruction and the establishment of bureaucratic institutions to oversee it. Underpinning the development ethos driving these international efforts was the assumption that the supposed success of the American developmental experience and the politico-economic ideals it championed – from the market economy to political pluralism – could offer a model the underdeveloped states should aspire to.[100]

While these ideas would become codified by social scientists into a "modernization theory" in the 1960s that posited the linear progression of societies from traditional to modern states of economic and political development through a distinct series of stages, in the 1950s they provided a lens that reduced the complex problems of a little-understood part of the world to something that the Americans could easily relate to and potentially solve.[101] This thinking clearly framed the Eisenhower

---

[99] This argument is made in James Scott, *Seeing Like a State: How Certain Schemes to Improve the Human Condition Have Failed* (New Haven, CT: Yale University Press, 1998), 6, but it has been reiterated and elaborated on by scholars like David Ekbladh, "Meeting the Challenge from Totalitarianism: The TVA as a Global Mode for Liberal Development, 1933–1945," *The International History Review* 32(1) (March 2010): 47–67 and Daniel Immerwahr, *Thinking Small: The United States and the Lure of Community Development* (Cambridge, MA: Harvard University Press, 2015), 40–44.

[100] See for example Latham, *Modernization as Ideology*, especially chapters 1 and 2.

[101] *Ibid.*, 30–46; and Gilman, *Mandarins of the Future*, 1–202.

administration's approach to Vietnam. On the one hand, it informed the ultimate goal of policy which was to deny the South to the communists and create a "showcase" state that would demonstrate that "the 'Miracle of Viet-Nam' [could] be converted into the prime example in Asia that loyal cooperation with the West pays, and pays handsomely." On the other, it made US policymakers think that South Vietnam's ability to defend itself against both internal and external aggression had to be built up to provide the necessary stability to allow the country to be able to develop economically.[102]

This would prove more problematic as many of the paternalistic assumptions about economic development found in the Eisenhower administration's developmental rhetoric were tempered by the fiscal conservatism that was at the heart of its New Look foreign policy. For the Democrats in the Truman administration the aid and technical assistance programs of Point Four offered the potential to extend the New Deal to the world, but the Republicans of the Eisenhower administration had a far more circumspect view of foreign aid.[103] While seeing the necessity of foreign aid for thwarting the spread of radicalism in the developing world, Eisenhower and his advisers believed that it should serve "as a catalyst for private initiative" in the recipient state to help promote its economic development.[104] This is best exemplified by the recommendations made by the Fairless Committee, or President's Citizen Advisors on the Mutual Security Program, which had been established in September 1956 to evaluate military, economic and other foreign assistance programs. On March 1, 1957 it released its report which contended that "in the long run" promoting economic development was "as important to the collective security of the Free World" as military measures.[105] The American economic assistance already provided to the developing world was helping these nations better use their resources and improve their standards of living, thereby reducing the risk that they might turn to communism or an even more radical alternative.

---

[102] Evaluation of Viet-Nam Program, August 15 1957, MSA 59, Box 40, CFS, CF, DDEL. See also Anderson, *Trapped by Success*, 3.

[103] David Eckbladh, "From Consensus to Crisis: The Postwar Career if Nation-Building in U.S. Foreign Relations," in *Nation-Building*, 22–24.

[104] See Michael R. Adamson, "'The Most Important Single Aspect of Our Foreign Policy'?: The Eisenhower Administration, Foreign Aid, and the Third World," in *The Eisenhower Administration, the Third World, and the Globalization of the Cold War*, ed. Kathryn C. Statler and Andrew L. Johns (Lanham, MD: Rowman & Littlefield Publishers, Inc., 2006), 48–55.

[105] Fairless Committee Report, March 1, 1957, FCPA 56–57, Box 76, CP, DDEL.

But there was still a significant danger. Such expenditures were a drain on the American economy and could pose a risk to the long-term economic health of the United States. Since "America's economic strength is the foundation of its total strength in the world" and "anything that undermines its economic security must necessarily weaken its national defense," the US government needed to "determine at what point the costs of collective security outweigh the results being achieved." The Fairless Committee recommended the government continue to make funds available for economic assistance, but concentrate this assistance "more upon long range economic development" to "help bring the recipient countries into the orbit of free society ... expand the economic activity of the Free world, and ... increase the capacity of our allies to carry their defense costs."[106]

With this in mind, members of the Eisenhower administration undertook an overall re-evaluation of its Vietnam program and came to the conclusion that the initial sense of urgency that had been hallmarked by the Hinh, sect and refugee crises of 1955 as well as the specter of a communist victory in the now cancelled elections had passed. Much of this success, they felt, was due in no small part to their own efforts, patronizingly contending that during this period American assistance had "performed the essential art of mid-wifery" to help Vietnam assert and establish "her identity as an independent member of the community of free nations." Since the overall objectives of American policy had been to support the Diệm regime and prevent a communist takeover, their efforts had been "exceedingly successful." Now that "the crisis of birth" was passed, the report continued, the United States had to "face, in its own interest, the difficult and unsought task of how best to use its resources to nurture and encourage the healthy development of its new-found ward." The objectives of policy changed from a "crash program" of denying the area to communism and starting Vietnam on a path to economic viability to maintaining "a strong defensive posture" and concurrently developing "a steadily expanding economy." Consistent with the assumptions of the New Look, this report contended that these

---

[106] *Ibid.* The same arguments are made in NSC 162/2 which outlined a national security policy to "meet the Soviet threat to U.S. security" without "seriously weakening the U.S. economy or undermining [its] fundamental values and institutions." Report to the National Security Council by the Executive Secretary, October 30, 1953, *Foreign Relations of the United States, 1952–1954*, Vol. 2, *National Security Affairs*, Part 1 (hereafter *FRUS*) (Washington, DC: United States Government Printing Office, 1984), 578, 582, 583–584, 588–589, 591, 592 and 593–594.

two objectives were intimately related since "the achievement of a rate of economic growth which holds promise in a reasonable period of time for the economic independence of Viet-Nam" would also allow the Sài Gòn government to assume "her own defense costs." Not only would this help relieve the United States of "the financial burden of Vietnam," but it would also reduce Vietnam's unhealthy dependency on American largesse, which the report warned could have a "debilitating effect ... on the vitality and determination of the Vietnamese people" that would lead to "frictions and frustrations" and "increasingly jeopardize U.S.-Vietnamese relations." The US government would need to "reassess its basic criteria for determining the nature and use of US aid and resources," and place a new emphasis on the extent to which it would "expand or facilitate efficient production" and augment government revenues while discouraging any aid programs that "encourage excessive demands on limited GVN [Government of Vietnam] budgetary resources."[107]

As the new community development aspect of Civic Action appeared to "have a fairly high domestic political content," the report recommended that USOM continue to avoid "direct association" with it "in terms of overall guidance or funding." In the event the Vietnamese did request any technical assistance, or "reasonable quantities of equipment" for this endeavor, the Mission "should be prepared to entertain and evaluate" these requests in terms of their overall contribution to Vietnam's economic development.[108] Clearly, as far as the Eisenhower administration was concerned, what passed for community development in Vietnam was only worthy of American support if it rigidly adhered to their prescription for the ills of the underdeveloped world. But the proposed remedy was not appropriate for the patient, as far as the Diệm regime was concerned.

What Eisenhower's advisers were championing was a high modernist approach to development that was intended to achieve the large-scale economic expansion necessary for the self-sustaining growth that they believed would make the South Vietnamese a sovereign people capable of achieving a relative level of self-sufficiency. But this approach was based on the model of the United States where a rich supply of natural resources and the supposed equality of opportunity and entrepreneurial spirit had fostered industrialization and created a relatively wealthy consumer-driven

[107] Evaluation of Viet-Nam Program, August 15 1957, MSA 59, Box 40, CFS, CF, DDEL.
[108] *Ibid.*

society that could absorb the results of this production. In a country like Vietnam in the 1950s many of the characteristics that such a model rested on were absent. The South Vietnamese economy lacked a sufficiently industrialized base to exploit its own limited natural resources, let alone satisfy the Eisenhower administration's demand for increased productivity.[109] More generally, South Vietnam was a developing country in a world of developed states. Its rate of development would be well behind that of the great powers. Countries like the United States could afford the luxury of protective tariffs and enjoy a massively expanding domestic market – particularly given the postwar affluence of the 1950s. But a state like the Republic of Vietnam could not withstand the effect of retaliatory tariffs, nor did it possess a middle class large enough to fuel any dramatic economic expansion. This imbalance meant that underdeveloped countries like the Republic of Vietnam would be perpetually reliant on the more developed nations for their economic growth and stability which was something the Ngôs were clearly not willing to allow.[110]

This highlights the fundamental difference in the Vietnamese and American conceptions of the means and ends of the developmental process. The US model focused on industrialization to achieve economic self-sufficiency and create a state that would fall neatly in line with an American-led world order. But the Diệm regime was dubious. Rather than self-sufficiency, it saw dependency. The community development plan would avoid this. It was a conceived as a vehicle to elevate South Vietnam's economy to a level of self-sufficiency that would allow it to stake out an independent place in the global arena. By embracing community development Diệm was situating his nation-building agenda within a transnational discourse of development where local state actors could lay claim to a global developmental vocabulary for their own

[109] Douglas Dacy contends that at the time Vietnam was partitioned in 1954 industrial production in the South was limited to beer, soft drinks and cigarettes, Dacy, *Foreign Aid, War, and Economic Development*, 77.
[110] Raúl Prebisch, *Change and Development – Latin America's Great Task: Report Submitted to the Inter-American Development Bank* (New York: Praeger Publishers, 1971), 154–156. See also Louis A. Pérez, Jr., "Dependency," in *Explaining the History of American Foreign Relations* 2nd ed., ed. Michael J. Hogan and Thomas G. Paterson (Cambridge: Cambridge University Press, 2004), 165–175. Though Dependency Theory evolved as a means to understand America's relationship with Latin America it is clearly relevant to Vietnam as well. For the Ngôs' concerns regarding dependency see Memorandum of a Conversation, April 4, 1957, *FRUS, 1955–57*, Vol. 1, *Vietnam* (Washington, DC: United States Government Printing Office, 1985), 770; Catton, *Diem's Final Failure*, 31, 34, 155 and 158.

ends – which were sometimes at odds with their great power backers.[111] While South Vietnam's developmental accomplishments were always framed in terms of its contribution to the Free World struggle against international communism, there was also a subtle, but conscious, effort to place these achievements in the context of a postcolonial renaissance of Asian civilization. Speaking in Thailand Diệm argued "the stake of the peaceful struggle in which Thailand and Vietnam are engaged is not only the liberty of the Thai and Vietnamese people: it is the existence of the Free World in Asia and even this Asian civilization from which we draw our own strengths."[112] In Seoul, South Korea, Diệm stated that "the stake of our common struggle is all the more important as we have not only to defend our independence and our liberties, but also to preserve the very foundations of Asian culture, to contribute to its renaissance by giving it a new orientation toward the active respect for the human person and thereby, within the limits of our responsibilities, to prevent the Asian revolution from being deprived of its efforts, its sacrifices and legitimate hopes."[113] The West offered solutions, as he acknowledged in India, the site of the world's first national community development plan, but because it was "highly industrialized and ahead of us in many fields, their problems are not our problems." Therefore, for "an Asian country whose legitimate ambition is to carry out its own national and social revolution yet remain faithful to Asian ideals," it "must deploy immense efforts of intelligence, generosity and imagination in order to find the most effective solutions to their current problems."[114]

Community development, the national plan for the social and economic development of Vietnam and the Personalist Revolution were all efforts to emulate "India's genius" in "endeavoring to adapt modern techniques in order to find smooth solutions to her great problems" that would fit local realities and preserve a discretely Asian way of life.[115] Unfortunately, Diệm did not elaborate on what this meant beyond indicating that this

---

[111] Cullather, "Development? It's History," 648–650; and David C. Engerman and Corina R. Unger, "Introduction: Towards a Global History of Modernization," *Diplomatic History* 33(3) (June 2009): 375–379.

[112] Office of the Presidency, *Towards a Better Mutual Understanding*, Vol. 1, *Speeches Delivered by President Ngo Dinh Diem during his State Visits to Thailand, Australia, Korea*, 2nd ed. (Saigon:Presidency of the Republic of Vietnam, Press Office, 1958), 6.

[113] *Ibid.*, 49.

[114] Office of the Presidency, *Towards a Better Mutual Understanding*, Vol. 2, *Speeches Delivered by President Ngo Dinh Diem during his States Visits to India and the Philippines* (Presidency of the Republic of Vietnam Press Office: Saigon, June 1958), 12.

[115] *Ibid.*, 7.

way of life would be distinct from the West and opposed to communism. Nevertheless, these claims of Asian solidarity demonstrate that Ngô Đình Diệm had an idea about South Vietnam's place in the postcolonial world. While it would be allied to the West, it would not be dominated by it. This principle would guide South Vietnam's approach to receiving foreign aid and advice for its economic development, even from its most important benefactor, the government of the United States. As the Diệm government moved forward with its community development plan it did so on its own terms.

FOUR

"Bettering the People's Conditions of Existence"

Civic Action and Community Development, 1957–1959

Despite American resistance to the idea, the South Vietnamese government went ahead with its plan of using the Special Commissariat for Civic Action as the "operating agency" for its community development plan. As far as the Diệm government was concerned, the CDV was the optimal choice for this task due to "its flexible organization and its past record of self-help in the villages." Indeed, the CDV offered a ready group of cadres who had an established presence at the local level.[1]

In principle, Kiều Công Cung agreed with the decision to adopt a community development plan. The community development idea of pursuing self-help initiatives that relied on local human and material resources to improve village institutions and infrastructure had been the basis of his approach to the Welfare Improvement component of Civic Action. However, Cung also felt that if the South Vietnamese government was going to employ community development, it should be a completely Civic Action-driven endeavor, not a scheme contrived by an inter-ministerial coordinating committee that only employed the Special Commissariat as a coordinating body. In Cung's mind, the Special Commissariat for Civic Action was gradually moving toward becoming a full-fledged community development agency.

Between 1957 and 1959, Kiều Công Cung fundamentally transformed the basic mission of the Special Commissariat for Civic Action in order to place South Vietnam's community development effort completely under the auspices of that organ. During that period, he began moving the

[1] Civic Action and Community Development, ND, Box 660, Folder 75, Michigan State University Vietnam Advisory Group (hereafter MSUVAG), Michigan State University Archives (hereafter MSUA).

Special Commissariat away from the village reconstruction focus which had been at the center of the Welfare Improvement concept toward a greater emphasis on local economic development which became the hallmark of Civic Action's new practice of "Bettering the People's Conditions of Existence." In this way, Cung could keep his hand on the tiller of South Vietnam's rural development effort and be sure he was steering it in a direction he believed most suitable for realizing the aims of Ngô Đình Diệm's Personalist Revolution at the local level.

KIỀU CÔNG CUNG, THE SPECIAL COMMISSARIAT FOR CIVIC ACTION AND THE COMMUNITY DEVELOPMENT PLAN

With the end of the Trương Tấn Bửu and Thoại Ngọc Hầu pacification campaigns in February 1957 the government announced plans for a major reorganization to occur the following month in anticipation of the Special Commissariat's new mandate.[2] Nguyễn Văn Châu requested Ngô Đình Diệm upgrade the Special Commissariat for Civic Action to a General Commission, or Commissariat for Civic Action. This was intended to give Kiều Công Cung and his office the necessary prestige to harmonize the activities of the various government ministries such as Agriculture, Land Development and Social Action with Civic Action for the community development program.[3] As part of the reorganization, all Civic Action cadres were to be recalled from the field and thirty-four community development province teams consisting of fifty cadres each were to be established and assigned to the provinces on a permanent basis. Unlike the current Civic Action teams whose Welfare Improvement work focused on reconstructing local institutions and infrastructure, the community development teams were supposed to determine how each community could contribute to the economic development of the state. These cadres would be trained to teach the villagers to identify what resources were available for agricultural or local industrial production and then mobilize them to develop these sectors of the local economy.

---

[2] Report on the Organization of the Special Commissariat for Civic Action, June 1957, Folder 82, Box 660, MSUVAG, MSUA.

[3] Phúc Trình về Công Dân Vụ [Report on Civic Action], February 28, 1957, Folder 1301, Phủ Tổng Thống Đệ Nhất Cộng Hòa [Office of the President of the First Republic] (hereafter PTTĐICH), Trung Tâm Lưu Trữ Quốc Gia II [National Archives 2] (hereafter TTLTQG2).

Kiều Công Cung was to be responsible for organizing the training assisted by instructors from the relevant ministries.[4]

The assignment of community development to the Special Commissariat for Civic Action was not met with enthusiasm by Kiều Công Cung. His initial response was half-hearted at best. The mass recall of cadres from the field did not occur and only eighty Civic Action cadres were transferred over to community development forming the basis for what would be the thirty-four province groups. In fact, the Special Commissariat did not initially assume its responsibility over the community development plan, leaving it temporarily under the authority of the Directorate of Planning, which began to prepare for the experimental phase of the community development plan. Staff were transferred from the government services and trained for "direction and executive" positions within the Central Committee for Community Development, the socioeconomic surveys that had been collected from the provinces were evaluated to determine appropriate sites for pilot projects, and a new training program was developed for community development cadres with the input of Uit Den Bogard from the United Nations.[5]

In the meantime, Kiều Công Cung appears to have bristled at the idea of subordinating the Special Commissariat for Civic Action to a centralized community development committee as was the desire of Huỳnh Văn Diệm, the Secretary General of the Central Committee for Community Development. As far as Kiều Công Cung was concerned, the Special Commissariat had been evolving along the lines of a community development program since 1956. He saw no need for the creation of a new and separate community development plan. The Civic Action cadres were gradually shifting away from rebuilding local infrastructure to economic development. His resistance was exemplified by his approach to training the Civic Action cadres who had been assigned to community development. The training began in March and lasted for two months, but it differed very little from what the cadres had "received on orientation for

---

[4] Report on the Organization of the Special Commissariat for Civic Action, June 1957, Folder 82; and Memorandum from Normand Poulin to Russell Frakes, March 20, 1958, Folder 75, Box 660, MSUVAG, MSUA.
[5] Airgram from USOM/Saigon to ICA/W, April 15, 1957; and Memorandum from D.C. Lavergne to Leland Barrows, May 22, 1957, Subject Files 1954–1958 (hereafter referred to as SF 54–58), Box 2, Record Group 469 (hereafter referred to as RG 469), National Archives and Records Administration, (hereafter referred to as NARA).

their work in civic action" which, as we shall see, led to some confusion down the road.[6]

Despite his opposition to Huỳnh Văn Diệm's community development plan, Cung did reluctantly accept that the Special Commissariat would have to play a subordinate role in it, most likely out of allegiance to Ngô Đình Diệm's broader nation-building agenda. As we have seen, Kiều Công Cung was fiercely loyal to Ngô Đình Diệm. Over the winter of 1957 Diệm demonstrated his enthusiasm for the community development program, celebrating its March 1957 launch in his Double Seven Day speech that summer.[7] The evidence suggests that Cung, attuned to the palace's desire to make the community development plan the backbone of its larger nation-building agenda, decided that he could exert more influence over it – and steer it in a direction he deemed more appropriate, possibly gaining total control – by toeing the party line rather than by standing on the outside looking in.

In May, as the community development cadres trained by Cung started to be deployed to the field, he sent a memorandum out to the province chiefs to explain the Special Commissariat's new role with regard to the program.[8] He opened by acknowledging the contribution of the province chiefs to all of the accomplishments made by the Special Commissariat in winning the people over to the government thus far. However, he conceded, this was not enough for Civic Action to achieve its goal of "assembling the people into a strong force" that could support the government in building a "national foundation and founding the state." The Special Commissariat was required to do more than simply mobilize the people to engage in Welfare Improvement. To date, their efforts of building bridges, roads and schools and "mobilizing production" were done on a regional basis and only dealt with the immediate "political requirements" of winning support for the Diệm government. What was now needed was a unified effort "guided closely from above" to realize the nation that Diệm envisioned. Therefore, he continued, in addition to the mission of

[6] Memorandum from Normand Poulin to Russell Frakes, March 20, 1958, Folder 75, Box 660, MSUVAG, MSUA.
[7] President Ngo Dinh Diem's Speech on Third Anniversary of Accession to Office, July 7, 1957, Item Number 2321507007, Texas Tech Virtual Vietnam Archive, www.virtualarchive.vietnam.ttu.edu (hereafter referred to as TTVVA) (accessed January 29, 2007); and Daniel Immerwahr, *Thinking Small: The United States and the Lure of Community Development* (Cambridge, MA: Harvard University Press, 2015), 126–127.
[8] Đặc Ủy Trưởng Công Dân Vụ Kính gởi Quý Ông Tỉnh Trưởng [Memorandum from the Special Commissariat for Civic Action to the Province Chiefs], May 25, 1957, Folder 16293, PTTĐICH, TTLTQG2.

winning the people over to the government, the Special Commissariat had also been entrusted with community development.

With the new responsibility, Cung indicated, there would now be two types of Civic Action cadres. Those cadres who would continue the regular work of winning the people over to the government would be placed into groups that would be assigned to each district in a province. They would help the regional authorities in each district build a foundation of civic responsibility amongst the people through popular education and propaganda so they would "carry out each program and policy of the government." As for community development cadres, each province would be assigned a separate community development group which would be under the authority of the provincial community development leadership committee and operate in a manner determined by the Central Services of the National Community Development Committee. These groups would move from district to district, rallying the people to carry out community development work – self-sustaining projects like animal husbandry or handicraft production intended to boost the local economy based on available resources rather than just the development of infrastructure. Both types of cadres would need to be willing to work together if the chief of the Civic Action provincial group deemed it necessary. This meant that they would follow a unified chain of command from the province chief down while demonstrating the flexibility to be able to concentrate and disperse their forces as needed, much like the mobile armed forces units assigned to the provinces.

Despite Cung's efforts to try to delineate the responsibilities of each type of cadre, considerable confusion occurred when the first groups of community development cadres trained by the Commissioner General were sent back out into the field as "initiating officers" to conduct the pilot projects that had been conceived by the central committee.[9] The problem appears to have originated with Kiều Công Cung and the distinction he was drawing between the regular Welfare Improvement work of the Civic Action cadres and the new work of community development. As we have seen, Kiều Công Cung was concerned first and foremost with winning the people's allegiance to the national cause of Ngô Đình Diệm's government. From an early stage, he had seen the self-help ideal behind the transnational community development movement as a means to achieve this end. Such thinking informed his conception of Civic Action

---

[9] Memorandum from D.C. Lavergne to Leland Barrows, May 22, 1957, SF 54–58, Box 2, RG 469, NARA.

under the guise of Welfare Improvement. But it also made it difficult for Cung to clearly articulate the difference between the work of Welfare Improvement and community development. While he was no doubt aware of the economic emphasis of community development work, his desire to see Civic Action gradually evolve in this direction meant that the focus remained on projects designed to improve local infrastructure such as building roads, embanking ditches, digging wells and erecting information halls to better prepare the peasantry for the leap to community development.

Compounding the problem was the fact that the community development training the cadres were receiving was inconsistent. The training of the first group of community development cadres differed very little from what they had received when they started out as Civic Action cadres. Subsequent groups were taught according to methodologies developed under the auspices of the Central Committee for Community Development and the UN community development advisers which focused on the development of the local economy. In the few provinces in central Vietnam which had not previously been assigned Civic Action groups this was not a problem and the community development pilot program proceeded relatively "smoothly." As for the other provinces, the local population could not make the distinction between Civic Action and community development, much as many in USOM had warned. In some provinces province chiefs simply treated the community development cadres as Civic Action cadres. They assigned them to participate in Welfare Improvement projects the province chiefs deemed imperative rather than anything related to agricultural or local industrial development.[10] In these cases, the community development program reportedly "lacked leadership and had no fundamental plan of action." The Civic Action teams quickly "lost their identity" and were unable to achieve many results.[11] This was hardly the auspicious start the government wanted for its community development program.

However, while community development faltered under the Special – now regular – Commissariat for Civic Action, the standard work of Raising the People's Intellectual Standards and Welfare Improvement proceeded apace. Following the Trương Tấn Bửu and Thoại Ngọc Hầu

---

[10] See for example Báo Cáo Thành Tích Hoạt Động Tháng 4 năm 1957 [Report of the Operational Achievements of April 1957], May 11, 1957, Folder 16295, PTTĐICH, TTLTQG2.

[11] Memorandum from Normand Poulin to Russell Frakes, March 20, 1958, Folder 75, Box 660, MSUVAG, MSUA.

pacification campaigns the cadres not assigned to community development teams were redistributed to twenty-two province groups in the south, three joint province groups acting in Quảng Nam province in the center, and five province groups in the highlands.[12] These cadres operated according to the procedures that had been laid out in the April 1956 reorganization which established province groups that operated on a district-by-district basis where teams of two cadres each were assigned to each village in the district. However, subtle changes were at work reflecting Kiều Công Cung's desire to transform Civic Action into its own bone fide community development program capable of realizing the nation-building aims behind the Personalist Revolution. In terms of Raising the People's Intellectual Standards the cadres continued to engage in communist denunciation to weed out undesirable elements or convert them to supporting the regime.[13] They also began holding political indoctrination sessions to explain the tenets of the Personalist Revolution following stints at the National Personalist Training Center at Vĩnh Long which had been inaugurated in October 1956.[14]

As for Welfare Improvement (*Cải Thiện Dân Sinh*), it became "Bettering the People's Conditions of Existence" (*Cải Tiến Dân Sinh*). In distinguishing between the two concepts for the province chiefs, Cung combined the language of community development experts with Personalist thought to argue that Bettering the People's Conditions of Existence was a long-term campaign that would be carried out "step by step" under "unified leadership" and "close coordination" to meet the goal of "elevating the lives of the people spiritually and materially, contributing to the cause of nation-building in every aspect." He explicitly equated it with community development, arguing that "outside the mission of winning the people over, the Government has entrusted Civic Action with the task of Bettering the People's Conditions of Existence (i.e. community development) (*gần đây,*

[12] Báo Cáo Thành Tích Hoạt Động Tháng 4 năm 1957 [Report of the Operational Achievements of April 1957], May 11, 1957, Folder 16295, PTTĐICH, TTLTQG2.

[13] Phương Thức Hoạt Động Mới của Tỉnh Đoàn Công Dân Vụ Hoạt Động tại Nam Phần Việt Nam [New Method of Action of the Civic Action Province Groups operating in the Southern Region of Vietnam], July 15, 1957, Folder 16293, PTTĐICH, TTLTQG2.

[14] See for example Sự Tiến Bộ Trong Việc Đào Tạo Cán Bộ Công Dân Vụ Qua Khóa XIV [Progress in Training the Fourteenth Class of Civic Action Cadres], July 4, 1958, Folder 16563, PTTĐICH, TTLTQG2. For details about the Personalist Training Center see Jessica Chapman, *Cauldron of Resistance: Ngo Dinh Diem, the United States, and 1950s Southern Vietnam* (Ithaca, NY: Cornell University Press, 2013), 121.

ngoài nhiệm vụ tranh thủ nhân dân, Chính Phủ còn giao cho Công Dân Vụ làm công tác Cải tiến Dân sinh (tức Phát triển Cộng đồng))." [15]

In addition to the new conceptualization of Welfare Improvement work, other changes emerged throughout 1957 that exemplified Kiểu Công Cung's efforts to foreground the community development ideal within the operational work of the Commissariat for Civic Action. In particular, Cung wanted the cadres to place a greater emphasis on self-reliance at the village level. A recurring problem the cadres had faced in a number of villages was that, try as they might, they ultimately bore the responsibility for coordinating, mobilizing and, in certain cases, carrying out much of the Welfare Improvement work themselves. These cadres found that the people in these locations worked "furiously" to get Civic Action cadres as they knew they would ultimately end up doing the work for them. One consequence of this was that additional cadres would have to be transferred to these locations to help bear the burden, bringing the work they were previously doing in their original villages to a crashing halt. [16] Cung introduced several new measures to remedy this problem. First, Cung refocused the work of the two cadres assigned to a village from coordinating the work of Bettering the People's Conditions of Existence to training the local cadres selected from the population to do this themselves – an integral part of community development. Second, they turned the responsibility of selecting these local cadres over to the village or hamlet chief – depending on the circumstances. Over the preceding two years, the Civic Action cadres had found that the capable village chiefs were very adept at selecting suitable individuals from the local population to help the cadres in their work. This showed respect for village administration on the behalf of the Civic Action cadres as they were no longer usurping the village chief's authority – something that went a long way to reducing a point of friction between the cadres and the village council. Finally, in addition to having a province group assigned to a particular province (or two provinces if they were small) on a permanent basis, Cung got the province group chief to assign the reserve cadres who remained at the provincial headquarters to a district

---

[15] Đặc Ủy Trưởng Công Dân Vụ Kính gởi Quý Ông Tỉnh Trưởng [Memorandum from the Special Commissariat for Civic Action to the Province Chiefs], May 25, 1957, Folder 16293, PTTĐICH, TTLTQG2.

[16] Phương Thức Hoạt Động Mới của Tỉnh Đoàn Công Dân Vụ Hoạt Động tại Nam Phần Việt Nam [New Method of Action of the Civic Action Province Groups operating in the Southern Region of Vietnam], July 15, 1957, Folder 16293, PTTĐICH, TTLTQG2.

on a permanent basis which would allow cadres to more easily follow up on the work of the local cadres.

As the effort to enlist the village chiefs in selecting appropriate local cadres to carry out the work of village improvement once the cadres left indicates Cung wanted the Civic Action cadres to download more of the responsibility for Bettering the People's Conditions of Existence to the village administration. In order to do this, he wanted to be certain his Civic Action cadres had capable counterparts at the administrative level. He got his cadres to weed-out those chiefs who were found to be too old or decrepit or failed to exhibit the requisite "culture" to effectively carry out their duties – the latter case being a reference to the "three enemies" formula. Cung wanted to remove those chiefs who were easily swayed by the propaganda or intimidation tactics of the opponents of the Diệm regime or those chiefs who did not exhibit the necessary virtues to lead by example such as avoiding graft or gambling. Those individuals found their responsibilities assumed by their deputies or the head of one of the interfamily groups. For those chiefs who were found to be efficient, Cung assigned "Hamlet Chief" cadres to the province groups. Their responsibility was to organize short training classes of five to seven days in duration where they would be educated about the importance of a self-reliant citizenry to the broader nation-building goals of the Diệm government and given techniques on how best to mobilize the villagers to work toward these ends. Every two months, the local chiefs would reconvene with these specialized cadres to critically evaluate their work and review the meaning of any new policies or decrees issued by the national or provincial authorities.[17]

These new procedures were intended to help shift the burden for building Diệm's South Vietnamese nation to where Cung felt it rightfully belonged: on the shoulders of the local population. The added permanence of the members of the CDV province groups at the district level would help to maintain the progress being made in building and consolidating effective village administration, while assisting the provincial administration in disseminating the policies of the central government. The greater emphasis on supervision and guidance at the village level would help to imbue the peasantry with the spirit of individual

---

[17] Phương Thức Hoạt Động Mới của Tỉnh Đoàn Công Dân Vụ Hoạt Động tại Nam Phần Việt Nam [New Method of Action of the Civic Action Province Groups operating in the Southern Region of Vietnam], July 15, 1957, Folder 16293; and Báo Cáo Tổng Kết Năm 1957 [1957 Comprehensive Report], January 10, 1958, Folder 16294, PTTĐICH, TTLTQG2.

self-sacrifice and communal self-help that lay at the heart of the community development ideal. This would create a hearty and virtuous citizenry that would work selflessly toward the common goal of realizing Ngô Đình Diệm's Personalist Revolution at the village level and create a viable, self-sufficient nation in the southern half of Vietnam.

Throughout 1957, the Civic Action cadres acted with alacrity to carry out Kiều Công Cung's mission. As mentioned above, their reach was expanded to the center of Vietnam where four province groups were combined into a three joint province groups that were concentrated in Quãng Nam province until June.[18] In the highlands, five province groups helped introduce the government's *Dinh Điền* (Agrarian) program to the indigenous highland communities. These groups were systematically relocated into *Dinh Điền* centers where they would reclaim the land from the jungle for agricultural development. In addition to promoting the region's agricultural sector, the program sought to further the work of ethnic assimilation into Vietnamese society.[19] Civic Action cadres equipped the settlers with provisions such as salt, raw rice and medicine along with portraits of Ngô Đình Diệm and the national flag to "instill" them with "respect and loyalty" for the their government.[20] In the south, twenty-two province groups operated in the south of Vietnam with great zeal to improve the people's well-being and bring them into them into the government's fold. Roads, canals and schools were built. Information centers were established. And communist denunciation proceeded. By June 2, 1957 opponents of the regime were reported to have voluntarily surrendered, "pledging loyalty to the regime," while an additional 980 had been caught up in "the net of the law."[21] So successful did the cadres

[18] Báo Cáo Thành Tích Hoạt Động Tháng 5 năm 1957 [Report of the Operational Achievements of May 1957], June 7, 1957; and Báo Cáo Thành Tích Hoạt Động Tháng 6 năm 1957 [Report of the Operational Achievements of June 1957], July 11, 1957, Folder 16295, PTTĐICH, TTLTQG2.

[19] Dennis J. Duncanson, *Government and Revolution in Vietnam* (New York: Oxford University Press, 1968), 246–247. See also Philip E. Catton, *Diem's Final Failure: Prelude to America's War in Vietnam* (Lawrence, KS: University Press of Kansas, 2002), 59.

[20] Tờ Trình Tháng Hai Năm 1957 Dại Biểu Chánh Phủ Cao Nguyên Trung Phần [February 1957 Statement from the Highland Delegate], April 15, 1957 DICH 16301, PTTĐICH, TTLTQG2.

[21] For the statistics on the number of opponents who surrendered or were captured see Tổng Kết Thành Tích 6–56 đến 6–57 [Summary of Achievements from June 1956 to June 1957], June 21, 1957, Folder 16294. For the reports of the other tasks conducted by the Civic Action cadres in 1957 and the zeal with which they brought to their work see Báo Cáo Thành Tích Hoạt Động Tháng 5 năm 1957 [Report of the Operational Achievements of May 1957], June 7, 1957; Báo Cáo Thành Tích Hoạt Động Tháng 6 năm 1957 [Report of the Operational Achievements of June 1957], July 11, 1957; Báo Cáo

appear in their overall work that by the end of the year the Commissariat
for Civic Action could report that the "cadres had crossed over from the
point of directly carrying out the work to the point of guiding the people
to automatically carry out the work" and achieve "a prosperous, peaceful
and happy life" both materially and spiritually.[22]

By all accounts, the cadres did comport themselves quite well during
1957 in those locations where they could operate (see Map 3). But significant obstacles remained for the program as a whole. In some of the remote
regions, such as the villages of Vĩnh Lợi, Vĩnh Trị and Vĩnh Thanh, the Civic
Action cadres tended to find themselves dangerously exposed to the enemies
of the regime and faced the threat of being kidnapped or assassinated.[23] In
others, like the far removed hamlets of Vĩnh Long and Vĩnh Bình provinces,
the "Viet Cong" – a derogatory term meaning Vietnamese communist that
was coined by the South Vietnamese government – continued to lurk in
the shadows, exerting enough of an influence over the local population to
impede the cadres' efforts to promote the "just cause" of the government.[24]
In Tây Ninh, which had been a Việt Minh stronghold during the war with
the French, the encountered a particularly entrenched communist presence
where children publicly celebrated "the enemy" through dance and song.[25]

Coordination between Civic Action cadres and the agents of the various technical services, ministries and local organizations was a persistent
problem, too, in some cases. Overall, it had been improving, but there
were still notable instances where cooperation was hampered by misunderstandings about the roles the various organs were supposed to play in
supporting the work of the Civic Action cadres.[26] As well, jurisdictional

Thành Tích Hoạt Động Tháng 10 năm 1957 [Report of the Operational Achievements
of October 1957], November 14, 1957; Báo Cáo Thành Tích Hoạt Động Tháng 11 năm
1957 [Report of the Operational Achievements of November 1957], December 7, 1957,
Folder 16295, PTTĐICH, TTLTQG2.

[22] Báo Cáo Tổng Kết Năm 1957 [1957 Comprehensive Report], January 10, 1958, Folder
16294, PTTĐICH, TTLTQG2

[23] Báo Cáo Thành Tích Hoạt Động Tháng 4 năm 1957 [Report of the Operational
Achievements of April 1957], May 11, 1957; and Báo Cáo Thành Tích Hoạt Động Tháng
7 năm 1957 [Report of the Operational Achievements of July 1957], August 10, 1957,
Folder 16295, PTTĐICH, TTLTQG2.

[24] Báo Cáo Thành Tích Hoạt Động Tháng 5 năm 1957 [Report of the Operational
Achievements of May 1957], June 7, 1957, Folder 16295, PTTĐICH, TTLTQG2.

[25] Báo Cáo Thành Tích Hoạt Động Tháng 3 năm 1957 [Report of the Operational
Achievements of March 1957], April 9, 1957, Folder 16295, PTTĐICH, TTLTQG2.

[26] See, for example Báo Cáo Thành Tích Hoạt Động Tháng 4 năm 1957 [Report of the
Operational Achievements of April 1957], May 11, 1957; Báo Cáo Thành Tích Hoạt
Động Tháng 5 năm 1957 [Report of the Operational Achievements of May 1957], June
7, 1957; Báo Cáo Thành Tích Hoạt Động Tháng 6 năm 1957 [Report of the Operational

MAP 3 Territory with Civic Action mobile groups as of June 1957 overlaid on a province map of the Republic of Vietnam ca. 1959–1960

disputes over bureaucratic turf were an issue. In one unnamed province the Civic Action group repeatedly interfered in the internal affairs of the various citizens' organizations like the Republican Youth Movement, the General Confederation of Labor and General Confederation of Workers.[27] Manpower continued to be a particular concern. As the Commissariat extended its reach into the countryside the demand for additional groups increased, particularly in the central provinces. However, the CDV simply lacked the personnel to fulfill these needs.[28] Finally, there was pronounced disillusionment with the nascent community development plan. Despite Cung's efforts to get the cadres to instill the people with a spirit of self-help the message remained lost.[29]

Against this backdrop, 450 delegates were invited to attend a National Conference on Civic Action at year's end in Sài Gòn to take stock of the direction the Commissariat was heading.[30] From December 21 to 25, cadres responsible for coordinating the work of the Civic Action groups in the provinces met with select "outstanding" cadres from the field to evaluate the strengths and weaknesses of the program and determine a plan of action for 1958.[31] They found that assigning mobile groups of two cadres each the responsibility for directing work in one to four villages in a given part of the province was paying significant dividends. The CDV could now establish a more permanent presence in the countryside and develop stronger bonds with the local population and village administration. This helped to encourage more fruitful exchanges of information and ideas between the Civic Action cadres and the local officials, allowing them to better determine the needs of any one village and the capabilities of its work force. Another

Achievements of June 1957], July 11, 1957, Folder 16295; and Ông Bộ Trưởng tại Phủ Tổng Thống Kính gởi Bộ Trưởng [Memorandum from the Secretary of State for the Office of the President to the Ministers], February 10, 1958, Folder 16563, PTTĐICH, TTLTQG2.

[27] Chỉ Thị [Directive], April 19, 1957, Folder 1463, PTTĐICH, TTLTQG2.

[28] Đặc Ủy Trưởng Công Dân Vụ Kính gởi Ông Bộ Trưởng tại Phủ Tổng Thống [Memorandum from the Commissioner General for Civic Action to the Secretary of State for the Office of the President], November 21, 1957, Folder 16301, PTTĐICH, TTLTQG2.

[29] See for example Báo Cáo Thành Tích Hoạt Động Tháng 4 năm 1957 [Report of the Operational Achievements of April 1957], May 11, 1957, Folder 16295, PTTĐICH, TTLTQG2.

[30] Báo Cáo Thành Tích Hoạt Động Tháng 11 năm 1957 [Report of the Operational Achievements of November 1957], December 7, 1957, Folder 16295, PTTĐICH, TTLTQG2.

[31] Tờ Trình về Đại Hội Công Dân Vụ [Report on the Civic Action Conference], January 11, 1958, Folder 16297, PTTĐICH, TTLTQG2.

positive was the general fortitude of the cadres. Because of the progress the Commissariat had made in nearly three years of work, they had engendered considerable resistance from the opponents of the regime ranging from intimidation to assassination. Through it all, they maintained their "duty to serve" the national cause and "resolutely" pursue their work.

These strengths, however, were matched by functional weaknesses that hindered the work of Raising the People's Intellectual Standards and Bettering their Conditions of Existence. In the former case, the cadres were having difficulty mobilizing the peasantry to study civics or engage in popular education and political indoctrination with any enthusiasm. Part of the problem was that a majority of the documents used for popular education were written at a level well beyond the comprehension of the people. Local communities were unable to obtain a proper foundation in the basics of politics, current events and, more significantly, the plans and policies of the government. This was a crucial step in informing the peasantry about their roles and responsibilities in the government's larger nation-building agenda. No doubt such a curriculum would have been informed by Personalist ideals of collective advance and self-sacrifice in the hope that it would elevate the community's cultural standards to a level in accordance with what Kiều Công Cung and the palace believed necessary to carry out its revolution. Unfortunately, we have no examples of the texts used by the CDV cadres in the Vietnamese archives to appraise their content. Even if we did, it is doubtful that the tenets of the Ngôs' cultural formula would have made much sense to those responsible for the peasantry. For one, the Ngôs never published a formal treatise on the subject.[32] For another, most of the palace's pronouncements on the subject were vague and obscure.[33]

As for Bettering the People's Conditions of Existence, the problem of coordination between the ministries and the Commissariat remained a major stumbling block. Some cadres were still having a difficult time

[32] Catton, *Diem's Final Failure*, 47.

[33] Robert Shaplen recounts a rather convoluted description of Personalism by Nhu that left him "bewildered." Robert Shaplen, *The Lost Revolution*, rev. ed. (New York: Harper Colophon Books, 1966), 131. See also John C. Donnell, "National Renovation Campaigns in Vietnam," *Pacific Affairs* 32(1) (March 1959): 86; John C. Donnell, "Personalism in Vietnam," in *Problems of Freedom: South Vietnam Since Independence*, ed. Wesley R. Fishel (New York: Free Press of Glencoe, 1961), 59 and 61; and Edward Miller, *Misalliance: Ngo Dinh Diem, the United States, and the Fate of South Vietnam* (Cambridge, MA: Harvard University Press, 2013), 46.

liaising with the ministries and technical services to get help down to the village level. For their part, the administrators in those ministries and services were not willing to use the Civic Action cadres to get any information down to the local level about their particular role in the government or how they could serve the village community. In some cases, this produced glaring inefficiency in human resource utilization that increased the workload of the cadres who felt compelled to cover the slack themselves, rather than enlist the services of experts from a particular ministry. In other cases, it led to wasteful power struggles between the cadres and their opposites in a particular ministry that delayed progress on any reconstruction work. As for the cadres who had been slated for community development work, those that had been granted "specialized" training by officials from a particular ministry found it was inadequate. They reported that they did not have enough time to learn the "fundamentals." When they tried to mobilize the people to carry out certain tasks they were often undertaken incorrectly, resulting in their having to be redone at public expense. The upshot of this was that while the cadres were keen on community development, the people were not. Rather than instilling the population with the sense of voluntarism Cung and the palace had anticipated, they found the people dispirited and less willing to participate. The conferees concluded the people as a whole were still not embracing the principles at the root of the community development ideal and voluntarily initiating measures to further the interests of the entire community. For the most part the people were complaining that they were simply getting explanations about the practical use of participating in self-help projects, when what they wanted was evidence of its merits. When people *did* participate, it was only in projects that were of direct interest to themselves and their family, not for the overall improvement of the community.[34] More would need to be done for the Commissariat to equip the cadres with the institutional and theoretical support they needed to ensure that spirit of communal self-help which lay at the root of the Personalist Revolution became ingrained the minds of the peasantry. As the New Year opened, the Commissariat clearly had its work cut out for it. Behind the scenes, however, significant changes were at work which would prove a boon for Kiều Công Cung and Civic Action.

---

[34] Tờ Trình về Đại Hội Công Dân Vụ [Report on the Civic Action Conference], January 11, 1958, Folder 16297, PTTĐICH, TTLTQG2.

KIỀU CÔNG CUNG'S COMMUNITY
DEVELOPMENT PLAN

As 1958 opened a combination circumstance and internal maneuverings helped to vault Kiều Công Cung into a commanding position with regard to South Vietnam's community development program. For some reason – quite possibly the rather dismal showing of the initial pilot program for community development – Huỳnh Văn Diệm, Director General of Planning for the Office of the President and Secretary General of the Central Committee for Community Development, "lost interest" in the community development plan over the latter half of 1957, turning it over to his assistant Nguyễn Bích Liên.[35] The loss of such a dominant force over the plan appears to have provided an opportunity for Kiều Công Cung to exert his influence over South Vietnam's community development movement.

In the wake of the Civic Action conference Kiều Công Cung approached Nguyễn Văn Châu, Secretary of State for the Office of the Presidency, with his own community development plan which would deal with some of the shortcomings he felt existed in the original plan, particularly the drift he saw at the provincial administrative level. He intended to use the experience he had garnered over three years of Civic Action work to provide his plan with "strong leadership and direction at the national level." He wanted to make the plan more relevant to the peasantry, focusing on what they perceived to be their felt needs, as opposed to what the province chiefs felt were in their best interest. Cung felt that in the past, too little "emphasis" had been placed "on effective improvement at the village level." What the people wanted, he claimed, was the "kind of help and guidance that will enable them to make a better living," improving their "daily pattern of living" – or the conditions of their existence. Clearly learning from past experience, such as the conclusions of the Civic Action conference surrounding the peasantry's self-interest, he argued they wanted "tangible" results from community development. They were "most interested" in action that would "enable them to increase their cash income" like "raising chickens, expanding garden plots, increasing agricultural production, fishing, handicraft, and the like." These were far more important to them than "receiving DDT, digging village wells, building privies, and similar projects that have been

[35] Memorandum from Normand Poulin to Russell Frakes, March 20, 1958, Folder 75, Box 660, MSUVAG, MSUA.

imposed on them in the past."[36] He intended to start slowly to provide real assistance that would demonstrate the power of communal self-help to improve the peasants' livelihood.[37] Once this foundation had been laid would the cadres turn to "the spheres of social and cultural action," and promoting the Personalist Revolution.[38]

The administrative set-up for Kiều Công Cung's community development plan (see Figure 5) remained much the same as the one proposed by Huỳnh Văn Diệm. It would be overseen by a National Committee for Community Development that would continue to be housed in the Office of the Presidency. The committee would be chaired by Nguyễn Hữu Châu with Kiều Công Cung and Huỳnh Văn Diệm acting as First and Second Vice-Chairmen respectively and they would oversee an interministerial body of Secretary Generals from the Ministries of Public Works, Agriculture, Health, Information, Land Development, Labor, Economics, Town Planning, Agricultural Reform and Social Action along with a delegate from the National Assembly. The National Committee would be responsible for the review and approval of all community development plans as well as allocating money for the program. The Commissariat for Civic Action would oversee implementation.

The community development project would be guided by the community development team which would be assigned to a particular district in a pre-selected province. These groups would be under the overall authority of the province chief, but the chain of command ran through the district chief. At the provincial level a delegate from Civic Action would sit on a committee with the province chief and province deputy chief. They would liaise with consultative committees consisting of chiefs of the technical services and ministries along with members of various citizens organizations to determine what kind of institutional assistance would be required to support the local community development initiatives. This organizational structure would be mirrored at the district level. These committees would formulate the plans based on the felt needs of a particular district and allocate resources accordingly. This was intended, in part, to avoid bureaucratic rivalry and any wasteful duplication of effort between the services. The first teams would consist of cadres from thirty-four community development teams currently located in the provinces.

[36] *Ibid.*
[37] Chi Thị [Instructions] Draft, April 1958, Folder 16560, PTTĐICH, TTLTQG2.
[38] Memorandum from Normand Poulin to Russell Frakes, March 20, 1958, Folder 75, Box 660, MSUVAG, MSUA.

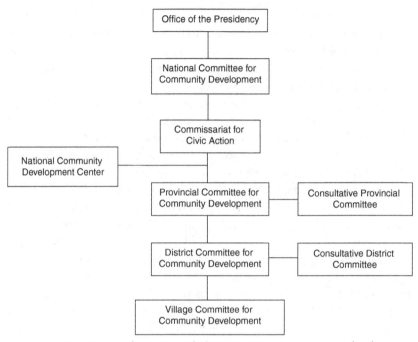

FIGURE 5 Organizational structure of Kiều Công Cung's community development plan

Cung planned to recall them to Sài Gòn where they would undergo an "intensive six month training program."[39]

The community development work involved transforming the community into a "model village" capable of contributing to the national economy through agricultural and small-scale industrial development, such as handicrafts, depending on the "family economics" of the village.[40] The village population would do the work on the project under the guidance of the Civic Action cadres and this work, where necessary, would be supported by the financial and material assistance of the village, province and requisite government organ, such as the Ministry of Agriculture or Land Development. As more trained cadres became available, new

[39] Memorandum from Normand Poulin to Russell Frakes, March 20, 1958, Folder 75, Box 660, MSUVAG, MSUA.

[40] See for example, Biên Bản Cước Hội Họp 12-6-58 về vấn đề Cải Tiến Dân Sinh và việc Cán Bộ Công Dân Vụ Kiên Giang [Minutes of a Meeting on June 16, 1958 about the problem of Bettering the People's Conditions of Existence and the Civic Action Cadres in Kiên Giang] June 16, 1958, Folder 16560, PTTĐICH, TTLTQG2.

projects would be initiated in other districts, while those teams already in a district would be free to circulate to help with other projects once their initial project had become self-sustaining. This way, each of South Vietnam's 135 districts would eventually have its own community development project, propelling the country toward a level of economic self-sufficiency.

A centerpiece of the plan was the National Community Development Center. It would be established on 4,000 hectares of land. One half of the land would be used as a training center for Civic Action cadres which would include a lecture theater, library, archive, mess, garden, stadium and camp to train cadres in animal husbandry. The other 2,000 hectares would serve as an experimental site for land and agricultural development. The infrastructure would consist of an "Agricultural Development Headquarters," a storehouse, electrical workshop and a water pump. Five hundred acres of jungle would be reclaimed for the cultivation and industrial development of coffee, pepper and rubber – which would take between three and six years to produce a return – and tobacco, camphor and kenaf for more immediate yields.

Select cadres would be stationed at the community development center on a permanent basis where they would live in a "model community" comprising a market, school, clinic and church. These cadres would each be allocated one hectare of property complete with a furnished home and given two years to develop it. If successful, they would receive "title ownership" to "the plot and house."[41] This was consistent with Nhu's "basic piece of property" idea. According to the president's brother, this was a "new conception of private ownership" where the government would work to provide the people with a minimum amount of property. Though he did not say how this would be achieved, Nhu envisioned each family obtaining a plot of one to three hectares of land which would be large enough for a garden and the cultivation of rice or other regular crops. This would contribute to a general increase in the economic productivity per family which would, in turn, result in larger tax revenues for the government that could be channeled into the industrialization process. It also offered a social safety net: it would give urban workers a means to provide for their own subsistence in the event of unemployment and to

---

[41] Chương Trình Hoạt Đông Phủ Đặc Ủy Công Dân Vụ năm 1958 [Program of Action for the Commissariat of Civic Action in 1958], March 3, 1958, Folder 16560; Huấn Luyện Thực Tập Cấn Bộ Công Dân Vụ tai Thành Tóa [Civic Action Cadre in Thanh Toa], July 4, 1958, Folder 16563, PTTĐICH, TTLTQG2;and Memorandum from Normand Poulin to Russell Frakes, March 20, 1958, Folder 75, Box 660, MSUVAG, MSUA.

rapidly absorb a massive number of refugees if and when the northern regime collapsed. Nhu thought that if the government could facilitate the means for each family to provide for their existence it would free up time for each member of the family to focus on the development of his or her democratic spirit – how they could contribute to the development of a socially and politically unified nation.[42]

Given the emphasis the government had placed on the Civic Action cadres being upstanding citizens, it is safe to assume that this model community was more than simply a comfortable place for exceptional cadres to live. This community was most likely intended to create model families of virtuous citizens who embodied the ideals of the Personalist Revolution. They would live pure lives, free of vice and graft. When assigned to work on particular community development projects in the provinces these cadres would serve as shining examples of the spirit of hard-work and self-sacrifice and dedication to national improvement that formed the basis of the national identity the Ngôs' were hoping to fashion.[43]

The South Vietnamese government wasted little time endorsing Kiểu Công Cung's plan. It granted Cung 20,000,000 piastres along with a tract of land at Thành Tóa near the village of Xuyên Mộc in Phước Tuy province to establish the community development center. Construction began in early 1958 and by March twenty houses had been built on recently cleared land and Cung began inviting members of the US mission to come and visit the site.[44] In August, Ngô Đình Diệm issued instructions for the specialized training of a number of Civic Action and Information cadres in agricultural development and political education to prepare them for their new responsibilities.[45] Particular attention would be paid to "encouraging a spirit of initiative" in the population to exploit their

---

[42] For a discussion of the "basic piece of property" idea see John C. Donnell, "Politics in South Vietnam: Doctrines of Authority in Conflict," Ph.D. diss. (University of California, Berkley, CA, 1964), 118–121. For a discussion of how these ideas fit with establishing a "democratic spirit" see Catton, *Diem's Final Failure*, 49–50.

[43] Chương Trình Hoạt Động Phủ Đặc Ủy Công Dân Vụ năm 1958 [Program of Action for the Commissariat of Civic Action in 1958], March 3, 1958, Folder 16560; Huấn Luyện Thực Tập Cán Bộ Công Dân Vụ tai Thành Tóa [Civic Action Cadre in Thanh Toa], July 4, 1958, Folder 16563, PTTĐICH, TTLTQG2; and Memorandum from Normand Poulin to Russell Frakes, March 20, 1958, Folder 75, Box 660, MSUVAG, MSUA.

[44] Memorandum from Normand Poulin to Russell Frakes, March 20, 1958, Folder 75, Box 660, MSUVAG, MSUA.

[45] Bản Tóm Lược các vấn để tại Phiên Họp Hội Đồng Nội 4.8.1958 [Summary of the August 4, 1958 Cabinet Meeting], August 6, 1958 Folder 1725, PTTĐICH, TTLTQG2.

"potential ability" to build villages and improve their communal standard of living.[46]

Over a series of interministerial meetings chaired by Kiều Công Cung throughout the fall of 1958, it was decided that Ministry of Information would train 300 Civic Action cadres to be able to teach the people about "the doctrine of personalism (*chủ nghĩa nhân vị*)" and "the theory of community development," among other things. These cadres would be used to establish "mobile political indoctrination committees" that would be assigned to particular provinces. Other cadres would be seconded to the Ministries of Land Development and Agriculture and Economics where they would receive three to six months of training in cultivation techniques, making fertilizer, animal husbandry, nutrition and veterinary medicine, the utility of agricultural cooperatives, establishing local industry, productivity, and the economics of the marketplace, such as instruction in how to sell produce and livestock in local markets and abroad.[47] Each community development team would be comprised of a complement of regular, or "multipurpose" Civic Action cadres along with four other types of cadres representing the specialized training that they had received: Political Indoctrination cadres – also known as Instruction and Organizational cadres – Agricultural cadres, Economic cadres and Social Action cadres who would be responsible for guiding construction, health and sanitation work.[48] In theory, these "specialized" cadres would work

[46] Nhiệm vụ chủ trương đường lối hoạt động thành tích và chương trình công tác của Phủ Đặc Ủy Công Dân Vụ [Achievements from the line of action and program of Action for the Commissariat for Civic Action], October 3, 1959, Folder 16919, PTTĐICH, TTLTQG2.

[47] Bộ Thông Tin và Thanh Niên kính gởi Ông Đặc Ủy Trưởng Công Dân Vụ, August 21, 1958 [Meeting on August 20, 1958 between the Minister of Information and Youth and the Commissioner General for Civic Action] August 23, 1958, Folder 1725; and Phiếu Trình về Việc Phân Phối Cán Bộ Công Dân Vụ [Report on the Distribution of Civic Action Cadres], ND, Folder 16291; Biên Bản Hội Nghị cửa Ủy Ban Trung Ương Phát Triển Cộng Đồng, [Conference Minutes of a Meeting of the Central Committee for Community Development], November 27, 1958, Folder 16563, PTTĐICH, TTLTQG2.

[48] See for example Tỉnh Trưởng Bình Long kính gởi Bộ Trưởng Phủ Tổng Thống, February 4, 1959 [Memorandum from the Binh Long Province Chief to the Secretary of State for the Office of the President]; Tỉnh Trưởng Long An kính gởi Bộ Trưởng Phủ Tổng Thống [Memorandum from the Long An Province Chief to the Secretary of State for the Office of the President], February 4, 1959; Tỉnh Trưởng Tỉnh Kiến Phong kính gởi Bộ Trưởng Phủ Tổng Thống [Memorandum from the Kien Phong Province Chief to the Secretary of State for the Office of the President], February 13, 1959; Tỉnh Trưởng Ba Xuyên kính gởi Bộ Trưởng Phủ Tổng Thống [Memorandum from the Ba Xuyen Province Chief to the Secretary of State for the Office of the President], March 2, 1959; and Tỉnh Trưởng Định Tường kính gởi Bộ Trưởng Phủ Tổng Thống [Memorandum from the Dinh Tuong

together with the Civic Action cadres to "mobilize the consciousness" of the people for "community development."[49]

Cung's community development plan picked up exactly where the preceding one left off. It rested on the communal voluntarism of an enlightened citizenry to build the nation from the ground up. Once imbued with the necessary spirit of self-help, the local population would be mobilized in community development projects consistent with the five-year plan for social and economic development. Land and agricultural development would be coupled with political education explaining each person's obligation to one another, the community and the state at large. The people would work together to exploit the local human and material resources to grow crops and livestock and develop the land and local industries that would make the community self-sufficient. It would start gradually, with an initial experimental phase in each province in early 1959 and then expand throughout the countryside, collectively contributing to the development of the national economy. In time, capital that would otherwise be diverted to rural development initiatives could then be channeled into more ambitious light industrialization projects – such as rice milling, sugar refining or textile production.[50] South Vietnam would then be dependent on its own resources for its continued viability, theoretically giving it greater control over its own destiny in the international arena.

To make this vision a reality, Kiều Công Cung used the Commissariat to prepare the people for the implementation of the community development plan through 1958. Model villages were established in select districts, the training program of the cadres was modified to include practicums where teams would be sent out to the villages for a trial period to gain real-life experience, and the reach of Civic Action was expanded so that by October each province in South Vietnam had its own province groups performing the dual tasks of Raising the People's Intellectual Standards and Bettering the Conditions of their Existence.[51]

Province Chief to the Secretary of State for the Office of the President], March 25, 1959, Folder 16922, PTTĐICH, TTLTQG2.

[49] Chương Trình Hoạt Đông Phủ Đặc Ủy Công Dân Vụ năm 1958 [Program of Action for the Commissariat of Civic Action in 1958], March 3, 1958, Folder 16560, PTTĐICH, TTLTQG2.

[50] Robert Scigliano, *South Vietnam: Nation Under Stress: An Important Look at the Trouble Spot of Asia* (Boston: Houghton Mifflin Company, 1964), 107–108.

[51] Biên Bản Cước Hội Họp 12-6-58 về vấn đề Cải Tiến Dân Sinh và việc Cán Bộ Công Dân Vụ Kiên Giang [Minutes of a Meeting on June 16, 1958 about the problem of Bettering the People's Conditions of Existence and the Civic Action Cadres in Kien Giang], June 16, 1958, Folder 16560; Sự Tiến Bộ Trong Việc Đào Tạo Cán Bộ Công Dân Vụ Khóa XIV [Progress During the Fourteenth Training Session of the Civic Action Cadres],

In areas where opponents of the regime still held considerable sway, the cadres would focus on "the political indoctrination of the people," communist denunciation and popular education to introduce the people to the government, what it stood for and how it was designed to serve them and promote their well-being. In the secure areas, the cadres would elaborate on the functioning of the constituent parts of the government, such as the ministries and technical services, and inform the peasantry how they could serve their interests. As well, they would promote a public campaign to fight illiteracy and "disseminate documents of public interest" dealing with "health, sanitation, agriculture, raising livestock, etc." – the latter two topics being the backbone of Vietnam's community development plan.[52] He also issued new instructions designed to further reframe the work of Bettering the People's Conditions of Existence "according to the principle of community development." Greater effort was to be made by the cadres to "inquire into the economic and social system of the village and the requirements and aspirations of the people" to determine exactly what they felt they needed. Increased focus was to be placed on explaining how the Civic Action cadres were there to guide them in the work needed to satisfy these needs. And more care was to be taken in planning the projects and statistically documenting their successes and failures to ensure the community was being mobilized as efficiently and effectively as possible to improve its overall well-being. This renewed focus on downloading the rural reconstruction work on the peasantry was essential, Cung believed, if each peasant were to see the merits of communal self-help and "build a consciousness of community development." With the psychological foundation the Civic Action cadres would lay in the minds of the peasantry, Kiều Công Cung anticipated the masses easily embracing the ambitious community development plan he was formulating and avoiding some of the confusion that had hampered the pilot work conducted in 1957.[53] By 1959, he hoped, all this groundwork would enable the entire Commissariat for Civic Action to be transformed into a genuine community development organ that would be national in its scope and capable of realizing the Personalist Revolution

Folder 16563; and Báo Cáo Thành Tích Hoạt Động Tháng 10 năm 1958 [Report of the Operational Achievements of October 1958], November 1958, Folder 16561, PTTĐICH, TTLTQG2.

[52] Chương Trình Hoạt Động Phủ Đặc Ủy Công Dân Vụ năm 1958 [Program of Action for the Commissariat of Civic Action in 1958], March 3, 1958, Folder 16560, PTTĐICH, TTLTQG2.

[53] Chỉ Thị [Instructions] Draft, April 1958, Folder 16560, PTTĐICH, TTLTQG2.

on the ground. Spiritually, the cadres would "imbue" the people with the "theories of Personalism and Community." Materially, the people would be given "the opportunity to obtain a minimum of private property and wealth" to develop their collective productive capacity to both raise their standard of living and contribute to the national economy.

APOTHEOSIS

As Kiều Công Cung's community development plan was put into action, the palace once again attempted to take stock of the situation. In January 1959, it issued a call to each of the province chiefs to submit an evaluation of the Civic Action group in the province paying particular attention to the strengths, weaknesses, attitudes of the cadres, summary of achievements and suggestions for improvements.[54] The reports which came in between February and May offer a revealing window into the early workings of community development in South Vietnam highlighting the potential and pitfalls of this ambitious plan. In virtually every province the province chief praised the Civic Action cadres and the good work they were doing. They acted zealously, were resourceful in the face of adversity, could withstand tremendous hardship and demonstrated an exemplary "spirit of service." Toward the people they were, for the most part, courteous, well-mannered and disciplined, earning their trust and respect. As for the village authorities, they comported themselves professionally, faithfully following the policy-lines of the government in terms of working closely with – not over – the local administration.[55] Indeed,

[54] Bộ Trưởng Tại Phủ Tổng Thống kính gởi Ông Tỉnh Trưởng [Memorandum from the Secretary of State for the Office of the President to the Province Chiefs], January 20, 1959, Folder 16922, PTTĐICH, TTLTQG2.
[55] See for example Tỉnh Trưởng Pleiku Kính gởi Ông Bộ Trưởng Tại Phủ Tổng Thống [Memorandum from the Pleiku Province Chief to the Secretary of State for the Office of the President], March 17, 1959; Tỉnh Trưởng Kiên Giang Kính gởi Ông Bộ Trưởng Tại Phủ Tổng Thống [Memorandum from the Kien Giang Province Chief to the Secretary of State for the Office of the President], March 30, 1959; Tỉnh Trưởng Vĩnh Bình Kính gởi Ông Bộ Trưởng Tại Phủ Tổng Thống [Memorandum from the Vinh Binh Province Chief to the Secretary of State for the Office of the President], April 2, 1959; Tỉnh Trưởng Quảng Ngãi Kính gởi Ông Bộ Trưởng Tại Phủ Tổng Thống [Memorandum from the Quang Ngai Province Chief to the Secretary of State for the Office of the President], April 13, 1959; Tỉnh TrưởngTỉnh Kontum Kính gởi Ông Bộ Trưởng Tại Phủ Tổng Thống [Memorandum from the Kontum Province Chief to the Secretary of State for the Office of the President], February 3, 1959; Tỉnh TrưởngTỉnh Đinh Tường Kính gởi Ông Bộ Trưởng Tại Phủ Tổng Thống [Memorandum from the Dinh Tuong Province Chief to the Secretary of State for the Office of the President], March 25, 1959; Tỉnh Trưởng Kiến Tường Kính gởi Ông Bộ Trưởng Tại Phủ Tổng Thống [Memorandum from the Kien Tuong Province Chief to the Secretary of State for the Office of the President], January 28, 1959; Tỉnh TrưởngTỉnh

the province chief of Long An stated that the number of clashes between the Civic Action cadres, the technical services and the village administration had virtually ceased over the past two years due to the changes in command structure which placed the Civic Action province group under the authority of the province chief.[56] In Phú Yên, the province chief instituted a new protocol making the district Civic Action group chief the assistant to the district chief. These new clearly delineated roles and respective responsibilities, he claimed, eliminated jurisdictional clashes between the various administrative organs and ensured the Civic Action district chief did not make arbitrary decisions that were inconsistent with local needs.[57]

Where concerns arose, they were generally directed at the youth and the inexperience of new cadres. In certain cases they tried too hard to mobilize the people; were standoffish, aloof and lacking in proper manners; or simply lacked proficiency in their particular specialty.[58] In the

Bình Tuy Kính gởi Ông Bộ Trưởng Tại Phủ Tổng Thống [Memorandum from the Binh Tuy Province Chief to the Secretary of State for the Office of the President], January 30, 1959; Tỉnh TrưởngTỉnh Thừa Thiên Kính gởi Ông Bộ Trưởng Tại Phủ Tổng Thống [Memorandum from the Thua Thien Province Chief to the Secretary of State for the Office of the President], February 14, 1959; Tỉnh TrưởngTỉnh Tây Ninh Kính gởi Ông Bộ Trưởng Tại Phủ Tổng Thống [Memorandum from the Tay Ninh Province Chief to the Secretary of State for the Office of the President], February 17, 1959;Tỉnh TrưởngTỉnh Darlac Kính gởi Ông Bộ Trưởng Tại Phủ Tổng Thống [Memorandum from the Darlac Province Chief to the Secretary of State for the Office of the President], February 28, 1959; Thị Trưởng Thành Phố Đà Lạt kiêm Tỉnh Trưởng Tỉnh Tuyên Đức Kính gởi Ông Bộ Trưởng Tại Phủ Tổng Thống [Memorandum from the Mayor of the City of Dalat and the Tuyen Duc Province Chief to the Secretary of State for the Office of the President], March 2, 1959; Tỉnh TrưởngVĩnh LongKính gởi Ông Bộ Trưởng Tại Phủ Tổng Thống [Memorandum from the Vinh Long Province Chief to the Secretary of State for the Office of the President], March 11, 1959; Tỉnh TrưởngTỉnh Bình Thuận Kính gởi Ông Bộ Trưởng Tại Phủ Tổng Thống [Memorandum from the Binh Thuan Province Chief to the Secretary of State for the Office of the President], March 14, 1959; Tỉnh TrưởngKhánh HòaKính gởi Ông Bộ Trưởng Tại Phủ Tổng Thống [Memorandum from the Khanh Hoa Province Chief to the Secretary of State for the Office of the President], March 17, 1959; Tỉnh TrưởngPhước LongKính gởi Ông Bộ Trưởng Tại Phủ Tổng Thống [Memorandum from the Phuoc Long Province Chief to the Secretary of State for the Office of the President], April 22, 1959; and Tỉnh TrưởngBình ĐịnhKính gởi Ông Bộ Trưởng Tại Phủ Tổng Thống [Memorandum from the Binh Dinh Province Chief to the Secretary of State for the Office of the President], April 23, 1959, Folder 16922, PTTĐICH, TTLTQG2.

[56] Tỉnh Trưởng Long An Kính gởi Ông Bộ Trưởng Tại Phủ Tổng Thống [Memorandum from the Long An Province Chief to the Secretary of State for the Office of the President], February 4, 1959, Folder 16922, PTTĐICH, TTLTQG2.

[57] Tỉnh Trưởng Phú Yên Kính gởi Ông Bộ Trưởng Tại Phủ Tổng Thống [Memorandum from the Phu Yen Province Chief to the Secretary of State for the Office of the President], March 6, 1959, Folder 16922, PTTĐICH, TTLTQG2.

[58] Tỉnh TrưởngTỉnh Thừa Thiên Kính gởi Ông Bộ Trưởng Tại Phủ Tổng Thống [Memorandum from the Thua Thien Province Chief to the Secretary of State for the Office

southwestern provinces of An Giang and An Xuyen the province chiefs complained that the majority of the cadres were from the North bearing thick accents that were alien to the southern population. Additionally, in the case of the latter province, the cadres were reportedly well-groomed, forsaking the black calico of the peasantry to wear ties and shoes.[59] The Kiến Phong province chief criticized his Civic Action group chief for showing poor leadership skills by micromanaging his cadres.[60] But for the most part these were exceptions which could easily be rectified by the monthly self-criticism sessions or timely discipline by the province group chief.[61]

of the President], February 14, 1959; Tỉnh Trưởng Long An Kính gởi Ông Bộ Trưởng Tại Phủ Tổng Thống [Memorandum from the Long An Province Chief to the Secretary of State for the Office of the President], February 4, 1959; Thị Trưởng Thành Phố Đà Lạt kiêm Tỉnh Trưởng Tỉnh Tuyên Đức Kính gởi Ông Bộ Trưởng Tại Phủ Tổng Thống [Memorandum from the Mayor of the City of Dalat and the Tuyen Duc Province Chief to the Secretary of State for the Office of the President], March 2, 1959; Tỉnh TrưởngTỉnh Bình Thuận Kính gởi Ông Bộ Trưởng Tại Phủ Tổng Thống [Memorandum from the Binh Thuan Province Chief to the Secretary of State for the Office of the President], March 14, 1959; Tỉnh Trưởng Pleiku Kính gởi Ông Bộ Trưởng Tại Phủ Tổng Thống [Memorandum from the Pleiku Province Chief to the Secretary of State for the Office of the President], March 17, 1959; Tỉnh TrưởngKhánh HòaKính gởi Ông Bộ Trưởng Tại Phủ Tổng Thống [Memorandum from the Khanh Hoa Province Chief to the Secretary of State for the Office of the President], March 17, 1959; Tỉnh TrưởngKiến HòaKính gởi Ông Bộ Trưởng Tại Phủ Tổng Thống [Memorandum from the Kien Hoa Province Chief to the Secretary of State for the Office of the President], March 25, 1959; Tỉnh Trưởng Kiên Giang Kính gởi Ông Bộ Trưởng Tại Phủ Tổng Thống [Memorandum from the Kien Giang Province Chief to the Secretary of State for the Office of the President], March 30, 1959; Tỉnh Trưởng Vĩnh Bình Kính gởi Ông Bộ Trưởng Tại Phủ Tổng Thống [Memorandum from the Vinh Binh Province Chief to the Secretary of State for the Office of the President], April 2, 1959; and Tỉnh Trưởng Quãng Ngãi Kính gởi Ông Bộ Trưởng Tại Phủ Tổng Thống [Memorandum from the Quang Ngai Province Chief to the Secretary of State for the Office of the President], April 13, 1959, Folder 16922, PTTĐICH, TTLTQG2.

[59] Tỉnh Trưởng An Giang Kính gởi Ông Bộ Trưởng Tại Phủ Tổng Thống [Memorandum from the An Giang Province Chief to the Secretary of State for the Office of the President], February 3, 1959; and Tỉnh Trưởng Tỉnh An Xuyen Kính gởi Ông Bộ Trưởng Tại Phủ Tổng Thống [Memorandum from the An Xuyen Province Chief to the Secretary of State for the Office of the President], March 5, 1959, Folder 16922, PTTĐICH, TTLTQG2.

[60] Tỉnh Trưởng Kiến Phong Kính gởi Ông Bộ Trưởng Tại Phủ Tổng Thống [Memorandum from the Kien Phong Province Chief to the Secretary of State for the Office of the President], February 13, 1959, Folder 16922, PTTĐICH, TTLTQG2.

[61] Tỉnh Trưởng An Giang Kính gởi Ông Bộ Trưởng Tại Phủ Tổng Thống [Memorandum from the An Giang Province Chief to the Secretary of State for the Office of the President], February 3, 1959; Tỉnh TrưởngTỉnh Tây Ninh Kính gởi Ông Bộ Trưởng Tại Phủ Tổng Thống [Memorandum from the Tay Ninh Province Chief to the Secretary of State for the Office of the President], February 17, 1959;Tỉnh Trưởng Tỉnh An Xuyen Kính gởi Ông Bộ Trưởng Tại Phủ Tổng Thống [Memorandum from the An Xuyen Province Chief to the Secretary of State for the Office of the President], March 5, 1959; Tỉnh Trưởng Long An Kính gởi Ông Bộ Trưởng Tại Phủ Tổng Thống [Memorandum from the Long An Province

Only two province chiefs complained significantly about the conduct of the Civic Action cadres. In Bình Dương the province chief conceded that the standard of the cadres was far from uniform. Those who demonstrated little ability were young, inexperienced, and consequently lacking the necessary "prestige" to educate the masses about the plans and policies of the central government.[62] Further south, in the Mekong Delta, the province chief of Phong Dinh bluntly stated that the cadres assigned to his province had failed in their efforts to win the people over. Citing a variety of problems including a haughty attitude, an absence of manners and little skill, he complained that they rarely attempted to get close to the people and therefore had not been able to gain any of their "sympathy." A majority of these cadres also apparently believed that they had the authority to exert their control over the village councils and demonstrated a tendency to interfere in the private affairs of many of the village council staff members.[63]

In terms of their achievements, the province chiefs indicated that they were very effective at propagandizing on behalf of the government through popular education classes. Ba Xuyen, Phú Yên and Tuyên Đức all reported that the cadres had raised the people's intellectual standards by explaining the structure, policies, programs and philosophy of the government, which, the latter province chief exuded, had instilled the people with "a consciousness of the Personalist Republic System" and an awareness of their responsibilities toward one another, the village and the nation.[64] In Long An, the cadres had dramatically reduced illiteracy

Chief to the Secretary of State for the Office of the President], February 4, 1959; Tỉnh Trưởng Phú Yên Kính gởi Ông Bộ Trưởng Tại Phủ Tổng Thống [Memorandum from the Phu Yen Province Chief to the Secretary of State for the Office of the President], March 6, 1959; Tỉnh TrưởngTỉnh Định Tường Kính gởi Ông Bộ Trưởng Tại Phủ Tổng Thống [Memorandum from the Dinh Tuong Province Chief to the Secretary of State for the Office of the President], March 25, 1959; and Tỉnh TrưởngPhước LongKính gởi Ông Bộ Trưởng Tại Phủ Tổng Thống [Memorandum from the Phuoc Long Province Chief to the Secretary of State for the Office of the President], April 22, 1959,Folder 16922, PTTĐICH, TTLTQG2.

[61] Tỉnh TrưởngBình DươngKính gởi Ông Bộ Trưởng Tại Phủ Tổng Thống [Memorandum from the Binh Duong Province Chief to the Secretary of State for the Office of the President], March 20, 1959, Folder 16922, PTTĐICH, TTLTQG2.

[63] Tỉnh TrưởngPhong ĐinhKính gởi Ông Bộ Trưởng Tại Phủ Tổng Thống [Memorandum from the Phong Dinh Province Chief to the Secretary of State for the Office of the President], March 18, 1959, Folder 16922, PTTĐICH, TTLTQG2.

[64] Tỉnh TrưởngBa XuyenKính gởi Ông Bộ Trưởng Tại Phủ Tổng Thống [Memorandum from the Ba Xuyen Province Chief to the Secretary of State for the Office of the President], March 2, 1959; Tỉnh Trưởng Phú Yên Kính gởi Ông Bộ Trưởng Tại Phủ Tổng Thống [Memorandum from the Phu Yen Province Chief to the Secretary of State for the Office of the President], March 6, 1959; and Thị Trưởng Thành Phố Đà Lạt kiêm Tỉnh Trưởng

to the point where it was nearly eliminated.[65] In Kiến Tường, they had
won many new adherents from the undecided population over to "the
National Cause" expounded by Ngô Đình Diệm. Elsewhere, the cadres
continued to organize the population against the communists.[66] In Định
Tường, for example, they established citizens' organizations – such as a
local branch of the National Revolutionary Movement, a mass political
party established by Ngô Đình Nhu created to politically indoctrinate
and mobilize the population on the behalf of the regime – and used the
village councils to denounce communists.[67]

Progress was also being made in the rural reconstruction work designed
to better the people's conditions of existence. In the lowland provinces
of the center and south, along with the Mekong Delta, the cadres' ability
to get close to the population and explain the policies of the government
was paying dividends as they could lay a foundation for "encouraging
and guiding the people to automatically carry out the useful and practical tasks" that would improve their well-being as was the case in Tây
Ninh.[68] In Thừa Thiên, improvements to local infrastructure such as the

Tinh Tuyên Đức Kính gởi Ông Bộ Trưởng Tại Phủ Tổng Thống [Memorandum from the
Mayor of the City of Dalat and the Tuyen Duc Province Chief to the Secretary of State
for the Office of the President], March 2, 1959, Folder 16922, PTTĐICH, TTLTQG2.

[65] Tinh Trưởng Long An Kính gởi Ông Bộ Trưởng Tại Phủ Tổng Thống [Memorandum
from the Long An Province Chief to the Secretary of State for the Office of the President],
February 4, 1959, Folder 16922, PTTĐICH, TTLTQG2.

[66] Tinh Trưởng Kiến Tường Kính gởi Ông Bộ Trưởng Tại Phủ Tổng Thống [Memorandum
from the Kien Tuong Province Chief to the Secretary of State for the Office of the
President], January 28, 1959, Folder 16922, PTTĐICH, TTLTQG2.

[67] Tinh TrưởngTinh Đinh Tường Kính gởi Ông Bộ Trưởng Tại Phủ Tổng Thống
[Memorandum from the Dinh Tuong Province Chief to the Secretary of State for the
Office of the President], March 25, 1959, Folder 16922, PTTĐICH, TTLTQG2. See also
Tinh Trưởng Gia Dinh Kính gởi Ông Bộ Trưởng Tại Phủ Tổng Thống [Memorandum
from the Gia Dinh Province Chief to the Secretary of State for the Office of the President],
February 13, 1959; and Tinh Trưởng Kiến Phong Kính gởi Ông Bộ Trưởng Tại Phủ Tổng
Thống [Memorandum from the Kien Phong Province Chief to the Secretary of State for
the Office of the President], February 13, 1959, Folder 16922, PTTĐICH, TTLTQG2.
For a description of the National Revolutionary Movement see Miller, *Misalliance*, 130.

[68] Tinh TrưởngTinh Tây Ninh Kính gởi Ông Bộ Trưởng Tại Phủ Tổng Thống [Memorandum
from the Tay Ninh Province Chief to the Secretary of State for the Office of the President],
February 17, 1959; see also Tinh TrưởngBa XuyenKính gởi Ông Bộ Trưởng Tại Phủ Tổng
Thống [Memorandum from the Ba Xuyen Province Chief to the Secretary of State for
the Office of the President], March 2, 1959; Tinh TrưởngBinh DươngKính gởi Ông Bộ
Trưởng Tại Phủ Tổng Thống [Memorandum from the Binh Duong Province Chief to
the Secretary of State for the Office of the President], March 20, 1959;Tinh Trưởng
Long An Kính gởi Ông Bộ Trưởng Tại Phủ Tổng Thống [Memorandum from the Long
An Province Chief to the Secretary of State for the Office of the President], February 4,
1959;TinhTrưởngTinh Đinh Tường Kính gởi Ông Bộ Trưởng Tại Phủ Tổng Thống

FIGURE 6 Another bridge built (through community development). Michigan State University Archives and Historical Collections

construction of bridges, roads and protective dykes were carried out by the community in the spirit of self-help (see Figure 6). Just as Kiều Công Cung intended, the province chief felt that this would help lay the foundation for community development projects in the future.[69]

Other province chiefs indicated that the transition to community development work was already underway. Định Tường, Kiến Phong, Long An and Ba Xuyen all had received specialized cadres in the fields of Agriculture, Training and Organization, Economics and Social Action – Rural Construction.[70] In Long An, where they constituted half of that

[Memorandum from the Dinh Tuong Province Chief to the Secretary of State for the Office of the President], March 25, 1959, Folder 16922, PTTĐICH, TTLTQG2.

[69] Tỉnh TrưởngTỉnh Thừa Thiên Kính gởi Ông Bộ Trưởng Tại Phủ Tổng Thống [Memorandum from the Thua Thien Province Chief to the Secretary of State for the Office of the President], February 14, 1959, Folder 16922, PTTĐICH, TTLTQG2.

[70] Tỉnh TrưởngTỉnh Đinh Tường Kính gởi Ông Bộ Trưởng Tại Phủ Tổng Thống [Memorandum from the Dinh Tuong Province Chief to the Secretary of State for the Office of the President], March 25, 1959; Tỉnh Trưởng Kiến Phong Kính gởi Ông Bộ Trưởng Tại Phủ Tổng Thống [Memorandum from the Kien Phong Province Chief to the Secretary of State for the Office of the President], February 13, 1959; Tỉnh Trưởng Long An Kính gởi Ông Bộ Trưởng Tại Phủ Tổng Thống [Memorandum from the Long An Province Chief to the Secretary of State for the Office of the President], February 4, 1959; and Tỉnh Trưởng Ba Xuyen Kính gởi Ông Bộ Trưởng Tại Phủ Tổng Thống [Memorandum from the Ba Xuyen Province Chief to the Secretary of State for the Office of the President], March 2, 1959, Folder 16922, PTTĐICH, TTLTQG2.

province's complement of 100 cadres, they engaged in agricultural and small-scale industrial development (handicrafts) which the province chief considered a solid framework for the future. In Ba Xuyen they had held a three-month agricultural class for fifty people from mid-November to January. Further north, in the coastal province of Phú Yên, which had only recently received a permanent Civic Action team the previous October, the province chief reported the introduction of one or two unspecified community development pilot projects in each district along with the proselytization by cadres elsewhere about the merits of this program.[71] And in the southwestern province of Kiên Giang, the chief boasted of an irrigation program for crops and the construction of highways, bridges and canals to improve transportation routes to ship them to the local markets and beyond.[72]

In the highland provinces the community development plan had the added component of "Vietnamizing" the ethnic minorities. Contingents of Civic Action cadres trekked deep into the mountainous jungle territory to uplift the indigenous groups through the gospel of community development. Their message was intended to make the highland populations forsake their "primitive and backward" lifestyle in the name of "renovation."[73] In Quảng Ngãi, in particular, the province chief praised the efforts of those Vietnamese cadres who "endured the difficulty of studying" the language and "practicing the customs of the Highland people in order to make contact" with them and earn their trust.[74] Elsewhere, the regular Civic Action cadres, in conjunction with the specialized cadres, established model villages for the highlanders to live in addition to their mobile work Raising the People's Intellectual Standards and Bettering the

---

[71] Tỉnh Trưởng Phú Yên Kính gởi Ông Bộ Trưởng Tại Phủ Tổng Thống [Memorandum from the Phu Yen Province Chief to the Secretary of State for the Office of the President], March 6, 1959, Folder 16922, PTTĐICH, TTLTQG2.

[72] Tỉnh Trưởng Kiên Giang Kính gởi Ông Bộ Trưởng Tại Phủ Tổng Thống [Memorandum from the Kien Giang Province Chief to the Secretary of State for the Office of the President], March 30, 1959, Folder 16922, PTTĐICH, TTLTQG2.

[73] The quotes are from Tỉnh TrưởngBình Longkính gởi Ông Bộ Trưởng Tại Phủ Tổng Thống [Memorandum from the Binh Long Province Chief to the Secretary of State for the Office of the President], February 4, 1959. See also Tỉnh TrưởngTỉnh Darlac Kính gởi Ông Bộ Trưởng Tại Phủ Tổng Thống [Memorandum from the Darlac Province Chief to the Secretary of State for the Office of the President], February 28, 1959, Folder 16922, PTTĐICH, TTLTQG2 for a discussion of the government's perception of the highlanders' conditions of existence.

[74] Tỉnh Trưởng Quảng Ngãi Kính gởi Ông Bộ Trưởng Tại Phủ Tổng Thống [Memorandum from the Quang Ngai Province Chief to the Secretary of State for the Office of the President], April 13, 1959, Folder 16922, PTTĐICH, TTLTQG2.

Conditions of their Existence.[75] In Bình Thuận the cadres helped demobilize and resettle Nùng soldiers who had previously enjoyed an autonomous position in Vietnam's wars of decolonization and were now willing to enter the national fold.[76] Every highland province chief celebrated the work of the Civic Action cadres and spoke favorably of the benefits their community development work was bringing to the indigenous population. Their main concern was that they had too few cadres versed in the customs and local dialects of the highland communities and the difficulty the Civic Action teams had traversing the mountains and penetrating the dense jungle.[77]

Logistics and manpower proved to be the source of the one complaint that transcended the regions of South Vietnam. Province chiefs everywhere voiced their apprehension about sheer size of the territories such a limited number of cadres were responsible for attending to. In the highland province of Tuyên Đức, for example, forty-one Civic Action cadres were responsible for a province with an area of over 4,800 square kilometers of mountainous jungle terrain that encompassed an urban center, Đà Lạt, and a population of nearly 110,000 people.[78] Likewise, An

[75] Tỉnh Trưởng Bình Long kính gởi Ông Bộ Trưởng Tại Phủ Tổng Thống [Memorandum from the Binh Long Province Chief to the Secretary of State for the Office of the President], February 4, 1959; Thị Trưởng Thành Phố Đà Lạt kiêm Tỉnh Trưởng Tỉnh Tuyên Đức Kính gởi Ông Bộ Trưởng Tại Phủ Tổng Thống [Memorandum from the Mayor of the City of Dalat and the Tuyen Duc Province Chief to the Secretary of State for the Office of the President], March 2, 1959; and Tỉnh Trưởng Tỉnh Kontum Kính gởi Ông Bộ Trưởng Tại Phủ Tổng Thống [Memorandum from the Kontum Province Chief to the Secretary of State for the Office of the President], February 3, 1959, Folder 16922, PTTĐICH, TTLTQG2.
[76] Tỉnh Trưởng Tỉnh Bình Thuận Kính gởi Ông Bộ Trưởng Tại Phủ Tổng Thống [Memorandum from the Binh Thuan Province Chief to the Secretary of State for the Office of the President], March 14, 1959, Folder 16922, PTTĐICH, TTLTQG2.
[77] See for example Tỉnh Trưởng Tỉnh Kontum Kính gởi Ông Bộ Trưởng Tại Phủ Tổng Thống [Memorandum from the Kontum Province Chief to the Secretary of State for the Office of the President], February 3, 1959; Tỉnh Trưởng Bình Long kính gởi Ông Bộ Trưởng Tại Phủ Tổng Thống [Memorandum from the Binh Long Province Chief to the Secretary of State for the Office of the President], February 4, 1959; Tỉnh TrưởngTỉnh Darlac Kính gởi Ông Bộ Trưởng Tại Phủ Tổng Thống [Memorandum from the Darlac Province Chief to the Secretary of State for the Office of the President], February 28, 1959; Tỉnh Trưởng Pleiku Kính gởi Ông Bộ Trưởng Tại Phủ Tổng Thống [Memorandum from the Pleiku Province Chief to the Secretary of State for the Office of the President], March 17, 1959; Tỉnh Trưởng Quảng Ngãi Kính gởi Ông Bộ Trưởng Tại Phủ Tổng Thống [Memorandum from the Quang Ngai Province Chief to the Secretary of State for the Office of the President], April 13, 1959;and Tỉnh TrưởngPhước LongKính gởi Ông Bộ Trưởng Tại Phủ Tổng Thống [Memorandum from the Phuoc Long Province Chief to the Secretary of State for the Office of the President], April 22, 1959, Folder 16922, PTTĐICH, TTLTQG2.
[78] Thị Trưởng Thành Phố Đà Lạt kiêm Tỉnh Trưởng Tỉnh Tuyên Đức Kính gởi Ông Bộ Trưởng Tại Phủ Tổng Thống [Memorandum from the Mayor of the City of Dalat and

Giang, in the Cà Mau peninsula, had a population of 700,000, but only seventy-seven Civic Action cadres.[79]

Nevertheless, by most accounts Kiều Công Cung's community development program was well on its way. Where the Civic Action cadres were operating the people were embracing the ideals of mutual self-help that underpinned the community development idea. Model villages were being established and rural reconstruction projects were being initiated under the guidance of the specialized cadres that were trained by the various ministries. Certainly some concerns remained about the conduct of the cadres. Some were too immature, imperious or officious; others were from the North with indecipherable accents to the ears of the southerners; in the case of the highlands, more indigenous cadres were required. Infrastructure and resources were an issue as well. Better roads and more means of transportation such as jeeps, trucks, motorbikes and canoes for the delta provinces were needed to connect the far-flung regions to the district centers where the bulk of the cadres were acting with regularity.[80]

None of these obstacles were insurmountable under the current conditions in the countryside. What was problematic was the overall reach of the cadres. For every town, village or hamlet which had a Civic Action presence there was another, more remote location that was more or less cut off from the government. In the delta province of Kiến Tường, for

the Tuyen Duc Province Chief to the Secretary of State for the Office of the President], March 2, 1959, Folder 16922, PTTĐICH, TTLTQG2.

[79] Tỉnh Trưởng An Giang Kính gởi Ông Bộ Trưởng Tại Phủ Tổng Thống [Memorandum from the An Giang Province Chief to the Secretary of State for the Office of the President], February 3, 1959 PTTĐICH, TTLTQG2.

[80] See for example Tỉnh Trưởng An Giang Kính gởi Ông Bộ Trưởng Tại Phủ Tổng Thống [Memorandum from the An Giang Province Chief to the Secretary of State for the Office of the President], February 3, 1959; Tỉnh Trưởng Long An Kính gởi Ông Bộ Trưởng Tại Phủ Tổng Thống [Memorandum from the Long An Province Chief to the Secretary of State for the Office of the President], February 4, 1959;Tỉnh Trưởng Kiến Tường Kính gởi Ông Bộ Trưởng Tại Phủ Tổng Thống [Memorandum from the Kien Tuong Province Chief to the Secretary of State for the Office of the President], January 28, 1959; Tỉnh Trưởng Bình Long kính gởi Ông Bộ Trưởng Tại Phủ Tổng Thống [Memorandum from the Binh Long Province Chief to the Secretary of State for the Office of the President], February 4, 1959; Tỉnh Trưởng Tỉnh Bình Thuận Kính gởi Ông Bộ Trưởng Tại Phủ Tổng Thống [Memorandum from the Binh Thuan Province Chief to the Secretary of State for the Office of the President], March 14, 1959;Tỉnh Trưởng Pleiku Kính gởi Ông Bộ Trưởng Tại Phủ Tổng Thống [Memorandum from the Pleiku Province Chief to the Secretary of State for the Office of the President], March 17, 1959; and Tỉnh TrưởngPhước LongKính gởi Ông Bộ Trưởng Tại Phủ Tổng Thống [Memorandum from the Phuoc Long Province Chief to the Secretary of State for the Office of the President], April 22, 1959, Folder 16922, PTTĐICH, TTLTQG2.

example, the province chief warned of a greater "Viet Cong" presence in the remote villages due mainly to family members with ties to the communists.[81] Despite the best efforts of the cadres, parts of the mountainous jungle proved impenetrable in some highland provinces. Every province chief requested more cadres. However there simply were not enough in the Commissariat of Civic Action to go around. In fact, this problem was exacerbated by community development's perceived successes. As the government attempted to extend the plan into the countryside, more multipurpose Civic Action cadres were recalled to Sài Gòn for specialized training. Province chiefs who were already feeling the burden of their cadres being spread too thinly felt a greater pinch as cadres were either withdrawn from the field or transferred to another district to fill a more pressing gap.[82] Under ideal circumstances, maintaining continuity as the program expanded would be difficult. But the situation in 1950s Vietnam was not ideal. Lurking in the shadows were the opponents of the regime, ready to obstruct and undermine the efforts of the Civic Action cadres whenever the opportunity presented itself. And, as the Commissariat for Civic Action attempted to deal with these manpower challenges in the second half of 1959, the regime's enemies moved increasingly into the light.

[81] Tỉnh Trưởng Kiến Tường Kính gởi Ông Bộ Trưởng Tại Phủ Tổng Thống [Memorandum from the Kien Tuong Province Chief to the Secretary of State for the Office of the President], January 28, 1959, Folder 16922, PTTĐICH, TTLTQG2.

[82] Tỉnh Trưởng Gia Dinh Kính gởi Ông Bộ Trưởng Tại Phủ Tổng Thống [Memorandum from the Gia Dinh Province Chief to the Secretary of State for the Office of the President], February 13, 1959; Tỉnh Trưởng Kiến Phong Kính gởi Ông Bộ Trưởng Tại Phủ Tổng Thống [Memorandum from the Kien Phong Province Chief to the Secretary of State for the Office of the President], February 13, 1959; Tỉnh Trưởng Tỉnh An Xuyen Kính gởi Ông Bộ Trưởng Tại Phủ Tổng Thống [Memorandum from the An Xuyen Province Chief to the Secretary of State for the Office of the President], March 5, 1959; Tỉnh Trưởng Phú Yên Kính gởi Ông Bộ Trưởng Tại Phủ Tổng Thống [Memorandum from the Phu Yen Province Chief to the Secretary of State for the Office of the President], March 6, 1959; Tỉnh Trưởng Khánh Hòa Kính gởi Ông Bộ Trưởng Tại Phủ Tổng Thống [Memorandum from the Khanh Hoa Province Chief to the Secretary of State for the Office of the President], March 17, 1959; Tỉnh Trưởng Phong Đinh Kính gởi Ông Bộ Trưởng Tại Phủ Tổng Thống [Memorandum from the Phong Dinh Province Chief to the Secretary of State for the Office of the President], March 18, 1959; and Tỉnh TrưởngTỉnh Đinh Tường Kính gởi Ông Bộ Trưởng Tại Phủ Tổng Thống [Memorandum from the Dinh Tuong Province Chief to the Secretary of State for the Office of the President], March 25, 1959, Folder 16922, PTTĐICH, TTLTQG2.

FIVE

Civic Action and Insurgency

From the moment Ngô Đình Diệm ascended to a position of leadership in Vietnam he had been faced with an array of political opponents ranging from dissident generals and the French to religious-political sects and an organized crime network. His first year in office was spent contending with these groups. Waiting in the wings were the communist supporters of the Hà Nội government who remained behind when Vietnam had been partitioned into two regroupment zones in 1954 and their sympathizers. The Special Commissariat for Civic Action had been established to meet this threat. The cadres' initial mission had been to extend the reach of the government down into the countryside to demonstrate to the people that they had more to gain by siding with the Diệm regime than agents of Hồ Chí Minh's government in the North. They pursued a two-track approach in their efforts. The first aimed at improving the well-being of the people through the distribution of gifts and medicine as well as coordinating the human and material resources of the community toward reconstructing local institutions and infrastructure. This was intended to demonstrate the government's concern with their welfare. The second track involved eradicating the clandestine communist menace at the village level. This required participating in the government's communist denunciation campaign, where cadres would mobilize the population to identify suspected communists who would then be either arrested or convinced to rally to the government. This proved to be very effective, but counterproductive as it could easily devolve into a local reign of terror in the hands of less-scrupulous officials and their supporters. It served to alienate many of the people the Civic Action cadres were supposed to help. Such alienation fueled anti-regime activity at the local level, perpetrated by opponents of the government of all political stripes. This periodically exploded in spectacular displays of malevolence from brazen attacks on local officials, including Civic Action cadres, to an assassination attempt against President Ngô Đình Diệm at the inauguration of the Ban Mê Thuột Fair on February 22, 1957.[1]

Community development offered a potential avenue to thwart this rising hostility. Seeing the communist regime in the North as the source of this unrest, both Kiều Công Cung and the Diệm regime had hoped the improvement brought about to the peasantry's standard of living through community development, along with the sense of pride and belonging to a larger cause that came from working for the communal good, would undercut the Hà Nội government's appeal. What they all failed to realize was that in addition to communist denunciation the government had been advancing other policies such as land reform and land development that, though well-meaning, were often poorly explained, ill-conceived and maladministered in such a way that they tended to add to the peasantry's misery. Despite the best efforts of the Civic Action cadres to rationalize the regime's actions their association with these endeavors, particularly the communist denunciation campaign, may have undermined much of the good work they were doing. By 1959, just as the Commissariat for Civic Action was on its way to becoming a community development organ, the resentment these policies incurred had become so entrenched in segments of the population that no amount of goodwill could turn the tide once an outlet for this frustration presented itself. Once this occurred, the Commissariat became increasingly reactionary, turning away from community development – and fomenting Diệm's Personalist Revolution throughout the countryside – toward security and propaganda work, quite possibly increasing the peasantry's sense of isolation.

THE ROOTS OF THE INSURGENCY

While Ngô Đình Diệm may have had a particular vision for a postcolonial Vietnam that ostensibly rested on principles of social justice insofar as it would protect the individual from the exploitative excesses of a liberal state or the oppressive order of a communist regime, the means with which he sought to impose it engendered a considerable amount of resistance. One of the pillars of this progressive republic was the free-holding

---

[1] *New York Times*, February 23, 1957, 1; and Philip E. Catton, *Diem's Final Failure: Prelude to America's War in Vietnam* (Lawrence, KS: University Press of Kansas, 2002), 58.

peasant. Collectively, this peasantry would comprise a new middle class of economically independent farmers.[2] In theory, this would bring stability to the countryside and a concomitant prosperity that would make the nation-building project to the south of the seventeenth parallel far more appealing that what was on offer in the North. From the beginning of its tenure, Diệm's regime began implementing agrarian policies intended to achieve this. One of the earliest was land reform.

In 1954, about 40 percent of the rice growing lands in the Mekong Delta belonged to approximately 2,500 persons – 0.025 percent of the rural population – making land redistribution a major propaganda device for southern communists. If Diệm could carry out his own reforms successfully, he stood to gain a powerful group of adherents. In January 1955 he promulgated a land ordinance that limited rent to a maximum of 25 percent of a farmer's major crop in fertile areas and smaller maximums in less fertile regions. In the event the owner provided the tenant with extras such as fertilizer or farm implements, the rent could be increased, but it was never intended to reach the rate of 50–70 percent, which had previously prevailed and reduced many tenant farmers to a position of virtual servitude. Unfortunately, Diệm was preoccupied with the Hinh and sect crises at this point and unable to provide the leadership to fully implement his reforms. As it turns out, very few of the 40 percent of the population of the South that were tenants were pleased with this new ordinance. During the war between the French and the Việt Minh rents had not been collected in some areas for nine years, whereas, in other areas that had been dominated by the Việt Minh, the land had essentially been expropriated outright to the tenants. When compared to the sweeping land transfers promised by the communists in the event of a Hà Nội victory in the July 1956 elections, Diệm's modest proposal seemed wholly inadequate.[3]

---

[2] David Elliott, *The Vietnamese War: Revolution and Social Change in the Mekong Delta, 1930–1975*, Vol. 1(Armonk, NY: M.E. Sharpe, 2003), 166 and 180.

[3] Land Reform Programs Before 1954 and Land Reform Program and Achievements Since July 1954, July 31, 1959, Item number 2322032034, Texas Tech Virtual Vietnam Archive,www.virtualarchive.vietnam.ttu.edu (hereafter referred to as TTVVA) (accessed January 29, 2007); Robert Scigliano, *South Vietnam: Nation Under Stress: An Important Look at the Trouble Spot of Asia* (Boston: Houghton Mifflin Company, 1964), 120–124; David L. Anderson, *Trapped by Success: The Eisenhower Administration and Vietnam, 1953–1961* (New York: Columbia University Press, 1991), 152–154; Catton, *Diem's Final Failure*, 54–55; Neil Sheehan, *A Bright Shining Lie: John Paul Vann and America in Vietnam* (New York: Random House, 1988), 182–183; Bernard Fall, "South Viet-Nam's Internal Problems," *Pacific Affairs* 31(3) (September 1958): 250–251; Dennis J. Duncanson, *Government and Revolution in Vietnam* (New York: Oxford University

In October 1956 Diệm augmented these measures with Ordinance 57. It was still very conservative, allowing land owners, who considered any land reform measures to be too radical, to retain about one hundred hectares of land – thirty times the limits set by American advisers in Japan, South Korea and Taiwan – leaving about one-third of the "tenanted land in South Vietnam" available for redistribution. Such conservatism, however, had both a pragmatic and an ideological component. From a pragmatic perspective, Diệm appreciated the fact that his grip on power was still fragile and feared alienating the landowning class who already resented the palace's agrarian reforms. Ideologically, since the regime's mantra was "collective advance," Diệm wanted to avoid pitting the social classes against one another.[4] He tried to balance the interests of the tenants and the landlords, a tactic that came to favor the landlords over the tenants. To make matters worse, Sài Gòn's provincial administrators proved to be incapable of carrying out these reforms due to incompetence, indifference or a lack of trained personnel. As a result, the Sài Gòn government only managed to transfer about 40 percent of the land that Ordinance 57 did make available.[5]

Far more ambitious was Diệm's land development program. One of his major concerns was the overpopulation of parts of the South Vietnamese countryside. Rather than pursuing a policy of radical redistribution of land to achieve this goal, as was occurring in the North, Diệm intended to redistribute the population.[6] In 1957, he attempted to relocate thousands of Vietnamese people to new *Dinh Điền* (Agrarian) centers on uncultivated or abandoned tracts of land in the vast, but thinly populated, Mekong Delta and the Central Highlands. In addition to alleviating South Vietnam's overpopulation, he believed that "pioneering, as a traditional way of life" would "give rise" to the type of sturdy, virtuous and civic-minded individuals that were an essential component of his infrastructure for democracy.[7] He hoped these land development centers would

---

Press, 1968), 242–246; and Douglas Pike, *Viet Cong: The Organization and Techniques of the National Liberation Front of South Vietnam* (Cambridge, MA: MIT Press, 1966), 73 and 276.

[4] Catton, *Diem's Final Failure*, 54.

[5] Land Reform Programs Before 1954 and Land Reform Program and Achievements Since July 1954, July 31, 1959, Item number 2322032034, TTVVA, (accessed January 29, 2007); Scigliano, *Nation Under Stress*, 121–123; Pike, *Viet Cong*, 62–63; Duncanson, *Government and Revolution in Vietnam*, 242–246; Fall, "South Viet-Nam's Internal Problems," 250–251; and Catton, *Diem's Final Failure*, 51–56.

[6] Edward Miller, *Misalliance: Ngo Dinh Diem, the United States, and the Fate of South Vietnam* (Cambridge, MA: Harvard University Press, 2013), 160–177.

[7] Duncanson, *Government and Revolution in Vietnam*, 247.

foster the communal solidarity and type of self-sacrifice his nation-building project demanded. At the same time, they could be used to promote the diversification of Vietnam's agricultural sector through the growth of new cash and industrial crops. While consistent with Diệm's goals for the social and economic development of the South Vietnamese countryside, these land development centers also had a security aspect to them. Part of their aim was to create a "human wall" of settlers along the frontier lands in both the delta and the highlands to thwart communist incursions through Cambodia and Laos. In the Central Highlands these centers were concentrated in the provinces of Darlac, Pleiku and Kon Tum, which all lay along the Cambodian border.[8]

Though land development was quite successful in certain cases, it did engender its own animosities. Many of these sites were located in inhospitable and malaria-ridden lands ill-suited for agriculture. Few would-be settlers wanted to move there, forcing some local officials to resort to either trickery or coercive measures to get them to move.[9] More problematic was that many were on lands that Vietnam's ethnic minorities had previously considered their own and were vital to their own "slash and burn pattern of agriculture."[10] As we have seen, during the colonial period, these ethnic minorities had been granted a significant amount of autonomy by the French. In certain cases they had even been encouraged to promote their own anti-Vietnamese brand of ethno-nationalism.[11] Some of the land development centers in the highlands had been specifically designated for the ethnic minorities to deal with this. The government hoped to relocate them into these centers in an effort to "Vietnamize" them by bringing them into the national, political and socio-cultural fold and granting them what the Ngôs conceived to be all the benefits of modern Vietnamese civilization such as "schools, hospitals, maternity clinics and the like."[12] Because this policy so blatantly replicated the French imperial project – complete with its own *mission civilisatrice* – it, not

---

[8] Land Reform Programs Before 1954 and Land Reform Program and Achievements Since July 1954, July 31, 1959, Item number 2322032034, TTVVA, (accessed January 29, 2007); Fall, "South Viet-Nam's Internal Problems," 252; Scigliano, *Nation Under Stress*, 104–105, and 114; Catton, *Diem's Final Failure*, 56–63; and Miller, *Misalliance*, 171–177.

[9] Duncanson, *Government and Revolution in Vietnam*, 247; and Catton, *Diem's Final Failure*, 60–61.

[10] George McTurnan Kahin, *Intervention: How America Became Involved in Vietnam* (New York: Alfred A. Knopf, 1986), 99.

[11] Catton, *Diem's Final Failure*, 57.

[12] The quotation is from Our Concept of Development: An Address by The Honorable Vu Van Thai, Director-General of the Budget and Foreign Aid, October 23, 1959, Item

surprisingly, ended up creating more problems than it solved. Some of the officials sent to perform these relocation tasks were unsympathetic to the sensitivities of the ethnic minorities. One province chief in Bình Long referred to the ethnic minorities as "primitive" and backward.[13] Other government representatives looked down upon them as "inferior" or "savage."[14] Often the government employed heavy-handed techniques to forcibly move these highland populations.[15] Consequently, the minority populations were rather suspicious of the ethnic Vietnamese settlers and officials sent to their territory from Sài Gòn and were quite vulnerable to communist influence. The Hà Nội government seized on this opportunity going to great lengths to court the ethnic minorities, they sent cadres versed in their ethnic dialects and customs to agitate for autonomy, as well as recruit members of the minority populations to travel to Hà Nội for guerrilla and political training. Compared to the relative autonomy they had enjoyed previously and the efforts of the communists to woo them, the practices of the Sài Gòn government appeared particularly harsh and resulted in many local armed rebellions.[16]

number 1780612031, TTVVA (accessed February 2, 2007). See also Catton, *Diem's Final Failure*, 57.

[13] Tỉnh TrưởngBình LongKính gởi Ông Bộ Trưởng Tại Phủ Tổng Thống [Memorandum from the Binh Long Province Chief to the Secretary of State for the Office of the President], February 4, 1959, Folder 16922, Phủ Tổng Thống Đệ Nhất Cộng Hòa [Office of the President of the First Republic] (hereafter PTTĐICH), Trung Tâm Lưu Trữ Quốc Gia II [National Archives 2] (hereafter TTLTQG2). See also Tờ Trình Tháng Hai Năm 1957 Dại Biểu Chánh Phủ Cao Nguyên Trung Phần [February 1957 Statement from the Highland Delegate], April 15, 1957, Folder 16301, PTTĐICH, TTLTQG2.

[14] Luther A. Allen and Pham Ngoc An, *A Vietnamese District Chief in Action* (Washington, DC: Department of State, Agency for International Development, 1963), 11 states that the Vietnamese are "chiefly an agricultural people of the plains and still have some fear of the mountainous regions where the water is unhealthy and the people are savage." See also Kahin, *Intervention*, 99; Fall, "South Viet-Nam's Internal Problems," 252; Scigliano, *Nation Under Stress*, 4; and Roy Jumper, "Problems of Public Administration in South Viet Nam," *Far Eastern Survey* 26(12) (December 1957): 188. Even the Ngôs viewed the Montagnards as ignorant and backwards. In a meeting with General Maxwell Taylor Diệm referred to the Montagnards as "child-like" and lacking "initiative and leadership qualities," Telegram From the Embassy in Vietnam to the Department of State, September 22, 1962 *Foreign Relations of the United States, 1961–1963*, Vol. 2,*Vietnam* (hereafter *FRUS*) (Washington, DC: United States Government Printing Office, 1990), 643. See also Catton, *Diem's Final Failure*, 49; and Thomas L. Ahern, Jr., *CIA and the House of Ngo* (Langley, VA: Center for the Study of Intelligence, declassified 2009), 153.

[15] Catton, *Diem's Final Failure*, 60.

[16] Scigliano, *Nation Under Stress*, 31 and 181–182; Kahin, *Intervention*, 99; and Catton, *Diem's Final Failure*, 57. See Hướng Công Tác Công Dân Vụ trong Giai Đoạn Hiện tại [Present Line of Action of Civic Action], September 30, 1960, Folder 17185, PTTĐICH, TTLTQG2 for a discussion of communist attempts to sabotage efforts to bring the highland populations into the South Vietnamese body politic.

It is unclear what impact these controversial policies like land reform and land development had on the Civic Action cadres' relationship with the people. The documents are silent on these matters, although it is unlikely that the state would blame its own policies for the rising unrest. The cadres were involved in these programs to one degree or another. In terms of land reform, they shared the responsibility for explaining the policies to the population either in village meetings, or through publications made available in the information rooms they helped to construct in the villages.[17] Regarding the land development centers, the cadres played a supporting role in the rather successful pilot project at Cái Sắn in the fall of 1956. Unfortunately the information available about Cái Sắn is fleeting and part of more general operation reports that merely acknowledge the CDV cadres' involvement.[18] What can be assumed is if the policy was unpopular so too would be those who were associated it.

More damning to the fortunes of the regime was its unwillingness to tolerate any opposition to its rule. It employed a variety of near-dictatorial means to quell any dissent including harsh restrictions on freedom of speech, the manipulation of the electoral process as seen in the referendum against Bảo Đại, the intimidation of political opponents, including arbitrary arrest, and, of course, the military clamp-down on the politico-religious sects and the Bình Xuyên criminal syndicate. Each of these measures served to disaffect significant noncommunist segments

---

[17] Thuyết Trình về dự án sắc lệnh thiết lập Phủ Đặc Ủy Công Dân Vụ [Lecture on establishing the Special Commissariat for Civic Action], September 24, 1955, Folder 1463; Sắc Lệnh [Decree], November 18, 1955, Folder 797, PTTĐICH; and Báo Cáo Tổng Quát Hoạt Động Tháng 9 1955 [September 1955 Comprehensive Operation Report], October 19, 1955, Phủ Thủ Tướng Chính Phủ [Office of the Prime Minister of the Government] (hereafter PTTCP), TTLTQG2.

[18] Báo Cáo Hoạt Động Tháng 10 1956 [October 1956 Operation Report], November 22, 1956; and Báo Cáo Hoạt Động Tháng 11 1956 [November 1956 Operation Report], December 11, 1956, Folder 16063, PTTĐICH, TTLTQG2. Evidence exists to indicate that this participation in resettlement activities continued through 1960 as cadres reported working on "Vietnamization" efforts of Montagnards in model villages. The report, however, only mentions this work in passing, revealing no details as to what this entailed or how it was received. Hướng Công Tác Công Dân Vụ trong Giai Đoạn Hiện tại [Present Line of Action of Civic Action], September 30, 1960, Folder 17185, PTTĐICH, TTLTQG2. In October 1960 a report from Tuyên Đức indicates the Civic Action group was establishing a land development center in his province the previous month, but again no specific details are provided. Báo Cáo Tình Hình Chung của Tỉnh Đoàn Công Dân Vụ 570 Đà Lạt Tuyên Đức về tháng 9 năm 1960 [General Situation Report of Civic Action Province Group 570 Dalat Tuyen Duc for September 1960], October 12, Folder 17181, PTTĐICH, TTLTQG2.

of the population who might otherwise have allied themselves with the government and actively supported its nation-building project.[19]

Of all the repressive tactics employed by the regime to root out its opponents, by far the most devastating in terms of turning people against it was the Denounce the Communist Campaign (*Tố Cộng*). While communist denunciation proved to be disastrous for the southern communists in the short-run, it had the long-term effect of driving many previously neutral or noncommunist Vietnamese who were either caught up in the sweeps, or had relatives that had been affected, into the communist camp.[20] Many of the people targeted in this campaign were not, in fact, communists. Initially, they were a collection of disenchanted elements of the population who found themselves categorized as one of the regime's "three enemies."[21] This was particularly true of former members of the Việt Minh who were still favorably regarded by much of the population for their sacrifices in achieving Vietnamese independence from the French.[22] According to one source from the Mekong Delta province of Định Tường:

People with no ties to the Viet Minh were regarded as good citizens and those who had relatives in the Viet Minh were regarded as "incomplete citizens" [*công*

---

[19] See, for example, Seth Jacobs, *Cold War Mandarin: Ngo Dinh Diem and the Origins of America's War in Vietnam, 1950–1963* (Lanham, MD: Rowman & Littlefield Publishers, Inc., 2006); Jessica Chapman, *Cauldron of Resistance: Ngo Dinh Diem, the United States, and 1950s Southern Vietnam* (Ithaca, NY: Cornell University Press, 2013); and Nhu-An Tran, "Contested Identities: Nationalism in the Republic of Vietnam (1954–1963)," Ph.D. diss. (University of California, Berkley, CA, 2013).

[20] Jeffrey Race, *War Comes to Long An: Revolutionary Conflict in a Vietnamese Province* (Berkeley, CA: University of California Press, 1972), 19; Catton, *Diem's Final Failure*, 64–65; Stanley Karnow, *Vietnam: A History*, 2nd rev. ed. (New York: Penguin, 1997), 243; and Sheehan, *Bright Shining Lie*, 186–193. The numbers of suspected communists—real or imagined—who were detained or executed varies widely between accounts of the period. Neil Sheehan, for example, reports that by 1957 of the 8,000 to 10,000 of the original cadres that stayed behind in the South following the resettlement of 1954 only 2,000 to 2,500 remained, Sheehan, *Bright Shining Lie*, 191. According to David Anderson, throughout 1957, the Diệm regime continued to arrest 5,000 suspects and execute over 150 each month, Anderson, *Trapped by Success*, 166. Robert Brigham argues that this denunciation campaign was followed by an even more repressive anti-communist campaign in the urban centers in 1958 that resulted in the jailing, torture and execution of many more thousands; Robert Brigham, *Guerrilla Diplomacy: The NLF's Foreign Relations and the Viet Nam War* (Ithaca, NY: Cornell University Press, 1999), 9. George Kahin cites official statistics from the Republic of Vietnam's Ministry of Information which states that between 1954 and 1960, 48,250 communist suspects were jailed. Kahin, *Intervention*, 96.

[21] Tran, "Contested Identities," 25–27.

[22] Sheehan, *Bright Shining Lie*, 190–192; and Kahin, *Intervention*, 96.

dân không hoàn toàn], who were kept under watch and given indoctrination. These families were isolated in every sphere. Even in going to the rice fields they had to report ... and "good citizen families" were not allowed to assist them.[23]

This stigma, undoubtedly, would have engendered lasting suspicion and resentment among those identified as "incomplete citizens," potentially making their lives untenable.

This was potentially quite problematic for the members of the Commissariat for Civic Action. At its most fundamental, the mission of the Civic Action cadres was to win adherents to the government's cause. Communist denunciation, while eliminating opponents of the regime, clearly alienated significant portions of the rural population. The reports indicate that the cadres actively participated in this campaign, organizing rallies, rooting out suspected communists and propagandizing against the perceived treachery of the enemy. However, these same reports provide no critical evaluation of how this activity was received by the population. If anything, they detail enthusiastic participation in the program by the peasantry.[24] There are several possible reasons for this rosy picture.

First, it could be a reflection of the general unwillingness of officials who feared losing their privileged positions by currying disfavor with the palace through negative reports. Criticism of cadres' involvement in communist denunciation would most likely have been dismissed, if not met with derision, in Sài Gòn given the palace's tendency to view communist supporters as nothing more than dupes of a foreign ideology.[25]

Second, the cadres themselves may have possessed little sympathy for the concerns of those who sided – or were suspected of siding – with the communists as some of their members were being targeted for assassination.[26] Finally, the campaign itself was becoming so widespread that those who opposed its more drastic measures felt it was better to hold their tongues lest they be suspected of harboring communist sympathies and end up in a re-education center. Whatever the reason for the silence on the

---

[23] Quoted in Elliott, *The Vietnamese War*, 189.

[24] See for example Báo Cáo Thành tích Hoạt Động tháng 10 1957 [October 1957 Report of Operation Achievements], November 14, 1957, Folder 16295, PTTĐICH, TTLTQG2; and Thomas L. Ahern, Jr., *CIA and Rural Pacification in South Vietnam* (Langley, VA: Center for the Study of Intelligence, declassified 2007), 19.

[25] Catton, *Diem's Final Failure*, 88–89. The palace's position on communism as an alien ideology is made explicitly clear in Speech of the Head of Vietnam's Delegation to the Bandung Conference, April 29, 1955, Item number 2321503034, TTVVA (accessed March 25, 2009).

[26] See for example Báo Cáo Hoạt Động Tháng 2 1957 [February 1956 Operation Report], March 6, 1957, Folder 16295, PTTĐICH, TTLTQG2.

negative impact of the communist denunciation campaign, its exclusion from the reports served to mask the reality that this program was not having the desired effect of pacifying the South Vietnamese population.

Indeed, even for the members of the South Vietnamese population who may not have been affected directly by the communist denunciation campaign, the regime's efforts to promote a revolutionary program to win adherents was running up against other, more germane societal forces at work. While Diệm may have been offering his particular vision of a postcolonial South Vietnamese state, David Hunt has demonstrated that members of Vietnam's southern peasantry had been wrestling with their own individualistic conceptions of what a postcolonial future should offer. A new, younger generation was rejecting the traditional familial relationships and village patterns of life and attempting to seize control of their own destinies on an individual basis. The disillusionment that was emerging from the failures of the Diệm regime's land reform policies and the increased resentment toward Sài Gòn's draconian security measures had served to fuel this restlessness among the South Vietnamese youth.[27] This created a potent mix for those loosely organized southern elements that were already disaffected by the regime to capitalize on. These opponents of the government, drawn from the remnants of the politico-religious sects, the Bình Xuyên, marginalized opposition parties, among others, joined with the remaining – though significantly depleted – stay-behind communists to do away with "the entire socioeconomic elite which constituted the foundation of the Saigon regime."[28] Acting on their own, they saw an opportunity to "appropriate" this discontent among the peasantry and mobilize it toward the fulfillment of "their vision of a new society."[29] They employed "a complex combination of appeals, incentives, psychological manipulation, threats and terror" to entice the peasantry to act. Not surprisingly, the boldest members of the village community could be found amongst its youth, so they were often targeted as a "key ingredient" to help entice "the hesitant majority" into becoming "fully engaged in the revolutionary movement."[30]

Since Vietnam had been divided at the seventeenth parallel in 1954 the area of greatest strength for opposition to the Diệm government was the

[27] David Hunt, *Vietnam's Southern Revolution: From Peasant Insurrection to Total War* (Amherst, MA: University of Massachusetts Press, 2008), 7–28.
[28] Chapman, *Cauldron of Resistance*, 189–193 and Hunt, *Vietnam's Southern Revolution*, 29–42; the quotation is taken from a Rand interview and can be found on page 7.
[29] Hunt, *Vietnam's Southern Revolution*, 7–8.
[30] Elliott, *The Vietnamese War*, 214.

Mekong Delta.[31] The region's scattered pattern of settlement significantly exacerbated the security problem; it was virtually without roads and thinly populated with villages and hamlets "strung out for miles along canals and waterways," long making it a haven for dissident elements.[32] During the war with the French, the communists had managed to establish a strong organization within the most heavily populated provinces of the Mekong Delta and had established two major bases of operations in Tây Ninh province along the Cambodian border and Phước Thành province northeast of Sài Gòn.[33] Such areas served as welcome bases for the South Vietnamese communist elements in the wake of Diệm's Denounce the Communist Campaign enabling them to easily re-entrench themselves and organize self-defense with the local population.[34] This was evident in the March 1957 monthly Civic Action Operation Report which stated that the cadres were still facing their greatest challenges in the provinces of Tây Ninh – which the month before had seen five CDV cadres assassinated – and Kiến Tường, which also lay along the Cambodian border west of Sài Gòn. Both provinces had reported that communist elements had been allowed to infiltrate from Cambodia for the previous nine years and were thoroughly entrenched in these regions.[35]

As 1957 progressed, more indications of unchecked enemy activity began permeating some of the other monthly reports. No doubt, some of this reporting was a reflection of Civic Action's limited reach in the countryside. However, it also coincided with changes in the strategy of the leadership of the southern communist party. Since the summer of 1954, the Democratic Republic of Vietnam had officially pinned its hopes for reunifying North and South Vietnam on the 1956 nationwide elections stipulated in the Geneva Accords. Weariness and a need to consolidate its hold on power in the North following the war with the French necessitated the communist regime wait for the elections to reunify the country.[36]

[31] Hướng Công Tác Công Dân Vụ trong Giai Đoạn Hiện tại [Present Line of Action of Civic Action], September 30, 1960, Folder 17185, PTTĐICH, TTLTQG2.

[32] Catton, *Diem's Final Failure*, 66 and 73; see page 66 for the quote; Sheehan, *Bright Shining Lie*, 72–74.

[33] David Kaiser, *American Tragedy: Kennedy, Johnson, and the Origins of the Vietnam War* (Cambridge, MA: The Belknap Press of Harvard University Press, 2000), 61.

[34] Kahin, *Intervention*, 108; Scigliano, *Nation Under Stress*, 137.

[35] Báo Cáo Thành tích Hoạt Động tháng 3 1957 [March 1957 Report of Operation Achievements], April 9, 1957, Folder 16295; and Báo Cáo Tổng Kết Năm 1957 [1957 Comprehensive Report], January 10, 1958, Folder 16294, PTTĐICH, TTLTQG2.

[36] Anderson, *Trapped by Success*, 165–166. Kahin, *Intervention*, 102. Robert Brigham concurs with these points, but argues that few party leaders in the North actually expected the elections to occur, Brigham, *Guerrilla Diplomacy*, 4. Pierre Asselin argues that while

This effectively meant that the government in Hà Nội would only sanction political struggle in the South and condemned armed struggle. The southern party apparatus attempted to adhere to these instructions to the best of its ability. According to one former member of the resistance "the policy of the Party headquarters was to block, slow down, and neutralize the implementation of policies by the enemy administration, and prepare to transform their government into our government when the general election came, and to use this government to protect our cadres."[37] In Định Tường (Mỹ Tho),[38] cadres were instructed to turn themselves in to the southern authorities and "legalize" themselves, confessing to their revolutionary past and "registering as citizens of the GVN [Government of Vietnam]." This would ease government suspicion of their activities, allowing them to more freely operate in a clandestine manner among the people. Unsurprisingly, this policy soon fell out of favor with the regional party authorities. They began to question the loyalty of the "legalized" cadres and appeared to drop them from the party rolls.[39] More troubling to the southern communists was that this passivity helped to enable the communist denunciation campaign and other subsequent draconian measures such as Ordinance Number 6, which was launched in January 1956 and called for the imprisonment or house arrest of anyone considered a danger to "the defense of the state and public order," to further deplete the party's ranks in the South.[40]

This posed a challenge for politburo in Hà Nội. Once it was clear the national plebiscite to unify Vietnam would not be held and the communist denunciation sweeps were taking their toll the southern party leadership, in June 1956, allowed for the use of arms in self-defense in certain cases. This was affirmed by Hà Nội, with a caveat that the emphasis was still to be placed on political struggle.[41] By the spring of 1957, armed propaganda and self-defense had gradually morphed into a limited, but more systematic, "extermination of traitors" program which involved the select kidnapping and execution of local officials and other government

"some revolutionaries believed" the elections would be held, "many others were skeptical, including Ho Chi Minh." Pierre Asselin, "Le Duan, the American War, and the Creation of an Independent Vietnamese State," *Journal of American-East Asian Relations* 10(1–2) (Spring–Summer 2001): 4.

[37] Quoted in Elliott, *The Vietnamese War*, 179.

[38] During the period of French rule this province was known as Mỹ Tho, following the end of the Franco-Việt Minh war it was called Định Tường.

[39] Elliott, *The Vietnamese War*, 220–221.

[40] Kahin, *Intervention*, 96–97. See also Karnow, *Vietnam*, 243.

[41] Elliott, *The Vietnamese War*, 218–219.

cadres.[42] This is quite possibly a reflection of events beginning to take on a life of their own in the South quite apart from the wishes of the leadership in the North. At this point the leadership in Hà Nội was still quite reluctant to advance any radical policy below the seventeenth parallel that could provoke an armed struggle against the southern regime that they felt they were too ill-prepared to support.[43]

According to the May 1957 operational report the more distant corners of Vĩnh Long and Vĩnh Bình provinces, where neither regional authority nor a military presence had been fully established, reported a heavy "Việt Cộng" influence, and the people were unable to see the "just cause" of the Sài Gòn government.[44] In the more removed locations in the coastal lowlands to the north there was also some cause for concern. The previous month, the Special Commissariat noted that in the mountainous regions of Quảng Nam, where the rice paddies produced weak harvests, the people were at the mercy of the extortive pressures of the "Việt Cộng", such as pillaging and taxes, and were vulnerable to communist efforts to disrupt the work of the Civic Action cadres.[45] Subsequent reports from the CDV indicated the situation was not improving. By the late summer of 1957 the reported communist presence in these remote regions was such that cadres were either unable to overcome this enemy influence in order to execute their programs and policies, or, in extreme circumstances did not even "dare to work."[46]

In the Central Highlands, the relative autonomy that the ethnic minorities had enjoyed during the French period had combined with the dense jungle and mountainous terrain of its border areas with Cambodia and Laos to make it another haven for communist insurgents in the South.[47]

[42] Kahin, *Intervention*, 107.

[43] Pierre Asselin, *Hanoi's Road to the Vietnam War, 1954–1965* (Berkeley, CA: University of California Press, 2013), 46–49. See also Elliott, *The Vietnamese War*, 223.

[44] Báo Cáo Thành tích Hoạt Động tháng 5 1957 [May 1957 Report of Operation Achievements], June 7, 1957, Folder 16295, PTTĐICH, TTLTQG2

[45] Báo Cáo Thành tích Hoạt Động tháng 3 1957 [March 1957 Report of Operation Achievements], April 9, 1957, Folder 16295, PTTĐICH, TTLTQG2

[46] Quote from Báo Cáo Thành tích Hoạt Động Tháng 7 1957, [July 1957 Report of Operation Achievements], August 10, 1957, Folder 16295, PTTĐICH, TTLTQG2. Báo Cáo Thành tích Hoạt Động tháng 10 1957 [October 1957 Report of Operation Achievements], November 14, 1957, Folder 16295, PTTĐICH, TTLTQG2 also discusses the difficulties in overcoming the communist presence.

[47] Memorandum from T.J. Farrell, Mission Liaison Representative for National Security to Joseph Starr, Chief, Public Administration Division, April 18, 1955, Subject Files, 1954–1958, Box 2, Record Group 469, National Archives and Records Administration; Catton, *Diem's Final Failure*, 73; Anderson, *Trapped by Success*, 162 and176; and Scigliano, *Nation Under Stress*, 139–141.

The following year sporadic attacks by disgruntled members of the ethnic highland population put pressure on their communist allies to help them organize an armed uprising in the Trà Bồng district of Quảng Ngãi.[48] In April 1958, three Civic Action cadres were killed in a marketplace attack in Kiến Tường.[49] Shortly thereafter, cadres of the southern party in Định Tường began to shift their tactics away from open political agitation toward clandestine struggle by secretly working to rebuild the party's base in the province.[50] Though by no means a sustained insurgency, these examples indicate that government control in the countryside was being increasingly contested, particularly on the periphery where its influence was quite circumscribed. By 1959 it was becoming increasingly clear that if something could not be done to establish order in these regions and provide substantive benefits for the welfare of the people in a way that the regime's opponents could not match resistance could grow and embolden more and more members of South Vietnamese society who were feeling disaffected by the policies of the government to join them.

CIVIC ACTION, COMMUNITY DEVELOPMENT AND THE BURGEONING INSURGENCY

Despite the increasing incidents of resistance in the countryside, Cung believed his community development plan was making headway in realizing the palace's vision for the national development of South Vietnam. In this he would have found assurance in the palace as Diệm saw this insurgent activity as an affirmation of his nation-building policies – the desperate last gasp of his enemies before they yielded before the "the superiority of the RVN model of economic and social development."[51] As far as Cung would have been concerned, his biggest problem was responding to the province chiefs' requests for more cadres in the field. The Commissariat claimed it had 2,162 active cadres in April 1959, but despite the best efforts of Kiều Công Cung this was not enough to reach the areas of the countryside removed from the district and provincial capitals and the major lines of communication that connected them.[52] Not

---

[48] Kahin, *Intervention*, 108–109.
[49] For the account of the ambush, see Elliott, *The Vietnamese War*, 234.
[50] *Ibid.*
[51] Miller, *Misalliance*, 178 and 188–189. The quote is from page 188.
[52] Nhiệm vụ chủ trương đường lối hoạt động thành tích và chương trình công tác của Phủ Đặc Ủy Công Dân Vụ [Achievements from the line of action and program of action for the Commissariat for Civic Action], October 3, 1959, Folder 16919, PTTĐICH, TTLTQG2.

all of these cadres could be expected to remain in the field. Many were routinely recalled from the field to undergo intensive training sessions from experts in agricultural and economic development, information and propaganda, and rural reconstruction and healthcare for Cung's ambitious community development plan. Accelerating the plan by recalling more and more cadres for specialization, however, placed an added stress on an already overstretched program. Province and district group chiefs were forced to transfer more and more individuals in and out of villages to fill the gaps left by the departed cadres. Many rural development projects were slowed or brought to an outright halt due to the consequent shortage in manpower.

Unfortunately, the Commissariat lacked the funding and institutional resources to recruit and train enough cadres to alleviate the situation. Diệm was reluctant, at this stage, to reach out to the Americans for additional funding as he felt it might jeopardize South Vietnam's closely guarded sovereignty and compromise the basic premise of self-sufficiency that undergirded the community development plan. Already he had run into problems with the American mission over his land development scheme. Where Diệm had seen the program as a vehicle for promoting South Vietnam's self-sufficiency through reliance on its human and material resources – much like community development – the American advisers felt Diệm should use it as an opportunity to win more adherents to the regime by demonstrating his benevolence. They wanted the Sài Gòn government to offer financial and technical assistance to help the farmers purchase and develop the newly available land, and they were willing to help fund it as long as it met this criterion. Diệm, however, believed the new settlers had certain obligations to fulfill toward the regime before he could offer such concessions. Only after they proved their worthiness to the regime by voluntarily adhering to the principles of communal self-help to make the land a productive commodity for the state would he be willing to give them title to their plots. Fearing this approach would only alienate these potential allies of the state, the American mission cut-off funding for the program in 1958.[53]

On April 24 the Commissariat issued new instructions to the provinces designed "to reorganize and close the ranks of the cadres" to deal with the manpower shortage.[54] All nonspecialized cadres were to be recalled from the field to be reconstituted into larger, mobile groups that would

[53] Miller, *Misalliance*, 175–177; and Catton, *Diem's Final Failure*, 62–63.
[54] Tờ Trình Kính gởi Ông Bộ Trưởng Tại Phủ Tổng Thống [Memorandum (from the Commissariat for Civic Action) to the Secretary of State for the Office of the President], April 4, 1959, Folder 16921, PTTĐICH, TTLTQG2. See also Phiếu Trình về Phát Triển

move from province to province for an indeterminate period of time. The size of the group and length of time they would spend in a particular place would be determined by the needs of the region and "the ability of the cadres to cope with the nature of the situation."[55] They would operate under the authority of the province chief, but only be responsible for three types of activities to try to streamline their activity: politics and organization, administration and training, and rural reconstruction.

Politics and organization referred to propagandistic and security related activities such as collecting intelligence on the enemy and convincing these opponents of the regime to turn themselves in; re-educating citizens who rallied from the enemy to the government through political indoctrination sessions; organizing citizens groups; and mobilizing the people to carry out the government's plans for social and economic development. Administrative and training work dealt with efforts undertaken by the cadres to help support the local authorities. It included assisting the village councils and their chiefs, strengthening the interfamily groups and training citizens' self-defense groups, and inspecting and keeping tabs on the population. Rural reconstruction referred to the nonspecialized tasks that supported community development work such as helping to build model villages, assisting in the development of irrigation projects and the construction and repair of bridges and roads.

Those cadres that had already received specialized training would continue to carry out their community development projects in the provinces in their capacity as representatives of the ministry that had trained them. Cung hoped that enough specialized cadres would be trained by the ministries in the near future to "guarantee" that these ministries would have their own representatives in the field so they would not have to be dependent on the already overextended nonspecialized cadres to continue the community development plan.[56] In May, he recalled 860 cadres for training in order to accelerate the plan.[57] Since this would leave just over

Cộng Đồng [Report on Community Development], ND, Folder 16922, PTTĐICH, TTLTQG2.

[55] Phủ Đặc Ủy Công Dân Vụ trực thuộc Phủ Tổng Thống Việt Nam Nam Cộng Hòa [(Memorandum) Commissariat for Civic Action, Office of the President of the Republic of Vietnam], April 24, 1959, Folder 16921, PTTĐICH, TTLTQG2.

[56] *Ibid.*

[57] Nhiệm vụ chủ trương đường lối hoạt động thành tích và chương trình công tác của Phủ Đặc Ủy Công Dân Vụ [Achievements from the line of action and program of action for the Commissariat for Civic Action], October 3, 1959, Folder 16919, PTTĐICH, TTLTQG2. It is unclear how many of these cadres were already doing specialized community development tasks. From the way the report is written, it is safe to assume that

1,300 cadres in the field this suggests the intent of these reforms was to give the work of the nonspecialized cadres more direction and focus at a time when the increased demand for the activities of fewer available cadres threatened to dilute their effectiveness.[58] This was particularly important as the restlessness in the countryside threatened to derail activities currently being coordinated by only a few cadres in remote settings. By concentrating a large number of cadres in one place for an indefinite period of time they stood a better chance of effecting meaningful change in that area and solidifying support for the regime at a time when it was coming increasingly into question.

One downside of the new instructions was that their implementation was going to be extremely disruptive. Many province chiefs resisted.[59] In Long An, for example, the province chief argued on two separate occasions that withdrawing a number of the cadres to the Central Services would interrupt the administrative work they were assisting the village officials with and hinder the implementation of community development as there would no longer be enough mobile cadres to go out and explain the theory behind this government policy.[60] In the Central Highlands, the Central Government Delegate complained that the absence of cadres would halt the assimilation of their "Highland compatriots."[61] One

---

some of these cadres were specialized, meaning that the 1,302 cadres the report indicated remained in the field were not all nonspecialized cadres.

[58] Phiếu Trình về Phát Triển Cộng Đồng [Report on Community Development], ND, Folder 16922, PTTĐICH, TTLTQG2.

[59] For general complaints against the request see, for example, Tỉnh TrưởngPhước ThanhKính gởi Ông Đặc Ủy Công Dân Vụ [Memorandum from the Phuoc Thanh Province Chief to the Commissariat for Civic Action], May 1959, Folder 16921, PTTĐICH, TTLTQG2, there was no date on the report beyond May 1959, though it is stamped as being received in the Office of the President of the Republic of Vietnam on May 19, 1959; and Tỉnh Trưởng Bình Định Kính gởi Ông Đặc Ủy Công Dân Vụ [Memorandum from the Binh Dinh Province Chief to the Commissioner General for Civic Action], May 12, 1959, Folder 16921, PTTĐICH, TTLTQG2.

[60] Tỉnh Trưởng Long An Kính gởi Ông Đặc Ủy Công Dân Vụ [Memorandum from the Long An Province Chief to the Commissioner General for Civic Action], May 6, 1959; and Tỉnh Trưởng Long An Kính gởi Ông Đặc Ủy Công Dân Vụ [Memorandum from the Long An Province Chief to the Commissioner General for Civic Action], May 13, 1959, Folder 16921, PTTĐICH, TTLTQG2. For similar concerns about the potential disruption of community development work following the reassignment of cadres see, for example, Tỉnh Trưởng Phước Thanh Kính gởi Ông Đặc Ủy Công Dân Vụ [Memorandum from the Phuoc Thanh Province Chief to the Commissioner General for Civic Action], May 1959, Folder 16921, PTTĐICH, TTLTQG2. In this report the province chief complained that the palace's request would leave his province with only six cadres, when he believed the minimum number required was one hundred.

[61] Đại Biểu Chánh Phủ tại Cao Nguyên Trung Phần Kính gửi Ông Bộ Trưởng Tại Phủ Tổng Thống [Memorandum from the Delegate for the Central Highlands to the Secretary

province chief argued that the reorganization would deprive him of indigenous highland cadres who served as a crucial counterweight to communist influence over the ethnic minorities.[62] Realizing the potential disruption the new orders could cause in the countryside the palace quickly made the Commissariat suspend the order. Instead, it asked Cung to get each province chief to inform him of the minimum number of cadres it believed necessary to maintain operations in the province while the Commissioner General attempted to figure out how to proceed.[63]

As these deliberations were going on, the Sài Gòn government implemented two new measures to deal with the stepped-up communist threat in the countryside: the Agroville Program and Law 10/59. Beginning in February 1959 the government started to forcibly regroup people living in insecure areas into one of two types of "agglomeration" centers. The first, called "regrouping zones," were for families that were considered favorably disposed, or at least vulnerable, to the communist insurgents because one or more of their members had moved north in 1954–1955. The second were called "regrouping hamlets" and were intended to provide protection from communist intimidation to peasants considered loyal to the government. Unfortunately, as one scholar notes, for the inhabitants of these regroupment centers, it was "an arbitrary and entirely security-oriented operation" that engendered bitter reaction in both groups of settlers, resulting in the program's overhaul later that spring.[64]

of State for the Office of the President], May 22, 1959, Folder 16921, PTTĐICH, TTLTQG2. Similar concerns were raised in Bình Định province. Tỉnh Trưởng Bình Định Kính gởi Ông Đặc Ủy Công Dân Vụ [Memorandum from the Binh Dinh Province Chief to the Commissioner General for Civic Action], June 5, 1959, Folder 16921, PTTĐICH, TTLTQG2.

[62] Tỉnh Trưởng Ninh Thuận Kính gởi Ông Đặc Ủy Công Dân Vụ [Memorandum from the Ninh Thuan Province Chief to the Commissioner General for Civic Action], May 20, 1959, Folder 16921, PTTĐICH, TTLTQG2.

[63] Tỉnh Trưởng Long Khánh Kính gởi Ông Bộ Trưởng Nội Vụ, [Memorandum from the Long Khanh Province Chief to the Minister of the Interior], May 22, 1959; Bộ Trưởng tại Tổng Thống kính Ông Đại Biểu Chánh Phủ tại Cao Nguyên Trung [Memorandum from the Secretary of State for the Office of the President to the Delegate for the Central Highlands], June 17, 1959; Tỉnh Trưởng Bình Tuy Kính gửi Đặc ỦyTrưởng Công Dân Vụ [Memorandum from the Binh Tuy Province Chief to the Commissioner General for Civic Action], June 25, 1959; Folder 16921, PTTĐICH, TTLTQG2.

[64] Quote from Catton, *Diem's Final Failure*, 65; Joseph J. Zasloff, *Rural Resettlement in Vietnam: An Agroville in Development* (Washington, DC: Department of State, Agency for International Development, 1963), 6–8; and Scigliano, *Nation Under Stress*, 178–179. See also Allen and Pham Ngoc An, *A Vietnamese District Chief in Action*, 44–45 for a description of regroupment into agglomeration centers in Quảng Nam province.

On July 7, 1959 the palace formally announced a new regroupment program that would relocate the peasantry into new "prosperity and density centers," or agrovilles. The Agroville Program, which concentrated its efforts on the Mekong Delta, reflected the regime's belief in population redistribution and land development as the keys to establishing a vibrant and self-sufficient agricultural sector. Though, unlike the land development program, which dealt with the overpopulation of the northern and central provinces by resettling people across vast swathes of uncultivated territory, the agrovilles focused on concentrating segments of the widely dispersed population of the Mekong Delta into confined and manageable tracts of land. It called for the construction of new model settlements that would be divided into residential, commercial and government sections according to a master plan. The new inhabitants would theoretically be provided with security from the insurgents and enjoy the amenities of modern urban life such as electricity, schools, maternity hospitals and market centers. The Sài Gòn government intended for these new centers to serve as rural showcases that would hopefully stimulate regional development and further the Ngôs' Personalist Revolution. Each agroville was projected to hold about 400 families, or around 2,000 to 3,000 people. These inhabitants would purchase small plots of land from the government at a low price and on credit for residences and gardens but they could also retain their old properties outside of the agroville to tend during the day.[65]

The initial plan called for the construction of twenty-four agrovilles with the expectation that the number would rise to as many as eighty new settlements encompassing up to half a million people if the program's most ambitious plans were ever carried out.[66] As a revolutionary project, Philip Catton observes, the agrovilles sought to put an end to the people's "physical and spiritual isolation" by integrating them into new, thriving and modern communities that would make them aware of the "larger national entity to which they belonged." Consistent with the Personalist ethos of communal self-improvement, the new inhabitants were expected to voluntarily prepare these sites by building access roads, canals and their new dwellings, often with their own tools. Through

---

[65] Zasloff, *An Agroville in Development*, 9–11; Scigliano, *Nation Under Stress*, 179; Catton, *Diem's Final Failure*, 63–64; and Miller, *Misalliance*, 177–180. Additionally, in June 1960 the government proposed the construction of a number of smaller agro-hamlets that would be clustered as satellites to the larger centers and house approximately 120 families each.

[66] Scigliano, *Nation Under Stress*, 179; and Catton, *Diem's Final Failure*, 63.

this popular participation the government believed the peasantry would "realize what the individual could achieve through united action" as well as develop "a new generation of rural leaders to replace the parochial and backward-looking ancient regime" which the government associated with feudalism.[67]

Whereas the Agroville Program attempted to separate the enemy from the peasantry, Law 10/59 sought to eliminate the enemy altogether. This draconian measure, passed in May, surpassed the previous excesses of the communist denunciation campaign by broadening the scope of what constituted a treasonous crime from past association with the Việt Minh to any form of political opposition. Not only did this narrow the already proscribed scope of what was deemed permissible dissent, but it further elevated the stakes for those who were considered offenders. In the past, under the communist denunciation campaign, some suspected communists had been executed or subject to torture, most of the accused, however, had only endured punishments ranging from little more than a few weeks in an indoctrination camp to a prison term of six months to three years. Under the new law special military courts had the power to sentence any transgressors to life imprisonment or death.[68] Roving tribunals began circulating throughout the countryside serving, at times, as judge, jury and executioner to any individual suspected of holding any political connections with the North.[69]

The introduction of these measures at a time when the mission and organization of the Commissariat were being debated ultimately affected the direction the Civic Action program would take in the second half of 1959. The Commissariat settled on maintaining its complement of province groups rather than completely reconstituting the nonspecialized cadres into larger interprovince groups, but they retained a degree of flexibility in the size of each group which allowed Sài Gòn to concentrate groups of cadres in certain areas. For example, some cadres were transferred en masse to the twelve provinces of the southeast to participate in a single pacification campaign.[70]

---

[67] Catton, *Diem's Final Failure*, 66–67. Quotes from page 67. See also Zasloff, *An Agroville in Development*, 1 and 10.

[68] Kahin, *Intervention*, 97–98; and Elliott, *The Vietnamese War*, 196. For a copy of Law 10/59 see Appendix A in Allen and Pham Ngoc An, *A Vietnamese District Chief in Action*, 69–71.

[69] William J. Duiker, *Ho Chi Minh: A Life* (New York: Theia, 2000), 518.

[70] Tờ Trình về việc Phân Phối Cán Bộ Công Dân Vụ [Report on the Distribution of Civic Action Cadres], May 29, 1959, Folder 16922, PTTĐICH, TTLTQG2.

In the western provinces of southern Vietnam, where the insurgents appeared most active, Civic Action cadres participated in stepped-up security and administration operations that were consistent with the harsh tenor of Law 10/59. In the eastern provinces, they helped the people establish agrovilles. To the north, in the central and highland provinces of South Vietnam, they attempted to consolidate Sài Gòn's control over the countryside by working with the citizens' organizations like the National Revolutionary Movement and venturing out on patrols with highland groups loyal to the government.[71] To be sure, they did not abandon their other responsibilities, like political organization, training and administration, and community development. In many ways this work complemented the new security measures. Participation in policing the countryside meant the cadres would work with the security forces to weed out opponents of the government for punishment or re-education. Partnering with the citizens groups to expand the government's reach involved a considerable amount of organization as new recruits were enlisted and new interfamily associations established. The basic developmental idea behind the Agroville Program adhered very much to the principles of self-help and self-sufficiency that underpinned the community development plan. Indeed, at this time South Vietnam was considered an important part of the "International Community Development Movement" and slated to host the Community Development Research Conference of East Asia the following year.[72] But the cadres' initial involvement in these security-oriented measures portended a subtle shift away from the fundamental mission of Civic Action which was to foment the palace's Personalist Revolution.

Whether this diversion would be permanent or temporary would ultimately depend upon the success of these measures and the cadres' own abilities to continue to perform the work of Civic Action and community development under these new conditions. Unfortunately, the records from the Commissariat for Civic Action are spotty for the next fifteen months. The available evidence indicates that the new measures implemented by the government failed to have the desired effect. Passage of Law 10/59 enabled all the discontent that had been building up in response to the excesses of the Diệm regime to boil over. According to David Elliott, Law 10/59 "negated whatever progress the GVN had made in legitimating its

---

[71] Sự Phát Triển của Cơ Quan Công Dân Vụ và Thành Tích 7 Năm [Development of Civic Action and Seven Years of Achievements], July 1961, Folder 444, PTTĐICH, TTLTQG2.

[72] Phiếu Trình về Phát Triển Cộng Đồng [Report on Community Development], ND, Folder 16922, PTTĐICH, TTLTQG2.

claim to rule and now made it clear that the regime would rest on naked power and coercion." Rather than stand before the kangaroo courts of the communist denunciation campaign, local offenders could be summarily executed on the spot for their alleged political beliefs – some by guillotine.[73] This had profound consequences for the government, particularly as corrupt local officials would exploit the law when arbitrarily accusing people who had fallen out of favor with them of harboring communist sympathies. Moderates who lay at the fringe of the revolutionary movement quickly came round to the conclusion that they had little to lose by throwing their lot behind the southern militants.[74]

In more and more areas across the country the balance began to shift away from the government as a tepid peasantry began to show their disaffection with the regime and actively support the revolutionary militants. In June, cadres began to agitate more openly, using megaphones to disseminate their propaganda, ripping down and destroying government flags and tearing up the hated house numbering signs which indicated a member or members of that dwelling were suspected of having ties to the regime's opponents.[75] These activities rapidly escalated to the point where insurgent groups began to contest some of the sweeps of the Sài Gòn military forces and even undertake offensive action against certain military outposts.[76] On July 8, 1959 insurgents executed a bold attack on an Army of the Republic of Vietnam (ARVN) base in Biên Hòa, just outside of Sài Gòn, resulting in the deaths of two American advisers and the wounding of one other.[77] At the end of August, sources in the Democratic Republic of Vietnam reported that sixteen villages in Quảng Ngãi had been "completely liberated" from South Vietnamese forces and the rebellion had begun to spread to adjacent districts.[78] By December, local members of the communist party in Long An province had reorganized and rearmed a number of province main force battalions, and rebuilt traditional base areas that had been used during the war against the French.[79]

Meanwhile, the Agroville Program was faltering in its ability to live up to the palace's expectations. Where Diệm had hoped the agrovilles would

---

[73] According to Edward Miller the Diệm regime employed the guillotines to execute supposed communists, including a portable device that could be brought by the special military tribunals to the villages. Miller, *Misalliance*, 201.

[74] Elliott, *The Vietnamese War*, 196–197. See also Hunt, *Vietnam's Southern Revolution*, 34.

[75] Elliott, *The Vietnamese War*, 231.

[76] Kahin, *Intervention*, 107–109. See also Catton, *Diem's Final Failure*, 70.

[77] Kahin, *Intervention*, 111.

[78] *Ibid.*, 111; Duiker, *Ho Chi Minh*, 518; and Kaiser, *American Tragedy*, 63.

[79] Race, *War Comes to Long An*, 113.

protect the peasantry of the Mekong Delta from the predations of the communist party while simultaneously saving them from the deprivations of what he saw to be their wretched existence, the peasants saw them quite differently. According to United States Ambassador Elbridge Durbrow, the Agroville Program was a major "cause of peasant disgruntlement."[80] For those southern revolutionaries who sought to make themselves "the subjects as well as the objects of modernization" such an initiative must have pointed to the further bankruptcy of the southern regime.[81] The last thing that would have resonated with them would have been a plan from the capitol that partnered the promise of a better future with a heavy-handed relocation effort. As for the uncommitted peasantry, this could only have increased their sense of alienation from the government. Robert Scigliano, a political scientist with the Michigan State University Group, contends that they were expected to leave their ancestral lands with their family tombs, established gardens and orchards "for a desolate plot of ground in a strange place" often located far from the rice fields they needed to work in order to make a living. Once there, they suffered tight budget limitations that provided the provinces with one million piastres (about 13,000 dollars) for each settlement – only about one-third of the estimated costs of the new centers. The peasant "had to build his new house from materials taken from his old one, and his only help from the government was a gift of about $5.50 and the offer of an agricultural loan."[82] To make matters worse, the Sài Gòn government set a fast pace for implementation of the program in the face of the mounting violence in the countryside. Local officials were left with little choice but to resort to the large-scale coercion of the peasantry in order satisfy the demands of their superiors.[83]

Yet, Diệm's Agroville Program should not be seen as a simple exercise of the regime's raw power. He legitimately believed they could offer the dispersed populace of the Mekong Delta a better future in a manner consistent with the Personalist Revolution. But he also clearly failed to understand why the peasantry would object to it. Accordingly, agrovilles

---

[80] Dispatch from the Ambassador in Vietnam to the Department of State, October 7, 1960, *FRUS, 1958–1960*, Vol. 1, *Vietnam* (Washington, DC: United States Government Printing Office, 1986), 590.

[81] Quoted in Hunt, *Vietnam's Southern Revolution*, 8–9.

[82] Quoted from Scigliano, *Nation Under Stress*, 180. See also Dispatch from the Ambassador in Vietnam to the Department of State, October 7, 1960, *FRUS, 1958–1960*, Vol. 1, 590–591; Zasloff, *An Agroville in Development*, 18–21; and Catton, *Diem's Final Failure*, 68 for corroborating accounts of the hardships the agrovilles placed on the peasants.

[83] Catton, *Diem's Final Failure*, 68

made ideal grist for the communist propaganda mills, where the settlements were referred to as "big prisons and hells on earth."[84] At the same time, their strategic value as a measure to cut the population off from dissident elements posed a legitimate threat to the regime's enemies that needed to be dealt with, particularly when some settlements, which were located along main road or water axes, obstructed their freedom of movement. As a result, they were often targets of harassment, sabotage or outright attack from opponents of the regime, further adding to the peasants' misery.[85]

The monthly Civic Action reports for 1960 offer a revealing, though fleeting, picture of the rise and fall of this government initiative. In February, Kiều Công Cung reported that some cadres in the south were reconcentrated to help in the construction of agrovilles.[86] The following month, an inauguration ceremony was held for the program's flagship center in Phong Dinh province.[87] Throughout the spring, the Commissariat regularly reported cadre participation in the "supervision" and "speeding up" of agroville construction.[88] In June, the Commissariat reported forty-two agrovilles were under construction.[89] In July the number had increased to forty-five. At this point, the program appeared to falter.[90] Rather than indicate more centers were being built, the August report simply noted cadres were "actively participating in the action in a number of agrovilles."[91] In September, the same month that Diệm informed the American embassy that he was scaling the program back due to doubts that were emerging in the efficacy of the program, the Commissariat stated they were helping to complete those that were still under construction and reinforcing activities in the spheres of livelihood

[84] Zasloff, *An Agroville in Development*, 25–27. The tract containing the quote is printed in Appendix IV, 39. See also Catton, *Diem's Final Failure*, 69.

[85] Zasloff, *An Agroville in Development*, 26; Catton, *Diem's Final Failure*, 69; Scigliano, *Nation Under Stress*, 180; and Duiker, *Ho Chi Minh*, 509–510.

[86] Báo Cáo Tháng 2, 1960 [February 1960 Report], March 10, 1960, Folder 17180, PTTĐICH, TTLTQG2.

[87] Miller, *Misalliance*, 180–181

[88] See, for example Báo Cáo Tháng 3 năm 1960 [March 1960 Report], April 20, 1960; Báo Cáo Tháng 4 năm 1960 [April 1960 Report], May 18, 1960; and Báo Cáo Tháng 5 năm 1960 [May 1960 Report], June 10, 1960, Folder 17180, PTTĐICH, TTLTQG2.

[89] Báo Cáo Tháng 6 năm 1960 [June 1960 Report], July 11, 1960, Folder 17180, PTTĐICH, TTLTQG2.

[90] Báo Cáo Tháng 7 năm 1960 [July 1960 Report], August 18, 1960, Folder 17180, PTTĐICH, TTLTQG2.

[91] Báo Cáo Tháng 8 năm 1960 [August 1960 Report], September 21, 1960, Folder 17180, PTTĐICH, TTLTQG2.

improvement, "social action and security" in the established facilities.[92] In October, the cadres were only completing agrovilles.[93] The following two months saw no mention of the program at all.[94]

The government came nowhere near completing the forty-plus agrovilles the Civic Action cadres were involved in. Diệm's initial plan had called for eighty agrovilles to be constructed to house half a million people. By the fall, he had limited it to twenty before he subsequently suspended the program as he no longer deemed it effective. It is unclear exactly why Diệm decided to abandon the Agroville Program. As Edward Miller contends, Diệm retained his belief that the program had its merits in terms of the possibilities it offered its inhabitants for a better life. The principle of communal self-help that lay at the heart of the program was a key tenet of the Personalist Revolution. Diệm's concerns, Miller continues, may have arisen from the reports that communist agents had infiltrated the established agrovilles giving them an opportunity to capitalize on, or at least foment, peasant discontent.[95]

It is difficult to determine with any certainty what impact the cadres' association with the increased security measures hallmarked by Law 10/59 and the Agroville Program had on the people's view of the Commissariat for Civic Action. It is not beyond reason to think that all the encouragement and fine sounding rhetoric of community development must have seemed out of step with the reality of the hardship the peasants had to endure, particularly in those cases where it was at the hands of corrupt or overly ambitious government officials.[96] Understandably, amidst the underlying social ferment that pervaded elements of the peasantry such reactionary measures on the behalf of the government most likely served to counteract any gains made by the community development plan. The tension that was emerging between the demands placed on the government by the insurgency and its desire to continue with the larger aims of the Personalist Revolution necessitated the CDV cadres begin to focus their efforts more on countering the former at the expense of the latter.

---

[92] Báo Cáo Tháng 9, 1960 [September 1960 Report], October 17, 1960, Folder 17180, PTTĐICH, TTLTQG2. See Miller, *Misalliance*, 182–183 for a discussion of Diệm's doubts about the program.

[93] Báo Cáo Tháng 10, 1960 [October 1960 Report], November 15, 1960, Folder 17180, PTTĐICH, TTLTQG2.

[94] Báo Cáo Tháng 11, 1960 [November 1960 Report], December 17, 1960; and Báo Cáo Tháng 12, 1960 [December 1960 Report], February 3, 1961, Folder 17180, PTTĐICH.

[95] Miller, *Misalliance*, 183–184.

[96] Catton, *Diem's Final Failure*, 68; and Zasloff, *An Agroville in Development*, 26 and 30–31.

Over the course of 1960 this shift toward a greater role in security was evident. In February, the Commissariat reported that due to the changing situation in the countryside the cadres were placing greater emphasis on "propagandizing" about the work of community development rather than mobilizing the people to engage in it.[97] Civic Action cadres in Sài Gòn became involved in population control efforts such as issuing plastic identity cards and organizing youth groups such as the Republican Youth Movement to challenge the appeal of the communists to what seemed a particularly vulnerable demographic.[98] Those in the frontier provinces of the Central Highlands and coastal lowlands found themselves attached to military patrols venturing into the dense jungle and mountainous terrain.[99] In the Mekong Delta more and more nonspecialized cadres were assigned to armed propaganda units that would coordinate with the administrative, security and military units in the delta provinces to help village and hamlet officials who were besieged by insurgents.[100] Consistent with Law 10/59, part of their role involved striking back at the enemy by helping to "lead the people" to denounce and "exterminate the communists."[101]

Despite this increased emphasis on security the community development effort continued, only under more challenging conditions for the Civic Action cadres. During this period of heightened unrest, the regions of each province were divided into one of three categories depending on the level of government control – secure, relatively secure, and insecure – while certain zones of each province were designated "essential" in terms of their economic, political and strategic value as communication hubs.

---

[97] Báo Cáo Tháng 2, 1960 [February 1960 Report], March 10, 1960, Folder 17180, PTTĐICH, TTLTQG2.

[98] Báo Cáo Tháng 7 năm 1960 [July 1960 Report], August 18, 1960; Báo Cáo Tháng 8 năm 1960 [August 1960 Report], September 21, 1960; and Báo Cáo Tháng 9, 1960 [September 1969 Report], October 17, 1960, Folder 17180, PTTĐICH, TTLTQG2. For a description of the interfamily family group see Catton, *Diem's Final Failure*, 14.

[99] Báo Cáo Tháng 3 năm 1960 [March 1960 Report], April 20, 1960, Folder 17180; Báo Cáo Tháng 7 năm 1960 [July 1960 Report], August 18, 1960; Báo Cáo Tháng 8 [August 1960 Report], September 21, 1960; and Báo Cáo Tháng 9 [September 1960 Report], October 17, 1960, Folder 17180, PTTĐICH, TTLTQG2.

[100] Báo Cáo Tháng 3 năm 1960 [March 1960 Report], April 20, 1960; Báo Cáo Tháng 6 năm 1960 [June 1960 Report], July 11, 1960; Báo Cáo Tháng 7 năm 1960 [July1960 Report], August 18, 1960; Báo Cáo Tháng 8 [August 1960 Report], September 21, 1960; and Báo Cáo Tháng 9 [September 1960 Report], October 17, 1960, Folder 17180, PTTĐICH, TTLTQG2.

[101] Báo Cáo Tháng 4 năm 1960 [April 1960 Report], May 18, 1960; see also Báo Cáo Tháng 5 năm 1960 [May 1960 Report], June 10, 1960, Folder 17180, PTTĐICH, TTLTQG2.

The *secure* areas were those regions that possessed villages where the enemy had little or no influence over the people. *Relatively secure* areas were subject to periodic enemy harassment, but managed to enjoy uninterrupted government service and the free movement of Civic Action cadres to the more remote regions. These areas were typically under the protection of nearby military posts. The *insecure* areas were those that suffered both constant "Việt Cộng terror" and exiled village or hamlet administrations and could only accommodate CDV cadres during the daytime.[102] Though vague on details, the reporting from 1960 indicates that in this environment the cadres were increasingly reconcentrated into larger groups to "do the work of Organization, Training" and community development.[103] In the latter capacity their activities included guiding the development of model villages and hamlets in the more secure areas of the countryside and mobilizing some of the highland groups to embrace the government's plans for their modernization in the mountainous regions.[104] Additionally, during this period, regular classes were held at the Cadre Training Center in Sài Gòn for secretarial staff, new cadres, and district and province group chiefs.[105]

Unfortunately, this increased focus on the security effort by the CDV appeared to be paying few dividends. In the autumn of 1960 a series of appraisals from the each of the provinces in the four regions of southern Vietnam – the Central Highlands, the coastal lowlands, the southeastern provinces and the southwestern provinces of the Mekong Delta – depicted a troubling scene overall. In the Central Highlands, where the cadres' work faced the least amount of disruption, the picture was the best. Aside from sporadic acts of resistance, antigovernment activists as a whole had not yet organized themselves into armed units. For the most part, the greatest challenge the Civic Action cadres encountered

---

[102] For a description of the various zones see Hướng Công Tác Công Dân Vụ trong Giai Đoạn Hiện tại [Present Line of Action of Civic Action], September 30, 1960, Folder 17185, PTTĐICH, TTLTQG2. For representative reports that refer to these areas see the February Report and the September Report.

[103] Báo Cáo Tháng 2, 1960 [February 1960 Report], March 10, 1960; see also Báo Cáo Tháng 3 năm 1960 [March 1960 Report], April 20, 1960, Folder 17180, PTTĐICH, TTLTQG2.

[104] See for example Báo Cáo Tháng 7 năm 1960 [July 1960 Report], August 18, 1960; and Báo Cáo Tháng 8 [August 1960 Report], September 21, 1960, Folder 17180, PTTĐICH, TTLTQG2.

[105] Báo Cáo Tháng 3 năm 1960 [March 1960 Report], April 20, 1960; Báo Cáo Tháng 7 năm 1960 [July 1960 Report], August 18, 1960; Báo Cáo Tháng 8 [August 1960 Report], September 21, 1960; and Báo Cáo Tháng 9 [September 1960 Report], October 17, 1960, Folder 17180, PTTĐICH, TTLTQG2.

was maintaining the loyalty of ethnic minorities who were agitating for regional autonomy.[106] But there were notable exceptions. In Quảng Đức, the CDV province group reported some insurgent activity in the remote villages along the border with Cambodia. In September, approximately 200 communists had crossed into Vietnam to try and build a base of support among the villagers.[107] The following month armed gangs were reportedly occupying schools and harassing villages in the more remote regions of the province.[108]

In the coastal lowland provinces to the east, antigovernment forces regularly intimidated villagers, assassinated local officials, and began ambushing patrols and attacking military posts.[109] In the southeast, the armed violence was widespread. A majority of the rural government organs were still able to function, though the provinces of Tây Ninh, Bình Dương and Phước Thành, which were the worst hit of the region, had seen their government officials and supporters withdraw to the sanctity of the district and provincial centers in the face of insurgent activity.[110] The cadres tried to counter this as best they could. In Quảng Ngãi they organized political indoctrination classes for known Communist Party members in order to convince them to switch allegiance, participate in rural construction projects, and provide information on antigovernment plots and activities.[111]

In the Mekong Delta antigovernment groups led by the communists had been actively promoting their struggle against the Sài Gòn regime

[106] Hướng Công Tác Công Dân Vụ trong Giai Đoạn Hiện tại [Present Line of Action of Civic Action], September 30, 1960, Folder 17185, PTTĐICH, TTLTQG2.

[107] Báo Cáo Tình Hình Chung (Tháng 9 năm 1960) Tỉnh Đoàn Công Dân Vụ 580 Quang Đức [General Situation Report of Civic Action Province Group 580 Quang Duc (for September 1960)], October 10, 1960, Folder 17181, PTTĐICH, TTLTQG2.

[108] Báo Cáo Tình Hình Chung (Tháng 10 năm 1960) Tỉnh Đoàn Công Dân Vụ 580 Quang Đức [General Situation Report of Civic Action Province Group 580 Quang Duc (for October 1960)], November 11, 1960, Folder 17181, PTTĐICH, TTLTQG2.

[109] Hướng Công Tác Công Dân Vụ trong Giai Đoạn Hiện tại [Present Line of Action of Civic Action], September 30, 1960, Folder 17185, PTTĐICH, TTLTQG2; and Báo Cáo Tình Hình Chung [Quảng Nam] (tháng 10 năm 1960) [General Situation Report (Quang Nam) (for October 1960)], November 16, 1960, Folder 17181, PTTĐICH, TTLTQG2.

[110] Hướng Công Tác Công Dân Vụ trong Giai Đoạn Hiện tại [Present Line of Action of Civic Action], September 30, 1960, Folder 17185, PTTĐICH, TTLTQG2. See Báo Cáo Tổng Tình Hình Chung Của Tỉnh Đoàn Công Dân Vụ 150 Phước Thành về Tháng 9-1960 [General Situation Report of Civic Action Province Group 150 Phuoc Thanh for September 1960], October 4, 1960, Folder 17181, PTTĐICH, TTLTQG2 for specific examples of the violence being perpetrated against the population and administration.

[111] Báo Cáo Tình Hình Chung Tháng 9-1960 của Tỉnh Đoàn CDV 660 Quảng Ngãi [General Situation Report for September 1960 of Civic Action Province Group 660,

among the people by compelling them to attend meetings and demonstrations in an effort to broaden the base of their underground network of agitators. These actions, according to an official report, had impacted heavily on the operation of many rural government organs. In the face of the threat of assassination provincial and local officials were resigning their posts or fleeing to the safety of the larger cities and towns, bringing the overall work of provincial reconstruction to a standstill. Here the CDV cadres were extremely circumscribed in their activities. In many places, they required the protection of the South Vietnamese military to be able to carry out their work or had to withdraw to the security of the district seat or a military post in the evening to avoid being assassinated in their sleep. Even when they were acting in villages and hamlets, they were hard-pressed to find local citizens willing to help them, due to the constant threat of a reprisal when the cadres left.[112]

Taken as a whole these reports indicate that by the fall of 1960, the insurgent activity that began in 1959 had taken a solid hold in parts of the countryside resulting in a decisive shift in the work of the cadres away from community development towards security and propaganda. This presented the palace with a fundamental problem. Civic Action was becoming more reactionary in the areas where government control was slipping and ceding the advantage in the struggle to spread its revolutionary ethos to that of its communist-led opponents. Theoretically the advantage should have gone to the CDV cadres. They were supposed to have the resources of the state behind this effort, while the opposition was more or less on its own, receiving limited, though growing support from the government in Hà Nội. But despite the effort to concentrate their forces the South Vietnamese cadres were still finding themselves spread far too thinly and up against an opponent that could move amongst the local population with relative impunity knowing the Civic Action presence in those regions would be fleeting.

Further complicating the situation was the question of what impact the work of community development that was being carried out actually had. There was some indication that the cadres were having a positive influence

Quang Ngai], October 11, 1960, Folder 17181, PTTĐICH, TTLTQG2. Unfortunately, the report does not provide any details regarding the response of the communists undergoing indoctrination, but the overall tone of the document is quite favorable, hinting that some communists or suspected communists may have actually been swayed whether by intimidation or the appeal of the cadres' message to switch their allegiance to the Sài Gòn government.

[112] Hướng Công Tác Công Dân Vụ trong Giai Đoạn Hiện tại [Present Line of Action of Civic Action], September 30, 1960, Folder 17185, PTTĐICH, TTLTQG2.

in some areas despite the stepped-up insurgency. Schools remained open in Gia Định and the illiterate were learning to read.[113] The CDV province group in Kiến Tường reportedly still enjoyed popular support.[114] And the cadres in the Central Highland province of Quảng Đức were said to have maintained their "zealous spirit" in the face of adversity.[115] But with the steady decline in the security situation elsewhere it is difficult to believe that under the existing circumstances much, if any, progress was being made in carrying out the palace's revolution, particularly when the Commissariat as a whole was shifting its emphasis to more heavy-handed counterinsurgency measures. Though the documents say nothing on the matter, it is quite possible that as their mandate became more militarized and therefore reactionary, they may, in the eyes of the peasantry, have been seen as complicit in the more reprehensible actions of the government. Regardless, the cadres found themselves reeling just at the time that the South Vietnamese government was beginning to face its greatest existential threat to date: the emergence of the National Liberation Front.

[113] Báo Cáo Tổng Tình Hình Chung [Gia Định] (Trong Tháng 10–1960) [General Situation Report (Gia Dinh) (for October 1960)], November 16, 1960, Folder 17181, PTTĐICH, TTLTQG2.

[114] Báo Cáo Tổng Tình Hình Chung Tháng 10 năm 1960 Tỉnh Đoàn 270 Kiến Tường [General Situation Report for October 1960 for Province Group 270, Kien Tuong], November 15, 1960, Folder 17181, PTTĐICH, TTLTQG2.

[115] Báo Cáo Tình Hình Chung (Tháng 10 năm 1960) Tỉnh Đoàn Công Dân Vụ 580 Quang Đức [General Situation Report (for October 1960) for Province Group 580, Quang Duc], November 11, 1960, Folder 17181, PTTĐICH, TTLTQG2.

SIX

The Strategic Hamlet Program and Civic Action in Retreat

By the autumn of 1960, the Diệm regime was in trouble. The surge in the level of organized violence that had been occurring throughout the year had begun to erode the ability of the Civic Action cadres to carry out the Personalist Revolution in the countryside. The Commissariat for Civic Action attempted to regroup the cadres into larger units that would either emphasize community development work or security and propaganda as the need dictated. Unfortunately, this reorganization failed to address the other problems that plagued Civic Action, namely the manpower shortages and the potential harm the cadres' association with the regime's heavy-handed security tasks had on their image in the eyes of the people. Civic Action was falling victim to the increasing desperation of the regime, losing its focus on development and becoming, more and more, an extension of the security apparatus of an unpopular government.

Violence in the countryside had become so prevalent that popular education classes were stopped in some regions as cadres were assigned to armed propaganda units. Instead of being rallied to improve village infrastructure, people were recruited to form village security details and build hamlet defenses. In the most vulnerable areas the focus on communist denunciation and political indoctrination of enemy prisoners and suspected insurgents superseded all other tasks. Even then the cadres could only stay in the outlying villages during the day, retreating to the protection of the district capitals or military posts when the enemy came out at night. In extreme cases, cadres could only work when accompanied by the South Vietnamese military. This further reduced their effectiveness as their deployment was contingent on troop availability. By early 1961 it was becoming impossible for the Commissariat to maintain a presence in the countryside that could carry-out the palace's Personalist Revolution, let alone convince the peasantry that their interests lay with the government rather than the opposition. A far more aggressive approach was required.[1] The resulting initiative was the Strategic Hamlet Program, and it ultimately became the Diệm government's final effort to build a viable, independent, noncommunist Vietnam.

THE NEW LINE OF ACTION

In September, the Civic Action province group chiefs had met in the Central Services in Sài Gòn to try to come to terms with the crisis the Commissariat was facing in the countryside.[2] At the conference, the attendees logically concluded that over the preceding six months the armed uprising of the antigovernment forces was compromising the security of the Civic Action cadres and preventing them from remaining in the remote hamlets where they were most urgently needed. The "enemy" was terrorizing the rural population, prohibiting them from participating in the work of rehabilitating the countryside and sabotaging the community development effort. The local village and hamlet authorities were unable to provide much assistance, having "lost their spirit" due to this enemy intimidation. More and more members of the peasantry were becoming content to sit on the fence in the struggle between the government and its opponents, believing that actively supporting the cadres might make them targets of the insurgents.

Taking their cue from Mao Zedong's metaphor for people's war, the Civic Action province group chiefs viewed their opponents as fish who were dependent on a sea of willing supporters for their survival, necessitating they take measures to "dry up the water" to eradicate the threat. They attempted to strike a better balance between security measures that would prevent the people from being "lured into following the enemy" and community development initiatives that would simultaneously encourage them to participate in the struggle against the insurgents on the side of the government. They also conceded that they lacked the necessary

[1] See A Strategic Concept for South Vietnam, February 2, 1962, *Foreign Relations of the United States, 1961–1963*, Vol. 2, *Vietnam* (hereafter referred to as *FRUS*) (Washington, DC: United States Government Printing Office, 1990), 73–90.

[2] Hướng Công Tác Công Dân Vụ trong Giai Đoạn Hiện tại [Present Line of Action of Civic Action], September 30, 1960, Folder 17185, Phủ Tổng Thống Đệ Nhất Cộng Hòa [Office of the President of the First Republic] (hereafter PTTĐICH), Trung Tâm Lưu Trữ Quốc Gia II [National Archives 2] (hereafter TTLTQG2).

manpower to maintain enough of a presence throughout the countryside to provide the people with sufficient assurance to trust the government.

They decided to further consolidate the work of the Civic Action cadres by reorienting their tasks to meet the security needs of the region they were being assigned – secure, relatively secure, insecure and essential. According to the Central Services, the majority of the villages in the center (or northern third of South Vietnam) fell into the secure category. Relatively secure areas were fairly widespread throughout the southeastern provinces, while limited to the district and provincial capitals of the southwest. Most of the villages in the southwestern provinces of the country, particularly the Mekong Delta, fell into the insecure category.

In the secure, relatively secure and "essential zones," the CDV cadres were charged with the three tasks of strengthening the village councils, coordinating and organizing defense and security for the villages, and building "model" areas – self-reliant communities that ascribed to the mutual aid philosophy that underpinned community development. These were a variation of the three activities of politics and organization, administration and training, and rural reconstruction that the cadres had been assigned back in the reorganization that had occurred in the spring of 1959. Strengthening the village councils involved personally assisting the village administrators and organizing self-criticism sessions to identify personal and bureaucratic shortcomings within the local administration. These would be overcome by "scientific administrative practices" and a "democratic style of work" where officials would lead by example by selflessly committing to policies and plans devoted to the betterment of the community. In cases where the councils were short-staffed, they would look to the local population for new recruits. The second task, organizing village defense and security, required the cadres to coordinate with the Ministry of Youth to mobilize the local youth into village defense organizations, reorganizing and broadening mutual aid interfamily groups to help identify and isolate potentially subversive elements, and working with the Civil Guard – a paramilitary force under the control of the province chief – to organize village and hamlet forces that would participate in patrols, guard duty and the establishment of village defenses such as digging ditches and erecting guard posts.[3]

---

[3] Hướng Công Tác Công Dân Vụ trong Giai Đoạn Hiện tại [Present Line of Action of Civic Action], September 30, 1960, Folder 17185, PTTĐICH, TTLTQG2. For a broader discussion of the Civil Guard see Robert Scigliano, *South Vietnam: Nation Under Stress: An Important Look at the Trouble Spot of Asia* (Boston: Houghton Mifflin Company, 1964), 138–140 and 163–167.

Building "model areas" posed the most interesting challenge for Civic Action given the mounting unrest in the countryside. It required putting the theory behind community development to the ultimate test in terms of its effectiveness in creating a "spirit of unity and defence" against an insidious enemy. The Commissariat appears to have hoped the spirit of mutual aid instilled by community development could be translated into a collective effort to strengthen village security. In each secure, relatively secure and "essential" village, the CDV envisioned designating one hamlet as a "model hamlet" where cadres would oversee the necessary tasks that would guarantee the people's material welfare such as ensuring good sanitation, providing adequate irrigation to increase the yields of individual gardens and improving the method of livestock breeding through the teaching of better animal husbandry techniques. At the same time, they would work to convince the community that only by standing together to resist enemy intimidation or entreaties for support could they prevent enemy encroachment. It took just one person to provide communist-led agitators with an opening through which they could infiltrate the community and the cadres needed to make the local inhabitants realize this. Where necessary, the members of the hamlet would be reassembled, reorganized and trained to fight for the government. If the cadres succeeded, these hamlets would then be considered "Strong Points" on which the remaining hamlets of the village could be patterned, leading to the gradual extension of zones loyal to the government across the countryside like an "oil-stain."

As for the insecure areas, the cadres would primarily be focused on participating in security oriented tasks, which included forming armed propaganda groups or coordinating their activities with local self-defense organizations like the regional militia, the Civil Guard, the local police or regular armed forces to eradicate the enemy. They were encouraged to try and bring relief to the beleaguered population by performing limited social and health work such as dispensing medical supplies or handing out awards and gifts to families that had suffered at the hands of the anti-regime forces as well as organizing cultural festivals and events, complete with patriotic songs, plays and movies. These efforts were intended to try and convey to the people a sense that the government was still quite concerned about their plight.

This "New Line of Action" must be seen as a definitive step backward for the Commissariat as it clearly resembled the initial work of the Civic Action cadres when the program was first started in 1955. Community development in the insecure areas had taken a back-seat to "psychological warfare" indicating the extent to which Diệm's opponents were now dictating the course of events in parts of the South Vietnamese countryside. Given this new reality, this reorientation in the direction of Civic Action appeared to offer the Commissariat the best chance to counter the insurgency given the cadres' increasingly circumscribed reach. But this was anything but progress. Previously, when reflecting on the development of the Civic Action program in his policy papers, Kiều Công Cung had described each reorganization of the organ as part of an evolutionary process. Each step marked a progressive milestone in the regime's efforts to extend its reach down to the countryside and build grassroots support for the Sài Gòn government and then its Personalist Revolution and broader nation-building plan.[4] This new policy line, in contrast, can only be described as reactionary – reflective of a failure, in one sense, of the South Vietnamese government to give the people who were increasingly siding with the insurgents a reason to eschew them and support it.

Unfortunately, just as these new measures were put into place, the Commissariat was rocked with the news of Kiều Công Cung's passing. In the summer of 1960 Cung had been sent to France for treatment of an undisclosed stomach ailment. He returned to Vietnam in October, succumbing to his illness on October 20. The president and many other officials from the Sài Gòn government visited Cung's home, where his body lay, to pay their respects.[5] It is unclear what immediate effect Cung's death had on the Commissariat for Civic Action. Western sources are equally as unhelpful. In fact, any American accounts of Cung's death, such as the *Pentagon Papers*, erroneously report it having occurred in 1957 with the remnants of the Special Commissariat coming under the influence of Ngô Đình Nhu.[6] This confusion is reflective of the disinterest the Eisenhower administration had begun to show toward the CDV in 1957. As for the actual timing of Cung's death, its occurrence at such a crucial moment for the organ's fortunes was hardly propitious. Gone

[4] See for example Báo Cáo Tổng Kết Năm 1957 [1957 Comprehensive Report], January 10, 1958, Folder 16294; and Nhiệm vụ chủ trương đường lối hoạt động thành tích và chương trình công tác của Phủ Đặc Ủy Công Dân Vụ [Achievements from the line of action and program of action for the Commissariat for Civic Action], October 3, 1959, Folder 16919, PTTĐICH, TTLTQG2.
[5] Ô Kiều Công Cung Đặc ủy Công Dân Vụ đã tạ thế [Kiều Cong Cung, Commissioner General for Civic Action dies], October 22, 1960, *Cách Mạng Quốc Gia* [National Revolution], 1.
[6] *The Pentagon Papers: The Defense Department History of United States Decisionmaking on Vietnam*, Vol. 1, The Senator Gravel ed. (Boston: Beacon Press, 1971), 306–307. Another work that indicates Kiều Công Cung died prior to 1960 is William Nighswonger, *Rural Pacification in Vietnam* (New York: Praeger, 1966), 36, which states he died in 1957.

was the architect of the government's community development plan. His actions as Commissioner General of the Civic Action program over the previous five years had demonstrated how in tune he had been with the government's nation-building plan. Under his guidance, the Commissariat had been molded into a vehicle for fomenting the Personalist Revolution at the local level. His presence would be sorely missed, particularly as other more ominous clouds were looming on the horizon to the north.

THE EMERGENCE OF THE NATIONAL
LIBERATION FRONT

The rapidly increasing pace of the insurgency in South Vietnam over 1960 both complemented and conflicted with the overall communist struggle for Vietnam, giving it, at times, a shape the party leadership in Hà Nội did not always anticipate or welcome. As we have seen, following the Geneva Accords the Political Bureau (Politburo), the most important policymaking body of the communist party, or Lao Động (the Vietnamese Worker's Party), in Hà Nội had elected to pursue a policy of perfecting socialism in the North before embarking on reunification in the South. This meant that the government in Hà Nội would support no form of resistance to the Sài Gòn regime beyond political agitation. Though the Politburo began to permit some armed resistance, primarily in self-defense, southern cadres were growing increasingly frustrated with the caution displayed by Hà Nội.[7]

This was made clear to one of the rising stars in the Lao Động: Lê Duẩn. Lê Duẩn was a southern-born revolutionary from Quảng Trị province who advocated armed violence in the South. Toward the end of 1958 he took a secret inspection trip below the seventeenth parallel to evaluate the situation there for a major policy review by the Central Committee of the communist party. He found that despite the rise in the level of insurgent activity, the situation was dire for the party in the South due to the communist denunciation campaign. He recommended the formation of a broad-based united front in the South to further the armed struggle and mobilize all the anti-government forces to resist the Sài Gòn regime. This resonated with like-minded members of the Politburo who felt that the rising level of violent resistance to the policies of the South Vietnamese government might overtake their ability to maintain influence over the revolutionary

[7] Pierre Asselin, *Hanoi's Road to the Vietnam War, 1954–1965* (Berkeley, CA: University of California Press, 2013), 46–49.

elements there. They were opposed, however, by moderates who feared a premature uprising in the South could divert attention away from their efforts to install socialist institutions in the North, or worse, precipitate a crisis that could draw the People's Army of Vietnam (PAVN, the North Vietnamese Army) in a conflict in the South for which Võ Nguyên Giáp, the chief military strategist of the PAVN, believed it was unprepared. For nearly two years the Politburo grappled with this question while the myriad elements of the southern resistance struggled to topple the Diệm regime on their own. Lê Duẩn's faction finally won out. In September 1960, he became the secretary general of the Central Committee of the Lao Động and the Politburo agreed to adopt the united front strategy in the South.[8]

That December a group of sixty revolutionaries met near the Cambodian border in Tây Ninh province and established the National Front for the Liberation of South Vietnam. Though the National Liberation Front (NLF) was established to unite all southern opponents of the government of Ngô Đình Diệm, and was open to any individual regardless of political affiliation, its leadership was dominated by the communists and they clandestinely used this organization "to promote the Party's ideological values and policies as widely as possible."[9] Two months later on February 15, 1961 the communist party organized the "People's Liberation Armed Forces," or "Liberation Army of South Vietnam," a military organization to bring under one unified command all of the militant liberation forces agitating against the Sài Gòn regime.[10]

For some in Hà Nội, the establishment of the NLF provided the party with the chance to try to establish control over what some members of the Politburo must have considered a spontaneous and increasingly violent revolt in the South.[11] For others, like Lê Duẩn, it was the culmination

[8] Lien-Hang T. Nguyen, *Hanoi's War: An International History of the War for Peace in Vietnam* (Chapel Hill, NC: University of North Carolina Press, 2012), 31–47; Pierre Asselin, "Le Duan, the American War, and the Creation of an Independent Vietnamese State," *Journal of American-East Asian Relations* 10(1–2) (Spring–Summer 2001): 5–11; Asselin, *Hanoi's Road to the Vietnam War*, 41–67, 76–78 and 82–87; William J. Duiker, *Ho Chi Minh: A Life* (New York: Theia, 2000), 499 and 503–505; Robert Brigham, *Guerrilla Diplomacy: The NLF's Foreign Relations and the Viet Nam War* (Ithaca, NY: Cornell University Press, 1999), 8–10; and David W.P. Elliott, *The Vietnamese War: Revolution and Social Change in the Mekong Delta 1930–1975*, Vol. 1 (Armonk, NY: M.E. Sharpe, 2003), 229.

[9] Brigham, *Guerrilla Diplomacy*, 9–11. See also Duiker, *Ho Chi Minh*, 523–527.

[10] Philip E. Catton, *Diem's Final Failure: Prelude to America's War in Vietnam* (Lawrence, KS: University Press of Kansas, 2002), 75.

[11] The following discussion about the different interpretations of the formation of the NLF is based on the studies of the southern revolution in Định Tường (Mỹ Tho) province

of the long and drawn out battle to finally get the official seal of approval from the DRV for a strategy that effectively recognized the need for armed struggle to bring about the overthrow of the South Vietnamese government. For the Lao Động as a whole, the decision to proceed with the establishment of the NLF allowed the party to subsequently claim credit for organizing an ultimately successful resistance effort against the Republic of Vietnam.

In the South, the establishment of the NLF had a somewhat different meaning. According to David Hunt, the "concerted uprising" that began in the South in 1959 "was the sum total of many hamlet revolts, each marked by its own lurches and delays" that "spread unevenly from hamlet to hamlet over a period of months and years." It emerged from "an encounter between a small number of instigators and a rural population that was ready to move." In Định Tường the creation of the NLF "came as an afterthought to revolutionaries who were already deciding on their own what sort of liberation they were striving to achieve."[12] Rather than an "inclusive coalition" of anti-Diệm elements that wanted to facilitate reunification with the North on Hà Nội's terms, these southern activists were striving to bring down the "entire socioeconomic elite which constituted the foundation of the Saigon regime."[13] Indeed, David Elliott concludes that the NLF, as conceived by the Lao Động, "never played a significant political role" in Định Tường. The resistance that started there in 1959 was seen as a " 'front,' which eventually disappeared from view."[14] It was only after the people became aware of the decisions made in Hà Nội regarding the resistance in the South did they begin to associate the NLF with the goal of national unification. At this point, Hunt argues, any use of the term NLF in Định Tường referred to "structures the party helped to install in 1961 and after" – a far different connotation than the "movement" that started to emerge in 1959 and "took an unqualified 'liberation' as its watchword."[15]

The decisions taken by the Lao Động to proceed with the establishment of such a broad-based organization provided an outlet for other southern elements which until then had remained silent in their

---

by David Hunt and David Elliott. David Hunt, *Vietnam's Southern Revolution: From Peasant Insurrection to Total War* (Amherst, MA: University of Massachusetts Press, 2008), 29–46 and Elliott, *The Vietnamese War*, 212–283.

[12] Hunt, *Vietnam's Southern Revolution*, 30–33.
[13] *Ibid.*, 7.
[14] Elliott, *The Vietnamese War*, 271–272.
[15] Hunt, *Vietnam's Southern Revolution*, 37.

displeasure with the Diệm government to openly resist. One group made up of noncommunist resistance fighters that included former leaders and members of the Việt Minh, representatives of the Buddhists, Cao Đài, Hòa Hảo, Catholics and individuals with no political affiliation, accused what they termed the "American-Diệm" (*Mỹ-Diệm*) regime of having declared "open war" against all opposition elements in the South. These oppositionists appealed to all classes of the population to join them in the struggle against this repression by putting an end to the Diệm government and liberating their country from what they saw as untoward American influence on Vietnamese affairs. In its stead, they proposed a broad coalition government composed of representatives from across the political and social spectrum that would rigorously apply the terms of the Geneva Accords and enter into discussions with North Vietnam over peaceful reunification.[16]

How the Commissariat responded to the changing circumstances depended on the relative level of security and preexisting social and economic conditions of the region in which the NLF and Civic Action cadres were acting. In the Central Highlands, the CDV province group chief of the more prosperous province of Tuyên Đức was able to maintain a positive air in his reports. Noting little change in the security situation between November and February, he claimed that the public still exhibited a "spirit of voluntarism" and readily participated in the work of community development throughout the province.[17] In neighboring Quảng Đức, the security situation had begun to deteriorate, which was particularly alarming as throughout the fall of 1960 this province had only been subjected to insurgent activity in its more remote areas, such as the border regions with Cambodia. Between January and April 1961 enemy activity escalated notably in districts and villages that had once been reported secure.[18]

[16] George McTurnan Kahin, *Intervention: How America Became Involved in Vietnam* (New York: Alfred A. Knopf, 1986), 112–113.
[17] Báo Cáo Tình Hình Chung của Tỉnh Đoàn Công Dân Vụ 570 Đa Lạt & Tuyên Đức về Tháng 12 Năm 1960 [General Situation Report of Civic Action Province Group 570, Da Lat and Tuyen Duc for December 1960], January 16, 1961, Folder 17182; and Báo Cáo Tình Hình Chung của Tỉnh Đoàn Công Dân Vụ 570 Đa Lạt & Tuyên Đức về tháng 02 Năm 1961 [General Situation Report of Civic Action Province Group 570, Da Lat and Tuyen Duc for February 1961], March 17, 1961, Folder 17443, PTTĐICH, TTLTQG2.
[18] This escalated activity included incidents of arson directed at government offices and the dwellings of individual citizens that allegedly resulted in the deaths of young children. Báo Cáo Tình Hình Chung (Tháng giêng Năm 1961) của Tỉnh Đoàn Công Dân Vụ 580 Quảng Đức [General Situation Report (for January 1961) of Civic Action Province Group 580, Quang Duc], February 8, 1961; Báo Cáo Tình Hình Chung (tháng hai Năm

In the coastal lowlands, the situation appeared slightly more promising than before. Province groups in the provinces of Quảng Ngãi and Quảng Nam reported some success in communist denunciation, arguing that the people were turning their backs on insurgent efforts to enlist their support in resisting the government.[19] In Phú Yên province, the Civic Action cadres were able to continue to work "zealously" in the regions that were devoid of any enemy presence. But in areas where there was an enemy presence they were forced to bring a halt to community development tasks and stop holding popular education classes as the cadres who organized these efforts were needed elsewhere.[20]

In the southeastern provinces, the province group chief of Phước Tuy reported a significant increase in enemy action in November while the chiefs of CDV groups in the capital of Sài Gòn and Gia Định maintained that no change had occurred in terms of the level of insurgent activity. Cadres in Bình Thuận reported that efforts to reinforce the rural security apparatus had begun to pay dividends with regard to destroying anti-regime strongholds in certain "essential" areas.[21] But in Tây Ninh, the

1961) của Tỉnh Đoàn Công Dân Vụ 580 Quảng Đức [General Situation Report (for February 1961) of Civic Action Province Group 580, Quang Duc], March 10, 1961; and Báo Cáo Tình Hình Chung (tháng 4 Năm 1961) của Tỉnh Đoàn Công Dân Vụ 580 Quảng Đức [General Situation Report (for April 1961) of Civic Action Province Group 580, Quang Duc], May 11, 1961, Folder 17443, PTTĐICH, TTLTQG2.

[19] Báo Cáo Tình Hình Chung Tháng 2 Năm 1961 của Tỉnh Đoàn Công Dân Vụ 660 Quảng Ngãi [General Situation Report for February 1961 of Civic Action Province Group 660, Quang Ngai], March 7, 1961; Báo Cáo Tình hình chung tháng 1 năm 1961 [Quảng Nam] [General Situation Report for January 1961 (Quang Nam)], February 21, 1961; Báo Cáo Tình Hình Chung (tháng 2 năm 1961) [Quảng Nam] [General Situation Report (for February 1961) (Quang Nam)], March 17, 1961; Báo Cáo Tình Hình Chung (tháng 3 năm 1961) [Quảng Nam] [General Situation Report (for March 1961) (Quang Nam)], April 13, 1961; and Báo Cáo Tình Hình Chung (tháng4 năm 1961) [Quảng Nam] [General Situation Report (for April 1961) (Quang Nam)], May 11, 1961, Folder 17443, PTTĐICH, TTLTQG2.

[20] Báo Cáo Tình Hình Chung tại Tỉnh Phú Yên Tháng 11.1960 [General Situation Report in Phu Yen Province November 1960], December 20, 1960; Báo Cáo Tình Hình Chung Tháng 12 năm 1960 tại Tỉnh Phú Yên [General Situation Report in Phu Yen Province December 1960], January 12, 1961, Folder 17182; Báo Cáo Tình Hình Chung tháng 1-1961của Tỉnh Đoàn 640 Phú Yên [General Situation Report for January 1961 for Province Group 640, Phu Yen], February 20, 1961; and Báo Cáo Tình Hình Chung Tỉnh Phú Yên (tháng 4 năm 1961) [General Situation Report for Phu Yen Province (April 1961)], May 16, 1961, Folder 17443, PTTĐICH, TTLTQG2.

[21] Báo Cáo Tình Hình Chung Hàng Tháng của Tỉnh Đoàn Công Dân Vụ 350 Phước Tuy (từ 1-11 đến 30-11-60) [General Monthly Report of Civic Action province Group 350, Phuoc Tuy (from November 1 to 30, 1960)], November 30, 1960; Báo Cáo Tình Hình Chung của Tỉnh Bình Thuận (Từ.11 cho đến 30.11.1960) [General Situation Report of Binh Thuan Province (From November 1 to 30, 1960)] (from November 1 to 30, 1960)]; Báo Cáo Tình Hình Chung Trong tháng 11-60 [Gia Định] [General Situation Report

birthplace of the National Liberation Front, the communists were making tremendous headway. By February, local village authorities could not
leave the government offices to get near to the people. Village and hamlet
infrastructure was "broken," and rice prices were rising as the peasants
were unable to go to their fields to harvest their crops. Rural improvement had come to a standstill and the people were rapidly losing confidence in their government.[22]

Finally, in the insurgent strongholds of the Mekong Delta, the New
Line of Action appeared to have had the least impact. The activities of
the antigovernment forces increased at a relentless pace. In Kiến Hòa,
the province group chief reported that the mounting terror campaign of
the government opposition meant that any progress made in community
development projects was short-lived and the sphere of action in which
the cadres could operate safely was severely limited.[23] More troubling
was Vĩnh Bình, where the province group chief conceded that in general
the people's morale was shaken in the face of the communist threat and
overall participation in community development activities and communist

    in November 1960 (Gia Dinh)], December 11, 1960, Folder 17182; and Báo Cáo Tình
    hình chung tháng 1 năm 1961 [Sài Gòn] [General Situation Report for January 1961
    (Saigon)], February 23, 1961, Folder 17443, PTTĐICH, TTLTQG2.

[22] Tờ Trình về Tình Hình Chung Hàng Tháng của Tỉnh Đoàn Công Dân Vụ 70 Tây
    Ninh (Tháng 11 năm 1960) [Monthly Report on the General Situation of Civic Action
    Province Group 70, Tay Ninh (November 1960)], December 9, 1960, Folder 17182; and
    Tờ Trình về Tình Hình Chung Hàng Tháng của Tỉnh Đoàn Công Dân Vụ 70 Tây Ninh
    Tháng 2 Năm 1961 [Monthly Report on the General Situation of Civic Action Province
    Group 70, Tay Ninh February 1961], March 10, 1961, Folder 17443, PTTĐICH,
    TTLTQG2.

[23] Báo Cáo Tình hình chung tháng 11–1960 của Tỉnh Đoàn Công Dân Vụ 180 Kiến Hòa
    [General Situation Report for November 1960 of Civic Action Province Group 180, Kien
    Hoa], December 16, 1960; Báo Cáo Tình Hình Chung Tháng 12 của Tỉnh Đoàn Công
    Dân Vụ 180 tại Tỉnh Kiến Hòa [General Situation Report for December 1960 of Civic
    Action Province Group 180 in Kien Hoa Province], January 6, 1961, Folder 17182;
    Báo Cáo Tình Hình Chung Tháng 01 của Tỉnh Đoàn Công Dân Vụ 180 Hoạt Động tại
    Tỉnh Kiến Hòa [General Situation Report for January 1961 of Civic Action Province
    Group 180 for Operating in Kien Hoa Province], February 11, 1961; Báo Cáo Tình Hình
    Chung Tháng 2 của Tỉnh Đoàn Công Dân Vụ 180 Hoạt Động tại Tỉnh Kiến Hòa [General
    Situation Report for February 1961 of Civic Action Province Group 180 Operating in
    Kien Hoa Province], March 3, 1961; Báo Cáo Tình hình chung tháng 3–1961 của Tỉnh
    Đoàn Công Dân Vụ 180 hoạt động tại tỉnh Kiến Hòa, April 6, 1961 [General Situation
    Report for March 1961 of Civic Action Province Group 180 Operating in Kien Hoa
    Province]; and Báo Cáo Tình Hình Chung Tháng 4 năm 1961 của Tỉnh Đoàn Công
    Dân Vụ 180, Hoạt Động tại Tỉnh Kiến Hòa [General Situation Report for April 1961 of
    Civic Action Province Group 180 Operating in Kien Hoa Province], May 4, 1961, Folder
    17443, PTTĐICH, TTLTQG2.

denunciation meetings was on the decline.[24] In Phong Dinh, site of the government's flagship agroville, Civic Action reports from October 1960 through to April 1961 regularly reported that both ordinary citizens and members of the various defense forces were suffering "Việt Cộng intimidation" to the point of impotence. In the remote areas, the regime's opponents brazenly stated that they would overthrow the government and guarantee the property and lives of the people who supported them. Here the people were constantly harassed and the fact that they saw little evidence that the government could prevent this meant very few individuals were willing to cooperate with the authorities to root them out. The province group chief conceded many disgruntled youth were readily enticed to join the National Liberation Front. Members of the Civil Guard, the provincial militia and the Army of the Republic of Vietnam were also regularly targeted by propaganda campaigns aimed at getting them to desert their posts or clandestinely join the NLF in order to create disorder and confusion within their ranks. These defense organs also possessed certain elements that became increasingly disillusioned and were no longer willing to leave their posts to engage the enemy.[25] In Định Tường, the CDV groups reported that anti-regime forces were inciting local vendors to strike, mobilizing villagers to demonstrate against the Sài Gòn regime, and appealing to government soldiers to surrender. Such activities, the group chief argued, were having a terrible impact on the peasantry as they were "alarmed and frightened" and unwilling to participate in the community development projects sponsored by the Civic Action cadres.

[24] Báo Cáo Tổng Tình Hình Chung Của Tỉnh Đoàn Công Dân Vụ 230 Vĩnh Bình trong tháng 10 năm 1960 [General Situation Report for Civic Action Province Group 230 Vinh Binh in October 1960], November 8, 1960, Folder 17181, PTTĐICH, TTLTQG2.

[25] Báo Cáo Tình Hình Chung Hàng Tháng 10 Năm 1960 của Tỉnh Đoàn 50 [Phong Đinh] [General Monthly Situation Report for October 1960 of Province Group 50 (Phong Dinh)], November 3, 1950, Folder 17181; Báo Cáo Tình Hình Chung Hàng Tháng 11 Năm 1960 của Tỉnh Đoàn 50 [Phong Đinh] [General Monthly Situation Report for November 1960 of Province Group 50 (Phong Dinh)], December 7, 1960; Báo Cáo Tình Hình Chung Tháng 12 Năm 1960 Tỉnh Đoàn 50 [Phong Đinh] [General Situation Report for December 1960 of Province Group 50 (Phong Dinh)], January 9, 1961, Folder 17182; Báo Cáo Tình Hình Chung Tháng 1 Năm 1961 Tỉnh Đoàn 50 [Phong Đinh] [General Situation Report for January 1961 of Province Group 50 (Phong Dinh)], February 7, 1961; Báo Cáo Tình Hình Chung Tháng 2 Năm 1960 Tỉnh Đoàn 50 [Phong Đinh] [General Situation Report for February 1961 of Province Group 50 (Phong Dinh)], March 6, 1961; Báo Cáo Tình Hình Chung Tháng 3 Năm 1961 Tỉnh Đoàn 50 [Phong Đinh] [General Situation Report for March 1961 of Province Group 50 (Phong Dinh)], April 1, 1961; and Báo Cáo Tình Hình Chung Tháng 4 Năm 1961 Tỉnh Đoàn 50 [Phong Đinh] [General Situation Report for April 1961 of Province Group 50 (Phong Dinh)], May 8, 1961, Folder 17443, PTTĐICH, TTLTQG2.

In response the CDV cadres tried to coordinate their actions with local militias and the armed forces to try and reassure the people that the government was capable of meeting their needs.[26] In Kiến Phong, as in Định Tường, these measures were wholly inadequate in the face of such an entrenched opposition, leaving many villages in near constant states of "alert," terror or even siege that could only be relieved by increasing the government's military presence.[27]

Taken together, these reports indicate that the overall impact of the October New Line of Action following the formation of the NLF was ambiguous at most. This is best illustrated by the situation in the Mekong Delta province of Kiến Tường. Following the October reorientation of the CDV, the province group chief observed a united spirit among the cadres that was helping to produce favorable results, particularly in the work of purging undesirable elements from local administrations and establishing reliable networks to help eradicate NLF cells in the small villages and hamlets. His province group offered many examples of novel propaganda efforts that were aimed at relieving the plight of the people from theatrical performances to sporting events to the more mundane group meetings and political indoctrination of antigovernment prisoners. These reports noted that Kiến Tường was a somewhat impoverished province, with upwards of 60 percent of the population lacking sufficient food due to a poor harvest and the plundering and terrorism of the "Việt Cộng gangs." For some of those who had been relocated to agglomeration zones for security purposes, the land could be considerably less fertile than that of their homes and, as a result, ill-equipped to provide them with the means to earn any type of a living. Thus, while it appeared that the Civic Action cadres were doing their utmost to provide for both the welfare and security of these people under increasingly difficult circumstances their efforts were ultimately falling short.[28] This is hardly surprising as the New Line

[26] Báo Cáo (Tình Hình Chung tháng 10–1960) [Định Tường] [(General Situation) Report for October 1960 (Dinh Tuong)], November 19, 1960, Folder 17181, PTTĐICH, TTLTQG2.

[27] Báo Cáo Tình Hình Chung Tháng 10 năm 1960 (Kiến Phong) [General Situation Report for October 1960 (Kien Phong)], November 30, 1960, Folder 17181, PTTĐICH, TTLTQG2.

[28] Báo Cáo Tình Hình Chung Tháng 11 năm 1960 Tỉnh Đoàn 270 Kiến Tường [General Situation Report for November 1960, Province Group 270 Kien Tuong], December 19, 1960; Báo Cáo Tình Hình Chung Tháng 12 Năm 1960 Tỉnh Đoàn 270 Kiến Tường [General Situation Report for December 1960, Province Group 270 Kien Tuong], January 13, 1961, Folder 17182; Báo Cáo Tình Hình Chung Tháng 01 Năm 1961 Tỉnh Đoàn 270 Kiến Tường [General Situation Report for January 1961, Province Group 270 Kien Tuong], February 12, 1961; and Báo Cáo Tình Hình Chung Tháng 02 Năm 1961

of Action failed to address one of the main shortcomings plaguing the work of the cadres: the manpower shortage. What was really needed was a massive increase in the number of cadres throughout the countryside. But the South Vietnamese government could not sustain this. As we have seen, Diệm's regime was barely able to meet the financial cost of Civic Action even before it faced a violent and growing insurgency. A bold new initiative would be required if the government hoped to turn the situation around in the countryside.

FROM CIVIC ACTION TO STRATEGIC HAMLETS

In February 1961, as the Civic Action cadres struggled to contend with the insurgency, Ngô Đình Diệm announced that the Commissariat for Civic Action, along with the Directorate General of Information and the Directorate General of Youth, Physical Activity and Sports, would be reorganized into a new Ministry of Civic Action. Their consolidation into one ministry at such a crucial time was an attempt to unify their efforts to better compete with the communist-led challenge in the countryside. It was part of a broader restructuring of the president's cabinet, which further centralized power in the hands of individuals who had demonstrated fidelity toward Diệm and his brother.[29]

The new Ministry of Civic Action officially came into existence on June 6, 1961 with Ngô Trọng Hiếu (see Figure 7) as its head. Hiếu was a devout Catholic, fervent anticommunist and particularly loyal to the president's brother, Ngô Đình Nhu. He had been born just north of Sài Gòn in Thủ Đầu Một in 1912, and had been educated in both Hà Nội and France, where he received degrees from the Universities of Paris and Toulouse, the latter a law degree. Hiếu returned to Vietnam and became a civil servant in the colonial government, where he started working in the Treasury Bureau in 1937, rising to the position of Director by 1954. Between 1956 and 1959 he had served as one of the Republic of Vietnam's representatives to Cambodia. While there he gained considerable notoriety for his alleged involvement in a plot to topple Sihanouk over his policy of neutrality. The intrigue, orchestrated at the apparent behest of Nhu, resulted in Hiếu's expulsion. In the meantime, Hiếu had asserted his anticommunist credentials as editor of the magazine *Sống (To Live)* and through

Tỉnh Đoàn 270 Kiến Tường [General Situation Report for February 1961, Province Group 270 Kien Tuong], March 10, 1961, Folder 17443, PTTĐICH, TTLTQG2.
[29] Edward Miller, *Misalliance: Ngo Dinh Diem, the United States, and the Fate of South Vietnam* (Cambridge, MA: Harvard University Press, 2013), 223.

FIGURE 7 Minister of Civic Action Ngô Trọng Hiếu with the Revolutionary Guard. Vietnam Center and Archive, Texas Tech University

his twenty-nine-year chairmanship of the Association of Victims of Communism.[30]

Despite Hiếu's anticommunism and fidelity to the Ngôs, he was a far cry from Kiều Công Cung. According to Edward Lansdale, he was a bit of a womanizer who was frequently "out on the town."[31] United States

[30] Tiểu sử các vì tân Bộ Trưởng trong chanh phủ VNCH [Biography of the new Minister in the government of the Republic of Vietnam], *Sàigòn Mới [New Saigon]*, May 31, 1961, 1,4; Current Intelligence by the Central Intelligence Agency Office of Current Intelligence, August 28, 1963, Countries: Vietnam 8/28/68 II, Box 3, Roger Hilsman Papers (hereafter RHP); Telegram From the Embassy in Vietnam to the Department of State (Part 2 of 2) Ambassador, June 1, 1961, General 5/25/61 – 5/31/61, Countries: Vietnam, Box 193A, National Security Files (hereafter NSF), John F. Kennedy Library (hereafter JFKL); and William Shawcross, *Sideshow: Kissinger, Nixon and the Destruction of Cambodia*, First Touchstone Edition (New York: Touchstone, 1981), 54–55.

[31] Notebook of Lansdale's from October 1961 trip to Vietnam, [possibly as part of Taylor-Rostow mission], ND, Folder: Materials returned from U.S. D.o.D. (Former) Box 6 Folders 1–2, Box 95, Edward G. Lansdale Papers (hereafter ELP), Hoover Institute (hereafter HI).

Ambassador to Vietnam Frederick Nolting doubted whether he had "the ideas and techniques for successful implementation of Civic Action."[32] And British counterinsurgency expert and adviser to the South Vietnamese government Robert Thompson called the ministry's operations under Hiếu "confused and diversified" with too much emphasis on "the intelligence and military aspects" of Civic Action.[33] This latter comment is particularly revealing, as one of the charges laid by Thompson against Hiếu at the time was that he was attempting to use the Civic Action teams as his own private army, somewhat along the lines of the Hitler Youth.[34]

Though the parallel with Nazi Germany may be a little excessive, there is evidence to support the allegation that following Cung's death the Civic Action cadres were adopting a strikingly military pose. Eight instructors from the Ministry of Civic Action attended a six-week "offshore" paramilitary and intelligence course at the end of 1961 in order to conduct their own training courses for Civic Action cadres at a center near the coastal city of Đà Nẵng.[35] Further reports indicate that between February and April 1962 at least 400 students attended these courses.[36] By late May, Diệm appeared to harbor some reservations about the direction in which the ministry was heading, and ordered the Civic Action teams to "cease functioning as aggressive combat units and be used only for self defense."[37]

[32] Telegram From the Embassy in Vietnam to the Department of State (Part 2 of 2), June 1, 1961, General 5/25/61 – 5/31/61, Countries: Vietnam, Box 193A, NSF, JFKL.

[33] Comments by Mr. R.K.G. Thompson to the Vietnam Task Force, Washington, April 4, 1962, April 9, 1962, Status Reports 4/4/62 – 7/11/62, Vietnamese Subjects, Box 203, NSF, JFKL.

[34] Peter Busch, "Killing the 'Vietcong': The British Advisory Mission and the Strategic Hamlet Programme," *Journal of Strategic Studies* 25(1) (2002): 142.

[35] Status Report on Covert Actions in Vietnam, January 11, 1962, Status Reports 1/4/62 – 4/4/62, Vietnamese Subjects, Box 203, NSF, JFKL. See also Phiếu Trình Kinh để Tống Thống Việt Nam Công Hòa [Report (from the Ministry for Civic Action) to the President of the Republic of Vietnam], December 23, 1961, Folder 17445; and Phiếu Trình Kinh để Tống Thống Việt Nam Công Hòa [Report (from the Ministry for Civic Action) to the President of the Republic of Vietnam], January 16, 1962, Folder 17697, PTTĐICH, TTLTQG2.

[36] This number was compiled from the following reports: Status Report on Covert Actions in Vietnam, January 11, 1962; Status Report on Covert Actions in Vietnam, March 7, 1962, Status Reports 1/4/62 – 4/4/62, Vietnamese Subjects; and Status Report on Covert Actions in Vietnam, April 18, 1962, Status Reports 4/4/62 – 7/1/62, Vietnamese Subjects, Box 203, NSF, JFKL.

[37] Kính gởi Ông Bộ Trưởng Công Dân Vụ, [Memorandum (from the President) to the Minister of Civic Action], May 31, 1962, Folder 17697, PTTĐICH, TTLTQG2; and Covert Annex to Status Report of Task Force Vietnam (29 May to 12 June 1962), ND, Central Intelligence Agency, Library, Freedom of Information Act Electronic Reading

Though it was a step back from the overtly paramilitary role the CDV cadres had been adopting, the overall trajectory of the ministry since Hiếu had taken it over was far removed from the direction Civic Action had been headed under Kiểu Công Cung. No doubt the changes in personnel from Cung to Hiếu were partly responsible for this more militant stance, but it was also a reflection of the demands placed upon the regime by the insurgency. Shortly after 1961 had opened, estimates by the palace placed less than half of the population of South Vietnam under the control of the Sài Gòn government.[38] With its limited resources and manpower, Civic Action was wholly incapable of competing with the insurgents. This increased militancy of the ministry was really a symptom of Civic Action's inadequacy and ultimately portended its end as the primary vehicle for fomenting the palace's Personalist Revolution across the South Vietnamese countryside. To be sure, the ideals of communal self-help which had motivated the Civic Action cadres' work under Kiểu Công Cung continued to animate the government's nation-building agenda. The spirit of community development lived on. But in the face of the sustained violence of the insurgency it had to occur under a new guise which appeared better suited to meet the communist challenge. This was the Strategic Hamlet Program and it became the Ngôs' most ambitious nation-building venture to date.

Placed under the supervision of Ngô Đình Nhu, the program was developed over the autumn of 1961. It attempted to fortify all of South Vietnam's existing hamlets by ringing them with hedges, ditches and fences of sharpened bamboo stakes to keep the insurgents out. In the event a hamlet was located in a supposedly "indefensible area" an entirely new one would be established in a more secure location.[39] Its approach was based on the assumption that most of the peasants who had embraced the insurgents "had been terrorized or duped into standing against" the Sài Gòn government.[40] Special teams were assigned to reorganize the local administration, determine the loyalties of the hamlet's inhabitants, re-establish various citizens' organizations where necessary, and ensure that the local people participated in their own defense. In fact, keeping with the emphasis on self-sufficiency, the palace placed

Room, www.foia.cia.gov/browse_docs.asp?doc_no=0000530481 (accessed February 4, 2009).

[38] Miller, *Misalliance*, 222.

[39] Milton Osborne, *Strategic Hamlets in South Viet-Nam: A Survey and a Comparison* (Ithaca, NY: Cornell University Southeast Asia Program, 1965), 29.

[40] Catton, *Diem's Final Failure*, 88.

the ultimate responsibility for maintaining hamlet security on the actual inhabitants of the hamlet. The residents were to establish their own self-defense forces, much like they had been expected to do with the help of the Civic Action cadres. To give the community a stake in bolstering its security the government initially armed the hamlet inhabitants for a period of six months before withdrawing the weapons. At that point, the defenders were supposed to be dependent on weapons they had captured from the enemy.[41]

This self-reliance reflected the larger purpose of the strategic hamlets in the minds of the Ngôs. They were not strictly a security endeavor. In fact, Nhu contended they were "seven-eighths political and social and only one-eighth military."[42] He and Diệm anticipated the strategic hamlets kindling "a new sense of communal solidarity and national consciousness" within the community capable of "gradually overcoming the isolated and atomized nature of rural life."[43] In other words, the strategic hamlets were intended to engender the people with the collective spirit that had been the hallmark of community development.[44]

In this light, then, the Strategic Hamlet Program can be seen as a direct outgrowth of the Civic Action program, modified to contend with a more sustained insurgency. Addressing the Civil Guard on the seventh anniversary of its founding in April 1962, Diệm echoed earlier statements about the Commissariat when he stated that the strategic hamlets represented the "foundation" of a "new Vietnamese society where values are reassessed according to the spirit of the personalist revolution where social, cultural and economic reform will improve the living conditions of the large working class down to the remotest villages."[45] By providing government cadres with a more secure environment in which to mobilize the rural population, the political, social and economic transformation of

---

[41] Directorate General of Information, *Vietnam's Strategic Hamlets*. (Saigon: Directorate General of Information, 1963), 4–5 and 10; and Catton, *Diem's Final Failure*, 119–121.

[42] Memorandum from Canadian Delegation ICSC, Saigon to the Under-Secretary of State for External Affairs, Ottawa (part 3), October 19, 1962, Folder 50052-A-1–40 pt 3, Box 4639, Record Group 25 (hereafter RG25), Library and Archives Canada (hereafter, LAC).

[43] The quotation is from Catton, *Diem's Final Failure*, 120–121. For the other details see Directorate General of Information, *Vietnam's Strategic Hamlets*, 3–21.

[44] Memorandum From the Department of State, Bureau of Intelligence for the Acting Secretary of State, July 1, 1963, Item number: 2321518004, Texas Tech Virtual Vietnam Archive, www.virtualarchive.vietnam.ttu.edu (hereafter referred to as TTVVA) (accessed February 2, 2007); and Miller, *Misalliance*, 234–235.

[45] Quotations from Osborne, *Strategic Hamlets in South Viet-Nam*, 28. See also, Directorate General of Information, *Vietnam's Strategic Hamlets*, 20–21.

the countryside that had been the fundamental mission of the CDV could still happen.

Socially, the strategic hamlets would establish a new order "built up from the rural areas to replace the elites left over from French colonial times."[46] According to the Canadian Delegate to the International Control Commission (ICC) – the body responsible for overseeing adherence to the provisions of the Geneva Accords – who met with the president's brother, Nhu wanted the hamlet inhabitants to "participate" in "vertical groupings and organizations with some political significance." These would be "small village organizations" that would take on a variety of tasks including "defence of the hamlet, protection of women and children and the organization of various social and possibly economic, and medical services." This would be "obligatory and participation in such organizations would be compulsory."[47] In Nhu's mind, these defense-minded communities would then become the crucible for an entirely new communal hierarchy. At the top would be the combatants and their families, followed by the hamlet leaders and locally elected officials, with the poor peasants and workers comprising the lowest stratum. Such a structure based on merit, Nhu contended, would displace those who received their privileged rank based strictly upon their wealth or level of education.[48] Much like the Civic Action cadres had been intended to replace the *fonctionnaires* Diệm had inherited from the French, Nhu believed the Strategic Hamlet Program could breed a new generation of administrative agents to replace the colonial holdovers "through an authentic Vietnamese revolution based on traditional community values."[49]

Once this "social revolution" was underway and the people had started to "win and earn" the right to enjoy democratic principles the political transformation of the hamlet could begin.[50] As we have seen, the Ngôs'

[46] William Colby with James McCargar, *Lost Victory: A Firsthand Account of America's Sixteen-Year Involvement in Vietnam* (Chicago: Contemporary Books, 1989), 99.

[47] Memorandum from Canadian Delegation ICSC, Saigon to the Under-Secretary of State for External Affairs, Ottawa (part 3), October 19, 1962, Folder 50052-A-1-40 pt 3, Box 4639, RG25, LAC.

[48] Directorate General of Information, *Vietnam's Strategic Hamlets*, 12–13 and 19.

[49] Mieczyslaw Maneli, *War of the Vanquished*, translated by Maria de Gorgey (New York: Harper & Row, 1971), 32–33. See also Memorandum from the Australian Ambassador to Vietnam to the Secretary, Department of External Affairs, Canberra, October 16, 1962, Folder 50052-A-1-40 pt 3, Box 4639, RG25, LAC.

[50] Memorandum from Canadian Delegation ICSC, Saigon to the Under-Secretary of State for External Affairs, Ottawa (part 3), October 19, 1962, Folder 50052-A-1-40 pt 3, Box 4639, RG25, LAC.

particular view of democracy held that the people had to demonstrate that they would be virtuous citizens willing to sacrifice personal interest for the greater good. The strategic hamlets would provide that opportunity. Only then would the government "give back to the hamlet the right of self-government with its own charter and system of community law."[51]

This decentralization of power to the village, as we have already seen, was a crucial element in the Ngôs' vision of postcolonial Vietnam. Under the Strategic Hamlet Program "the basic institutions of direct democracy" would be introduced at the local level through the controlled election of hamlet committees and councils. This system of democracy would then extend outward toward the urban centers and upward through various levels of government. Hamlet members would elect hamlet committees and leaders of local organizations. These would then elect village councils and the leaders of village organizations, and so on up through the district to the province and ultimately national level. Eventually, according to Nhu, the strategic hamlets would "become the real nucleus of national organization" causing the state, in the words of Marx, to "wither away."[52]

Economic change would come last. Nhu felt that security had to be a priority before economic development could occur. As well, he was concerned that without the proper socio-political foundation any initiatives to improve the local economy would tend to favor the wealthy village elites. Once the government was able to turn to the local economy, its efforts were driven by the community development plan. Within the supposedly safe confines of the hamlet's defensive perimeter the people would collectively focus their energy on developing village agriculture and cottage industries that required little external support.[53] Once the insurgency had been defeated, it was hoped that these self-reliant communities would be able flourish through the ingenuity of their enterprising inhabitants.[54]

[51] Quoted in "The Strategic Hamlet Program, 1961–1963," in *The Pentagon Papers: The Defense Department History of United States Decisionmaking on Vietnam*, Vol. 2, Gravel ed. (Boston: Beacon Press, 1971), 148.

[52] The quotes are from Maneli, *War of the Vanquished*, 145. According to the Polish Diplomat, Nhu actually invoked Marx. See also Telegram From the Central Intelligence Agency Station in Saigon to the Agency, November 26, 1962, and Telegram From the Central Intelligence Agency Station in Saigon to the Agency, November 29, 1962, General 11/26/62 – 11/30/62, Countries: Vietnam, Box 197, NSF, JFKL; Catton, *Diem's Final Failure*, 127–128; and Osborne, *Strategic Hamlets in South Viet-Nam*, 29.

[53] Directorate General of Information, *Vietnam's Strategic Hamlets*, 11–12.

[54] Catton, *Diem's Final Failure*, 123–124 and Miller, *Misalliance*, 237–238.

The thread that tied all of this together was Personalism's emphasis on combining individual rights and initiative with collective responsibility. For Nhu, the Strategic Hamlet Program was the "purest formulation of the Personalist philosophy." According to Milton Osborne, an adviser with the Michigan State University Group who performed a study of the Strategic Hamlet Program, the president's brother considered the hamlets to be central to the "moral" development of the population where an "enthusiastic movement of solidarity and self-sufficiency" would flourish.[55] Not only would this eventually bring material benefits, but, as Nhu believed, it could instill the people with a sense of struggle and self-reliance that would help "develop the leadership of a free and authentic Vietnam, neither Communist nor Western in culture or character."[56] As Diệm described it, it was the "quintessence of our truest traditions" and an "outgrowth of our ancestral virtues."[57] Nhu argued that the program sought to "integrate all our policies in the historical movement of the nation" in order to tap into Vietnam's "heritage of struggle" and compel the people to "march toward progress."[58] Just as Civic Action had once been conceived as the vanguard of the Personalist Revolution, now the Strategic Hamlet Program would take up that mantle.

The Strategic Hamlet Program was officially launched on April 17, 1962. Like the community development plan it was coordinated by an inter-ministerial committee – in this case the Interministerial Committee for Strategic Hamlets, chaired by Ngô Đình Nhu. It aimed to convert all of the Republic of Vietnam's 16,000 hamlets into strategic ones.[59] The

---

[55] Osborne, *Strategic Hamlets in South Viet-Nam*, 28. Nhu's quote may be found on the same page.

[56] Colby, *Lost Victory*, 100.

[57] Osborne, *Strategic Hamlets in South Viet-Nam*, 32.

[58] Nhu, Friendly Talk to the Militants, Item number 0440728001, TTVVA (accessed February 2, 2007). See also Telegram From the Embassy in Vietnam to the Department of State, August 23, 1962, General 8/23/62 – 8/31/62, Countries: Vietnam, Box 196A, NSF, JFKL for an earlier account of Nhu placing the Strategic Hamlet Program into a much larger context of Vietnamese history.

[59] Memorandum of a Conversation, May 24, 1962, FRUS, 1961–1963, Vol. 2, 428–30 reports that the palace intended to implement the Strategic Hamlet Program throughout the countryside. The Vietnamese Secretary of State to the President Thuan, who was the source of the information "wryly" noted that the palace intended to complete the program in six months. Memorandum for the Record, September 14, 1962, FRUS, 1961–1963, Vol. 2, 639 reports Nhu telling General Taylor that he envisioned the program encompassing all 16,000 of South Vietnam's hamlets, a process which he envisioned taking three years. See also Catton, *Diem's Final Failure*, 97.

Ministry of Civic Action was included in this inter ministerial committee and its cadres made up one component of the Rural Rehabilitation Teams that were charged with going out into the countryside to implement the program.[60]

These teams were organized and trained by each province to establish strategic hamlets. Each consisted of between ten and twenty individuals drawn from the existing provincial administration, technical services, Civil Guard and Self-Defense Corps – a small local militia intended to defend each village throughout the country – and was led, in some cases, by a member of the Provincial Office of the Ministry of Civic Action.[61] These teams would be responsible for mobilizing the hamlet occupants to transform their community into a strategic hamlet. The Civil Guard and Self-Defense Corps personnel were generally responsible for leading the population in constructing defenses and organizing and training its youth as militia. Similar to the tactics of the Civic Action cadres, other members of the team would be charged with gathering information about all aspects of hamlet life, such as a detailed breakdown of the population by age and sex, the names and attitudes of families with known members in the National Liberation Front, production figures for agriculture and livestock and the conditions of schools, medical dispensaries, temples and other aspects of the hamlet's infrastructure. The Rural Rehabilitation Team would then begin social and political development, explaining the philosophy and objectives of the program, organizing residents into action groups, developing a hamlet charter and arranging for the election of officials by secret ballot. Once these steps had been carried out to the satisfaction of the cadres, the hamlet officials and the district chief, an inauguration ceremony would be held, usually presided over by the province chief, after which the Rural Rehabilitation Team would move

[60] Briefing Paper for a Presentation by the Director of the Vietnam Task Force (Cottrell) Before the Special Group (Counterinsurgency), March 22, 1962, *FRUS, 1961–1963*, Vol. 2, 260. Also see Trình Văn Kính đệ Tổng Thống Việt Nam Công Hòa, [Report (from the Ministry of Civic Action) to the President of the Republic of Vietnam], September 8, 1962, Folder 3406, PTTĐICH, TTLTQG2 which states that the Ministry of Civic Action had periodic monthly meetings with representatives from all levels of the three branches within the ministry to coordinate work to support the national policy of strategic hamlets.

[61] John B. O'Donnell, "The Strategic Hamlet Program in Kien Hoa Province, South Vietnam: A Case Study of Counter-Insurgency," in *Southeast Asian Tribes, Minorities, and Nations*, Vol. 2, ed. Peter Kunstadter (Princeton, NJ: Princeton University Press, 1967), 716–717 where he states that strategic hamlet construction cadres in his province were generally led by young men from the Provincial Office of the Ministry of Civic Action.

on to the next hamlet. The entire process of establishing the strategic hamlet tended to take anywhere from three to eight weeks depending on the attitude of the population toward the government and the degree of NLF penetration.[62]

Once the Rural Rehabilitation Team had moved on, the local strategic hamlet council would be responsible for mobilizing the population to carry out rural rehabilitation work and defense, to make the hamlet as self-reliant as possible. Exemplifying this was the Hamlet Self-Help Program. Much like the community development projects, the Self-Help Program aimed to use the human resources of the hamlet in a collective effort to improve the overall standard of living for the community. The strategic hamlet council would organize a mass-meeting where inhabitants would gather to discuss their social and economic needs and then decide by a vote which were the most pressing. Following the vote, a cost estimate would be submitted along with a request for materials up to the province chief for consideration. Supplies, if available, would be provided by the province or the US aid mission. The manpower would voluntarily come from the hamlet population. This was what was supposed to instill the people with a collective sense of accomplishment and interest in the "development" of their community.[63]

Unfortunately, the available documentary record offers little additional information of the role of the Civic Action cadres in the Strategic Hamlet Program. One initiative was the ministry's establishment of Basic Cadre Teams over the fall of 1962. These three member teams were organized to go out to the strategic hamlets and work alongside the people just as the original Civic Action cadres had. These groups would stay in a hamlet for a period of ten weeks before moving on to another one, returning periodically to oversee the work going on and report back up to the ministry. While in the hamlets, they would assist the people in their daily tasks, help coordinate and carry out hamlet improvements, work

---

[62] USOM Counterinsurgency Program for FY 1963, July 20, 1962; Proposed USOM Counterinsurgency Organization, July 20, 1962; A Report on Counter-Insurgency in Vietnam, August 31, 1962, General, 1961–63 (2), Subject File: Vietnam, Box 49, ELP, HI; A Strategic Concept for South Vietnam, February 2, 1962, *FRUS, 1961–63*, Vol. 2, 78–79, 82–85 and 86–88; O'Donnell, "The Strategic Hamlet Program in Kien Hoa Province," 716–718; and John O'Donnell, "Life and Times of a USOM Prov Rep," in *Prelude to Tragedy: Vietnam 1960–1965*, ed. Harvey Neese and John O'Donnell (Annapolis, MD: Naval Institute Press, 2001), 221.

[63] Bert Fraleigh, "Counterinsurgency in South Vietnam: The Real Story," in *Prelude to Tragedy*, 103; and A Report on Counter-Insurgency in Vietnam, August 31, 1962, General, 1961–63 (2), Subject File: Vietnam, Box 49, ELP, HI.

FIGURE 8 Vietnamese working in a field of plants that is fenced in by a sharp wooden spiked fence. Vietnam Center and Archive, Texas Tech University

with the hamlet council and spend a good deal of time propagandizing on the behalf of the Sài Gòn government.[64]

As a counterinsurgency measure, the palace anticipated the program putting its communist-led opponents on the defensive by cutting them off from the ultimate source of their strength, the people (see Figure 8). This, the government hoped, would force the insurgents to escalate the conflict further by attacking the hamlets directly to get at the peasantry, thus revealing them "as the aggressors" and "the enemy of the people."[65] Deprived of sanctuary and now facing a hostile population, Nhu believed the NLF would then be vulnerable to ambush by special government guerrilla forces which would include "armed villagers."[66] In time, the strategic hamlets

---

[64] Thảo Điều Lệ và Nội Quy Đoàn Cán Bộ Cơ Sở Công Dân Vụ, [Regulations and Statutes for Detachments of Cadres from the Civic Action Group], September 29, 1962, Folder 3016, PTTĐICH, TTLTQG2.

[65] Directorate General of Information, *Vietnam's Strategic Hamlets*, 7.

[66] Memorandum from Canadian Delegation ICSC (part 3), Saigon to the Under-Secretary of State for External Affairs, Ottawa, October 19, 1962, Folder 50052-A-1-40 pt 3, Box 4639, RG25, LAC.

would enable the South Vietnamese government to go on the offensive and "switch from a counter-guerrilla concept to a genuine guerrilla operation against the enemy."[67]

Management would be the key. By the spring of 1962 the government of South Vietnam was on its heels in the face of the insurgency. The palace felt that time was of the essence, lest they completely lose control of the South Vietnamese countryside. The Ngôs rushed to implement the Strategic Hamlet Program as broadly and rapidly as possible. But managing the program would become a complex issue as once again the Ngôs were confronted with the interests of their foremost ally, the United States. While the enemies of the Diệm regime had been coalescing into what would become the National Liberation Front a new presidential administration was coming to power in Washington. It was comprised of what were supposed to be the "best and the brightest" minds in public service, dedicated to stopping international communism wherever they perceived it to be rearing its ugly head.[68] By 1962, Vietnam had become the place to make this stand. With that commitment, some members of the new presidential administration had taken a particular interest in the Strategic Hamlet Program and its potential to quell the communist-led insurgency.

THE KENNEDY ADMINISTRATION AND
THE STRATEGIC HAMLET PROGRAM

The Strategic Hamlet Program dovetailed nicely with American aims for dealing with the insurgency in the Republic of Vietnam that emerged when John F. Kennedy succeeded Dwight Eisenhower as the president of the United States in 1961. A staunch Cold Warrior, Kennedy believed that South Vietnam was a critical battleground in America's ideological contest with the forces of international communism and Diệm, who he had met in 1953, was the best man to lead it.[69] In the autumn of 1961,

---

[67] Memorandum for the Record, September 14, 1962, *FRUS 1961–1963*, Vol. 2, 636. See also Memorandum from Canadian Delegation ICSC, Saigon to the Under-Secretary of State for External Affairs, Ottawa (part 3), October 19, 1962; and Memorandum from the Australian Ambassador to Vietnam to the Secretary, Department of External Affairs, Canberra, October 16, 1962, Folder 50052-A-1-40 pt 3, Box 4639, RG25, LAC.

[68] This quote is taken from the title of David Halberstam's account of America's descent into Vietnam. David Halberstam, *The Best and the Brightest*, twentieth anniversary ed. (New York: Ballantine Books, 1992).

[69] Arthur M. Schlesinger, Jr. *A Thousand Days: John F. Kennedy in the White House* (Boston, MA: Houghton Mifflin, 1965), 321; Lawrence J. Bassett and Stephen E. Pelz, "The Failed Search for Victory: Vietnam and the Politics of War," in *Kennedy's*

as the insurgency was increasing in its intensity, Kennedy sent a fact-finding mission to Vietnam led by his military adviser, General Maxwell Taylor, and Deputy National Security Advisor Walt Rostow, to determine an appropriate course of action to help the Sài Gòn government. They recommended the deployment of 8,000 American troops as a "logistical" task force to provide flood relief to areas of the Mekong Delta, along with a dramatically stepped-up military advisory effort. Concomitant with this was a proposal for a change in the nature of the relationship between the two countries to "limited partnership and working collaboration." Taylor and Rostow believed that American advisers ought to be inserted into the Vietnamese administrative and military apparatus.[70] The first recommendation for the introduction of combat troops was subsequently rejected as it was little more than a guise to commit the American military directly to the war effort which the president of the United States considered to be premature. The latter two, however, were accepted, dramatically increasing the overall commitment to Vietnam from the days of the Eisenhower administration.[71]

As part of this increased commitment many State Department officials, notably director of the State Department's Bureau of Intelligence and Research, Roger Hilsman, began advocating a stronger Civic Action-type effort to demonstrate to the villager what the government "had to offer him was something better than what the enemy could."[72] Like the Ngôs, Hilsman believed such an approach was essential for defeating the insurgency, but his frame of reference was a far cry from the idiosyncrasies of the Ngôs' Personalist Revolution. Hilsman had been a guerrilla leader against the Japanese in Burma during World War II and was motivated by the same concerns about the revolution of rising expectations

Quest for Victory: American Foreign Policy, 1961–1963, ed. Thomas G. Paterson (New York: Oxford University Press, 1989), 226; Lawrence Freedman, *Kennedy's Wars: Berlin, Cuba, Laos and Vietnam* (New York: Oxford University Press, 2000), 306; Seth Jacobs, *Cold War Mandarin: Ngo Dinh Diem and the Origins of America's War in Vietnam, 1950–1963* (Lanham, MD: Rowman & Littlefield Publishers, Inc., 2006), 121; and Fredrik Logevall, *Choosing War: The Lost Chance for Peace and the Escalation of the War in Vietnam* (Berkeley, CA: University of California Press, 1999), 25–26.

[70] Letter From the President's Military Representative (Taylor) to the President, November 3, 1961, *FRUS, 1961–1963*, Vol. 1, *Vietnam* (Washington, DC: United States Government Printing Office, 1988), 479–480 and 489–493. The quote is from page 489.

[71] Draft National Security Action Memorandum, November 13, 1961, *FRUS, 1961–1963*, Vol. 1, 591–594.

[72] Roger Hilsman, *To Move a Nation: The Politics of Foreign Policy in the Administration of John F. Kennedy* (Garden City, NY: Doubleday, 1967), 432.

that had animated the Eisenhower administration's commitment to the Third World.

This position was articulated in a Policy Research Study on Counterinsurgency published by the bureau on November 20, 1961 entitled "Internal Warfare and the Security of the Underdeveloped States." The study contended that although the rural populations of "underdeveloped lands" were still "indifferent, apathetic, and lacking political interests," they were beginning to experience "an increase in political consciousness and a mounting restiveness" which made them vulnerable to "the subversive apparatus of a revolution-by-export." Modernization, the study continued, could have a particularly destabilizing effect on the existing social order as it "inevitably uproots established social systems, dislocates established political and economic patterns, and produces tension" without providing "results quickly enough to relieve the short term pressures it creates." Communists would specifically target these societies to "manipulate these conditions, pressures and demands" so they could "demoralize the population and ... set the government against its people."[73] Applying this model to Vietnam just over a year later Hilsman observed that the villagers would "be prudently cooperative with the Viet Cong if they are not given physical security."[74]

This is what made the Strategic Hamlet Program so appealing to the members of the Kennedy administration. They saw it as a means to channel the forces of modernization in Vietnam in a direction more conducive to wider American Cold War interests. The Rural Rehabilitation Teams fit

[73] Internal Warfare and the Security of the Underdeveloped States, November 20, 1961, Subjects, Counterinsurgency Fred Greene Study (PRS-1) 11/20/61, Box 5, RHP, JFKL. See also Irene L. Gendzier, *Managing Political Change: Social Scientists and the Third World* (Boulder, CO: Westview Press, 1985), 102–104; Michael E. Latham, "Introduction: Modernization, International History, and the Cold War World," in *Staging Growth: Modernization, Development and the Global Cold War*, ed. David C. Engerman, Nils Gilman, Mark H. Haefele and Michael E. Latham (Amherst, MA: University of Massachusetts Press, 2003), 2; and Gilman, *Mandarins of the Future*, 3 for a discussion of the "revolution of rising expectations." A similar argument was made by George Kennan in the Long Telegram; see the Chargé in the Soviet Union (Kennan) to the Secretary of State, February 22, 1946, *FRUS, 1946*, Vol. 6, *Eastern Europe, the Soviet Union* (Washington, DC: United States Government Printing Office, 1969), 703–706. In this telegram Kennan also argues that the Soviet Union would attempt to weaken the influence of the Western nations in the colonial areas to create vacuum that would "favor Communist-Soviet penetration," page 702.
[74] See Memorandum From the Director of the Bureau of Intelligence and Research (Hilsman) and Michael V. Forrestal of the National Security Council Staff to the President, January 25, 1963, *FRUS, 1961–63*, Vol. 3, *Vietnam* (Washington, DC: United States Government Printing Office, 1991), 53 for the quote.

with Hilsman's concept of an "institutional generation" of Vietnamese functionaries to "produce favorable attitudes, active popular cooperation against the Viet Cong, and cadres to execute the government's programs intelligently."[75] These individuals – sometimes referred to as a "national cadre" – consisted of "the officers and noncommissioned officers of the armed services, the government bureaucrats, the functionaries at the province and district level, the teachers, the tiny strata of business entre-preneurs and labor leaders, and the small number of professional men."[76] They could serve as "reformers to organize mass parties and social and political programs that could become the basis for modernization"; ulti-mately contributing to a "long-range development program" to help Vietnam "press ahead into an era of self-sustaining economic growth" once the "Communist menace has been brought under control."[77]

Hilsman proposed a three-phased approach to defeating the insur-gency, with each phase adopting "a combination of military, political, civic action, economic, and social measures." The first would establish zones of strategic villages, while the Army of the Republic of Vietnam would employ guerrilla tactics to clear out selected areas of NLF insur-gents and keep those in the remaining areas "off balance." The self-de-fense forces would protect the villages and the Civil Guard would defend the area in between the villages. The Civic Action teams would go to work in the villages improving security and modernizing the village insti-tutions and infrastructure to prevent the NLF from hijacking the pro-cess. The second phase would see the extension of the zones of strategic hamlets to include the remaining densely populated areas, as well as "a stepped-up program of economic and social development ... designed to achieve maximum effect at the village level and to build up the progress made by the Civic Action teams during Phase I." The third phase would involve the relocation of "suitably hardy, loyal and tough villagers" to permanently defended strategic villages in the frontier areas to seal off

[75] Memorandum From the Deputy Secretary of Defense (Gilpatric) to the President, May 3, 1961, *FRUS, 1961–63*, Vol. 1, 103. Hilsman referred to the Rural Rehabilitation Team, which he referred to as a "Civic Action Team" as the "single most important element in eliminating the Viet Cong." A Strategic Concept for South Vietnam, February 2, 1962, *FRUS, 1961–63*, Vol. 2, 86.

[76] Hilsman, *To Move a Nation*, 459.

[77] See Hilsman, *To Move a Nation*, 426 for the first quote regarding finding reformers who could form a basis for modernization; and Memorandum From the Deputy Secretary of Defense (Gilpatric) to the President, May 3, 1961, *FRUS, 1961–63*, Vol. 1, 98 for the quote about a long range development plan for Vietnam. Pages 102–106 further outline the plan and the role of Civic Action "Task Force Teams" in the project.

the border with Cambodia, much as the previous land development centers had attempted to do. Hilsman's plan focused on more densely populated and secured areas of the countryside of the Mekong Delta and the area around Huế, gradually extending into the more insecure regions as the security situation improved.[78] If this succeeded, the march of communism could be halted in Southeast Asia and American credibility as a staunch ally of the oppressed and determined opponent of Marxist-Leninist tyranny in the Cold War battle over the future of the developing world would be secured.[79]

Unfortunately, Hilsman's efforts to introduce his concept to Vietnam on a rational and gradual basis that could be closely coordinated with civil-military operations ran up against the Ngôs' attempts to implement the Strategic Hamlet Program on a wide-scale as rapidly as possible. Part of the urgency stemmed from the palace's fear of the growing strength of the NLF. As the insurgency mounted, the Ngôs believed they had to transform all of South Vietnam's hamlets into strategic ones before the guerrillas had the opportunity to overwhelm the program and consolidate their hold over a "liberated zone" below the seventeenth parallel.[80] Initially, this strategy created many more problems than it solved. John O'Donnell, a USOM Province Representative for Kiến Hòa, observed that many of "the intangibles involved in winning the peasantry over to the government's cause were often sidetracked or lost in the rush to *get things done*."[81] Hamlets were often reported as being completed even though they still remained under NLF control.[82] In many cases, Nhu's vision of creating a more equitable society that privileged patriotism and sacrifice was undermined by hard economic realities. Often the poorest inhabitants of the communities ended up doing the brunt of the unpaid work of erecting defenses. The more well-to-do were able to avoid work by donating cash directly to the cause

[78] A Strategic Concept for South Vietnam, February 2, 1962, *FRUS, 1961–63*, Vol. 2, 82–88. See also Hilsman, *To Move a Nation*, 431–435.

[79] Michael E. Latham, *Modernization as Ideology: American Social Scientists and "Nation Building in the Kennedy Era"* (Chapel Hill, NC: The University of North Carolina Press, 2000), 152–153 and 163–164.

[80] Catton, *Diem's Final Failure*, 134.

[81] O'Donnell, "The Strategic Hamlet Program in Kien Hoa Province," 720, (emphasis in the original).

[82] Memorandum From Assistant Director for Rural Affairs of the United States Operations Mission (Phillips) to the Director of the United States Operations Mission in Vietnam (Killen), September 7, 1964, Box 34, CBP, HI. Some Comments on the Counterinsurgency Program of Vietnam and USOM, March 1964, Counterinsurgency, Box 46, ELP, HI; and Colby, *Lost Victory*, 101–102.

or paying someone else to do their share.[83] This clearly did not have the desired effect of undermining privilege and creating an egalitarian democracy on the ground. Making matters worse was the poor state of cadres selected to guide this effort. The Ministry of Civic Action is particularly revealing here. In May 1962, shortly after the launch of the Strategic Hamlet Program, Diệm chastised Hiếu for the quality of Civic Action personnel, informing him that he needed to start selecting "worthy people."[84] Malcolm Browne, an Associated Press reporter covering the conflict in Vietnam, agreed: the new cadres showed "a reluctance to face dangerous situations, unwillingness to take initiative and flagrant corruption." He accused them of looking down on "the peasants" they were "expected to convert as inferior beings" and showing a "lamentable lack of planning and coordination with related agencies."[85] While it would be too much to suggest that the cadres Diệm was referring to in the spring of 1962 were representative of the Strategic Hamlet Program overall, it is indicative of one of the larger weaknesses of the program which resembled the problems that plagued Civic Action: the scope of the program far exceeded the number of trained cadres available. Thousands of young men and civil servants were "recruited off the streets" and organized into mobile cadre teams, often with too little training to be effective. Many of the real concerns of the rural population simply went unaddressed.[86]

As early as July 1962, policymakers in Washington expressed concern over the fact that the Vietnamese government "had not decided on any priorities for [the] strategic hamlet program" and feared that if it was

[83] Letter From the Ambassador in Vietnam (Nolting) to the Deputy Assistant Secretary of State for Far Eastern Affairs (Cottrell), October 15, 1962, *FRUS, 1961–1963*, Vol. 2, 700; and Memorandum for the Record of a Conversation Between the Assistant Director for Rural Affairs of the United States Operations Mission (Phillips) and Prime Minister Tho, November 13, 1963, *FRUS, 1961–1963*, Vol. 4, *Vietnam* (Washington, DC: United States Government Printing Office, 1991), 596–597.

[84] Kinh gọi Ông Bộ Trưởng Công Dân Vụ [Memorandum (from the Office of the President of the Republic of Vietnam) to the Minister of Civic Action], May 31, 1962, Folder 17697, PTTĐICH, TTLTQG2.

[85] Malcolm Browne, *The New Face of War* (New York: The Bobbs-Merrill Company, Inc., 1965), 152.

[86] Quote from Memorandum From Assistant Director for Rural Affairs of the United States Operations Mission (Phillips) to the Director of the United States Operations Mission in Vietnam (Killen), September 7, 1964, Box 34, CBP, HI. See also Some Comments on the Counterinsurgency Program of Vietnam and USOM, March 1964, Counterinsurgency, Box 46, ELP, HI; O'Donnell, "The Strategic Hamlet Program in Kien Hoa Province," 737–738; and Robert Thompson, *Defeating Communist Insurgency: The Lessons of Malaya and Vietnam* (London: Chatto & Windus, 1967), 80.

"spread too thin and too fast" the "resultant failures may be fatal" to the Sài Gòn regime.[87] Milton Osborne concurred, flatly stating that "the over-extension of the hamlet program was clearly a problem."[88] Five months later, near the end of 1962, American reviews of the program remained mixed. Theodore Heavner, the Deputy Director of the State Department's Vietnam Working Group, upon returning from a forty-day trip to Vietnam, stated that he believed the Strategic Hamlet Program had got off to a good start everywhere but in central Vietnam.[89] Hilsman, in a year-end assessment of the counterinsurgency effort, noted that in areas where the strategic hamlets were being implemented in conjunction with military pacification plans, they were "generally well organized and defended." However the program "as a whole has been precipitous and uncoordinated."[90]

Such concerns reflected the fact that the US government and the Diệm regime had fundamentally different views about the role of the Strategic Hamlet Program in the nation-building process. For the South Vietnamese, semi-autonomous, self-reliant strategic hamlets exemplified the much larger social revolution the palace was attempting. As we have seen, the Ngôs viewed "self-reliance" as both a virtue and a necessity: it was virtuous because the palace believed that a "people forced back upon their own resources would develop the inner strength and common bonds of unity necessary to build a new society"; it was necessary given South Vietnamese budget restrictions and the government's reluctance to rely on foreign aid.[91]

This perspective conflicted with American views that Diệm's method placed undue hardship on the peasantry at a time when the regime needed to demonstrate what it "could do to help the people" rather than emphasize "what the people should do for the government."[92] As the State Department saw it, the Strategic Hamlet

---

[87] Telegram From the Department of State to the Embassy in Vietnam, July 16, 1962, *FRUS, 1961–1963*, Vol. 2, 520.

[88] Osborne, *Strategic Hamlets in South Viet-Nam*, 38.

[89] Report by the Deputy Director of the Vietnam Working Group (Heavner), December 11, 1962, *FRUS, 1961–1963*, Vol. 2, 765.

[90] Memorandum From the Director of the Bureau of Intelligence and Research (Hilsman) to the Assistant Secretary of State for Far Eastern Affairs (Harriman), December 19, 1962, *FRUS, 1961–1963*, Vol. 2, 791.

[91] Catton, *Diem's Final Failure*, 119.

[92] Telegram From the Embassy in Vietnam to the Department of State, March 23, 1962, *FRUS, 1961–1963*, Vol. 2, 268. See also Telegram From the Embassy in Vietnam to the Department of State, April 9, 1963, *FRUS, 1961–1963*, Vol. 3, 218.

Program should showcase the South Vietnamese government's benevolence.[93] This would meet the dual aims of providing the peasantry with physical security and tying "the villagers into the network of government administration and control."[94] That said, Washington clearly did not fail to take grassroots development seriously. As we have seen, the Rural Rehabilitation Teams gelled nicely with Roger Hilsman's notions of a national cadre leading the countryside toward his vision of modernity. But Hilsman's vision was rooted in the same high modernist conceptions that had informed individuals like Leland Barrows. In particular, Hilsman's thinking embraced elements of the "modernization theory" that underpinned much of the Kennedy administration's approach to the developing world.[95]

A manifestation of the discourse of development discussed earlier, modernization theory attempted to chart "the social, economic and technological process of progressive historical change" between societies defined as "traditional" and "modern."[96] It conceived of modernization as an evolutionary process where "traditional" societies follow a unidirectional, gradual and irreversible path toward modernity through a series of progressive phases. The process is immanent where economic, political and social changes are all interdependent, making all developing societies more alike as they proceed along the path of evolution.[97] For US policymakers like Hilsman, the end stage they

---

[93] Hilsman, *To Move a Nation*, 431–435 and 451–452; and Notes on Strategic Hamlets, August 15, 1963, Subject File: "Notes on Strategic Hamlets," Box 61, ELP, HI; A Strategic Concept for South Vietnam, February 2, 1962, *FRUS, 1961–63*, Vol. 2, 75 and 78.

[94] The quote is from A Strategic Concept for South Vietnam, February 2, 1962, *FRUS, 1961–63*, Vol. 2, 78. Hilsman makes the connection with the Philippines explicit in Internal Warfare and the Security of the Underdeveloped States, November 20, 1961, Subjects, Counterinsurgency Fred Greene Study (PRS-1) 11/20/61, Box 5, RHP, JFKL.

[95] Hilsman, *To Move a Nation*, 424–426; and Latham, *Modernization as Ideology*, 180.

[96] Gilman, *Mandarins of the Future*, 7.

[97] By the 1960s, these ideas had been translated by American social scientists into a full-blown model for development known as modernization theory, Latham, *Modernization as Ideology*, 30–46. This theory, in the words of Nils Gilman, attempted to chart "the social, economic and technological process of progressive historical change" between societies defined as "traditional" and "modern," Gilman, *Mandarins of the Future*, 7. It borrowed from evolutionary theory by arguing that "traditional" societies follow a unidirectional, gradual and irreversible path toward modernity through a series of progressive phases. The process is immanent where economic, political and social changes are all interdependent, making all developing societies more alike as they proceed along the path of evolution, Alvin Y. So, *Social Change and Development: Modernization, Dependency and World-System Theories* (Newbury Park, CA: Sage Publications, 1990), 33–34. Representative works include Talcott Parsons and Edward A. Shils, eds., *Toward*

posited resembled an idealized rendering of American society based on the ideals of free enterprise, social mobility and a liberal, free market economy. Just as had occurred with the Eisenhower administration's prescriptions for development so did Hilsman's vision failed to mesh with the Ngôs' conception of a modern South Vietnamese state. The solipsistic assumptions that informed individuals like Hilsman served to make matters worse.

As we have seen, the Ngôs were very sensitive to the appearance of any overt Western influence in their affairs. They were caught in a pitched conflict with the communist-led insurgents over who would be the true heirs to Vietnam's nationalist tradition and lead the Vietnamese people toward a brighter, independent future. The increased American presence that came with the limited partnership they had entered into only served to reinforce communist propaganda that Diệm was a lackey of a colonial power.[98] Nhu in particular saw such reliance as humiliating, dangerous and uncharacteristic of a genuinely independent nation.[99] Such an outside role, he feared, would "corrupt" the process of developing the indigenous leadership necessary to fulfill the palace's vision of a modern nation.[100] Not only did the Strategic Hamlet Program provide a means to instill the peasantry with the communal strength and fortitude that lay at the heart of the Ngôs' national revolution, but it did so in a manner that would involve a minimum of outside interference. An important rationale in making the villages self-reliant was to avoid any overt dependence on the Americans to make the program work.[101] The stage was set, therefore, for a clash of wills between the two governments over the nature of the American commitment to Vietnam.

a General Theory of Action: Theoretical Foundations for the Social Sciences (New Brunswick, NJ: Transaction Publishers, 2001); Edward A. Shils, *Political Development in the New States* (Gravenhage: Mouton & Co., 1962); Daniel Lerner, *The Passing of Traditional Society: Modernizing the Middle East* (New York: The Free Press of Glencoe, 1958); Gabriel A. Almond and James S. Coleman, eds., *The Politics of the Developing Areas* (Princeton, NJ: Princeton University Press, 1960); and W.W. Rostow, *The Stages of Economic Growth: A Non-Communist Manifesto* (Cambridge: Cambridge University Press, 1960).

[98] Colby, *Lost Victory*, 110.
[99] Catton, *Diem's Final Failure*, 153–157.
[100] Colby, *Lost Victory*, 99–100.
[101] Dennis J. Duncanson argues that Nhu found a means of counteracting the increasing American influence on Vietnamese affairs in the Strategic Hamlet Program. Dennis J. Duncanson, *Government and Revolution in Vietnam* (New York: Oxford University Press, 1968), 312. See also Miller, *Misalliance*, 234; and Catton, *Diem's Final Failure*, 94–97.

DENOUEMENT

Ironically, this clash came just as the Strategic Hamlet Program appeared to be turning the corner. In August 1962, the Canadian Delegate to the ICC informed Ottawa that the "general impression" of the Western embassies in Sài Gòn regarding the direction of the counterinsurgency effort was "qualified optimism" but pessimists could still "point to signs of continued deterioration in the security situation."[102] By October, however, the sense of "guarded optimism" could be reported as "optimism." The enemy had "suffered a sharp increase in their casualty rate" due to stepped up military operations, particularly in the Mekong Delta, which included the use of helicopters. Strategic hamlets now protected roughly one-third of the population with another third expected to come under government protection by the end of the year. While their "development" on the whole was still "uneven" – there were "some first class hamlets" along with "others" that were "little more than villages surrounded by light fence work" – the program appeared to be "going better than expected." Indeed, "in many areas" it was "proving popular" marked by "villagers ... beginning to provide intelligence concerning the Viet Cong" which was "proving invaluable in mounting operations against them." There were even some indications that "Northern leaders and the Viet Cong themselves" were becoming "increasingly concerned about how to deal with the renewed government efforts."[103]

This bubble of optimism was punctured by the release of a negative appraisal of the situation in Vietnam by Democratic Senate Majority Leader Mike Mansfield in February 1963. Mansfield had been a friend and longtime supporter of Ngô Đình Diệm, going so far as to virulently back him when the Eisenhower administration contemplated withdrawing its support during the so-called "sect crisis" in 1955.[104] By the end of 1962 Mansfield contended that he had seen little progress made in the past seven years, despite the vast expenditure of billions of American dollars.[105] Such a "sobering appraisal" served as a harsh reminder to

[102] Memorandum from Canadian Delegation ICSC, Saigon to the Under-Secretary of State for External Affairs, Ottawa, August 14, 1962, Folder 50052-A-1-40 pt 3, Box 4639, RG25, LAC.

[103] Memorandum from Canadian Delegation ICSC, Saigon to the Under-Secretary of State for External Affairs, Ottawa (part 1), October 19, 1962, Folder 50052-A-1-40 pt 3, Box 4639, RG25, LAC.

[104] Memorandum for the Record, April 21, 1955, *FRUS 1955–1957*, Vol. 1, *Vietnam* (Washington, DC: United States Government Printing Office, 1985), 277.

[105] Report by the Senate Majority Leader (Mansfield), December 18, 1962, *FRUS, 1961–1963*, Vol. 2, 779.

Diệm's brother Nhu of the pitfalls of becoming too dependent on the United States.[106]

Nhu feared Mansfield's harsh report portended a "shift" in American strategy away from support of the South Vietnamese government.[107] Though Nhu resented South Vietnam's reliance on American largesse, he was well aware of his country's limited resources and, like his brother, recognized that in the face of the insurgency some American assistance was essential.[108] He was wary, however, about the level of commitment the Kennedy administration would continue to show its beleaguered ally. In meetings with the Canadian Delegate to the ICC and the Australian Ambassador, Brian Hill, in the fall of 1962 he cited Laos – where the United States had agreed to respect Laotian neutrality rather than assist in the fight against the communist-led Pathet Lao – and the situation in Cuba as signs that the "American relationship with Vietnam could not be counted on as a permanent relationship."[109] Nhu, therefore, went to great lengths to speed his country along in preparing it for the day when the Americans departed. First, he tried to "avoid 'institutionalizing' certain substantive relationships and procedures jointly engaged in by the Vietnamese and by American personnel."[110] Second, he pushed for a re-evaluation of the American aid program. Finally, he suggested that the United States dramatically reduce the size of its advisory presence in Vietnam by as much as 50 percent.[111]

Such concerns were matched by those of his brother who had come to believe that the insertion of so many American advisers at every level of the Vietnamese government had created the impression that the United

[106] Telegram From the Embassy in Vietnam to the Department of State, March 28, 1963, *FRUS, 1961–1963*, Vol. 3, 183–184.

[107] *Ibid.*

[108] Memorandum from Canadian Delegation ICSC, Saigon to the Under-Secretary of State for External Affairs, Ottawa, October 19, 1962, Folder 50052-A-1-40 pt 3, Box 4639, RG25, LAC; and Miller, *Misalliance*, 230–231.

[109] Memorandum from Canadian Delegation ICSC, Saigon to the Under-Secretary of State for External Affairs, Ottawa, October 19, 1962; and Memorandum from the Australian Ambassador to Vietnam to the Secretary, Department of External Affairs, Canberra, October 16, 1962, Folder 50052-A-1-40 pt 3, Box 4639, RG25, LAC. The quote can be found in the former document.

[110] Memorandum for the Record of a Conversation With the Presidential Counselor (Ngo Dinh Nhu), April 12, 1963, *FRUS, 1961–1963*, Vol. 3, 224. See also Catton, *Diem's Final Failure*, 159.

[111] Telegram From the Central Intelligence Agency Station in Saigon to the Agency, April 24, 1963, General 4/19/63 – 4/30/63, Countries: Vietnam, Box 197A, NSF, JFKL; *Washington Post*, May 12, 1963, A1 and A14; and Telegram From the Embassy in Vietnam to the Department of State, May 23, 1963, *FRUS, 1961–1963*, Vol. 3, 324–326.

States was turning South Vietnam into a "protectorate," an idea that was clearly playing into the hands of the communists.[112] Since the 1950s communist propaganda had labeled the Ngôs and their supporters as *tai say* (lackeys) of the imperialists and the regime *Mỹ-Diệm* (American-Diệm). This became so insidious that peasants who were conducting business with Sài Gòn officials used this latter epithet with all due respect when addressing them.[113]

As the US–South Vietnamese relationship appeared to stumble into the summer of 1963, the NLF began a massive and coordinated assault on the Strategic Hamlet Program.[114] Militarily this had been the whole point of the program. The government *wanted* to bring the NLF out into the open and escalate the insurgency before physically isolating and then crushing it. But despite the sense of optimism that was emerging regarding the program the hamlets were nowhere near ready for this kind of assault. According to a March 1964 report on the counterinsurgency, the rapid pace "forced by the GVN [Government of Vietnam] outstripped the capabilities of those charged with its implementation."[115] This should hardly be surprising, given that in the convoluted explanations Nhu presented to explain the program, much was lost in translation. For example, in a meeting with visiting American congressmen, Nhu argued that the Strategic Hamlet Program attempted to combine democracy and authoritarianism in order to combat underdevelopment.[116] In the Ngôs' eyes this concentration of power in Sài Gòn was justified as a temporary measure to promote a greater good down the road.[117] Meeting with Ramchundur Goburdhun, the Indian Delegate to the ICC, Nhu responded to the diplomat's concern about the Strategic Hamlet Program's "regimentation of the peasants" by stating "one must fight fire with fire."[118] This attitude backfired, naturally, as many at the provincial level interpreted it as simply another example of the authoritarian policies that emanated from

[112] Telegram From the Embassy in Vietnam to the Department of State, April 5, 1963, *FRUS, 1961–1963*, Vol. 3, 207.

[113] Catton, *Diem's Final Failure*, 28; Scigliano, *Nation Under Stress*, 158; Pike, *Viet Cong*, 88–89; and Sheehan, *A Bright Shining Lie*, 192–193.

[114] Catton, *Diem's Final Failure*, 192.

[115] Some Comments on the Counterinsurgency Program of Vietnam and USOM, March 1964, Counterinsurgency, Box 46, ELP, HI.

[116] Memorandum of a Conversation, December 1, 1962, *FRUS, 1961–1963*, Vol. 2, 751.

[117] Catton, *Diem's Final Failure*, 128; Maneli, *War of the Vanquished*, 145; and Directorate General of Information, *Vietnam's Strategic Hamlets*, 20–21.

[118] Telegram from Canadian High Commission, Delhi to Department of External Affairs, Ottawa, May 8, 1963 Folder 50052-A-6-40 pt 3, Box 4643, RG25, LAC.

the palace.[119] As the March 1964 report continued, "it was apparent that many of these officials did not fully understand the concept, and were so frightened by the pressures from the president and his brother that they would employ any measures, from forced labor and confiscation to false reporting, to achieve the quantitative goals set."[120] While not necessarily a reflection of the situation in every strategic hamlet, it does suggest that ideologically the program failed to establish a solid foundation across the countryside. Consequently, under the Strategic Hamlet Program, many of the tenets of the regime's Personalist Revolution had failed to resonate with the rural population.

The full bankruptcy of the Strategic Hamlet Program would not become evident until after the Ngôs were toppled from power in a military coup in the fall of 1963. The coup occurred as a result of the political fallout from the Buddhist Crisis that had erupted throughout the cities of South Vietnam in the spring of 1963. In May, eight protesters were killed in the melee following government attempts to quash a Buddhist protest in the imperial city of Huế over what appeared to be religious persecution by a Catholic minority government in a Buddhist majority country. The demonstration was organized by a group of Buddhist revivalists who possessed their own particular vision of a postcolonial Vietnam that would be rooted in their country's past Buddhist traditions. By 1963 they felt increasingly under threat by what they perceived to be the "pro-Catholic chauvinism" of South Vietnam's bureaucracy. In the fallout to the incident at Hue, these Buddhist leaders blamed the government for the deaths of the protesters, while the government countered that NLF saboteurs were responsible.[121]

With both sides refusing to back down, the Buddhists upped the ante on June 11, when Thích Quảng Đức immolated himself at a busy Sài Gòn intersection in front of a large crowd, which included Malcolm Browne. The grisly photos that Browne took that day made international headlines and drew global condemnation of the South Vietnamese government. International opprobrium afforded the urban opponents of the Sài Gòn government in South Vietnam an outlet for their anger. Emboldened by this solidarity, the militant Buddhist bonzes engaged in a well-orchestrated campaign with the foreign press corps to bring down

---

[119] Thomas L. Ahern, Jr., *CIA and the House of Ngo* (Langley, VA: Center for the Study of Intelligence, declassified 2009), 117.

[120] Some Comments on the Counterinsurgency Program of Vietnam and USOM, March 1964, Counterinsurgency, Box 46, ELP, HI.

[121] Miller, *Misalliance*, 260–268.

the Diệm regime. As the press attacks mounted, more and more opponents from the cities came forward to join the Buddhists and protest the authoritarian policies of the Diệm regime over the summer of 1963.

This provided an opportunity for individuals like Roger Hilsman who had grown increasingly dismayed by what he saw as the Ngôs' seeming inability to effectively counter the insurgents to move against the regime from Washington. Though Kennedy was initially reluctant to see Diệm removed from power, he was quite concerned about the impact such opposition toward the Sài Gòn government would have on its ability to build a viable, noncommunist nation around the South Vietnamese president. Prompted by Hilsman and his allies within the administration, the president of the United States pushed for the regime to make amends with the Buddhists while searching for alternative leadership. After several months of intrigue and coup rumors the Kennedy administration tacitly approved a change in the regime plotted by a cabal of South Vietnamese generals who also claimed to fear for the future of the war effort under the Diệm regime in the face of its repression of the Buddhist Crisis. The coup came on November 1, resulting in the assassination of Diệm and his brother Nhu the following day.[122]

Ironically, the turmoil that gripped South Vietnam in the summer of 1963 does not appear to have played into the NLF's decision to mount its sustained campaign against the Strategic Hamlet Program. Documents indicate that the NLF, as well as the Hà Nội government, were as surprised by the Buddhist Crisis as the leadership in Sài Gòn.[123] Yet, the NLF took advantage of the opportunity provided when Diệm withdrew his forces from key areas around Sài Gòn to shore up security in the capital, leaving these places, such as the military zone to the north of the capital, where the Strategic Hamlet Program had been inaugurated, vulnerable to attack.[124] In September, Rufus Phillips reported that the hamlets

[122] For more detailed accounts of the Buddhist Crisis and its impact on American-South Vietnamese relations see such works as Miller, *Misalliance*, 260–318; Rust, *Kennedy in Vietnam*, 94–178; Kahin, *Intervention*, 146–181; Ellen Hammer, *A Death in November: America in Vietnam, 1963* (New York: E.P. Dutton, 1987), 103–311; Francis X. Winters, *The Year of the Hare: America in Vietnam, January 25, 1963–February 15, 1964* (Athens, GA: The University of Georgia Press, 1997), 29–113; David Kaiser, *American Tragedy: Kennedy, Johnson, and the Origins of the Vietnam War* (Cambridge, MA: The Belknap Press of Harvard University Press, 2000), 213–283; Jacobs, *Cold War Mandarin*, 142–181; Logevall, *Choosing War*, 1–74.
[123] Pike, *Viet Cong*, 352–53; NLF Document, June 29, 1963, VC Docs 1962–1963, Box 5, CBP, HI; and Catton, *Diem's Final Failure*, 205.
[124] Catton, *Diem's Final Failure*, 202–207.

were getting "chewed to pieces by the Viet Cong" in the Mekong Delta and 60 percent of those in Long An province had been overrun.[125] One month earlier, when the NLF campaign was still in its early stages, an American appraisal of the military situation in South Vietnam reported that 2 percent – at least 144 hamlets depending on the figures used for calculation – had been attacked directly by the insurgents over the previous eight months.[126] Three months later the situation was dramatically worse. Philip Catton's evidence shows Sài Gòn received reports from half the country in mid-November that contended, in the two weeks following the coup, at least 199 strategic hamlets had been attacked and damaged. Catton concluded that the NLF had "virtually defeated the program" in large portions of the Mekong Delta as well as the area to the north of Sài Gòn – including the location where the Strategic Hamlet Program had been launched eighteen months before.[127]

Politically the Strategic Hamlet Program was moribund as well. Without the Ngôs at the helm, both the program and the Personalist Revolution at its heart lost their driving force. The provisional government established in the wake of the Diệm regime, the Military Revolutionary Council (MRC), tried to distance itself from the ideas and policies of its predecessor. Initially, it sought to continue the Strategic Hamlet Program, but under a new name, so as not to be associated with the Ngôs.[128] But this effort was half-hearted at best, and the program gradually ground to a halt. In December, the government elected not to construct any additional

---

[125] Memorandum of a Conversation, September 10, 1963, *FRUS, 1961–1963*, Vol. 4, 165.

[126] The 2 percent figure is printed in Telegram From the Commander in Chief, Pacific (Felt) to the Joint Chiefs of Staff, August 17, 1963, General 8/1/63 – 8/20/63, Countries: Vietnam, Box 198, NSF, JFKL. Statistics vary widely for the Strategic Hamlet Program, so the 144 figure represent a very loose estimation, but provides a rough indication of the state of the Strategic Hamlet Program at the beginning of the NLF's stepped-up campaign. The higher number comes from data presented by Robert Scigliano which states that by the end of June 1963 7,205 strategic hamlets had been constructed throughout South Vietnam, Scigliano, *Nation Under Stress*, 181. By November, the number of strategic hamlets had allegedly grown to over 8,300 according to a memorandum prepared for the Secretary of Defense to refute a negative October 1963 appraisal of the military situation in Vietnam. Memorandum From the Director of the Bureau of Intelligence and Research (Hilsman) to the Secretary of State, November 8, 1963 *FRUS, 1961–1963*, Vol. 4, 585.

[127] Catton, *Diem's Final Failure*, 207.

[128] Telegram From the Central Intelligence Agency Station in Saigon to the Agency, November 5, 1963, General 11/3/63 – 11/5/63 CIA Reports, Countries: Vietnam, Box 201, NSF, JFKL.

hamlets, and the following March, the Interministerial Committee for Strategic Hamlets was unceremoniously disbanded.[129]

As for the Ministry of Civic Action, it also met an ignominious end in the autumn of 1963. Ngô Trọng Hiếu, the Minister for Civic Action, remained loyal to the palace to the end, though it appears more for personal than political reasons. When those conspiring against Diệm approached Pham Xuon Nung, the Director of Plans, Training and Operations, General Group for Civic Action about the coup in early July, Nung warned them against divulging their plans to the minister as "Hieu would be likely to report the coup plans to Ngô Đình Nhu in order to secure his own future, or at the very least, Hieu would take preventative action to avoid arrest by the coup group."[130]

Following the coup, the Ministry for Civic Action ceased to exist.[131] Hiếu sought asylum in the Philippine embassy, where mobs of angry protestors gathered to seek his arrest. After two attempts by the protesters to sack the embassy, the Philippine Ambassador asked the American Ambassador, Henry Cabot Lodge, Jr., if the United States would fly Hiếu to the Philippines, where he would be granted sanctuary for life.[132] Initially, the MRC had informed the Philippine embassy that they would be willing to "look the other way" in the event that Hiếu could be secretly spirited out of the country. However, in the face of the angry mobs being held back from attacking the embassy by South Vietnamese troops, the MRC later recanted "on [the] grounds that [the] surreptitious departure of Hieu from [an] embassy surrounded by troops would make [the] military look ineffective."[133] Lodge recommended that the United States not get involved in the matter, while the State Department encouraged the

[129] Osborne, *Strategic Hamlets in South Viet-Nam*, 40; Telegram From the Central Intelligence Agency Station in Saigon to the Agency, November 5, 1963, General 11/3/ 63 – 11/5/63 CIA Reports, Countries: Vietnam, Box 201; Telegram From the Embassy in Vietnam to the Department of State (2), November 9, 1963; and Telegram From the Embassy in Vietnam to the Department of State, November 12, 1963, General 11/6/ 63 – 11/15/63 State Cables, Countries: Vietnam, Box 202, NSF, JFKL.

[130] Telegram From the Central Intelligence Agency Station in Saigon to the Agency, July 3, 1963, General 7/1/63 – 7/20/63, Countries: Vietnam, Box 198, NSF, JFKL.

[131] Department of State Briefing Memorandum, November 1, 1963, General 11/1/63 – 11/ 2/63 Memos and Misc, Countries: Vietnam, Box 201, NSF, JFKL.

[132] Telegram From the Embassy in Vietnam to the Department of State, November 15, 1963, General 11/6/63 – 11/15/63 State Cables, Countries: Vietnam, Box 202, NSF, JFKL.

[133] Telegram From the Embassy in Vietnam to the Department of State (2), November 15, 1963, General 11/6/63 – 11/15/63 State Cables, Countries: Vietnam, Box 202, NSF, JFKL.

Philippines to turn Hiếu over to the new government in Sài Gòn provided they would "ensure his physical safety and a fair trial."[134] In the end, the Philippine embassy assented to the MRC's demands on November 15. On that day they turned Hiếu over to the new Sài Gòn government which subsequently tried and jailed him on charges of gross corruption, an unfortunate coda to a program that nine years earlier had begun rather promisingly and declined most precipitously in conjunction with the fortunes of South Vietnam's ruling family.[135]

---

[134] Lodge's recommendation may be found in Telegram From the Embassy in Vietnam to the Department of State, November 15, 1963; while the State Department position is quoted from Telegram From the Department of State in Vietnam to the Embassy in Vietnam, November 15, 1963, General 11/6/63 – 11/15/63 State Cables, Countries: Vietnam, Box 202, NSF, JFKL.

[135] Telegram From the Embassy in Vietnam to the Department of State, November 16, 1963, General 11/16/63 – 1/22/63 State Cables, Countries: Vietnam, Box 202, NSF, JFKL; and Malcolm Browne, *The New Face of War*, 151.

Conclusion

Vietnam's Lost Revolution

For nearly a decade the government of Ngô Đình Diệm attempted to build a viable nation in the southern half of Vietnam. In Diệm's mind it would be capable of standing independently among the powers of the "free world" and serve as a beacon to his Vietnamese compatriots who lived under the communist regime in Hà Nội. Though this nation that Diệm imagined was an anticommunist one, it was not entirely a Cold War construction. The vision he put forward of a self-reliant Southeast Asian nation capable of charting its own course in the international system was consistent with that of many leaders of the developing world at the midpoint of the twentieth century. The majority of these leaders shared a colonial history and each was attempting to assert an independent voice for their nations in a world being shaped by the twin forces of the Cold War and decolonization. That these forces intersected in Vietnam was a reality the Sài Gòn regime had to contend with in its quest for nationhood.

The story of the Special Commissariat for Civic Action stands as a testament to this difficult course. Originally conceived as a temporary expedient to establish a central government presence in the rural areas following Vietnam's war of decolonization with the French, it evolved into an organ responsible for fomenting the palace's Personalist Revolution throughout the countryside. Unfortunately, the Special Commissariat for Civic Action was incapable of carrying this task out. Though it got off to a promising start it was constantly plagued by a tight budget and chronic shortage of manpower. This resulted in an unfavorable ratio of cadres to civilians which was further exacerbated by the harsh geographic settings of many of the provinces in the Mekong Delta and the borderlands with Cambodia – areas that provided sanctuary for the state's opponents.

Adding to the Civic Action cadres' difficulties in promoting the revolution were the psychological effects of the other nation-building schemes the palace attempted to implement between 1955 and 1959: the land reform, land development, and agroville programs. Whatever noble intentions these may have they also had weaknesses that served to estrange significant portions of the rural population. The land reform program was tepid, poorly implemented, and failed to match the scope of the earlier Việt Minh efforts. Land development was more successful, but foundered on the suitability of locations for certain land development centers and the employment, at times, of coercive measures to get new inhabitants to populate these centers – particularly against the ethnic minorities whom the regime were attempting to assimilate into the mainstream of South Vietnamese society. As for the agrovilles, they became particularly unpopular as they attempted to relocate members of existing hamlets into one of two types of regroupment centers based on whether they were considered trustworthy or potentially subversive elements – a distinction that was arbitrary at times. The new locations were undeveloped when their new inhabitants arrived and required extensive work to make them even habitable. All of this pales in comparison to the detrimental impact of the regime's ruthless communist denunciation campaign. Though the Civic Action reports are silent on the effect this campaign had on the cadres' efforts to win adherents to the new regime, one cannot escape the fact that this was a brutally repressive campaign that created, in the Republic of Vietnam, the aura of a police state, and the Special Commissariat for Civic Action was a crucial part of it. This was not lost on the peasantry.

But these material limitations, common to the nation-building efforts of most postcolonial states, were more profoundly complicated by the flawed assumptions and ideological contradictions that were manifest in the Diệm regime's revolutionary project. Diệm's revolution was intended to mobilize South Vietnam's rural population to self-reliantly participate in his nation-building project. It was predicated on the belief that there was a vast reservoir of untapped manpower at the local level that, with the appropriate guidance, would become willing to volunteer its time and energy for this great undertaking. In Diệm's mind, this potential was rooted in Vietnam's precolonial structure of autonomous villages that had formed the bedrock of rural society.

Unfortunately, for Diệm such a conception of rural life accorded more with the experiences of northern village communities than those in the south. Diệm's northern view of the village is reflected in the work of James Scott who argues that peasants operated on a reciprocal basis with each other to share in the labor and the bounty that it provided in order to ensure their collective survival.[1] This was not the case in the south – a phenomenon which dates back to Vietnam's expanding southern frontier in the seventeenth and eighteenth centuries. As Li Tana demonstrates, the more densely populated north of Vietnam created conditions for the existence of long-standing, "relatively immobile," close-knit, corporate communities. Even there, she argues, it was only in the "land-scarce" Red River Delta and Thanh Hoá-Nghệ An region that it approached the ideal that would later be envisioned by Diệm. From Quảng Nam south, the situation was quite different. Li Tana contends that Vietnamese moving into the south found abundant land, creating conditions where the settlers' "relationships to a particular village or area of land could be far less close and far more mutable than in a majority of northern villages."[2]

This evidence suggests that the rural population of South Vietnam adhered far more closely to traits exhibited by Samuel Popkin's theory of the "rational peasant," which rejects Scott's notion of a "moral peasant," and posits that "the peasant is a rational problem solver with a sense of his own interests and a need to bargain with others to achieve mutually acceptable outcomes."[3] According to Popkin's theory, peasants possess a sense of self-interest that stood in sharp contrast to that developed by Diệm. These peasants actually "see sufficient uncertainty or threat in one another to make social actions difficult." They are more inclined to make sacrifices that benefit the "welfare and security of self and family" than the community at large.[4] This was particularly evident in Bà Rịa in 1956, where the inhabitants complained that volunteering for the Welfare Improvement work was keeping them from earning a living.[5]

[1] James Scott, *The Moral Economy of the Peasant* (New Haven, CT: Yale University Press, 1976), vii.
[2] Li Tana, *Nguyễn Cochinchina: Southern Vietnam in the Seventeenth and Eighteenth Centuries* (Ithaca, NY: Southeast Asia Program Publications, Southeast Asia Program, Cornell University 1998), 110.
[3] Samuel Popkin, *The Rational Peasant: The Political Economy of Rural Society in Vietnam* (Berkeley, CA: University of California Press, 1979), ix.
[4] *Ibid.*, 30–31.
[5] Tỉnh Tưởng Bária Kính gởi Ngài Bộ Trưởng tại Phủ Tổng Thống [Memorandum from the Province Chief of Baria to the Secretary of State for the President in the Office of the President], August 29, 1956, Folder 16065, Phủ Tổng Thống Đệ Nhất Cộng Hòa [Office

It was seen again in the findings of the December 1957 Conference on Civic Action which indicated that the people only participated in Welfare Improvement projects that were of direct interest to themselves or their families.[6] It was even present under the auspices of the Strategic Hamlet Program where John Heble, the American Consul in Huế, reported that the "villagers in Central Vietnam can see no advantage in the strategic hamlet program and they complain because work on the hamlets takes them away from their fields."[7]

As Popkin's argument suggests, the implications of this are profound for Diệm's conception of nation-building. The "overly sanguine view of the ability of villagers to cooperate ... leads to false hopes for community development schemes requiring voluntarism or a broad concern with welfare."[8] Any attempt to organize group action needed to account for the difference between individual and group interest and "provide effective leadership as well as sufficient incentives to overcome individual resistance to collective action."[9] Personalism, with its emphasis on individual self-sacrifice for the common good, might have provided a philosophical foundation in the minds of the peasantry that would overcome this resistance. However, for reasons that will be elaborated on shortly, the Ngôs' faith in such an abstract dogma proved misplaced.

Compounding the problem was the fact that Diệm's most basic assumption about the corporate character of the Vietnamese village as a latent source of nationalist energy in the South was grossly misplaced. According to the Dutch sociologist Jan Bremen, this corporate image of the village is little more than a myth. He argues that it emerged in the early reports of European colonialists and it offered a universal view of the village based on a number of shared characteristics, specifically "political autonomy, economic autarchy, social homogeneity and, finally, the tenacious immutability of this closed collectivity."[10] Anticolonial nationalists

of the President of the First Republic] (hereafter PTTĐICH), Trung Tâm Lưu Trữ Quốc Gia II [National Archives 2] (hereafter TTLTQG2).

[6] Tờ Trình về Đại Hội Công Dân Vụ [Report on the Civic Action Conference], January 11, 1958, Folder 16297, PTTĐICH, TTLTQG2.

[7] Memorandum From Robert H. Johnson of the Policy Planning Staff to the Counselor of the Department of State (Rostow), October 16, 1962, *Foreign Relations of the United States, 1961–1963*, Vol. 2, *Vietnam* (hereafter referred to as *FRUS*) (Washington, DC: United States Government Printing Office, 1990), 704.

[8] Popkin, *The Rational Peasant*, 29.

[9] *Ibid.*, 252.

[10] Jan Bremen, *The Shattered Image: Construction and Deconstruction of the Village in Colonial Asia* (Providence, RI: Forbis Publications, 1988), 1–2 and 18–19. The quote is on page 2. A similar argument is made in Jeremy Kemp, "The Dialectics of Village

and postcolonial leaders, he continues, appreciated the symbolism "of the intrinsic struggle of a much older pattern of social organization." In their efforts to "denounce the injurious effects of colonial rule," they seized upon this image to try to form a national culture by claiming this "ageless and immutable" structure "had forcibly resisted foreign occupation and been reasonably successful in maintaining its own identity."[11] Thus, the assumption that there were "village traditions" Diệm could draw upon in the south of Vietnam was patently false, and merely reproduced the universalist assumptions about the village that had their origins in the European colonial project.

Finally, there was the efficacy of Personalism as the basis for Diệm's revolution. To begin with, it was far too convoluted to be easily understood by most government officials, much less articulated to the peasantry. Worse was the fact that its central ideas, when applied to the Ngôs' nation-building designs for South Vietnam, were inherently contradictory. Personalism arose as an organic and conservative European philosophy that defined the person as distinct from the individual in terms of his or her relationship with the state. It holds that the person is a spiritual and inherently social being who is part of a larger community and therefore obligated to secure the common good of all its constituent elements. The individual, on the other hand is an atomistic entity that is prone to either pursuing selfish goals in a liberal society, or standing helpless as part of a collective in a powerful totalitarian state. In its broadest sense it attempted to amalgamate various secular and theistic interpretations of the person's relationship with society. These included, in the words of Clive Christie:

the liberal notion of the free individual as the core of any acceptable political or social system; the Christian notion of the individual conscience as the basis of the moral order; and the broad socialist concept that society itself was a moral entity that not only had to balance the right of the individual against the welfare of the whole society, but had to take positive steps to ensure that individuals increasingly behaved as social beings.[12]

and State in Modern Thailand," *Journal of Southeast Asian Studies* 22(2) (September 1991): 312–315.

[11] Bremen, *The Shattered Image*, 38. It is not clear from Bremen's argument whether this was a deliberate attempt to co-opt the European model for anticolonial purposes, or if Asian nationalists legitimately believed this mythical image of the corporate village was a latent source of strength to be tapped into for nation-building. In the case of the Ngôs, Diệm's romanticized view of the village strongly suggests he believed this to have been a valid depiction of the traditional Vietnamese village.

[12] Clive J. Christie, *Ideology and Revolution in Southeast Asia, 1900–1975: Political Ideas of the Anti-Colonial Era* (Richmond, UK: Curzon, 2001), 147.

The whole point of Personalism, Christie continues, was to "protect the individual's freedom of action as a moral entity" from both the
"abstract power of market forces" on the one hand, and the tendency
of the impersonal state to assume all "social, moral and sometimes even
political responsibility" on the other. Politically, Personalists believed
federalism could achieve this. Federalism devolved considerable political responsibility to the regions, thereby serving as a check on central
power. Nhu envisioned this being achieved by the autonomous corporate
village. Socially, Personalists saw this occurring through a form of pluralism, where institutions like the trade union, or the family could shield
the individual from the direct power of larger collectivities. In Vietnam,
where pluralism was far less prominent, Diệm called for the community
to balance the power of the state.[13]

For European Personalists, these ideas made tremendous sense as the
state was indeed a powerful institution.[14] However in the Republic of
Vietnam the Ngôs' conception of a *Vietnamese* state was still in its infancy
relative to the Europeans' and not yet resonating with enough of the
population to be considered a genuinely *national* political entity, which
accounts for the many contradictions in the Ngôs' revolution.[15] First, the
Personalist Revolution tried to develop a heightened sense of national
consciousness while cultivating a politically decentralized state comprised
of autonomous village communities. Second, these autonomous village
communities were supposed to foster a new type of grassroots democracy that would further erode the power of the state to promote national
unity. Third, this new system of direct democracy was being forced on
the villages by a highly centralized and increasingly authoritarian state.
Fourth, the government expected this to be implemented by members of
an existing village elite that would then be overturned by the new social
order to emerge from the crucible of the strategic hamlet and its novel
form of hierarchy. The ends and means of their entire project were fundamentally incompatible. It is therefore small wonder that when various

---

[13] Christie, *Ideology and Revolution in Southeast Asia*, 148; Mieczyslaw Maneli, *War of
the Vanquished*, translated by Maria de Gorgey (New York: Harper & Row, 1971), 145;
and John C. Donnell, "Politics in South Vietnam: Doctrines of Authority in Conflict"
(Ph.D. diss., University of California, Berkeley, 1964), 89–90.

[14] Personalism had only begun to emerge in European thought in the 1930s, scarcely two
decades before Diệm had promulgated it as a revolutionary formula. While prevalent
among European intellectuals during this period, it never reached the mainstream of
political thought to the point where a state was run along these lines—leaving the Ngôs
devoid of any concrete examples from which to draw upon for guidance.

[15] Christie, *Ideology and Revolution in Southeast Asia*, 151.

cadres and government officials attempted to embrace Personalism and relay its tenets to the people its message was ultimately lost.[16]

Collectively this demonstrates that the Ngôs' revolution was deeply troubled before it faced its greatest threat in the communist-led insurgency. When this reached a sustained level of violence by 1960, the Special Commissariat for Civic Action was quickly overwhelmed. The focus on community development soon shifted to an emphasis on security and propaganda as the insurgents began dictating the pace of events in the countryside. The southern regime became even more reactionary, increasing the militancy of the Civic Action campaign until it was forced to adopt the more drastic policy of the Strategic Hamlet Program to create conditions more favorable to fomenting the Personalist Revolution and try to succeed where the Civic Action cadres could not.

Unfortunately, the Strategic Hamlet Program also contained a set of flawed assumptions that ultimately undermined the Ngôs' entire agenda. To begin with, it failed to account for the genuine appeal of the communist-led opposition amongst the peasantry. The notion of separating the rural population from the insurgents to facilitate community development was premised on the belief that the peasantry was an otherwise passive group that had been either duped or intimidated.[17] Other than a policy of exclusion, it offered no palliative to that portion of the population who legitimately believed that some variant of Marxist-Leninism may have offered a better prospect for Vietnam's future than the palace's inchoate formula for Personalism.

According to David Hunt, as the concerted uprising gained momentum it unleashed the pent-up frustration felt by much of the rural population. It ushered in what one observer called a "golden period" that fundamentally questioned the existing sociopolitical order in the South. It was "filled with debate over the organization of material life, the relationship between religion and politics, the function and control of print communication, the proper use of entertainment and leisure, the roles of youth and elders and of women and men."[18] Many of the people who shared these sentiments were the disaffected youth who felt themselves caught

---

[16] David Halberstam, who covered the denouement of the Diệm regime for the *New York Times* referred to Personalism as "a confusing counterideology to Communism, which no one else in Vietnam ever understood." David Halberstam, *The Making of a Quagmire*, Third Printing (New York: Random House, 1965), 50.

[17] Philip E. Catton, *Diem's Final Failure: Prelude to America's War in Vietnam* (Lawrence, KS: University Press of Kansas, 2002), 130.

[18] David Hunt, *Vietnam's Southern Revolution: From Peasant Insurrection to Total War* (Amherst, MA: University of Massachusetts Press, 2008), 21.

between the village and the city in their search for answers.[19] Throughout 1960, many of the southern revolutionaries who would take leadership roles in the National Front for the Liberation of South Vietnam appeared far more able to capitalize on this discontent than any officials in the Diệm government. Rather than the embrace the concepts of Welfare Improvement and Bettering the Conditions or Existence or community development that Diệm's Personalist Revolution offered, southern revolutionary cadres chose to interpret Marxist-Leninism, or various aspects of it, to meet their needs and fashion their own "modernist credo" that was able to resonate with these youth.[20]

Equally as problematic, the Strategic Hamlet Program offered no provisions to undo the excesses of the palace's other anticommunist policies, arguably the real cause of the insurgents' popularity. In the minds of some, the prospect for strategic hamlets' forcibly isolating supposedly loyal people into armed camps served to reinforce the draconian image that had been developed and propagated in communist propaganda against the regime.[21]

In the end, the Personalist Revolution ultimately failed because it could not impart the legitimacy of Ngô Đình Diệm and his nation-building plan on the people. If the cadres of the Special Commissariat for Civic Action had been able to reach enough of the population and convince them to buy into, or at least accept, the Ngôs' Personalist Revolution, the people would not have had cause to side with, tolerate or endure the forces that opposed the Sài Gòn government. That they could not was made evident by the fact that the insurgency was able to erupt with such force and durability in 1960–1961. At that the point the American commitment deepened, further eroding Diệm's credibility as a national leader. In the midst of this, the Diệm regime was overturned with the quiet approval of the American government, giving Washington a greater obligation to ensure the survival of the nation than it ever had under Ngô Đình Diệm.[22] Each of the many successor regimes would now be partially beholden to the US government. The downward spiral would continue as the US government assumed more and more responsibility for shoring these regimes

---

[19] *Ibid.*, 27.

[20] *Ibid.*, 27–30.

[21] Philip Catton discusses how in the response to the rapid pace of construction emphasized by the palace provincial officials often employed highly coercive measures to get the populace to comply with the program, often alienating many; Catton, *Diem's Final Failure*, 133–137.

[22] William J. Rust and the Editors of U.S. News Books, *Kennedy in Vietnam* (New York: Charles Scribner's Sons, 1985), xii–xiii.

up. In the end it took the final step of committing its own troops to the task of fighting the communist insurgency. In doing so, these foreign troops assumed the role of convincing the South Vietnamese people that they had more to gain by supporting their own government than siding with the NLF – a task that had already proved impossible for the indigenous cadres of the Special Commissariat for Civic Action to fulfill.

Bibliography

Archival Collections

Central Intelligence Agency Library, Langley, Virginia
    Freedom of Information Act Electronic Reading Room
Dwight D. Eisenhower Library, Abilene, Kansas
    Collins, James Lawton, Papers
    National Security Staff Papers
    U.S. Council on Foreign Economic Policy, Office of the Chairman, Records
    White House Central Files
Hoover Institute, Stanford, California
    Bohannan, Charles T.R., Papers
    Lansdale, Edward G., Papers
John F. Kennedy Library, Boston, Massachusetts
    Hilsman, Roger, Papers
    National Security Files
Library and Archives Canada, Ottawa, Ontario
    Record Group 25, Records of the Department of External Affairs
Michigan State University Archives
    Michigan State University Vietnam Advisory Group
National Archives and Record Administration, College Park, Maryland
    Record Group 469, Records of U.S. Foreign Assistance Agencies, 1948–1961
Texas Tech Virtual Vietnam Archive, Lubbock Texas
Trung Tâm Lưu Trữ Quốc Gia II [National Archives Number 2], Hồ Chí Minh
    City, Vietnam
    Phủ Thủ Tướng Chính Phủ [Office of the Prime Minister of the Government]
    Phủ Tổng Thống Đệ Nhất Cộng Hòa [Office of the President of the First
    Republic]

Government Publications

Directorate General of Information. *Vietnam's Strategic Hamlets*. Saigon:
    Directorate General of Information, 1963.

Foreign Relations of the United States, 1946. Vol. 6, *Eastern Europe, the Soviet Union.* Washington, DC: United States Government Printing Office, 1969.

Foreign Relations of the United States, 1952–1954. Vol. 2, *National Security Affairs*, Part 1. Washington, DC: United States Government Printing Office, 1984.

Foreign Relations of the United States, 1955–1957. Vol. 1, *Vietnam.* Washington, DC: United States Government Printing Office, 1985.

Foreign Relations of the United States, 1958–1960. Vol. 1, *Vietnam.* Washington, DC: United States Government Printing Office, 1986.

Foreign Relations of the United States, 1961–1963. Vol. 1, *Vietnam.* Washington, DC: United States Government Printing Office, 1988.

Foreign Relations of the United States, 1961–1963. Vol. 2, *Vietnam.* Washington, DC: United States Government Printing Office, 1990.

Foreign Relations of the United States, 1961–1963. Vol. 3, *Vietnam, January – August 1963.* Washington, DC: United States Government Printing Office, 1991.

Foreign Relations of the United States, 1961–1963. Vol. 4, *Vietnam, August – December 1963.* Washington, DC: United States Government Printing Office, 1991.

Nha Tổng Giảm Đốc Kê Hoạch. *Phát Triển Công Đong [Community Development].* Sài Gòn: Việt Nam Cộng Hòa Phủ Tổng Thống, n.d.

Office of the Presidency. *Toward Better Mutual Understanding.* 2nd ed. 2 vols. Saigon: RVN Office of the Presidency, 1958.

Rostow, W.W. "Guerrilla Warfare in the Underdeveloped Areas." *The Department of State Bulletin*, Vol. 155, No. 1154 (August 7, 1961): 233–238.

Truman, Harry S. "Recommendations on Greece and Turkey." *The Department of State Bulletin*, Vol. 16, No. 403 (March 23, 1947): 534–537.

Vietnamese-Language Sources

Newspapers

Cách Mạng Quốc Gia [National Revolution]
Sàigòn Mở [New Saigon]

Books and Articles

Đoàn Thêm, *Hai Mươi Năm Qua: Việc từng ngày (1945–1964) [Twenty Years Past: Events Day by Day (1945–1964)].* Sài Gòn: Nam Chi Tùng Thư, 1966.

Hồ Chí Minh. *Hồ Chí Minh: Toàn Tập 2: 1924–1930 [The Complete Works of Ho Chi Minh Vol. 2: 1924–1930].* Hà Nội: Nhà Xuất Bản Chính Trị Quốc Gia, 1995.

Western-Language Sources

Newspapers and Magazines

Life
New Republic

New York Times
Washington Post

Books and Articles

Adamson, Michael R. "'The Most Important Single Aspect of Our Foreign Policy'? The Eisenhower Administration, Foreign Aid, and the Third World." In *The Eisenhower Administration, the Third World, and the Globalization of the Cold War*. Eds. Kathryn C. Statler and Andrew L. Johns. Lanham, MD: Rowman & Littlefield Publishers, Inc., 2006, 47–72.

Adas, Michael. *Dominance by Design: Technological Imperatives and America's Civilizing Mission*. Cambridge, MA: The Belknap Press of Harvard University Press, 2006.

Ahern, Thomas L. Jr. *CIA and Rural Pacification in South Vietnam*. Langley, VA: Center for the Study of Intelligence, declassified 2007.

   CIA and the House of Ngo. Langley, VA: Center for the Study of Intelligence, declassified 2009.

Allen, Luther, and Pham Ngoc An. *A Vietnamese District Chief in Action*. Washington, DC: Department of State, Agency for International Development, 1963.

Almond, Gabriel, and James S. Coleman, eds. *The Politics of Developing Areas*. Princeton, NJ: Princeton University Press, 1960.

Anderson, Benedict. *Imagined Communities: Reflections on the Origin and Spread of Nationalism*. Rev. ed. London: Verso, 1991.

   The Spectre of Comparisons: Nationalism, Southeast Asia and the World. London: Verso, 1998.

Anderson, David L. *Trapped by Success: The Eisenhower Administration and Vietnam, 1953–1961*. New York: Columbia University Press, 1991.

Arnold, James. *The First Domino: Eisenhower, The Military and America's Intervention in Vietnam*. New York: W. Morrow, 1991.

Asselin, Pierre. "Le Duan, the American War, and the Creation of an Independent Vietnamese State." *Journal of American-East Asian Relations*, Vol. 10, Nos. 1–2 (Spring–Summer 2001): 1–27.

   A Bitter Peace: Washington, Hanoi, and the Making of the Paris Agreement. Chapel Hill, NC: University of North Carolina Press, 2002.

   Hanoi's Road to the Vietnam War, 1954–1965. Berkeley, CA: University of California Press, 2013.

Baritz, Loren. *Backfire: A Brief History of How American Culture Led Us into Vietnam and Made Us Fight the Way We Did*. New York: Morrow, 1985.

Bassett, Lawrence J., and Stephen E. Pelz. "The Failed Search for Victory: Vietnam and the Politics of War." In *Kennedy's Quest for Victory: American Foreign Policy, 1961–1963*. Ed. Thomas Paterson. New York: Oxford University Press, 1989, 223–252.

Bell, Daniel. *The End of Ideology: On the Exhaustion of Political Ideas in the Fifties*. Glencoe, NY: The Free Press, 1960.

Biersack, Aletta, and Lynn Hunt, eds. *The New Cultural History: Essays.* Berkeley, CA: University of California Press, 1989.

Binder, Leonard. "The Natural History of Development Theory." *Comparative Studies in Society and History,* Vol. 28 (1986): 3–33.

Boot, Max. *The Savage Wars of Peace: Small Wars and the Rise of American Power.* New York: Basic Books, 2002.

Bouscaren, Anthony Trawick. *The Last of the Mandarins: Diem of Vietnam.* Pittsburgh: Duqesne University Press, 1965.

Bradley, Mark Philip. *Imagining Vietnam and America: The Making of Postcolonial Vietnam, 1919–1950.* Chapel Hill, NC: University of North Carolina Press, 2000.

Vietnam at War. Oxford: Oxford University Press, 2009.

Bremen, Jan. *The Shattered Image: Construction and Deconstruction of the Village in Colonial Asia.* Providence, RI: Forbis Publications, 1988.

Brigham, Robert K. *Guerrilla Diplomacy: The NLF's Foreign Relations and the Viet Nam War.* Ithaca, NY: Cornell University Press, 1999.

ARVN: Life and Death in the South Vietnamese Army. Lawrence, KS: University Press of Kansas, 2006.

Browne, Malcolm. *The New Face of War.* New York: The Bobbs-Merrill Company, Inc., 1965.

Bui Diem, and David Chanoff. *In the Jaws of History.* Boston: Houghton Mifflin, 1987.

Busch, Peter. "Killing the 'Vietcong': The British Advisory Mission and the Strategic Hamlet Programme." *Journal of Strategic Studies,* Vol. 25, No. 1 (2002): 135–162.

Buttinger, Joseph. *Vietnam: A Dragon Embattled.* 2 vols. New York: Frederick A. Praeger, 1967.

Carter, James. *Inventing Vietnam: The United States and State Building, 1954–1968.* New York: Cambridge University Press, 2008.

Catton, Philip E. *Diem's Final Failure: Prelude to America's War in Vietnam.* Lawrence, KS: University Press of Kansas, 2002.

Chapman, Jessica M. "Staging Democracy: South Vietnam's 1955 Referendum to Depose Bao Dai." *Diplomatic History,* Vol. 30, No. 4 (September 2006): 671–703.

Cauldron of Resistance: Ngo Dinh Diem, the United States, and 1950s Southern Vietnam. Ithaca, NY: Cornell University Press, 2013.

Christie, Clive J. *Ideology and Revolution in Southeast Asia, 1900–1975: Political Ideas of the Anti-Colonial Era.* Richmond, UK: Curzon, 2001.

Colby, William, with James McCargar. *Lost Victory: A Firsthand Account of America's Sixteen-Year Involvement in Vietnam.* Chicago: Contemporary Books, 1989.

Collins, J. Lawton. *Lightning Joe: An Autobiography.* Baton Rouge, LA: Louisiana State University Press, 1979.

Connelly, Matthew. "Taking Off the Cold War Lens: Visions of North-South Conflict during the Algerian War for Independence." *The American Historical Review,* Vol. 105, No. 3 (June 2000): 739–769.

A Diplomatic Revolution: Algeria's Fight for Independence and the Origins of the Post-Cold War Era. Oxford: Oxford University Press, 2002.

Cooper, Chester L. *The Lost Crusade: America in Vietnam.* New York: Dodd, Mead, 1970.

Cullather, Nick. *Illusions of Influence: The Political Economy of United States-Philippines Relations, 1942–1960.* Stanford, CA: Stanford University Press, 1994.

"Development? It's History." *Diplomatic History,* Vol. 24, No. 4 (2000): 641–653.

The Hungry World: America's Cold War Battle Against Poverty in Asia. Cambridge, MA: Harvard University Press, 2010.

Currey, Cecil B. *Edward Lansdale: The Unquiet American.* Boston: Houghton Mifflin, 1988.

Dacy, Douglas C. *Foreign Aid, War, and Economic Development: South Vietnam, 1955–1975.* New York: Cambridge University Press, 1986.

Donnell, John C. "National Renovation Campaigns in Vietnam." *Pacific Affairs,* Vol. 32, No. 1 (March 1959): 73–88.

"Personalism in Vietnam." In *Problems of Freedom: South Vietnam Since Independence.* Ed. Wesley R. Fishel. New York: Free Press of Glencoe, 1961, 29–67.

Donoghue, John D. *My Thuan: A Mekong Delta Village in South Vietnam.* N.P.: MSU Viet Nam Advisory Group, 1961.

Duiker, William J. *The Rise of Nationalism in Vietnam, 1900–1941.* Ithaca, NY: Cornell University Press, 1976.

The Communist Road to Power in Vietnam. 2nd ed. Boulder, CO: Westview Press, 1996.

Ho Chi Minh: A Life. New York: Theia, 2000.

Duncanson, Dennis J. *Government and Revolution in Vietnam.* New York: Oxford University Press, 1968.

Eisenstadt, S.N. "Studies of Modernization and Sociological Theory." *History and Theory,* Vol. 13, No. 3 (1974): 225–252.

Ekbladh, David. "To Reconstruct the Medieval: Rural Reconstruction in Interwar China and the Rise of an American-Style Modernization, 1921–1961." *Journal of American-East Asian Relations,* Vol. 9, Nos. 3–4 (Fall–Winter 2000): 169–196.

"From Consensus to Crisis: The Postwar Career if Nation-Building in U.S. Foreign Relations." In *Nation-Building: Beyond Afghanistan and Iraq.* Ed. Francis Fukuyama. Baltimore: The Johns Hopkins University Press, 2006, 19–41.

The Great American Mission: Modernization and the Construction of an American World Order. Princeton, NJ: Princeton University Press, 2010.

"Meeting the Challenge from Totalitarianism: The TVA as a Global Mode for Liberal Development, 1933–1945." *The International History Review,* Vol. 32, No. 1 (March 2010): 47–67.

Elliott, David W.P. *The Vietnamese War: Revolution and Social Change in the Mekong Delta, 1930–1975.* 2 vols. Armonk, NY: M.E. Sharpe, 2003.

Engerman, David C., and Corina R. Unger. "Introduction: Towards a Global History of Modernization." *Diplomatic History*, Vol. 33, No. 3 (June 2009): 375–385.

Ernst, John. *Forging a Fateful Alliance: Michigan State University and the Vietnam War*. East Lansing, MI: Michigan State University Press, 1998.

Fall, Bernard B. "South Viet-Nam's Internal Problems." *Pacific Affairs*, Vol. 31, No. 3 (September 1958): 241–260.

     The Two Viet-Nams: A Political and Military Analysis. 2nd rev. ed. New York: Frederick A. Praeger, 1968.

     ed. *Ho Chi Minh on Revolution, Selected Writings, 1920–66* (Reprint). Boulder, CO: Westview Press, 1984.

Finkle, Jason L., and Tran Van Dinh. *Provincial Government in Vietnam: A Study of Vinh Long Province*. Saigon: Michigan State University Viet Nam Advisory Group and National Institute of Administration, 1961.

Fishel, Wesley R., ed. *Vietnam: Anatomy of a Conflict*. Itasca, IL: F.E. Peacock Publishers, 1968.

Fitzgerald, Frances. *Fire in the Lake: The Vietnamese and Americans in Vietnam*. Boston: Little, Brown and Company, 1972.

Fraleigh, Bert. "Counterinsurgency in South Vietnam." In *Prelude to Tragedy: Vietnam, 1960–1965*. Eds. Harvey Neese and John O'Donnell. Annapolis, MD: Naval Institute Press, 2001, 86–128.

Freedman, Lawrence. *Kennedy's Wars: Berlin, Cuba, Laos, and Vietnam*. New York: Oxford University Press, 2000.

Frey, Marc, and Sönke Kunkel. "Writing the History of Development: A Review of the Recent Literature." *Contemporary European History*, Vol. 20, No. 2 (2011): 215–232

Gellner, Ernest. *Nations and Nationalism*. Ithaca, NY: Cornell University Press, 1983.

Gendzier, Irene L. *Managing Political Change: Social Scientists and the Third World*. Boulder, CO: Westview Press, 1985.

Gibbons, William Conrad. *The U.S. Government and the Vietnam War: Executive and Legislative Roles and Relationships Part 1, 1945–1960*. Princeton, NJ: Princeton University Press, 1986.

     The U.S. Government and the Vietnam War: Executive and Legislative Roles and Relationships Part 2, 1961–1965. Princeton, NJ: Princeton University Press, 1986.

Gilman, Nils. *Mandarins of the Future: Modernization Theory in Cold War America*. Baltimore, MD: Johns Hopkins University Press, 2003.

     "Modernization Theory, the Highest Stage of American Intellectual History." In *Staging Growth: Modernization, Development and the Global Cold War*. Eds. David C. Engerman, Nils Gilman, Mark H. Haefele and Michael E. Latham. Amherst, MA: University of Massachusetts Press, 2003, 47–80.

Haefele, Mark H. "Walt Rostow's Stages of Economic Growth: Ideas and Action." In *Staging Growth: Modernization, Development and the Global Cold War*. Eds. David C. Engerman, Nils Gilman, Mark H. Haefele and Michael E. Latham. Amherst, MA: University of Massachusetts Press, 2003, 81–105.

Halberstam, David. *The Making of a Quagmire: America and Vietnam During the Kennedy Era.* Third Printing. New York: Random House, 1965.

The Best and the Brightest. Twentieth anniversary ed. New York: Ballantine Books, 1992.

Hammer, Ellen J. "Progress Report on Southern Viet Nam." *Pacific Affairs*, Vol. 30, No. 3 (September 1957): 221–235.

The Struggle for Indochina, 1940–1955: Viet Nam and the French Experience. Stanford, CA: Stanford University Press, 1966.

A Death in November: America in Vietnam, 1963. New York: Oxford University Press, 1987.

Harrison, James P. *The Endless War: Vietnam's Struggle for Independence.* New York: Columbia University Press, 1989.

Hellman, John. *Emmanuel Mounier and the New Catholic Left, 1930–1950.* Toronto: University of Toronto Press, 1981.

Henderson, William. "South Viet Nam Finds Itself." *Foreign Affairs*, Vol. 35 (January 1957): 283–294.

Hendry, James B. "American Aid in Vietnam: The View from a Village." *Pacific Affairs*, Vol. 33, No. 4 (December 1960): 387–391.

The Small World of Khanh Hau. Chicago: Aldine Publishing, 1964.

Herring, George C. *America's Longest War: The United States and Vietnam, 1950–1975.* New York: Wiley, 1979.

Hess, Gary R. "Commitment in the Age of Counterinsurgency: Kennedy's Vietnam Options and Decisions, 1961–1963." In *Shadow on the White House: Presidents and the Vietnam War, 1945–1975.* Ed. David L. Anderson. Lawrence, KS: University Press of Kansas, 1993, 63–86.

Vietnam and the United States: Origins and Legacy of War. Rev. ed. New York: Twayne Publishers, 1998.

Higgins, Marguerite. *Our Vietnam Nightmare: The Story of U.S. Involvement in the Vietnamese Tragedy, with Thoughts on a Future Policy.* New York: Harper & Row, 1965.

Hilsman, Roger. *To Move a Nation: The Politics of Foreign Policy in the Administration of John F. Kennedy.* Garden City, NY: Doubleday, 1967.

Hoang Lac. "Blind Design." In *Prelude to Tragedy: Vietnam, 1960–1965.* Eds. Harvey Neese and John O'Donnell. Annapolis, MD: Naval Institute Press, 2001, 58–85.

Hue-Tam Ho Tai. *Radicalism and the Origins of the Vietnamese Revolution.* Cambridge, MA: Harvard University Press, 1996.

Hunt, David. *Vietnam's Southern Revolution: From Peasant Insurrection to Total War.* Amherst, MA: University of Massachusetts Press, 2008.

Hunt, Michael H. *Ideology and U.S. Foreign Policy.* New Haven, CT: Yale University Press, 1987.

Hunt, Richard A. *Pacification: The American Struggle for Vietnam's Hearts and Minds.* Boulder, CO: Westview Press, 1995.

Huntington, Samuel P. *Political Order in Changing Societies.* New Haven, CT: Yale University Press, 1968.

Huynh Kim Khanh. *Vietnamese Communism, 1925–1945.* Ithaca, NY: Cornell University Press, 1986.

Immerman, Richard H. *The CIA in Guatemala: The Foreign Policy of Intervention.* Austin, TX: University of Texas Press, 1982.

Immerwahr, Daniel. *Thinking Small: The United States and the Lure of Community Development.* Cambridge, MA: Harvard University Press, 2015.

Jacobs, Seth. *America's Miracle Man in Vietnam: Ngo Dinh Diem, Religion, Race, and U.S. Intervention in Southeast Asia.* Durham, NC: Duke University Press, 2004.

Cold War Mandarin: Ngo Dinh Diem and the Origins of America's War in Vietnam, 1950–1963. Lanham, MD: Rowman & Littlefield Publishers, Inc., 2006.

Jamieson, Neil L. *Understanding Vietnam.* Berkeley, CA: University of California Press, 1993.

Jian, Chen. *Mao's China and the Cold War.* Chapel Hill, NC: The University of North Carolina Press, 2001.

Joiner, Charles A., and Roy Jumper. "Organizing Bureaucrats: South Viet Nam's National Revolutionary Civil Servants' League." *Asian Survey* (1963): 203–215.

Jones, Howard. *Death of a Generation: How the Assassinations of Diem and JFK Prolonged the Vietnam War.* Oxford: Oxford University Press, 2003.

Jumper, Roy. "Mandarin Bureaucracy and Politics in South Viet Nam." *Pacific Affairs*, Vol. 29, No. 4 (December 1957): 47–58.

"Problems of Public Administration in South Viet Nam." *Far Eastern Survey*, Vol. 26, No. 12 (November 1957): 183–190.

Kahin, George McTurnan. *The Asian-African Conference: Bandung, Indonesia, April 1955.* Port Washington, NY: Kennikat Press, 1956.

Intervention: How America Became Involved in Vietnam. New York: Alfred A. Knopf, 1986.

Kaiser, David. *American Tragedy: Kennedy Johnson, and the Origins of the Vietnam War.* Cambridge, MA: The Belknap Press of Harvard University Press, 2000.

Karnow, Stanley. *Vietnam: A History.* 2nd revised and updated ed. New York: Penguin, 1997.

Kaufman, Burton I. *Trade and Aid: Eisenhower's Foreign Economic Policy, 1953–1961.* Baltimore, MD: The Johns Hopkins University Press, 1982.

Kemp, Jeremy. "The Dialectics of Village and State in Modern Thailand." *Journal of Southeast Asian Studies*, Vol. 22, No. 2 (September 1991): 312–326.

Kershaw, Roger. *Monarchy in South-East Asia: The Faces of Tradition in Transition.* London: Routledge, 2001.

Kimball, Jeffrey P., ed. *To Reason Why: The Debate About the Causes of U.S. Involvement in the Vietnam War.* New York: McGraw-Hill Publishing Company, 1990.

Klein, Christina. *Cold War Orientalism: Asia in the Middlebrow Imagination, 1945–1961.* Berkeley, CA: University of California Press, 2003.

Kolko, Gabriel. *Anatomy of a War: Vietnam, the United States, and the Modern Historical Experience.* New York: Pantheon Books, 1985.

Kwon, Heonik. *The Other Cold War.* New York: Columbia University Press, 2010.

Lacouture, Jean. *Vietnam: Between Two Truces.* Translated by Konrad Kellen and Joel Carmichael. New York: Vintage Books, 1966.

Lansdale, Edward G. *In the Midst of Wars: An American's Mission to Southeast Asia.* New York: Harper & Row, 1972.

Latham, Michael E. *Modernization as Ideology: American Social Science and "Nation Building" in the Kennedy Era.* Chapel Hill, NC: The University of North Carolina Press, 2000.

"Modernization, International History, and the Cold War World." In *Staging Growth: Modernization, Development and the Global Cold War.* Eds. David C. Engerman, Nils Gilman, Mark H. Haefele and Michael E. Latham. Amherst, MA: University of Massachusetts Press, 2003, 1–23.

Lerner, Daniel. *The Passing of Traditional Society: Modernizing the Middle East.* New York: The Free Press of Glencoe, 1958.

Little, Douglas. *American Orientalism: The United States and the Middle East since 1945.* Chapel Hill, NC: The University of North Carolina Press, 2002.

Logevall, Fredrik. *Choosing War: The Lost Chance for Peace and the Escalation of War in Vietnam.* Berkeley, CA: University of California Press, 1999.

Embers of War: The Fall of an Empire and the Making of America's Vietnam. New York: Random House, 2012

Manela, Erez. "Imagining Woodrow Wilson in Asia: Dreams of East-West Harmony and the Revolt against Empire in 1919." *The American Historical Review,* Vol. 111, No. 5 (December 2006): 1327–1351.

Maneli, Mieczyslaw. *War of the Vanquished.* Translated by Maria de Gorgey. New York: Harper & Row, 1971.

Mann, Robert. *A Grand Delusion: America's Descent into Vietnam.* New York: Basic Books, 2001.

Marcus, John T. "Social Catholicism in Postwar France." *South Atlantic Quarterly* (1957): 299–313.

Marlay, Ross, and Clark Neher. "Part II: Vietnam." In *Patriots and Tyrants: Ten Asian Leaders.* Eds. Ross Marlay and Clark Neher. Lanham: Rowman & Littlefield Publishers, Inc., 1999.

Marr, David G. *Vietnamese Anticolonialism, 1885–1925.* Berkeley, CA: University of California Press, 1971.

Vietnamese Tradition on Trial, 1920–1945. Berkeley, CA: University of California Press, 1984.

Masur, Matthew. "Exhibiting Signs of Resistance: South Vietnam's Struggle for Legitimacy." *Diplomatic History,* Vol. 33, No. 2 (April 2009): 293–313.

Maung, Maung. "Pyidawtha Comes to Burma." *Far Eastern Survey,* Vol. 22, No. 9 (August 1953): 117–119.

McAlister, John T. Jr. *Vietnam: The Origins of Revolution.* New York: Alfred A. Knopf, 1970.

McAlister, John T., and Paul Mus. *The Vietnamese and Their Revolution.* New York: Harper & Row, 1970.

McAlister, Melani. *Epic Encounters: Culture Media, and U.S. Interests in the Middle East, 1945–2000.* Berkeley, CA: University of California Press, 2001.

Mecklin, John. *Mission in Torment: An Intimate Account of the U.S. Role in Vietnam.* Garden City, NY: Doubleday, 1965.

Miller, Edward. "Vision, Power and Agency: The Ascent of Ngô Đình Diệm." *Journal of Southeast Asian Studies,* Vol. 35, No. 3 (October 2004): 433–458.

Misalliance: Ngo Dinh Diem, the United States and the Fate of South Vietnam. Cambridge, MA: Harvard University Press, 2013.

Millikan, Max F., and W.W. Rostow. *A Proposal: Key to an Effective Foreign Policy.* New York: Harper & Brothers, 1957.

Montgomery, John D. *The Politics of Foreign Aid: American Experience in Southeast Asia.* New York: Frederick A. Praeger, 1962.

Mounier, Emmanuel. *Personalism.* Translated by Philip Mairet. London: Routledge & Kegan Paul Ltd., 1952.

Moyar, Mark. *Triumph Forsaken: The Vietnam War, 1954–1965.* Cambridge: Cambridge University Press, 2006.

Mus, Paul. "The Role of the Village in Vietnamese Politics." *Pacific Affairs,* Vol. 22, No. 3 (September 1949): 265–272.

Nashel, Jonathan. *Edward Lansdale's Cold War.* Amherst, MA: University of Massachusetts Press, 2005.

Nguyen, Lien-Hang T. *Hanoi's War: An International History of the War for Peace in Vietnam.* Chapel Hill, NC: University of North Carolina Press, 2012.

Nguyen-Marshall, Van. *In Search of Moral Authority: The Discourse on Poverty, Poor Relief, and Charity in French Colonial Vietnam.* New York: Peter Lang, 2008.

Nighswonger, William A. *Rural Pacification in Vietnam.* New York: Praeger, 1966.

Ninkovich, Frank. *Modernity and Power: A History of the Domino Theory in the Twentieth Century.* Chicago: The University of Chicago Press, 1994.

Nolting, Frederick. *From Trust to Tragedy: The Political Memoirs of Frederick Nolting, Kennedy's Ambassador to Diem's Vietnam.* New York: Praeger, 1988.

O'Donnell, John B. "The Strategic Hamlet Program in Kien Hoa Province, South Vietnam: A Case Study of Counter-Insurgency." In *Southeast Asian Tribes, Minorities and Nations.* Ed. Peter Kunstadter. Princeton, NJ: Princeton University Press, 1967, 703–744.

"Life and Times of a USOM Prov Rep." In *Prelude to Tragedy: Vietnam 1960–1965* Eds. Harvey Neese and John O'Donnell. Annapolis, MD: Naval Institute Press, 2001, 210–236.

Olson, James S., and Randy Roberts. *Where the Domino Fell: America in Vietnam, 1945–1990.* New York: St. Martin's Press, 1991.

Osborne, Milton E. *Strategic Hamlets in South Viet-Nam: A Survey and a Comparison.* Ithaca, NY: Cornell University Southeast Asia Program, 1965.

Packenham, Robert A. *Liberal America and the Third World: Political Development Ideas in Foreign Aid and Social Science.* Princeton, NJ: Princeton University Press, 1973.

Parsons, Talcott and Edward A. Shils, eds. *Toward a General Theory of Action: Theoretical Foundations for the Social Sciences.* New Brunswick, NJ: Transaction Publishers, 2001.

The Pentagon Papers: The Defense Department History of the United States Decisionmaking on Vietnam. Senator Gravel ed. Vols. 1 and 2. Boston: Beacon Press, 1971–1972.

Pérez, Louis A., Jr. "Dependency." In *Explaining the History of American Foreign Relations.* 2nd ed. Eds. Michael J. Hogan and Thomas G. Paterson. Cambridge: Cambridge University Press, 2004, 162–175.

Phillips, Rufus. "Before We Lost in South Vietnam." In *Prelude to Tragedy: Vietnam, 1960–1965.* Eds. Harvey Neese and John O'Donnell. Annapolis, MD: Naval Institute Press, 2001, 7–57.

Why Vietnam Matters: An Eyewitness Account of Lessons Not Learned. Annapolis, MD: Naval Institute Press, 2008.

Pike, Douglas. *Viet Cong: The Organization and Techniques of the National Liberation Front of South Vietnam.* Cambridge, MA: MIT Press, 1966.

Popkin, Samuel. *The Rational Peasant: The Political Economy of Rural Society in Vietnam.* Berkeley, CA: University of California Press, 1979.

Porter, Gareth. "Proletariat and Peasantry in Early Vietnamese Communism." *Asian Thought and Society,* Vol. 1, No. 3 (December 1976): 335–342.

Prashad, Vijay. *The Darker Nations: A People's History of the Third World.* New York: The New Press, 2007.

Prebisch, Raúl. *Change and Development – Latin America's Great Task: Report Submitted to the Inter-American Development Bank.* New York: Praeger, 1971.

Prochnau, William. *Once Upon a Distant War: David Halberstam, Neil Sheehan, Peter Arnett – Young War Correspondents and Their Early Vietnam Battles.* First Vintage Books ed. New York: Vintage, 1996.

Quinn-Judd, Sophie. *Ho Chi Minh: The Missing Years, 1919–1941.* Berkeley, CA: University of California Press, 2002.

Race, Jeffrey. *War Comes to Long An: Revolutionary Conflict in a Vietnamese Province.* Berkeley, CA: University of California Press, 1972.

Rostow, W.W. "The Take-Off into Self-Sustained Growth." *The Economic Journal,* Vol. 66, No. 261 (March 1956): 25–48.

The Stages of Economic Growth: A Non-Communist Manifesto. 2nd ed. Cambridge: Cambridge University Press, 1971.

Rotter, Andrew J. *The Path to Vietnam: Origins of the American Commitment to Southeast Asia.* Ithaca, NY: Cornell University Press, 1987.

Rubin, Barry. *Paved with Good Intentions: The American Experience and Iran.* New York: Oxford University Press, 1980.

Rust, William J., and the editors of U.S. News Books. *Kennedy in Vietnam.* New York: Charles Scribner's Sons, 1985.

Said, Edward. *Orientalism: Western Concepts of the Orient.* London: Penguin Books, 1995.

Schlesinger, Arthur M., Jr. *A Thousand Days: John F. Kennedy in the White House.* Boston: Houghton Mifflin, 1965.

Schulzinger, Robert. *A Time for War: The United States and Vietnam, 1941–1975.* New York: Oxford University Press, 1997.

Scigliano, Robert. *South Vietnam: Nation Under Stress: An Important Look at the Trouble Spot of Asia.* Boston: Houghton Mifflin Company, 1964.

Scott, James. *The Moral Economy of the Peasant*. New Haven, CT: Yale University Press, 1976.

Seeing Like a State: How Certain Schemes to Improve the Human Condition Have Failed. New Haven, CT: Yale University Press, 1998.

Shafer, D. Michael. *Deadly Paradigms: The Failure of U.S. Counterinsurgency Policy*. Princeton, NJ: Princeton University Press, 1988.

Shaplen, Robert. *The Lost Revolution: The U.S. in Vietnam, 1946–1966*. Rev. ed. New York: Harper Colophen, 1966.

Shawcross, William. *Sideshow: Kissinger, Nixon and the Destruction of Cambodia*. New York: Touchstone, 1981.

Sheehan, Neil. *A Bright Shining Lie: John Paul Vann and America in Vietnam*. New York: Random House, 1988.

Shils, Edward. *Political Development in the New States*. Gravenhage: Mouton & Co., 1962.

Smith, Roger M. "Prince Norodom Sihanouk of Cambodia." *Asian Survey*, Vol. 7, No. 6 (June 1967): 353–362.

So, Alvin Y. *Social Change and Development: Modernization, Dependency and World-System Theories*. Newbury Park, CA: Sage Publications, 1990.

Spector, Ronald H. *Advice and Support: The Early Years of the U.S. Army in Vietnam, 1941–1960*. New York: Free Press, 1985.

Statler, Kathryn. "The Diem Experiment: Franco-American Conflict over South Vietnam, July 1954–May 1955." *The Journal of American-East Asian Relations*, Vol. 6, Nos. 2–3 (Summer–Fall, 1997): 145–173.

Replacing France: The Origins of American Intervention in Vietnam. Lexington, KY: The University Press of Kentucky, 2007.

Stewart, Geoffrey C. "Hearts, Minds and Công Dân Vụ: The Special Commissariat for Civic Action and Nation-Building in Ngô Đình Diệm's Vietnam, 1955–1957." *Journal of Vietnamese Studies*, Vol. 6, No. 3 (Fall 2011): 44–100.

Sutton, Francis X. "Nation-Building in the Heyday of the Classic Development Ideology: Ford Foundation Experiences in the 1950s and 1960s." In *Nation-Building: Beyond Afghanistan and Iraq*. Ed. Francis Fukuyama. Baltimore, MD: The Johns Hopkins University Press, 2006, 42–63.

Tana, Li. "An Alternative Vietnam? The Nguyen Kingdom in the Seventeenth and Eighteenth Centuries." *Journal of Southeast Asian Studies*, Vol. 29, No. 1 (March 1998): 111–121.

Nguyễn Cochinchina: Southern Vietnam in the Seventeenth and Eighteenth Centuries. Ithaca, NY: Southeast Asia Program Publications, Southeast Asia Program, Cornell University, 1998.

Tarling, Nicholas. *Nationalism in Southeast Asia: "If the People are with Us."* London: RoutledgeCurzon, 2004.

Taylor, Milton C. "South Viet-Nam: Lavish Aid, Limited Progress." *Pacific Affairs*, Vol. 34, No. 3 (August 1961): 242–256.

Thompson, Robert. *Defeating Communist Insurgency: The Lessons of Malaya and Vietnam*. London: Chatto & Windus, 1967.

Tran Van Don. *Our Endless War: Inside Vietnam*. San Rafael, CA: Presidio Press, 1978.

Truong Buu Lam. *Patterns of Vietnamese Response to Foreign Intervention: 1858–1900*. New Haven, CT: Southeast Asian Studies, Yale University, 1967.

Truong Nhu Tang, David Chanoff, and Doan Van Toai. *A Viet Cong Memoir*. New York: Vintage Books, 1985.

Vũ Văn Thái. "Vietnam's Concept of Development." In *Problems of Freedom: South Vietnam Since Independence*. Ed. Wesley R. Fishel. New York: Free Press of Glencoe, 1961, 69–73.

Waite, James. *The End of the First Indochina War: A Global History*. London: Routledge, 2012.

Walinsky, Louis J., ed. *Agrarian Reform ad Unfinished Business: The Selected Papers of Wolf Ladejinsky*. New York: Oxford University Press, 1977.

Warner, Dennis. *The Last Confucian: Vietnam, South-East Asia, and the West*. New York: Macmillan, 1963.

Westad, Odd Arne. *The Global Cold War: Third World Interventions and the Making of Our Times*. Cambridge: Cambridge University Press, 2007.

Winters, Francis X. *The Year of the Hare: America in Vietnam, January 25, 1963–February 15, 1964*. Athens, GA: University of Georgia Press, 1997.

Woodruff, Lloyd W. *My Thuan: Administrative and Financial Aspects of a Village in South Vietnam*. Saigon: Michigan State University Vietnam Advisory Group, 1961.

Woodside, Alexander B. *Community and Revolution in Modern Vietnam*. Boston: Houghton Mifflin, 1976.

Young, Marilyn B. *The Vietnam Wars, 1945–1990*. New York: HarperCollins, 1991.

Young, Robert J.C. *Postcolonialism: An Historical Introduction*. Oxford: Blackwell Publishers, Inc., 2007.

Zasloff, Joseph J. *Rural Resettlement in Vietnam: An Agroville on Development*. Washington, DC: Department of State, Agency for International Development, 1963.

Theses and Dissertations

Donnell, John C. "Politics in South Vietnam: Doctrines of Authority in Conflict." Ph.D. diss., University of California, Berkeley, CA, 1964.

Holdcroft, Lane E. "The Rise and Fall of Community Development: 1950–1965." M.Sc. thesis, Michigan State University, East Lansing, MI, 1976.

Miller, Edward Garvey. "Grand Designs: Vision, Power and Nation Building in America's Alliance with Ngo Dinh Diem, 1954–1960." Ph.D. diss., Harvard University, Cambridge, MA, 2004.

Sackey, Nicole. "Passage to Modernity: American Social Scientists, India, and the Pursuit of Development, 1945–61." Ph.D. diss., Princeton University, Princeton, NJ, 2004.

Tran, Nhu-An. "Contested Identities: Nationalism in the Republic of Vietnam (1954–1963)." Ph.D. diss., University of California, Berkley, CA, 2013.

Index